Studies in the History of Law and Justice

Volume 15

The purpose of this book series is to publish high quality volumes on the history of law and justice.

Legal history can be a deeply provocative and influential field, as illustrated by the growth of the European universities and the *ius commune*, the French Revolution, the American Revolution, and indeed all the great movements for national liberation through law. The study of history gives scholars and reformers the models and courage to question entrenched injustices, by demonstrating the contingency of law and other social arrangements.

Yet legal history today finds itself diminished in the universities and legal academy. Too often scholarship betrays no knowledge of what went before, or why legal institutions took the shape they did. This series seeks to remedy that deficiency.

Studies in the History of Law and Justice will be theoretical and reflective. Volumes will address the history of law and justice from a critical and comparative viewpoint. The studies in this series will be strong bold narratives of the development of law and justice. Some will be suitable for a very broad readership.

Contributions to this series will come from scholars on every continent and in every legal system. Volumes will promote international comparisons and dialogue. The purpose will be to provide the next generation of lawyers with the models and narratives needed to understand and improve the law and justice of their own era.

The series includes monographs focusing on a specific topic, as well as collections of articles covering a theme or collections of article by one author.

More information about this series at http://www.springer.com/series/11794

Flavia Lattanzi · Emanuela Pistoia
Editors

The Armenian Massacres of 1915–1916 a Hundred Years Later

Open Questions and Tentative Answers in International Law

Springer

Editors
Flavia Lattanzi
University LUISS-Guido Carli
Rome
Italy

Emanuela Pistoia
University of Teramo
Teramo
Italy

ISSN 2198-9842 ISSN 2198-9850 (electronic)
Studies in the History of Law and Justice
ISBN 978-3-030-08631-2 ISBN 978-3-319-78169-3 (eBook)
https://doi.org/10.1007/978-3-319-78169-3

Printed on acid-free paper

This Springer imprint is published by the registered company Springer International Publishing AG part of Springer Nature
The registered company address is: Gewerbestrasse 11, 6330 Cham, Switzerland

Homo sum, humani nihil a me alienum puto
Publius Terentius Afer,
Heautontimorùmenos, verse 77 (165 B.C.)

Contents

Introduction 1
Flavia Lattanzi and Emanuela Pistoia

Historical Introduction: World War I and the Dynamics of the Armenian Genocide 11
Marcello Flores

Part I Searching for a Legal Definition

The Armenian Massacres as the Murder of a Nation? 27
Flavia Lattanzi

On the Applicability of the Genocide Convention to the Armenian Massacres 105
Chiara Cipolletti

Is Customary Law on the Prohibition to States to Commit Acts of Genocide Applicable to the Armenian Massacres? 125
Alessandra Gianelli

Part II Which Possible Legal Consequences?

Metz Yeghern and the Origin of International Norms on the Punishment of Crimes 143
Antonio Marchesi

Armenian Cultural Properties and Cultural Heritage: What Protection under International Law One Hundred Years Later? 161
Federica Mucci

What Reparations for the Descendants of the Victims of "the Armenian Genocide"? 181
David Donat Cattin

Part III Denying the Armenian Massacres

The Armenian Massacres and the Price of Memory: Impossible to Forget, Forbidden to Remember 195
Agostina Latino

Denying the Armenian Genocide in International and European Law 237
Monica Spatti

Criminalizing the Denial of 1915–1916 Armenian Massacres and the European Court of Human Rights: *Perinçek* v *Switzerland* 251
Carmelo Domenico Leotta

Part IV The Armenian Massacres and the European Union: Active Player or *Festin de Pierre*?

Is the Denial of the "Armenian Genocide" an Obstacle to Turkey's Accession to the EU? 275
Pierluigi Simone

The European Parliament as the Human Rights Gatekeeper of the Union? 299
Alessandro Rosanò

The EU and the Turkish Recognition of the Armenian "Genocide" in the Broader Framework of the EU External Action: A Tale of Possibilities Yet to Be Explored 313
Emanuela Pistoia

Contributors

Chiara Cipolletti International and European Union Law Fellow, University of Teramo, Teramo, Italy

David Donat Cattin Adjunct Professor of International Law, Center for Global Affairs, New York University (NYU), New York, USA; Secretary-General, Parliamentarians for Global Action (PGA), New York, USA

Marcello Flores Historian, Siena, Italy

Alessandra Gianelli Full Professor of International Law, University of Teramo, Teramo, Italy

Agostina Latino Assistant Professor of International Law, University of Camerino, Camerino, Italy

Flavia Lattanzi Full Professor of International Law, University LUISS-Guido Carli, Rome, Italy; Former Judge at the International Criminal Tribunal for Rwanda and at the International Criminal Tribunal for the Former Yugoslavia, Rome, Italy

Carmelo Domenico Leotta Associate Professor of Criminal Law, European University of Rome, Rome, Italy

Antonio Marchesi Associate Professor of International Law, University of Teramo, Teramo, Italy; Chairperson, Amnesty International Italy, Teramo, Italy

Federica Mucci Associate Professor of International Law, University of Rome "Tor Vergata", Rome, Italy

Emanuela Pistoia Associate Professor of European Union Law, University of Teramo, Teramo, Italy

Alessandro Rosanò Research Fellow, University of Turin, Turin, Italy

Pierluigi Simone Assistant Professor of International Law, University of Rome "Tor Vergata", Rome, Italy

Monica Spatti Assistant Professor of International Law, University "Cattolica del Sacro Cuore", Milan, Italy

Introduction

Flavia Lattanzi and Emanuela Pistoia

Abstract The introduction explains the objectives of the collection of essays, clarify the specificity of the volume against the background of the existing bibliography on the so-called "Armenian genocide", justify the adopted methodology and details the legal issues addressed in the various essays.

The massacre of a large part of the Armenian population perpetrated in Anatolia in 1915–1916 is known as the first genocide of the XXth century. It is also said to have been brought up by Adolf Hitler in his 1939 Obersalzberg speech to army commanders prior to the German invasion of Poland, in support for his planned extermination policy of the Polish people. Despite having occurred a century ago, the 1915–1916 Armenian massacres[1] are still a reason for tensions between, on the one hand, Turkey, i.e. the successor State of the Ottoman Empire, and, on the other hand, the Republic of Armenia and the Armenian diaspora, as well as those international entities and national institutions who refer to those massacres as "genocide" and/or urge Turkey to acknowledge the roughly one million persons murdered.

Decades after the massacres, the earliest sign of such a tension was probably the opposition by the Turkish delegation against a reference to the facts of 1915–1916

[1]We refer to the years 1915–1916 because the political and operative decisions on the elimination of the Armenians from the territory of the Ottoman Empire were all taken in this range of time. Moreover, the core of the deportations and the killings took place in those two years. Many refer to 1923 as the final year of the "Armenian genocide", when the Treaty of Lausanne was concluded. Others refer to 1918, i.e. the end of World War I.

F. Lattanzi (✉)
University LUISS-Guido Carli, Rome, Italy
e-mail: fllattanzi@luiss.it

E. Pistoia
University of Teramo, Teramo, Italy
e-mail: epistoia@unite.it

F. Lattanzi and E. Pistoia (eds.), *The Armenian Massacres of 1915–1916 a Hundred Years Later*, Studies in the History of Law and Justice 15,
https://doi.org/10.1007/978-3-319-78169-3_1

in the work of the Sub-Commission on Prevention of Discrimination and Protection of Minorities, which had been entrusted by the United Nations Committee on Human Rights with conducting a study on the question of the prevention and punishment of the crime of genocide. The preliminary study presented in 1978 by Nicodème Ruhashyankiko, Special Rapporteur,[2] did not refer to the Armenian massacres, which did appear in earlier drafts, following pressures by the Turkish delegation. Over time, a number of international and national bodies and institutions have urged Turkey to acknowledge the facts, to admit that a genocide of part of the Armenian nation had been perpetrated and/or to take steps vis-à-vis the victims or their descendants. Particularly on the occasion of the centenary of the massacres, solemnly commemorated on 24 April 2015 and for the rest of that year, the reactions of the Turkish governments have been harsh. A few years after gaining independence from the former Soviet Union, the Republic of Armenia placed the "recognition of the genocide" at the top of its international agenda. The two major attempts to induce the two parties to commence a dialogue on the matter failed badly. The first was the establishment of the Turkish-Armenian Reconciliation Commission (TARC), in July 2001. The TARC's membership included Armenian and Turkish civil society representatives who acted in a private capacity. The Commission's terms of references did not even mention the 1915–1916 events, but they alluded to "serious differences" between Armenians and Turks and to "obstacles to normal relations" between Armenia and Turkey. The TARC faced multiple difficulties and was subject to the opposition by groups from both sides. In April 2004, it closed its work with a set of seven recommendations to the parties and concluding that there were "substantial differences" between them, so that rapprochement and reconciliation between Turks and Armenians would "be a process, not an event, and the difficulty of that process should not be underestimated." Against this background, one could well believe that the TARC's work was a step in the right direction. Admittedly, it does not appear to have had any follow-ups, which is the reason for considering it, overall, a failure. In 2009, tremendous diplomatic efforts led to the historic conclusion of two Protocols between Turkey and Armenia with the primary aim to begin and normalize the international relations between the two countries. In one of them, the contracting parties agreed on the establishment of an intergovernmental bilateral commission, to be organized in sub-commissions, whose task was *inter alia* to "implement a dialogue on the historical dimension" "with the aim to restore mutual confidence between the two nations, including an impartial and scientific examination of the historical records and archives to define existing problems and formulate recommendations". This provision raised harsh criticism from part of the Armenian civil society and tensions in Turkey. The two Protocols never entered into force for lack of ratification by both countries, and the bilateral commission was obviously never established.

[2]Nicodème Ruhashyankiko, Study on the Question of the Prevention and Punishment of the Crime of Genocide, UN Doc. E/CN.4/Sub.2/416, 4 July 1979.

The topic is naturally of considerable interest in historical studies, both in the past and still in recent times. Historians, whose task is researching the relevant facts, have sometimes reached contradictory results insofar as they have either relied on documents which others discredited or considered facts in an acritical fashion. What is more, several historians combined their research on the historical facts with a legal analysis on their qualification, which they are not properly equipped to do.

In international legal studies, the events in which approximately one million Armenians lost their lives and properties at the outset of World War I pose a number of challenging questions, their legal qualification being the most prominent but not the only one. The aftermath of the massacres in recent times also raise stimulating issues. Whether or not the 1915–1916 massacres qualify as "genocide", as claimed by the Armenian Republic and community and rejected by Turkey, is controversial mainly because that term surfaced in international law only decades later. Indeed, as everyone agrees, the term "genocide" was coined by a scholar during World War II and was officially admitted in international law only with the 1948 "Convention on the Prevention and Punishment of the Crime of Genocide". Hence, we believe that question is limited and misrepresentative of the relevant legal framework insofar as it leads to the assessment of the 1915–1916 events in the light of norms in force at present times, while ignoring any other source. It is not accidental that both historians and international lawyers have reached opposite solutions on the matter. One hundred years after the 1915–1916 events and contrary to the determination of the opposite parties of the dispute to reject or take advantage of the "g" word, we consider that a difference approach is needed, in which the focus is placed on the circumstances within which the facts occurred. In this new perspective, the "mother" of all legal questions raised by the "genocide row" is, beyond terminology, whether the massacres and deportations can be factually identified as the destruction of a nation. Whether an international unwritten norm prohibiting genocide existed already in 1915–1916 and whether the 1948 "Convention on the Prevention and Punishment of the Crime of Genocide" can be applied retroactively are different legal issues that should be dealt with separately. This approach has led us to opt for avoiding the word "genocide" in the title of the book. Our ambition is not to take sides in the "genocide row", but first and foremost, whatever our conclusions, to convey the idea that it does not help understand the matter. Moreover, we are convinced that the word "genocide" would automatically stimulate our readers to approach the book either with a critical or with a supporting attitude, which we arc equally determined to avoid.

The several other legal questions triggered by those tragic events—with some being unrelated to the passage of time and others having arisen from conducts undertaken recently as a follow-up or as reaction to those occurred in the past—deserve to be dealt with individually, which is the approach taken so far by both historians and international lawyers. However, we also believe that those legal questions are interrelated: hence, the need, while keeping the analysis of each of them separate, to gather them in a comprehensive volume.

As obvious as it may be, our legal analysis needed to take advantage of the scrutiny of relevant facts. As lawyers, we are not familiar with the tools aimed at collecting data if not in the context of legal proceedings or criminal trials, where documents and witnesses can be proved true by means of appropriate procedures. We therefore had to rely heavily on the work of historians. The Authors of the essays in this volume committed to consider contrasting historical reconstructions, which has proven a major difficulty in the legal assessment. We considered most reliable those historians who wrote on the massacres during or immediately after they occurred, which makes their reports and comments essentially neutral, especially if they happened to be eye-witnesses due to their role in the Ottoman Empire.

We do not dare to claim that we and all the Authors have considered all aspects with equal carefulness and that all previous views have been equally understood and taken into account. Yet, we do claim that we as Editors and Authors and all of the other Authors have been guided by international law as a tool for fully understanding the 1915–1916 tragic events. After years of research and teaching international and European Union law, we the Editors developed the idea, which someone may well deem a bias on our side, that those events did not take place in a legal *vacuum* and that the justifications that sometimes scholars and politicians have put forward are nothing but specious and untenable, even at a time when human rights were still unknown to international law.

As members of the Academia with no personal links with either the Turkish or the Armenian community, we have sought to gather scholars equally committed to the task of understanding the several legal issues directly or indirectly arising from the 1915–1916 events in a unbiased manner. Our ambition has been to take into account the norms existing already at the time and norms arisen later, with due attention to *tempus regit actum*. Beyond the massacres perpetrated in 1915–1916, the Volume also covers facts and conducts occurred in recent times. We also considered the standpoints of national and international institutions, as well as of States on the matter, including the opposing parties, i.e. the Republic of Turkey, the Republic of Armenia and the Armenian diaspora. We have been committed to ensuring that all Authors, including ourselves, followed those guidelines and took a non-judgmental approach. This does not mean that there might not be slight differences among the essays given that in principle we have not interfered with everyone's independent assessment.

This peer reviewed collection of legal essays is introduced by a focused analysis on a historical issue which is crucial in the legal analysis: the *intention* of the political class leading the Ottoman Empire to eliminate the Armenians in Anatolia, which is behind the 1915–1916 massacres. We are grateful to one of the most distinguished historians of those events, Marcello Flores, who took responsibility for this task. In his "Il genocidio degli Armeni", first published in 2006 and successively re-published in 2015 with further elaborations, Flores had already investigated the politics of the "ittihadist" party that ruled the Ottoman Empire at the time, as well as the way the Ottoman government (headed by the triumvirate of Talât Pasha, Enver Pasha and Djemal Pasha) organized the Armenian massacres. As an introduction to this collection of essays, he further elaborates on the objectives of eliminating the Armenians from the Empire and on how those objectives fitted into a political agenda monopolized by the outbreak of World War II.

The legal questions getting to the heart of the "genocide row" are dealt with in Part I of the Book. The legal assessment of the 1915–1916 events opens it up, under the responsibility of Flavia Lattanzi. As a former judge at the International Criminal Tribunal for Rwanda and at the International Criminal Tribunal for the Former Yugoslavia, Lattanzi borrows the determinants used by those two Tribunals and earlier by the Occupying Tribunals in Germany, as well as by the International Court of Justice, to carry out a thorough analysis of the facts and the specific required moral element. The analysis includes a careful discussion of disclaimers, justifications and explanations put forward by modern Turkey and/or writers who distance themselves from the "genocide" narrative (regardless of the term "genocide" as such). An impressive number of factors leads the Author to conclude that a deliberate destruction in part of the Armenian Christian nation did take place in 1915–1916. Since the 1948 Convention on the determinants of genocide is inapplicable to facts occurred in 1915–1916, the next step was to identify the applicable law. This issue is addressed in the second half of Lattanzi's essay. Pursuant to the principle of *lex specialis derogat generali*, she first considers the conventional rules applicable to the relations between the Sublime Porte and some European States concerning Non-Muslim Minorities in the Ottoman territories and, particularly, the Armenians: the Treaties of San Stefano and Berlin, stipulated in 1878 at the conclusion of the Russo-Turkish war, and the Treaty of Sèvres, i.e. the Peace Treaty with Turkey signed by the Allied Powers—UK, France, Italy, Japan—, and the other so-called Allied Associated Powers. While the obligations of Turkey laid down in the Treaty of Sèvres (which never entered into force) are nothing but the detailing of the reparations for the international wrongful acts committed by the Ottoman Empire, as regulated by general international law, the Treaties of San Stefano and Berlin do constitute law applicable to the Armenian massacres. They deal with the protection of minorities, hence they do not even mention the destruction of a religious or ethnic group or other groups. However, protection of a minority necessarily encompasses the prohibition of its destruction. Next, Flavia Lattanzi takes up the assumption that the Armenian massacres took place in the context of a civil war, which had broken out as a consequence of the Armenians' uprising against the Empire and their fighting with the Russian enemy. She believes that this assumption does not reflect reality. Yet, this is a favourite argument of modern Turkey, occasionally upheld also by some writers, against the qualification of the massacres as the destruction of a minority for discriminatory reasons and, more generally, in opposition to any Turkish responsibility for them. The Author shows that, in the context of a civil war, the Martens clause would be a safe ground for establishing the international responsibility of the Ottoman Empire, which was a party to the 1899 Hague Convention. Lattanzi's final argument is that, whatever context one may consider (civil war or not), the Armenian massacres marked a massive breach of the laws of humanity, independently from the existence of specific international norms on the protection of minorities and/or the prohibition of certain behaviors. The Martens clause refers to them as principles of international law, i.e. of general application. In addition, the Author shows that applying the laws of humanity exclusively in a war context, is illogic and ill-founded.

The two questions most commonly underpinning the legal qualification of the 1915–1916 events are then dealt with in the two successive essays: at that time, did any international unwritten rule exist regarding what will be later defined as genocide? Can the Genocide Convention apply to the massacres, i.e. retroactively? Given that the *Meds Yegern*, as the massacres are referred to in the Armenian language, indeed qualifies as genocide within the modern meaning of the term, and that it constitutes a serious breach of rules of international law applicable at that time, those two questions do not appear as crucial as at a *prima facie* consideration. However, a full legal analysis of the 1915–1916 events requires an answer, which is negative in both cases. For Alessandra Gianelli, the "genocide rulings" of the International Court of Justice, the preparatory works of the International Law Commission's Articles on the Law of the Treaties and on State Responsibility, the preparatory works of the 1948 Genocide Convention and the behavior of the different States involved during and after the 1915–1916 massacres, unequivocally demonstrate the absence, in 1915–1916, of a customary rule prohibiting States from committing genocides. She then addresses the further question as to whether the current peremptory rule on the prohibition of genocide is retroactive. She argues that it is not, and that neither does it involve obligations concerning Turkey and other States with regard to their current conduct. This conclusion in no way detracts from the contribution of the Armenian massacres to the quick raising of a universally shared opinion on the prohibition of genocide a few decades later, which determined the instant rise of the corresponding peremptory norm in customary law. Yet, no responsibility of Turkey on ground of commission of genocide can be asserted. Cipolletti deals with the issue of the retroactivity of the Genocide Convention by relying on the Vienna Convention on the Law of the Treaties, which rules such retroactivity out. She also carefully explores the argument of an exception with regard to the Genocide Convention, which has been upheld in legal literature, only to convincingly dismiss it.

Part II brings together three essays that explore three different sets of possible legal consequences of the massacres.

Less than three decades later, the individual criminal responsibility of those responsible for serious crimes against humanity similar to those related to *Metz Yeghern* was established. Has *Metz Yeghern* nothing to deal with such an achievement? Antonio Marchesi investigates to what extent the international reactions caused by the Armenian massacres represented an advancement towards the development of the broader notion of international crimes and of a special legal regime applicable to the punishment of crimes falling within that notion. He focuses on the Joint Declaration by the Allied Powers of 24 May 1915, on the proposals of the Commission on Responsibility of Authors of the War and on Enforcement of Penalties (the so-called "Commission of the Fifteen"), set up in the context of the Paris Peace Conference, and on the provisions in Part VII, particularly in Article 230, of the Treaty of Sèvres. Those provisions lay the ground for the construction of a truly innovative legal framework, which became reality after a short period of time, though unfortunately after another world war.

Federica Mucci addresses the destruction of the Armenian cultural heritage associated with the 1915–1916 massacres. She argues that the 1899 II Hague Convention did not cover the intentional destruction of cultural sites by territorial States. The Martens clause did not extend to it either. The protection of cultural heritage in international law is considerably higher today. Beginning with the 1954 Hague Convention, the protection of cultural heritage and cultural diversity has been highlighted as a common fundamental interest of the international community, both in times of war and in peacetime. Against this background, Mucci notes Turkey' efforts to restore Armenian damaged properties, among which the renovation and re-opening of three sites that have become the object of socio-political discussion in the last decade. A different issue is that of the exit of movable Armenian cultural properties out of Turkey in violation of relevant domestic and international regulations. This phenomenon was not covered by the 1899 Hague Convention either, which applies exclusively to acts committed by the enemy. Mucci's bitter conclusion is that the absence of an effective overall regulatory framework leaves each restitution request to its own destiny, in consideration of the peculiar circumstances of each case.

Is there an international legal case for reparations to the advantage of the descendants of the Armenian genocide? David Donat-Cattin takes on responsibility for answering this question. He explains that while contemporary public statements, resolutions or political agreements affirming the "Armenian genocide" may, as such, be an acceptable and feasible form of *collective* reparation provided by the entities that adopt/issue/produce them, the general principle of non-retroactivity under international law is a major obstacle to *inter-individual* reparations. The law of armed conflicts, instead, already existed in 1915 and it may provide a firm legal basis for claims to obtain forms of reparations, which may be inherited by descendants of victims. Such forms of reparations are of two kinds: those aimed at trying to partially restore the harm and losses of victims through material and immaterial means of reparation provided to their descendants, and those aimed at preventing that atrocities are repeated in the future, also via the proper memorialization and recognition of the gross abuses of the past and the enactment of strict guarantees of non-repetition through legislative means and international cooperation against impunity for international crimes. As a conclusion of his analysis, Donat-Cattin advocates ratification of the Rome Statute of the International Criminal Court by both Armenia and Turkey as a meaningful and effective step to guarantee non-repetition, and one most suitable to address multi-generational harm.

In current times, the most striking feature of those 1915–1916 events that represented almost the murder of the Armenian nation is the determination of modern Turkey to refuse to acknowledge their extent and impact, and hence to acknowledge any responsibility as the successor State of the Ottoman Empire. Part III of this Volume looks closely at this attitude by means of three essays respectively devoted to the "right of memory" of the Armenians, to the legal assessment of the Armenian "genocide" denial in international and European law, and to an analysis of the *Perinçek* v. *Switzerland* judgment of the European Court of Human Rights. The first essay, written by Agostina Latino, examines the position of Turkey and provides a thorough picture of the widespread practice concerning the recognition of the massacre of the Armenians, often the recognition of the "genocide" of Armenians, in the international community. Latino's analysis draws on a legal framework first developed in regional and local contexts, and later elaborated at the level of the United Nations. The need to achieve protection of the individual and collective right to memory leads the Author to put forward proposals aimed at a shared memory based on a reconstruction of the events accepted by both sides, though respectful of the historical truth. The second essay, authored by Monica Spatti, provides an overview of the main international and European legal acts on the criminal prosecution of speeches that deny, condone or minimize international crimes, i.e. on the possible legal tools aimed at the repression of negationism. Spatti highlights the technical difficulties of applying the European Union Framework Decision on the matter to conducts related to the Armenian massacres, and, more generally, the difficulties encountered by criminal legislation on negationism in the light of the European Convention of Human Rights. Carmelo Domenico Leotta's comment on *Perinçek* focusses on the latter question, as emerged specifically with regard to the Armenian massacres. Leotta's accurate comment of the judgment against the background of the previous Court's case-law on the Holocaust denial ends up with a severe criticism of the Court.

The last Part of the Book focuses on the European Union. Turkey has been a candidate country for many years and Turkey's relations with the then European Economic Community flourished even earlier. As the requirements for candidate States to accede the Union include respect of human rights and democracy, while the Community has been championing human rights in its external relations far before they began an objective formally established by the founding Treaties, it seemed interesting to explore the reasons why the Community/Union proved entirely ineffective in cooling the "genocide row" down. Pierluigi Simone explains that the Turkish negationist position is not *per se* an obstacle to the country's accession to the Union: admitting past massive breaches of norms protecting principles of humanities, human rights and/or minorities is not included in Article 2 TEU and does not constitute one of the so–called "Copenhagen criteria". However, Simone also demonstrates that the criminalisation in the Turkish legal order of any dissenting opinion on the matter could indirectly affect the Copenhagen *legal* criteria, as well as Articles 2 and 49 TEU, and the Copenhagen *political* criteria. So far, neither the Commission nor the Council have relied upon those potential tools. Authoritative standpoints on the matter are due to the European Parliament, which Alessandro Rosanò accordingly describes as the "human rights gatekeeper" of the Union. In three different resolutions on the matter, the Parliament has made the Turkish attitude vis-à-vis the Armenian massacres, including the current treatment of Armenian cultural heritage, a key issue. According to Rosanò, this amounts to establishing an additional criterion for membership of the Union which could not be ignored as, based on art. 49 TEU, the Council decides on the accession of new members following the Parliament's approval. Ultimately, Emanuela Pistoia provides a legal assessment of the total lack of dialogue between the Community/ Union and Turkey on the "Armenian genocide row" in decades of partnership, aimed at obtaining the cessation of the international wrongdoings currently committed by modern Turkey upon the basis of the denial of any responsibility of the predecessor State for the 1915–1916 massacres. The European (Economic) Community lacked the power to bring up the matter with Turkey for decades, while human rights awareness in the Community's external relations only emerged in the early Nineties. It is only with the Treaty of Maastricht that the European Union has been endowed with a foreign policy aimed *inter alia* at developing and consolidating democracy and respect for human rights and fundamental freedoms. However, the Treaty of Maastricht did not mark any change in the EU/Turkey relations in connection with the Armenian massacres, neither did the Treaty of Lisbon, which made democracy, respect of human rights and international law the objectives of the Union's external relations in all areas. It is in this context that Pistoia puts the Parliamentary resolution passed on the occasion of the "Genocide" centenary, on April 15, 2015, into perspective. Despite its great moral value, the resolution does not convey *the Union's* point of view and will on the matter, but merely those of the Parliament. Moreover, since it addresses *Turkey* rather than the Union's Council, as it could have done pursuant to art. 36 TEU, it has no legal value while it could have had one. The Union has been even more shy in encouraging relations between Turkey and the Republic of Armenia, most probably due to the broader political scenario in the region and the prominent role of Russia in the Caucasus. However, in Pistoia's view, the way to reconciliation between the two peoples and States in the medium-long run, could unfold precisely from a multilateral scenario promoted by the Union in the framework of its Eastern Partnership, provided that it is developed in such a way as to involve Turkey.

During our time in preparing this Book, our compassion for the victims of the massacres has increased enormously. In a way, the hard work that we and all the Authors put into the Book is a tribute to their suffering and their lost future. By means of this work, we would like to pay tribute also to the Turkish people, who are the victims of an official biased reconstruction of the 1915–1916 events. Our tribute also extends to the Circassians and the Kurds. They too have been victims of those responsible for the planning and the organization of the massacres, who took advantage of them by inciting them to take an active role in perpetrating the massacres on the basis of a misrepresentation of the Armenians' role in the Ottoman society and upon promise of the Armenians' wealth.

We share the TARC's view that reconciliation between Turks and Armenians, and necessarily between the Republic of Turkey and the Republic of Armenia, is a process that takes time and efforts. We are convinced that a sound and durable reconciliation cannot but rely on a thorough and rigorous analysis of the circumstances back in 1915–1916, and on their objective and accurate legal assessment. Our wish is that the present collection of essays could give a contribution in this direction.

Historical Introduction: World War I and the Dynamics of the Armenian Genocide

Marcello Flores

Contents

References 22

Abstract Against the backdrop of the contended lack of continuity among the Hamidian massacres of 1984–1896, the massacres of the first years of the 1900s and the slaughters and deportation of 1915 and afterwards, the essay focuses on the factors that led the Ottoman leadership to take the decision to engage in the annihilation of the Armenian people in Anatolia in early 1915. The analysis shows the existence of a precise intention in this connection, which represents a historical introduction to the legal analysis carried out in the Volume.

Up to twenty years ago, one of the most controversial and unresolved questions concerning the history of the Armenian genocide, which represented the framework for many other questions, was whether or not the genocide resulted from the "continuity" which linked the hamidian massacres of 1894–1896 to the massacres of the first years of the 1900s (mainly Adana) and finally to the slaughters and deportations of 1915 and afterwards, which was to be considered the "peak" of the genocide itself.

This issue was extremely interesting, not only with respect to the Armenian genocide, but also in view of a wider understanding of all genocides perpetrated

M. Flores (✉)
Siena, Italy
e-mail: floresmarcello@gmail.com

F. Lattanzi and E. Pistoia (eds.), *The Armenian Massacres of 1915–1916 a Hundred Years Later*, Studies in the History of Law and Justice 15,
https://doi.org/10.1007/978-3-319-78169-3_2

over the years. It was not by chance that, for both the Jewish genocide and the genocide against the Tutsis in Rwanda, there had been a similar polarisation of two different interpretations: one concentrating on the research of the long wave of genocidal violence and the ideologies and cultures of hatred that supported and promoted it; the other concentrating on understanding the mechanisms that made such events possible—events that the main protagonists of those years could neither conceive nor envisage.

It was difficult ten years ago to support the thesis of "continuity", and it is even more so today for the following reasons. Between the hamidian massacres and 1915 there are significant discontinuities on the level of regime and government (there are at least two significant ruptures in 1909 and 1913), on the level of political organisation (the "ittihadist" party, the Committee of Union and Progress—at the end of the '800s the CUP had not exist yet, while in 1915 it was almost a state-party) and on an ideological level (Turkish nationalism starts and consolidates between the end of the '800s and the First World War, especially in its most radical and exclusivist forms). The massacres of 1894–96 were certainly a new way of responding to some of the effects of the process of modernisation that had been affecting the Ottoman Empire too (new Turkish immigration, economic crisis, contrasts between Muslims and non-Muslims). However, a strong collective identity had not formed yet (but it was in its nascent stage), an identity capable of opposing the other ones in an ever more radical and exclusivist way. It is only because of the first territorial losses, suffered between the years of the hamidian massacres and the genocide, that Eastern Anatolia became fundamental for the geopolitical needs of Turkish nationalism, as well as for its mythical and ideological construction. Most importantly, all genocides (this is suggested by their comparative analysis) were implemented in the context of war. In order to implement a genocide, in addition to intentionality and the questions it raises, "capabilities" and a strong "opportunity" are also needed, the latter often being an incentive and a spur to move from violent but not extreme nor total projects for the organisation and implementation of genocide. The war, and especially the First World War, represents a significant historical rupture that rearranges any previously pre-existing order. It is not a coincidence that the beginning of the repressive phase that led to the Armenian genocide was happening at the same time in which the European war began to be more and more insistently called the Great War, signifying its tragic grandeur and the profound differences from traditional conflicts of the past: its character—in fact—of total war. "The failure of the Allied landing at Gallipoli was the proximate cause of the succession of repressive measures taken in the subsequent months against Armenian civilians. Had the Allied landing succeeded, leading to a rapid advance to Costantinople, the Armenian tragedy would not have occurred. But the failure of the Allies to break out of their beachheads doomed the Armenians to exile and indescribable suffering. Once the Gallipoli landing had occurred, the Turkish regime was indeed besieged on all sides. The decision to expel the Armenians from their homes was taken in this environment of wartime invasion and heavy loss of life among Turkish forces, with Turkish forces engaged both at Gallipoli in the west and against Russian and Armenian troops in the Caucasus”.[1]

The discussion on the importance of the context of World War I in shaping the Armenian genocide found a decisive turning point with Jay Winter's already cited essay:

> In effect, total war did not produce genocide; it created the military, political, and cultural space in which it could occur, and occur again. Another way of putting the central point is to see total war as both the context and the outcome of genocide. Indeed genocide helped create total war.[2]

Within the accepted interpretation that war and genocide are inextricably intertwined, posited in many important volumes published in the last years, new questions have been raised, which can help us to better understand the connection between war and genocide, the intentionality of the latter, the moment(s) of the decision(s) taken, the responsibilities but also the justifications that had such importance in the lasting contrast of memory and history which followed between the Armenians and the Turks.

Not all scholars have accepted Winter's thesis that the war inaugurated and provided the space in which genocidal crimes could and did take place: some of them have linked genocide to the Ottoman imperial policy, to the “culture of hatred” that had been sown against the Christian population, and to the ethnoreligious plan of homogenizing Anatolia around the Turkish and Muslim presence alone. This last aspect will likely be studied and analyzed more profoundly in new volumes, taking advantage of the new documents that Taner Akçam and others have discovered and used with great precision and cleverness.

Akçam has certainly stressed how today

> the clear-cut separation and opposition of continuity and contingency cannot be very meaningful. To be sure, historical processes include both dimensions, and in this sense both sides of the debate make some correct points and have contributed significantly to our understanding of the genocidal process. More important, however, is the interaction of these themes during the process of annihilation.[3]

It should be noted, against the preoccupation that placing the Armenian genocide within a general pattern of violence—that of the first total war—could undermine either the responsibility or the peculiarity of this event as the first genocide of the twentieth century, that only in the broader context of the war—the continuum of the Balkan wars of 1912–1913 and of the first year of World War I in 1914–1915—can we fully appreciate and understand the radicalisation that occurred within CUP's nationalism and its plan for Anatolia's Turkification. Mark Levene has suggested that

[1]Winter (2003), p. 208.
[2]Winter (2003), p. 191.
[3]Akçam (2012), p. 128.

> the violence perpetrated in the Balkan wars might be read as an adjunct to the main matter of genocide. Ethnic cleansing aggravated repeatedly by instances, if not sequences, of diverse atrocity, including communal massacre, is clearly evident.[4]

That all the State powers involved in the Balkan Wars claimed to have learnt deportation from their neighbouring enemies makes it perhaps difficult to establish a hierarchy of responsibility, but certainly does not undermine that of the Ottoman power both in this respect and in the initiation of World War I. The process of demonization of the enemy, that constitutes one of the noteworthy aspects of the World War, makes the outburst of hatred education, that several nationalisms were spreading for years in every country, particularly virulent. It is the war that allows the ethnic, national and religious hatred to turn violence into massacres and war crimes, and which raises the level of tolerance towards violence of the people implicated.

The process of the formation of Turkish national identity—that Gökalp more than anybody else tried obsessively to introduce in the collective soul of the Turkish people—was largely based on a sense of cultural and religious superiority and of political preponderance; but this was happening precisely when the state and the elite were losing power both in in terms of territory and in the strife with the Great Powers after the Balkan Wars.

During this period, the CUP leadership "closely mirrors the sort of psycho-cultural pathologies and obsessions which we have elsewhere identified as key preconditions for genocide: not least the subjective insistence on the regaining of power in an international context as set against the objective reality of weakness."[5] The coup d'ètat, the raid on the Sublime Porte that the new CUP triumvirate (Talât, Enver, Cemal) carried out in late January 1913, was justified with the refusal to accept the peace terms offered by Great Powers and, thanks to the selfish shortsightedness of Bulgaria that started the second Balkan War, allowing for the reconquering of Edirne and rewarding national pride. The goal of "saving the Empire" instantly became a different rallying cry "Turkey for the Turks".

The idea of the national homogenization of Ottoman Anatolia as the homeland of Turkism began to assume now a different vision from that of a mass population transfer or population exchange like the one with respect to the Greeks or Bulgarians before and during the Balkan Wars. Regarding the Armenians, who in 1914 were diminished from one-third to one-quarter of the total population in Anatolia after the waves of millions of Muslim migrants settled there from the second half of 19th century, the fulfillment of the demographic vision of the Unionists meant necessarily expulsion, deportation and, in the context of the war, annihilation. Taner Akçam wrote:

> The course of the war and accompanying security fears powerfully shaped decision about the annihilation of the Armenians. Had the Ottomans not been defeated at Sarıkamiş, and if, in March 1915, the loss of Istanbul had not been looming in a mere matter of days, the final,

[4]Levene (2013), p. 104.

[5]Levene (2013), p. 113.

> fatal blow against the Armenians might have been stayed. Talât Paşa's memorandum of 26 May indicates, however, that removal of the threat known as the 'Armenian reform issue' was widely considered a necessity among the Unionists even before the war, and the efforts were made to eliminate this perceived threat.[6]

In the first phase of the development of the Young Turk movement, Ottoman patriotic citizenship was emphasized; in the second (from 1889 to 1913) Muslim nationalist activism was characterized by competition with liberals, Islamist conservatives and Armenian revolutionaries. Gradually the Young Turks conquered hegemony and the third phase started in 1912–13, within the Balkan wars:

> Ethnic separatism on the part of non-Turks and the rise of Turkiash nationalism were two processes that only served to strengthen each other. These processes of disidentification represented the contracting shifts from Ottoman to Muslim to Turkish nationalism. They are richly documented in the sources and examples of this shift are plentiful.[7]

It is natural that, in this process, opposition against the Armenians was accentuated and radicalized in a psychological sense, in the dimension of everyday life, pushing the Christian communities to withdraw into themselves as a means of self-defense and to look towards the foreign policy of the Great Powers for the support to achieve (this being the goal, the hope, the illusion) the "reform" that was announced too late (February 1914) and would therefore be impossible to implement. The project of ethnic homogenization and demographic engineering, when intertwined with the military defeats, fear of loss of empire, the context of violent total war brought back and accentuated, with the contribution of increasingly radicalised turkish nationalism, the ethnic and religious hatred that for a long time Armenian historians have seen in a somewhat abstract and ahistorical way as the essence and the raison d'etre of the genocide. The ethnic expulsion policy, begun against the Greeks before the deportation of the Armenians, had represented a kind of dress rehearsal for the ethnic cleansing mechanism against the Armenians that—unable to reach a "homeland" nearby—could only manifest itself and turn into annihilation. The "intentionality" in the destruction of the Armenians by the Ottoman authorities (a central theme in the possibility of legitimately using the term genocide with reference to this historic event) can find a more solid explanation on the basis of studies and documentation which have appeared in recent years. The issue of intentionality is often confused with that of planning even by scholars of value, but the two, albeit intertwined, belong to two moments which are often different and that strengthen each other. The intention of the Ottomans to "get rid" of the Armenians shared partial and limited characteristics in the period between the nineteenth and twentieth centuries, when it was already beginning to feel the first effects of Turkish immigration from countries that had belonged to the Ottoman Empire and that had conquered their independence in the second half of the nineteenth century. The victory of the Young Turks' revolution and then, within it, of the heated nationalist faction, had been accompanied by the construction of

---

[6]Akçam (2012), p. 227.

[7]Üngör (2012), p. 29.

Turkey's national identity. In order to succeed, they had to stigmatize as "foreign" all non-Muslim populations, and consider non-Muslim Turks lower grade citizens. The rapid growth of turkish nationalism found in the defeats of the First Balkan War a moment of radicalization and despair, fear and desire for revenge, which were the breeding grounds for the coup of the triumvirate and the final victory of most intense and radical nationalism, at the precise moment when Turkish immigration resumed massively from the lost territories. The decision to rely on Germany and the Central Powers in the War, which was taking shape and which would explode in the late summer of 1914, permanently favored the "intention" to ethnically cleanse Anatolia, Cilicia (but also other regions) from non-Turkish groups beginning with Christian groups, initially directed against the Greek population. The intention to get rid of the Armenians in Anatolia, which was already part of the demographic and social project of the Young Turks made explicit by the triumvirate in power, became an urgent necessity at a time when the events of the war were characterized by unexpected and heavy defeats at the hands of the Russian army on the Eastern front (the battle of Sarıkamiş was the crucial moment) and the assault on the Dardanelles by British forces which aroused the fear that the Ottoman Empire could not survive. The fear that the Russian advance could establish *de facto* in Eastern Anatolia—and especially in the six *vilayets* where the Armenian presence was greater—that "reform" that the great powers had belatedly imposed on the Sublime Porte in February 1914, without enacting mechanisms that could ensure implementation, triggered the intention of ethnically homogenizing Anatolia during the deportation and annihilation project directed towards the Armenians who lived there. The Russian conquest of Anatolia, part of which did take place in the following months, could result in strong Armenian autonomy or even an independent Armenian state under Tsarist Control; while any defeat in the Dardanelles, which seemed certain in late April and led to preparation of evacuation plans for Istanbul, appeared to be the background for the final loss of Anatolia, the very land that Turkish nationalism had placed at the center of its own battle for identity and state building.

War was a catalyst. The CUP immediately decided to free the country from all Great Powers' control, both political and economic, revoking the Capitulatory system and launching—better, pushing the Caliphate to declare—the jihad, singling out Christians, and Armenians in particular, as the likely enemies. War brought a final shift from the previous Ottoman nationalism, at the heart of the Young Turk revolution, to Muslim nationalism and now to Turkish nationalism. The theoretical rejection by the Young Turks of Ottomanism and Islamism in favour of Turkish nationalism hastened the spread of a radical ideology. It is possible, as Ümit Üngör suggested, that "Turkish national identity was constructed by exclusion and violence" and that rather "than identity leading in a linear manner to violence, violence had produced identity."[8] If this was the case, it was the violence of the war—the violence suffered by the Turks in the battles against the external enemy and the

[8]Üngör (2012), p. 52.

violence pursued by them on the Christians, seen as the internal enemy—that strengthened the nationalism of a defeated people, allowing in 1920–1923 Kemal to carry on in a new nationalist war that led to the establishment to the Republic of Turkey and to the collective justification of the violence committed in name of their own national identity.

All scholars agree that the battle of Sarıkamiş was a critical turning point, enhanced a few months later by the landing in Gallipoli and the evacuation of Istanbul. It was in that first moment that Enver started to blame the Armenians, their cowardice and their treason in order to avert his own responsibility in the defeat; they were soon disarmed and forced into labor battalions. "Can we ascertain—asks Mark Levene—that it was in these early winter months of 1915 that parallel decisions were being taken at the highest level for some comprehensive resolution of the Armenian question?"[9] We know from different sources and documents—even if we lack the documents of the official discussions of the CUP's central committee—that it was around February and March that it seems possible to establish this moment as the turning point. Even if it is clear that the early measures (the disarming of Armenians and their transfer to labor battalions, the search for weapons and the raids against villages) could not be seen as the first steps towards genocide, it is in these months that Talât, Enver, and Bahaeddin Şakir stated many times that it was necessary to "eliminate" the Armenian danger, threat, presence in Anatolia and especially in the east border disctrict. Raymond Kevorkian recalls the CUP's meeting of that period when Dr. Nâzim explained he was astonished that "few of our comrades still preserve a protective attitude towards Armenians" and Talât concluded it was "his personal responsibility to use all the means he considered suitable towards Armenians."[10]

Akçam stressed that in the winter of 1915, the advance of the Russian armies into the provinces which were the subject of western imposed reform, could lead to the establishment of an independent Armenia that was to be halted with the cleansing of the Armenians from Anatolia. An official note of the Ottoman Interior Ministry dated 26 May to the grand vizierate explained the necessity of eliminating the Armenian problem in a comprehensive and absolute manner, it also stated that "deliberations were under way as to how to prepare and implement the means for eliminating this trouble"[11]; and similar reasoning was better expressed by Tâlat to the German consul general Mordtmann and to the American ambassador Morgenthau, according to whom "Tâlat said that they had discussed the matter thoroughly and arrived at a decision to which they would adhere."[12]

According to Levene, on the contrary, "none of this evidence, however, nails the case for a premeditated campaign of destruction of the entire Armenian community —and certainly not in February or March 1915. What it instead suggests is a

[9]Levene (2013), p. 141.

[10]Kevorkan (2006), p. 312.

[11]Akçam (2012), p. 133.

[12]Morgenthau (2004), p. 27.3.

deliberate set of actions being considered against the Armenians as a political entity [...]. In other words the committee had opted instead for an alternative plan: that of a targeted but nevertheless large-scale politicide."[13] I must confess I am uneasy with the concept of politicide, since all genocides and crimes against humanity are the result of political decisions taken against enemies (either national, ethnic or religious) considered to be politically dangerous for the existing power. In this case, moreover, the Armenians could hardly be seen as a political entity, since the divided Armenian political parties—Dashnaks and Hnchaks—represented a minority within their people.

Levene, however, admits that "the late April emergency situation also saw a marked radicalization of CUP animus and, with it, exterminatory violence towards Armenians"[14] but is still uncertain whether this was a point of no return. It is he, anyway, who stresses the gradual building up of the deportations programme until the general deportation law (27 May) also as an answer to the Joint Great Powers Declaration of few days before. Even if Levene establishes the date of late May as the "ultimate watershed" that implemented genocide, he agrees with Akçam that it is impossible to fix a particular moment when everything crystallized into a decision to launch genocide. Taner Akçam, anyway, has identified an essential document in solving the question of the moment when the decision was taken to "get rid" of the Armenian question definitively—a letter that Interior Minister Talât wrote to the grand vizier in May 26, 1915. "According to this document, the deportation of the Armenians had created the possibility of eliminating the problem in a manner that is comprehensive and absolute".[15] In discussions with the German Embassador, Talât repeated his reasoning, explaining to him that the deportation did not have "merely" a military motivation. Talât had told the German consul general Mordtmann that he wished "to use the world wars a pretext for cleansing the country of its internal enemies—namely, its Christian population—without having to face the diplomatic interventions of foreign countries",[16] adding that Germany itself would benefit since the Turkish state would be stronger and more stable. The accounts of repeated meetings between US Ambassador Henry Morgenthau and Talât confirm the attitude of the main architect of the genocide. The solution to the "Armenian question" was justified as an act of defense that was inevitable in a context marked by defeats in the east (November-December 1914) and the expected success of the landing at Gallipoli (which did not take place) that would lead to the surrender of the Ottoman Empire. In the memories that Celal Bey, the General Governor of the province of Aleppo, published in December 1918, we have the confirmation of what would be decided in the 1919 trial of the leaders of

[13]Levene (2013), p. 143.

[14]Levene (2013), p. 147.

[15]Akçam (2012), p. 132.

[16]Akçam (2012), p. 133.

the CUP, namely that the decision to kill and destroy the Armenians had been taken after a long debate within the Party Central Committee:

> Since the decision in this matter was arrived at by the Central Committee only after long and in-depth discussions, it would be impossible to change it, and the deportation of the Armenians was necessary for the sake of our national ideals, and thus I should put aside my own personal consideration of this matter; finally, he said they would get rid of me were I to oppose their point of view on this question.[17]

The measures against the Armenians taken in the first months of 1915, although later justified as responses to the needs of war, testify the will of the unionist leaders to definitively resolve the issue raised in the previous February Agreement on Armenian reforms. The issue of identifying within the CUP leadership a clear intent in wanting to permanently get rid of the Armenian presence should not make us forget how the choice of genocide is the result of an evolution. "For this reason, it is better to think in terms of a process than a 'continuum'. This avoids predetermining an outcome and implies a variable dynamics of destruction that is liable to change at any point".[18]

But if we agree with the latter interpretation of the Armenian genocide as a "process", as a cumulative radicalization, we cannot avoid to put together the winter and spring months of 1915 as the fundamental steps in this process. To which we must add the decision in the summer to limit the presence of Armenians to 5% of population in the Western provinces and to 10% in the Eastern ones, establishing the conditions for the second wave of massacres in late 1915 and 1916 in the camps of the Syria desert, that added half a million more deaths to the first genocidal wave of spring-summer 1915.

Through new documentation which has emerged in recent years, the identification of the process of "radicalization" that takes the form of the deportation and annihilation of Armenians (March 1915), provides insight on the intertwining of a project which had already been suggested with the context of the war, that would allow it to be implemented and make it operational. That project was the ambitious goal of making Anatolia and Cilicia homogeneous and turkisized after having expelled the ethnoreligious Christians groups—of which the Armenians constituted the majority—and having forcibly assimilated the remaining Muslim groups (especially the Kurds). A project that was born in some way already because of the demographic dynamics that preceded and accompanied the massacres of the late nineteenth century, but had found a pulse, acceleration and, above all, a new clarity of purpose around the ideological construction of turkish fundamentalist nationalism in the late 20th century; a project that had become compelling, urgent and decisive with the losses and defeats in the first Balkan war.

The implementation mechanisms for this decision, which we have seen repeatedly tried and tested in the testimonies and documents recently acquired by scholars, were followed by multiple and converging trends: on the one hand, the

[17]Akçam (2012), p. 135–136.
[18]Akçam (2012), p. 137.

decision of the Central Committee of the CUP as well as the orders addressed to the secretaries and party officials; on the other, the central role of the Special Organization, which was autonomous and linked directly with the more radical and intransigent leaders of the CUP and the army that operated directly both in the killings and massacres phase and in that of deportation.

In a nutshell we ask: What happened in the Ottoman Empire in the days of the First World War, when the siege of Gallipoli and the landing of Anglo-Australian-New Zealand troops had seemed to threaten the very existence of the Empire, and were felling overwhelmed by the simultaneous victories of the Russian armies on the front of the Caucasus? The 24 April 1915 arrest of over two thousand Armenians in Istanbul (community leaders, intellectuals, political leaders, businessmen, journalists, students, civil servants), citizens of the Ottoman state, constitutes the starting point for the genocide of the Armenians, that US ambassador to Istanbul Henry Morgenthau called the "death of a nation".

A month later, on 24 May, the Great Powers (Britain, France and Russia) simultaneously released a joint statement in London, Paris and Petrograd that said:

> In view of those new crimes of Turkey against humanity and civilization, the Allied governments announce publicly to the Sublime-Porte that they will hold personally responsible [for] these crimes all members of the Ottoman government and those of their agents who are implicated in such massacres.[19]

On 27 May 1915, three days later, the Ottoman government (headed by the triumvirate of Talât Pasha, Enver Pasha and Djemal Pasha who had seized power in 1913) promulgated the "Temporary Law of Deportation", which legitimized and legalized the Armenian deportations and massacres which had been taking place from the end of April and that would have a further development in June and July. Two weeks later, on 10 June, a new "Temporary law of expropriation and confiscation" made the political and military intention behind the massacres and deportation to the Syrian Desert clear. The two laws combined together make clear the goal to expel—and not temporarily, but definitely—the Armenians from their historical settlement areas, cleansing the state of their presence throughout Eastern Anatolia and Cilicia. The total number of Armenians who survived the deportations and in the fall 1915 found themselves settled in the deserts of Syria were about eight hundred thousand, just over 40% of the Armenians who had been living in the Ottoman Empire. Just as many are those who had already been killed or who had died during the deportations in late 1915, while approximately three hundred thousand were able to save themselves because they managed to escape or because they had not been deported. A new law established at that time that the presence of minorities, including Armenians, could not exceed 5% in every region, and 10% in the Aleppo district. The new law represented the legal framework and administrative reference to overcome the resistance of the more moderate officials (who were removed or killed when they refused to follow orders). Since the detention

[19] Garibian (2010), p. 87.

camps where the Armenians were locked up were all near Aleppo, this law allowed the killing of another half million Armenians.

At the end of the war the new Ottoman governments tried to bring those responsible for the Armenian massacres to court so they could rid themselves of the weight of nationalism and meet the winners' requests. They wanted to target some of the top executives of the Committee of Union and Progress and of the Special Organization, as well as the military leaders who were mostly involved; not an easy task since the night between 1 and 2 November functionaries who were on top of the list of war criminals were on board a German destroyer. The new Ottoman Justice subsequently encountered other obstacles that made the continuation of the trial difficult. Firstly, the international climate, in which the idea of a special tribunal to try all those who had "committed acts contrary to the laws and customs of war" but also against the "principles of humanity" was dropped after the arduous and full-bodied work done by a committee of fifteen jurists belonging to Great Britain, France, Italy, United States and Japan. The war waged by Turkey (and Bulgaria) was considered "barbaric" and conducted with "illegal methods" while the violence against Armenians, considered "primitive barbarism", entered into the category of crimes against the "laws of humanity", according to the Hague Convention in 1907 which strengthened the famous Martens clause approved within the Hague Convention of 1899.

American intransigence prevented an international tribunal from being establish, and it was determined that war crimes were to be dealt with by the military courts of the individual states. The trials, which started in Istanbul and other cities (Yozgat, Trabson, Harput, Bayburt, Erzincan and other smaller centers), had in turn clashed with the climate marked by the growing resurgence of nationalist impulses that the government fostered in Ankara through Mustafa Kemal. This climate was further exasperated by the Greek occupation of Izmir, and then by the retreat and military victories the Turkish nationalists were able to gather, playing with the psychological refusal of the population to consider the winners and occupying armies as standard-bearers of freedom and democracy.

Reactions to the first death sentence—the one imposed by the military court in Yozgat on Mehmed Kemal, the local Kaimakan (in the city of Yozgat 88 of the 1,800 Armenians present survived and in the district almost all 33,000 Armenians were killed or deported), which was executed on 10 April 1919—were likely to worry the government and the allied occupation authorities themselves. The debate that had taken place in the months previous to the trials, which helped the population to become aware of the horrors committed against the Armenians, was reduced now to a conviction handed down simply to please the victorious powers. Few voices defended the justness and morality of the punishment imposed by the court martial. In the documentation of the trials, and especially in those documents pertaining to the defendants who were CUP and Special Organization leaders, as well as in the documents directed to the CUP regional secretaries and officials, Talât made specific requests to ascertain the status of deportations, the number of remaining Armenians, the number of arrivals and from where in the camps. This was a repeated recurrence and many times the term "deportation" appears to be a clear synonym of annihilation. Some important witnesses—such as the commander of the 3rd Army from 1916 Vehip Paşa—confirmed during the trial that the decision to "liquidate" the Armenians had been taken by the CUP Central Committee and that local political leaders, military commanders, senior officers of the gendarmerie, gave strict orders to kill groups of Armenians before and during the deportation. Although many telegrams were destroyed immediately afterwards, there remained a sufficient amount, in addition to those copied and signed as equal to the originals, to show the complex organization of terror that the CUP had organized with the Special Organization, and in close cooperation with the army regiments led by the most trusted officers. The question that in these past years had been an element of uncertainty in identifying the genesis of the genocide (when it began and when the decision to initiate it was taken) and that had especially driven many Armenian historians to interpret the history of the Armenian massacres as a continuum starting from the late 19th century massacres and connecting them to those perpetrated in the World War II, has found in recent studies a convincing reinterpretation shared by a substantial group of historians focusing on this issue.

> As for Armenian policy, what we now know as the genocide emerged from a series of more limited measures implemented regionally. It developed into an empire-wide programme through a process of cumulative policy radicalization. Only by the early summer of 1915 may we speak of a crystallized policy of general killing [...] informed by ideology but according to shifts of circumstance.[20]

The genocides were perpetrated differently from region to region, from district to district, city to city: the central level merely established the key features of the "repression" of Armenians from Anatolia and from Cilicia. The actual genocidal plan was then put into practice with a good deal of autonomy by individual CUP and SO leaders of CUP, while the central level intervened primarily—as told by many of the large number of telegrams with which Talât ruled at that time—in places where it encountered delays or difficulties.

This is the story that comes to us today by an articulate and mature historiography, where Turkish, Armenian, American, European historians are continuing to try to explore the still uncharted territory of research, to provide insight into local experience and diversity, the attitudes of individuals and social and ethnic groups that were involved, to understand the influences, interference, and dynamics which also result from the randomness which history is often subjected to. There is no need for these historians to show that what happened in 1915–1916 was indeed genocide because it is a long since recognised result.

[20]Bloxham (2005), p. 69.

References

Akçam T (2012) The Young Turks' crime against humanity: The Armenian genocide and ethnic cleansing in the Ottoman Empire. Princeton University Press, Princeton

Bloxham D (2005) The great game of genocide: imperialism, nationalism, and the destruction of the Ottoman Armenians. Oxford University Press, Oxford

Garibian S (2010) From the 1915 joint declaration to the 1920 treaty of Sèvres. Armen Rev 52:87–102

Kevorkan R (2006) Le génocide des Arméniens. Odile Jacob, Paris

Levene M (2013) The crisis of genocide, vol. I: Devastation: The European Rimlands 1912–1938. Oxford University Press, Oxford

Morgenthau H (2004) United States diplomacy on the Bosphorus: the diaries of Ambassador Morgenthau, 1913–1916. Taderon Press, London

Üngör, UÜ (2012) The making of modern Turkey: nation and state in Eastern Anatolia, 1913–1950. Oxford University Press, Oxford

Winter J (2003) Under cover of war: The Armenian genocide in the context of total war. In: Gellately R, Kiernan B (eds) The specter of genocide. mass murder in historical perspective. Cambridge University Press, Cambridge, pp 189–214

Part I
Searching for a Legal Definition

The Armenian Massacres as the Murder of a Nation?

Flavia Lattanzi

Contents

1 Introduction 28
2 A Preliminary Legal Question: The Deliberate Destruction of a Group Protected by the Genocide Convention of 1948 Before Its Entry into Force 39
2.1 The Non-applicability of the Convention to the Destruction of a Group Protected Before Its Entry into Force 39
2.2 Genocide as a State Violation of International Law and as a Crime of International Concern Before 1948 40
3 The Determinants of the Armenian Massacres and Deportations in Light of the Genocide Convention Criteria as Applied by the ICTY/ICTR and ICJ Jurisprudence 43
3.1 The Facts 43
3.2 The Specific Moral Element 57
4 The Applicable Law 73
4.1 The San Stefano and Berlin Treaties 73
4.2 The Applicability of the *Martens Clause* to the Alleged Armenian Uprising 76
4.3 The Applicability of the Laws of Humanity to the Events of 1915–16 78
4.4 The Laws of Humanity at the Paris Peace Conference 81
4.5 Crimes Against Humanity and the Issue of Competent Jurisdiction 83
4.6 The Reparation Obligations 90
5 Final Remarks 96
6 Post scriptum 101
References 101

Abstract Starting from the claim by the Armenian community and the majority of historians that the 1915–1916 Armenian massacres and deportations constitute genocide as well as Turkey's fierce opposition to such a qualification, this paper investigates the possibility of identifying those massacres and deportations as the destruction of a nation. On the basis of a thorough analysis of the facts and the

---

F. Lattanzi (✉)
University LUISS-Guido Carli, Rome, Italy
e-mail: fllattanzi@luiss.it

F. Lattanzi and E. Pistoia (eds.), *The Armenian Massacres of 1915–1916 a Hundred Years Later*, Studies in the History of Law and Justice 15,
https://doi.org/10.1007/978-3-319-78169-3_3

required mental element, the author shows that a deliberate destruction, in a substantial part, of the Armenian Christian nation as such, took place in those years. To come to this conclusion, this paper borrows the very same determinants as those used in the case-law of the Military Tribunals in occupied Germany, the International Court of Justice and the International Criminal Tribunals for the Former Yugoslavia and Rwanda in genocide cases. Based on the principle of *tempus regit actum*, this essay also discusses the law applicable to such a deliberate destruction, and tries to demonstrate that, far from falling in a legal vacuum, the 1915–1916 Armenian massacres and deportations constituted a serious breach of various international norms in force at that time. Indeed, it consisted in "the murder of a nation", which is the proper meaning of the word "genocide".

1 Introduction[1]

It is historically undisputed that the different cultural-religious communities of the Ottoman Empire have lived together quite peacefully for centuries. This stemmed from a rule that, while recognising a privileged status to the Muslim community identified as the "real believers" (*umma*), ensured a status of autonomy to other communities, the Jewish and the Christian. The members of these communities did not enjoy the same civil and political rights as Muslims. However, belonging to the "religion of the book" and identified as "the protected" (*dimmi*), they were free to follow their religion and traditions.[2]

At one point in time, that autonomy was reinforced through the creation of the *Millet* (the Nations) rule, which identified the nation proper with a community's religious belief and formally improved the *status* of non-Muslim communities inhabiting the Ottoman territory. However, these reforms (*tanzimat*), which occurred in particular in 1839 and 1856, did not become really effective, given that the disregard from Muslims towards the "infidels" (*kâliv*) was progressively growing in strength and scope as the Empire was weakening.

The "Armenian question" especially developed after the Balkan crisis and the Russian-Ottoman war, when thousands of Muslim refugees (*Muhacir*), in particular Circassians and Turks, arrived in the Empire and were relocated in Anatolia by the

[1]In this introduction I refer to the historical context preceding the Armenian massacres of 1915–16 in a very brief and even sketchy way. For an accurate illustration of these precedents, numerous and significant historical studies can be consulted. Some of them are quoted in this paper as in other contributions of this Volume.

[2]The Armenian community was for a long time considered the *millet-y-sadyka*, "the most loyal millet" (see, inter alios, Lewy (2005a), pp. 3, 7).

Refugee Commission (*Muhacirin Komisyonu*).[3] At that point in time, the Christian Armenians began to be perceived as "others" in a territory that had been their motherland for centuries.[4]

Moreover, facing a gradual disintegration following both further military defeats under the rule of the Sultan Abdul-Hamīd II and the European Great Powers' expansion ambitions, the Ottoman Empire reacted with carrying out massive killings of Armenians, who were claiming more rights (1894–96).[5] Over-optimistically, the Armenian community, in its claims against the Sublime Porte, relied on the support and protection by some among the major European Powers of that time, as this was provided in the 1878 Berlin Treaty.[6]

It should also be noted that the *coup d'état* against the Sultan and the takeover by the "Young Turks" in 1908 was at first perceived as a project of modernization and democratization of the Ottoman rule. The Armenian community, sensitive to new liberal ideals, welcomed this takeover. However, the "Young Turks", organised in the Committee of Union and Progress (CUP) (*Ittihadve Terakki*), started, already in 1909, their turkification policy. This process worsened in 1913, when the triumvirate of the three Pasha–Mehmed Talât, the future Minister of Interior, Ismail

[3]See on this movement of populations Van Hear (1998). See also the interview given by the Turkish historian, professor at the Sabanci University in Istanbul, Halil Berktay, on 1 November 2000 after a Symposium in Chicago on the Armenian tragedy (http://www.atour.com/~aahgn/news/20001101c.html).

[4]As T. Akçam, a Turkish scholar, who went into exile in '70s after having escaped from jail in Turkey as human rights activist, significantly stresses, "the era of nation-state ushered in a new period of defining 'the other'": Akçam (2012), p. IX. For an objective understanding of the events of 1915–16 in the Ottoman Empire, is also interesting what Halil Berktay says, inter alia: "Th[e] period of the second half of the 19th century and the beginning of the 20th century was a time of rapacious, social-Darwinist nationalisms in Europe, in which it was 'kill or be killed'. It was a time in which massacres, large and small, were carried out, and in which the Turkish Muslim population was also very much a victim." (quoted supra fn. 3).

[5]The crushing of an Armenian rebellion by some revolutionists, although it did not have much success within their community, caused in 1894 about 4.000/6.000 victims mostly among innocent mountaineers in the region of Sasun and was followed by other massacres in Constantinople, Trebizond and Urfa in 1895 and in the District of Van in 1896. See, inter alios, Lewy (2005a), p. 20 ff.

[6]See, Sect. 4.1.2. Indeed, in 1878 the first Armenian political parties – *Hunchak* and *Dashnak* – were organized to claim civil rights and parity with Muslims. These two parties were then represented in the Ottoman National Assembly until the fraudulent elections of 1912 (the so called "Elections of clubs") and were peacefully and legally fighting for the democratization of the Empire together with the Liberal Union and other parties opposing the Young Turks rule. Armenian parliamentarians were amongst the members of the leadership massacred in 1915, as was Krikor Zohrab, a personal friend of Talât Pasha!

Enver, the Minister of the war and Ahmed Gemal, the Minister for the Navy–took power to hold it until the end of WWI.[7]

When the conflict approached, the Armenian leadership supported the neutrality of the Ottoman Empire. Eventually, the members of the community could not but fight for their country against the European Powers of the Entente. This sometimes led to difficult situations, given that Russian–Armenian citizens were also enrolled in the Tsarist Army. Some Ottoman Armenians may have sympathized with them and some may have deserted for enrolling in the Russian-Armenian battalions fighting in Caucasus.[8] However, this is no evidence that the community as such would have betrayed their country, as the CUP alleged then and Turkey still does nowadays in trying to justify the massacres of 1915–16.

At any rate, what is relevant here is that, especially during WWI, the Armenian "massacres and deportations"—for now I prefer to use only these terms, given that the fact that those tragic events occurred is accepted even by those who deny the genocide—escalated to such proportions and characteristics to possibly reveal the intent of the ruling power to destroy in whole or in part the biggest community in Anatolia whose religion, ethnicity, culture were different from those of the

[7]On this historical background, see also Flores in this Volume, and the literature he refers to, as well as all the literature quoted in the present paper. I limit myself to underline what the Turkish historian Halil Berktay says about the Triumvirate members: "It's necessary to understand something not just about the Ittihatve Terakki, but also about the three-man military dictatorship of Enver, Cemal, and Talât that headed it. These were not traditional Ottoman notables. They were a new type of elite [...]. They were extremely ambitious and predatory. They were positivists, without roots, and had risen only as a result of their education and thanks to the army. They lived a life of violence. This violence was of a sort that had been imposed on them by the great powers and the revolts in the Balkans, and as a result they became extreme nationalists. They were fighting desperately for the survival of the Empire [...]. The Ittihatve Terakki triumvirate of Enver, Cemal, and Talât was an extraordinary administration that had been born in these conditions of war and struggle" (supra, fn. 3). See also Morgenthau (1918), p. 106–109.

[8]There were some Ottoman Armenian deserters fighting during WWI in volunteer units of the Russian Army. But these were sporadic instances (see on this question and on the attempt of the Ottoman leadership to solve the problem in cooperation with the Turkish authorities Payaslian (2006), p. 156 ff.) These units had been indeed created and mostly composed of and commanded by Russian Armenians (as commander Drastamat Kanayan) or by Ottoman Armenians who had left their homeland after the first persecutions and massacres, at the end of the XIX and beginning of the XX century (as did both Andranik in 1907, when disagreeing with the cooperation of the Armenian leadership with the "Young Turks", and Hamazasp Srvandztyan in 1914 (he then participated in the Armenian resistance in Van).

Turks-Muslims.[9] This would imply, according to some commentators and the Armenian claim, the qualification of such massacres as the first genocide of the XX century.[10]

The characterization of these tragic events as "genocide" has widely been discussed among historians, politicians, political scientists, lawmakers and jurists, who have however reached controversial conclusions. They have conducted their researches and analyses on the basis of historic, diplomatic, photographic and media documentation that is still substantially available, even though the tragic events have occurred more than a century ago and many Ottoman documents have disappeared or are still hidden.[11] Also available are the testimonies of many eye-witnesses, including victims-survivors, which were collected by some

[9]The fact that the war represented the real opportunity for the atrocities against Armenians is discussed by many scholars. See, in particular, Flores, in this volume. Talât himself affirmed, on 6 January 1915: "Turkey is taking advantage of the war in order to thoroughly liquidate its internal foes, i.e., the indigenous Christians, without being thereby disturbed by foreign intervention", quoted by Dadrian (1989), p. 258. Interesting is also the interpretation of these events in the context of WWI given by Halil Berktay: "The Allied landing at Gallipoli during the First World War [the night of 24/25 April 1915] created the fear among the Ottomans, who had suffered continuous losses throughout the 19th century and were now left with little but Anatolia, that 'Now we're even going to lose Istanbul, and we won't even be able to hang on to Anatolia'. For this reason, there's an integral connection between the Ottoman psychosis of having its back to the wall, being desperate and harassed, and the policy that the military dictatorship of the Committee of Union and Progress (Ittihatve Terakki) would launch against the Armenians on the eastern front. The 24/25 April date was when this desperation was crystallized." (quoted supra fn. 3).

[10]The massacres and deportations of Armenians were characterized as genocide also by Pope Francis, who was warned by President Erdogan not to make "such a mistake again", while the Prime Minister Davutoglu accused the Pope of "blackmail" and of having joined an "evil front". On the qualification of the "Armenian genocide" see also, inter several *alios,* Weitz (2015), as well as the interesting sentence of the Permanent Peoples' Tribunal on the Armenian Genocide, issued in Paris on 16 April 1984 (http://permanentpeoplestribunal.org/11-armenian-genocide-paris-13-16-april-1984/?lang=en). See also T. Akçam, who, on the basis of first-hands documents, conducted a new research on the "Armenian question" after his previous ones. This research resulted in the volume Akçam (2012), where there is also, in the first Chapter, a detailed illustration of Turkish archives and other relevant sources, together with an in-depth discussion of their reliability. Indeed, Akçam also accurately discusses how the archives have been purged from the documents concerning the Armenian massacres, how they disappeared or are perhaps still hidden.

[11]It must also be stressed that Ottoman documents cannot be read by present day Turks, save by some scholars, after the nationalistic reform of the Turkish language started in 1928 (see Metz (1995)). As to the photographic documents, several of these come from Armin T. Wegner, a paramedic, member of the German Army, present on Ottoman territory in 1915–16. There are also some photos of the Armenian concentration camps, taken by him during a military mission in Mesopotamia. He succeeded to hide only some of the numerous photos of the massacred, starved and suffering victims and send them to Germany and the U.S. But his activity was discovered and eventually he was recalled to Germany, where, two decades later, he tried to fight against the criminal rule of the Nazis. Persecuted by them, he went on exile to Italy. I have read some of his very emotional interviews to Italian newspapers, where he was giving direct testimony on the Armenian massacres and deportations.

historians even as the events were unfolding[12]—or reported in writing before the end of WWI, in particular by diplomats and missionaries present on the field of the atrocities.[13] Among the available documentation, particularly significant are the decrees issued and the open and secret orders given by the ruling Ottoman power

[12]I particularly refer to the Official Report on the Armenian massacres prepared by J. Bryce, a British historian and diplomat, for the Secretary of State for Foreign Affairs. The Report was later edited by the (then) young historian A. J. Toynbee and published in Bryce and Toynbee (1916). In the very words of J. Bryce (Preface, p. XXI), "the evidence here collected comes from various sources. A large, perhaps the largest, part has been drawn from neutral witnesses who were living in or passing through Asiatic Turkey while these events were happening, and had opportunities of observing them. Another part comes from natives of the country, nearly all Christians, who succeeded, despite the stringency of the Turkish censorship, in getting letters into neutral countries, or who themselves escaped into Greece, or Russia, or Egypt and were there able to write down what they had seen. A third but much smaller part comes from subjects of the now belligerent Powers (mostly Germans) who were in Turkey when these events were happening, and subsequently published in their own countries accounts based on their personal knowledge." In his Preface, J. Bryce also discusses the reliability of this documentation and its sources. The Bryce/Toynbee compilation was accused by Turkey of being war propaganda and some Western commentators were convinced of this as Bryce had also authored a Report on the atrocities of Germans in Belgium, which were not considered credible! Needless to say, this type of criticisms reveals a discriminatory and racist approach, as if Germans (or other Europeans) could not be put on the same footing of Turks, Kurds and Circassians in respect of the commission of atrocities. In fact, these German atrocities of 1914 in Belgium (and France) were instead proved (see Horne and Kramer (2001)). WWII proved even better, as the former Yugoslavia conflict did, that Europeans are also capable of perpetrating mass atrocities. So, I consider the Bryce/Toynbee compilation reliable. I further refer to the Report by L. A. Davis, the U.S. Consul of Harput (1914–1917), to the State Department, written in 1918 upon his return in the United States. The Consul had directly witnessed the bodies of thousands of slaughtered Armenians and, with the help of a medical doctor, tried to understand the causes of deaths. This Report, which contains several pictures of the victims, was found in the U.S. National Archives only in 1988 by a researcher, Susan Blair, who then published it with a commentary (2001). The experiences referred to in are also relevant.

[13]I refer here to Morgenthau (1918). In this landmark book, the former U.S. Ambassador in Constantinople (1913–1916) recorded all his talks with the CUP members of the Triumvirate and other diplomats and military present at that time in the Ottoman capital. He was indeed a direct witness of the top rulers decisions and intentions. He likewise recorded in this *Story* many reports he received from the US consuls present in all districts of the Empire and from the numerous US religious missionaries operating in the entire Ottoman territory. US consuls and missionaries were direct witnesses of the massacres and deportations. In this *Story,* Morgenthau also discusses the events with a surprisingly modern approach. Indeed, he constantly stresses the elements characterizing the Murder of a Nation, as he labels the 1915–16 events in Chapter XXIV of his *Story* according to the same determinants of the current legal notion of genocide. Given his continuous contacts with direct sources, I consider that, together with Bryce/Toynbee compilation and the Report of Davis (1918), Morgenthau's Story is one of the most important documents for reference on what really happened in 1915–16 (however, I do not share some malicious observations by Morgenthau on "Turks", even if there are understandable when they were directed towards the triumvirate's members). I have also found very useful Kévorkian and Ternon (2014). The synthetic narration of all that happened in 1915–16 contained in a Report of 1916 is also impressive. It is published in Niepage (1917).

for the execution of the massacres and deportations.[14] Little information is likewise available on the Ottoman criminal trials held in 1919–1920 against some of the individuals responsible for those atrocities.[15]

On the basis of such a documentation, more recently, the Turkish official denial or understatement of the massacres, as their justification, seem to be losing ground.[16] Their characterization as genocide seems instead increasingly accepted.[17] Among those who argue against the characterization of those tragic events as genocide, some admit to the large scale and the state-sponsored nature of the

---

[14]There is, however, a very heated debate about the reliability of documentation related to these orders. In addition to their discussion by T. Akçam mentioned supra, see Sarafian (1999) and Lewy (2005b), p. 3 ff. (but on this latter, see below, fn. 166).

[15]See on this Marchesi, in this volume, Akçam (2012), Dadrian (1997). Some proceedings are also commented by Cassese (2008) and Cassese (2009), pp. 575, 757 f., 806, 897.

[16]The historian J. McCarthy reveals to be the most fervent denier of the genocide and defender of the massacres (sic!) as a result of a civil war: see *The Armenian-Turkish Conflict*, Speech given by him at the Turkish Grand National Assembly on 24 March 2005 (https://wilson.engr.wisc.edu/Armenia/justin.html), McCarthy (2006, 2015) and McCarthy et al. (2006), as well as the Conference of Prof. McCarthy quoted below, fn. 88. From a scientific point of view all thesis have, of course, their dignity if supported by historical data and logical arguments. Yet, acknowledging massacres and attributing them to a civil war situation as well as to criminal bands represent an incoherent reading of the facts, since massacres are massacres and nothing else. In his numerous conferences in which he appears as an ardent propagandist of the Turkish positions, this historian does not bring evidence, but only makes categorical statements on the civil war justification, where Turks would have massacred Armenians and the latter would have massacred the former. It is a pity that he ignores the fact that even in the hypothetical civil war context of 1915–16 there were some domestic and international rules that the Ottoman Empire had to comply with. Furthermore, the tu quoque argument can never be used to justify a very serious wrongdoing. In arguing the tu quoque defense he refers to "thousands of Turks' killed by Armenians", not considering that in the events of 1915–16 there are, at any rate, even assuming those killings did take place, two different elements that testify the destruction of the Armenian community by the Ottoman Empire: deportations without return of elders, women and children, and the involvement of the Turkish rulers against innocent victims. Indeed, when prof. McCarthy is a lone speaker on "the Armenian question", as it frequently occurs, the weaknesses of his thesis may not appear, but, after a serious comparison between different views, they are clear. After all, even prof. McCarthy admits to half a million of Armenians perished, as "sickness, exhaustion following long marches, immediate change of climate", i.e. nothing else than the destructive modalities of deportations of children, women and elders!

[17]See Flores and Latino in this book and, in particular, Robertson (2009): His opinion deserves special attention as it comes from a British counsel in leading criminal cases and an International Judge on genocide, war crimes and crimes against humanity (first President of the Special Court for Sierra Leone) and an author of books in this field. See also Robertson (2016).

massacres.[18] There are also those who deny the massacres altogether, scale down their extent, or only acknowledge some murders and deaths as "collateral damages" of a lawful repressive reaction against Armenian rebels, and/or justify deportations of Armenian civilians by military necessity and their tragic outcomes by the difficult war conditions, which also Muslims would have suffered.[19] The latter are in particular the most frequent official positions of Turkey.[20]

Considering that the controversial qualification of the 1915–16 massacres and deportations as genocide is the crucial issue at stake here, and that the definition of genocide is included in the 1948 Convention, the first and preliminary legal

---

[18]For instance, B. Lewis, Interview of 14 April 2002, https://www.ataa.org/reference/lewis.pdf, specifically questions the analogy with the holocaust, while in 1915–16 only a deportation policy would have occurred. Apart from the under-estimation of the killings, he also does not consider that deportations and their modalities were the most relevant components of the destruction of the Armenian nation. In 1994, on account of his denial of the Armenian genocide, Lewis was convicted in France to paying a symbolic sum of 1 franc for "grievous prejudice to truthful memory". I have some reservations on the criminalization of denialism, in particular when not accompanied by instigating to hatred or racist behaviour, which is frequent but was not the case of Lewis.

[19]Among those who deny the massacres of 1915–16 or justify them in the context of a civil war or simply war conditions, in addition to McCarthy (2006, 2015) and McCarthy et al. (2006), there are Shaw and Shaw (1977), Gürün (1985). I would put amongst them also Lewy (2005a). This latter historian attempts to give an objective illustration of the facts occurred, as he purportedly states that other historians have not. The accuracy and objectivity of his research is however convincingly contested by Akçam (2008). Its weakness also appears in Lewy (2005b) (see about this above, fn. 166).

[20]Turkish authorities, anxious to deny massacres and death marches or at least to find some justification, give contradictory versions of the atrocities occurred during the war. Inter alia: 1. the Armenian population was attacked by "bandits", 2. it was attacked by people of the Ottoman provinces where Armenians were fighting with the enemy (in particular with Russia), 3. some killings of Armenian men or their "relocation" constituted a lawful defense of the Empire against their uprising and collaboration with the enemy, 4. some suffering of the civilian members of the Armenian community was caused by the "relocation" (or "resettlement") organized by the authorities in time of war for military necessity or security reasons (even for the Armenians' security!), 5. the suffering of Armenian civilians was caused by war conditions, which also affected thousands of Muslim Turks. On 29 April 2014, President Erdogan asked: if a genocide had been occurred, would there still be Armenians in Turkey? In so doing, he clearly showed his complete ignorance of the determinants of genocide, while also implicitly denying the Jews and Tutsi genocides, which were legally ascertained by criminal courts, notwithstanding the presence of Jews even in Germany and Tutsi in Rwanda after the genocide. For a recent Turkish view on the "Armenian question", see Tacar and Gauin (2012). The two authors, a former Turkish Ambassador and an expert in strategic issues, discuss International Law issues, but clearly show that these matters are not in the realm of their areas of competence. In particular, they do not see the difference between international responsibility pursuant to general International Law and competence of international bodies to deal with it. Their writing is a reply to a contribution by Avedian (2012) in the European Journal of International Law (EJIL). Although he is an historian, Avedian seems to be more familiar with International Law issues. However, why did the EJIL not ask experts of International Law to deal with such complex and delicate issues that do not only concern the reconstruction of historical truth in the "Armenian question"?

question is whether this international agreement is applicable to the tragic events occurred in 1915–16. On this, I will confine myself to some short observations, essentially referring to an essay in this volume that concludes for the temporal inapplicability of the Genocide Convention to such events.[21]

I should mention that the inapplicability of the Convention to the *Shoah*, which is almost universally and consensually labelled as genocide, would also be worth discussing. At any rate, the inapplicability of the Genocide Convention, whether to the massacres and deportations of Armenians or the *Shoah* does not automatically mean, as we shall see, that these two tragic events cannot be labelled as genocide. This notion could have also been a legacy of international law prior to 1948, although it is indisputable that in 1915, a State or individual behaviour aimed at destroying a group for racial, national, ethnical, religious reasons was not termed as genocide. This term was coined for the "crime of crimes" by a young Polish-Jewish Prosecutor in 1943 and legally adopted by a United Nations General Assembly Resolution in 1946[22] and by the Genocide Convention only in 1948.[23] In my view, however, it is relevant here that, in 1918, the massacres of Armenians were labelled —we could say "politically" labelled—by an authoritative and credible eye witness as a premeditated "murder of a nation", which means nothing else than "genocide" (*genos* in old Greek = nation; *cidium* in Latin = murder).[24]

On the other hand, it is difficult—or perhaps impossible, as another contributor to this Volume argues[25]—to trace back to the WWI both the prohibition of such a specific conduct, defined according to the characteristics that are specifically relevant to genocide, and the obligations for States as they are regulated in the 1948 Convention. This does not mean, however, that the mass-killings and deportations of 1915–16 cannot be labelled as deliberate destruction of the Armenian community, or that some of those conventional obligations did not exist at that time pursuant to other applicable international rules. On the latter issue, it is worth stressing from the outset that, on the basis of my decades-long experience in studying and teaching International Law, I am firmly convinced that those who assert that massacres and deportations of Armenians took place in a legal vacuum

---

[21]Cipolletti, in this Volume.

[22]UNGA Resolution, 1946. 96 (I).

[23]As correctly underlined by Sir Geoffrey Robertson, the destruction of a substantial part of the Armenians in Turkey became, in the years before the Holocaust, the paradigm for those who argued for the creation of a new crime to be called genocide: Robertson (2009), p. 3.

[24]Morgenthau (1918). Also in German the word "Völkermord" (the murder of a nation) is often used instead of "genozid".

[25]Gianelli, in this Volume.

which went as far as allowing barbarism, are essentially wrong. This is (inter alia) what I want to demonstrate in this paper.

However, on the question of the possibility of labelling the events of 1915–16 as "genocide", I intend to follow a different approach than the usual "genocide yes/genocide no" approach. Indeed, given the general acceptance of both the non-retroactive effect of the 1948 Convention and the inexistence, at the time of the Armenians tragic events, of the legal term "genocide", the "genocide yes/genocide no" vision leads to irreconcilable outcomes.[26] I will therefore confine my discussion to examining whether the massacres and deportations could be factually identified as a deliberate destruction in whole or in part of the Armenian community, on one of the same grounds as those indicated in the Convention.[27] Leaving aside the question of its legal qualification and labelling, this is, in my opinion, the actual key issue of the dispute, and it constitutes the keystone of this paper.

More precisely, after over a century since the mass-killings and deportations of 1915–1916, the question as to whether these events may or may not be labelled as the destruction—in whole or in part—of the Christian Armenian community has to be seen from the perspective of the conduct of the Ottoman Empire rather than from that of the individual perpetrators. Moreover, the Genocide Convention deals not only with the individual crime, but also with acts of genocide by States, which would equally consist in the acts enumerated in the Convention's Articles II and III.

---

[26]However, the 1948 Convention, by "recognizing that at all periods of history genocide has inflicted great losses on humanity" (Preamble), allows to assume that, according to States Parties, the term genocide can be used for such a conduct whenever it has occurred.

[27]An analogous approach was already followed by the International Center for Transitional Justice and it resulted in the following conclusion: "The Events [...] can [...] be said to include all of the elements of the crime of genocide as defined in the Convention, and legal scholars as well as historians, politicians, journalists and other people would be justified in continuing to so describe them" (quoted by Phillips (2015)). I do not agree with W.A. Schabas' suggestion to qualify the tragic events of 1915–16 only as crime against humanity (Schabas 2011, p. 256). I agree that genocide is a crime against humanity, but a specific one, and this specificity needs to be reflected in the way it is labelled. Furthermore, in labelling those events only as crime against humanity, one loses their twofold characterization: In addition of consisting in an individual crime, genocide is also a state violation of International Law. The ILC has rejected the term "crime" with regard to States' violations of fundamental international rules, in view of avoiding a sort of "criminalization" of States' conducts. Moreover, labelling the 1915–16 events as crimes against humanity could implicitly be read as simply and automatically considering them as conduct by bandits or, perhaps, by (incompetent) State agents and not an overall State-decided/planned/organized destruction of a community. This approach would render worthless any discussion on these events, given that no individual perpetrator is still alive.

In the *Genocide* case, the International Court of Justice (ICJ), a Court which is competent to assess States' and not individuals' conduct, was just requested to assess, pursuant to the 1948 Convention, whether a State—Serbia-Montenegro—committed genocide and/or did not prevent and suppress it. The Court stated that:

> State responsibility can arise under the Convention for genocide and complicity, without an individual being convicted of the crime or an associated one.[28]

This means that, although some perpetrators of the Armenian massacres and deportations were indeed tried and convicted before Ottoman Martial Courts, the potential destructive intention of the Ottoman State, as represented by its rulers, can be enquired independently of any criminal proceeding against the individual perpetrators. Therefore, in exploring the question whether the Ottoman Empire destroyed in whole or in part the Armenian community, it is necessary to enquire both the conduct of the Turk rulers[29] and the facts occurred on the field of the 1915–16 events.

Of course, I am aware that facts and law always find themselves in a dialectic relation and that in the present case this relation cannot be discussed on the basis of the Genocide Convention. It is however also true that facts logically precede the law that would subsume them where appropriate. Concerning the facts of 1915–16, I will thus confine myself to borrowing both the determinants of the destruction of a national, racial, ethnical or religious group provided for by the Genocide Convention and the factual criteria utilized by international tribunals in genocide cases in order to verify whether the radical nationalistic Ottoman power—in the hands of the CUP—did accomplish the destruction in whole or in part of the

[28] *Case Concerning Application of the Convention on the Prevention and Punishment of the Crime of Genocide*, Bosnia and Herzegovina *v.* Serbia and Montenegro, Judgment of 26 February 2007 (here ICJ *Genocide case*), para. 182. The Court also stressed that "The different procedures followed by, and powers available to, this Court and to the courts and tribunals trying persons for criminal offences, do not themselves indicate that there is a legal bar to the Court itself finding that genocide or the other acts enumerated in Article III have been committed. Under its Statute the Court has the capacity to undertake that task" (para. 209–210). The Court competence in relation to State responsibility for genocide is apparent by the content of Article IX of the Convention: "Disputes between the Contracting Parties relating to the interpretation, application or fulfilment of the present Convention, including those relating to the responsibility of a State for genocide or for any of the other acts enumerated in art. III, shall be submitted to the ICJ at the request of any of the parties to the dispute".

[29] On the attribution to the State of the acts of the Ottoman rulers - and likely also of the Special Organization – see below fn. 30, 86, 89 and 177.

Armenian nation, with the executive help of the semi-secret Special Organisation (*Teskilat-iMahsusa*).[30]

The issue of analysing the events of 1915–16 from the perspective of the same determinants provided by the Genocide Convention is not the object of a purely abstract and intellectual exercise. Apart from the fact that the issue retains great relevance from the historical and political point of view, the potential ascertainment of a deliberate—hence, likely, state-decided or state-sponsored—destruction of the Armenian community would also entail important consequences in respect of the position taken by Turkey and other States, international institutions and some historians.[31]

In exploring the facts I also have to consider whether, according to the positions of current Turkish authorities (as of the Ottoman authorities), the "1915–16 events" only reveal a repression of an uprising by members of an Ottoman minority plotting with the enemy and, concerning the massacres and deportations of elders, women and children, a mere vengeance by some "bandits".

If, on the contrary, the facts explored lead to ascertain the determinants provided for by the Genocide Convention, I will need to first verify whether such determinants would have been subsumed under a law applicable at that time to States and/ or to individuals. Even if no international rule specifically prohibited the destruction of a group on the basis of the said determinants, it would still be relevant to explore whether the atrocities committed against Armenians were attributable to the Ottoman Empire and whether they have infringed other international rules in force at that time, such as, inter alia, conventional rules in the matter of the protection of religious minorities and/or general international rules.

[30]The *Teskilat-iMahsusa* was a semi-secret para-military organization created in 1914, put under the orders of Dr. Bahaettin Sakir and charged with the task of coordinating massacres and deportations. It resorted to hundreds of Turks, Circassians and Kurds for carrying out criminal activities on the field. It already had an experience with the forced expulsion of 200.000 *Rûm* from the Aegean coast in 1914: see on this the Introduction to Kieser, Oktem and Reinkowski (2015); see also Üngör (2016). On the links of this Organisation with the Ottoman rulers and on its composition, see, inter alia, what the Turkish historian, Halil Berktay writes: "It is clear that Bahaettin Sakir, who operated as the Teskilat-i Mahsusa's man for Enver, Cemal, and Talât, set up death squads in the region. Some of these people were convicted criminals who were saved from the gallows and released from prison just to carry out such activities" (supra, fn. 3). Such an evaluation of the Special Organisation was also made by the Martial Courts' Trials held in 1919–20. Being this Organisation directly connected with the CUP members, it was indeed a state organ of the Ottoman State, even though only a de facto organ.

[31]This ascertainment is relevant not only for the Armenian community, but also for the Kurdish and Turkish peoples. These peoples would need to oppose an official biased reconstruction of the Armenian events. They too are the victims of such a reconstruction, which represents "them" as the unique culprits, without taking into account that religious authorities had convinced them that killing Armenians was an order from God. Indeed, Leslie Davis recalls the feeling of Muslims living near the Consulate in these words: "We could all hear them piously calling upon Allah to bless them in their efforts to kill the hated Christians." Davis (1918), p. 69. On the proclamation of Jihad see Payaslian (2006), p. 156.

Furthermore, even if the allegation by Turkish authorities and some historians about the Armenian uprising would not be grounded on facts, I would still need to enquire, in the section on applicable law, whether the facts, as alleged by them, could have been legally justified.

The possible determination of violations of international law by The Sublime Porte in the one or the other context—destruction of a peaceful community or repression of an uprising—will bring me to also explore whether such violations were considered at that time individual crimes of international concern or merely crimes according to the Ottoman legislation. This question is of course no longer relevant *in se*, but has a certain link, as we will see, with the responsibility of the State concerned and even the responsibility of other States.

I hope I will be able to demonstrate that the atrocities amounted to violations of International Law in force at that time. The question of the responsibility of the Ottoman Empire and of Turkey, as successor State, would therefore arise.[32] The question of the responsibility of Turkey *per se* for having, inter alia, adopted and implemented the Law of 27 June 1926 and the follow-up Regulation of 1928 concerning Armenian properties seized during the deportations would also arise.

The issue of the State's responsibility, which in any case I will only briefly touch upon, is particularly important in view of the fact that the individuals who were active protagonists of the mass-killings and deportations have passed away, while the community and the heirs of "direct victims" are still waiting for justice.

2 A Preliminary Legal Question: The Deliberate Destruction of a Group Protected by the Genocide Convention of 1948 Before Its Entry into Force

2.1 The Non-applicability of the Convention to the Destruction of a Group Protected Before Its Entry into Force

On the temporal non-applicability of the Genocide Convention to the 1915–16 events, I share the conclusion reached in the relevant contribution to this volume.[33] The Convention's non-applicability does not rely on the long temporal distance of those tragic events from the adoption of the treaty, but simply on the fact that the Convention only applies to future genocides.[34] Thus, this Convention does not

---

[32]On the question of the continuity between the Ottoman Empire and present-day Turkey or succession of this latter State to the former, see V. Avedian (2012), pp. 799–805.

[33]Cipolletti in this Volume.

[34]Thus, Article IX of the 1948 Convention cannot be a basis for the Court jurisdiction on the dispute about labelling the massacres and deportations of Armenians as genocide. For an opposite view, see de Zayas (2010).

apply either to the Nazi atrocities commenced in the 1930s against German Jews and continued during the war against all Jews in the Nazi occupied territories.

Does this imply that those atrocities did not constitute genocide? Or, rather, was genocide already a prohibited act and a crime of international concern before the beginning of the massive destruction of the Jewish world community for racial/ethnic/religious reasons? Only in this latter case, one could understand why the labelling of the *Shoah* as genocide is undisputed. In exploring this question, I will devote particular attention to the jurisprudence of the Nuremberg IMT and the criminal justice bodies that operated in Germany as occupying jurisdictions after WWII.

2.2 Genocide as a State Violation of International Law and as a Crime of International Concern Before 1948

It is not by chance that tragic events resulting in the destruction of a community were the object, after WWI, of a research by Raphael Lemkin, a young Polish-Jewish Prosecutor. His studies were in particular focused on "the premeditated destruction of national, racial, religious, social collectivities".[35] Firmly convinced of the criminal nature of such behaviour, Lemkin intended to submit to the League of Nations a proposal in view of the adoption of an international instrument criminalizing such "offenses of barbarity and vandalism" as constituting a "transnational" danger. We know that the proposal, submitted in 1933—at the beginning of Hitler's rule, when this criminal dictator had just made known his intentions towards the Jews[36]—, was rejected. Needless to say, this was only for political reasons. But the influence of such kind of reasons on the development of international rules cannot be ignored.

The political reasons that had led to under-estimate the Nazi and Fascist atrocities in their early stages, could not prevent from providing, in the Nuremberg and Tokyo Statutes, for crimes against humanity as crimes under pre-existing general international law, as explicitly affirmed in the Nuremberg judgement.[37] Yet, among these crimes against humanity, genocide was not specifically envisaged, notwithstanding that this term, coined in 1943, had become publicly known in 1944.[38]

[35]Lemkin (1933).

[36]The first anti-Semite law was issued in Germany in April 1933.

[37]See the arguments developed in the Nuremberg Judgement on the principle of legality: International Military Tribunal (IMT), Trial of the Major War Criminals before the International Military Tribunal, Nuremberg 14 November 1945–1 October 1946, Published at Nuremberg, Germany 1947, p. 462. For an interesting comment of those arguments see Acquaviva (2011).

[38]This new word is contained in the Preface (of October 1943) of Lemkin (1944).

However, it is noteworthy that the Prosecutor of the Nuremberg IMT evoked the term "genocide" one time in his indictment and not only with respect to Jews. In his presentation of count three "War Crimes: Murder and Ill-Treatment of Civilian Populations…", he stated: "In some occupied territories the defendants interfered in religious matters, persecuted members of the clergy and monastic orders, and expropriated church property. They conducted deliberate and systematic genocide, viz., the extermination of racial and national groups, against the civilian populations of certain occupied territories in order to destroy particular races and classes of people and national, racial, or religious groups, particularly Jews, Poles, and Gypsies and others."[39] Through this statement, the Nuremberg Prosecutor, in resorting to the term coined by Raphael Lemkin, intended to characterise, in a non-technical way, the Nazi criminal discriminatory behaviour that had brought to the elimination of millions of individuals on racial, ethnic, national and other grounds. This discriminatory behaviour was considered in the Nuremberg Statute under the counts of persecution and extermination as crimes against humanity, two offenses that described such behaviour inadequately.

It is also relevant in the context of the present discussion that the Nuremberg Judges, in illustrating the tragic events suffered by Jews and Pols, preferred to quote the word "elimination" contained in the Nazi orders[40] and used themselves this term when giving their succinct legal arguments in the Judgement.[41] In convicting the accused, they ignored the term "genocide" and only resorted—of course—to the statutory terms of extermination and persecution.

The term "genocide" has instead been frequently used in the proper sense of crime against humanity aimed at the destruction of Jews not only by the Prosecutors, but also by the Judges in the Judgements of the other Nuremberg Tribunals, the jurisdiction of which was provided for the same counts of the IMTs Statutes by the Control Council Law No. 10, issued in Berlin the 20 December 1945 for the occupied territories of Germany.

Indeed, these trials began after the adoption of the first UNGA Resolution on genocide, in which this crime is considered as already recognized by international customary law. The Judgments in the *Justice* case referred to this Resolution as follows: "The General Assembly is not an international legislature, but it is the most authoritative organ in existence for the interpretation of world opinion. Its recognition of genocide as an international crime is persuasive evidence of the fact. We

---

[39]IMT, Trial of the Major War Criminals before the International Military Tribunal, p. 43–44.

[40]IMT, Trial of the Major War Criminals before the International Military Tribunal, pp. 202 and 340.

[41]IMT, Trial of the Major War Criminals before the International Military Tribunal, p. 272: Judges referred to "the elimination of all inferior races", borrowing the Nazi language.

approve and adopt its conclusions."[42] This view was also adopted in the Genocide Convention proper.[43] Therefore, for sure, among the crimes against humanity, "the crime of crimes", "the crime without a name",[44] in its specific characteristic of deliberate destruction, in whole or in part, of a racial, national, ethnic, religious group as such, was already a legacy of general international law before the UNGA Resolution, perhaps even before WWII.

Yet, in an attempt to reinforce deterrence by giving more certainty to its determinants, after WWII, states decided to move to a written binding ascertainment of the prohibition and criminalisation of genocide. They further created new conventional rules concerning the objective and subjective elements of the crime, as well as the states' obligation to prevent and repress it pursuant to the territorial jurisdictional link. The provision in the Convention of the only territorial link was justified by the envisaged concurrent jurisdiction of an international criminal court. However, the then fragmented international community prevented from establishing such an international court and the mere territorial jurisdictional link proved to be useless.

It is not easy to determine when genocide became a legacy of general international law. Probably not at the time of the Armenians massacres or of that of Herero and Nama, carried out by German soldiers in South-West Africa in 1904–1907, which some other historians consider the general test for the *Shoah* and the first genocide of the Twentieth Century, instead of that of Armenians.[45]

[42]Military Tribunal III, *Opinion and Judgement*, vol. 3, p. 963. The Judges go on to state: "As set forth in the indictment, the acts charged as crimes against humanity were committed before the occupation of Germany. They were described as racial persecutions by Nazi officials perpetrated upon German nationals. The crime of genocide is an illustration" (p. 983). In the same Judgment, they convicted the defendant *Lautz* stating that he "was criminally implicated in enforcing the law against Poles and Jews which we deem to be a part of the established governmental plan for the extermination of those races. He was an accessory to, and took a consenting part in, the crime of genocide" (p. 1128). More or less in similar terms, still referring to genocide, they assessed the responsibility of *Rothaug* for having applied "the cruel and discriminatory law against Poles and Jews" and having so participated "in the crime of genocide" (p. 1156).

[43]Indeed, see the following statement included in the Genocide Convention: "The Contracting Parties confirm that genocide [...] is a crime under international law" (Article 1). If the States had adopted a new international rule criminalizing ex-novo the destruction of a national, racial, ethnical or religious group as such, they should have undertaken, and not only confirmed, "to consider genocide as a crime under international law".

[44]The horrendous acts committed by the German occupation forces were labelled as such by Churchill in a broadcast from London on 24 August 1941: http://www.preventgenocide.org/genocide/crimewithoutaname.htm.

[45]This extermination came weakly to the fore after the start of negotiations between Germany and Namibia over possible reparation payments. See Bruneteau (2006), who discusses in the 1st Chapter the massacres of indigenous peoples by imperialist Europe.

At any rate, independently of their legal qualification, the mass-killings and deportations of Armenians could have constituted, in their essence, a massive and deliberate destruction of a religious/ethnical community, i.e. a Murder of a Nation, in line with their characterization provided by a direct witness.[46] This is what I intend to verify.

3 The Determinants of the Armenian Massacres and Deportations in Light of the Genocide Convention Criteria as Applied by the ICTY/ICTR and ICJ Jurisprudence

3.1 The Facts

In addressing the issue of whether the facts that occurred to the Armenians in 1915–16 constituted a deliberate destruction in whole or in part of a group as such on one of the discriminatory grounds envisaged in the Genocide Convention and replicated *verbatim* in the Statutes of International Criminal Tribunals for the former Yugoslavia (ICTY) and Rwanda (ICTR), I will be guided both by the features of genocide according to the Convention and by the factual criteria utilised in genocide cases by ICJ and, in particular, the two ad hoc International Criminal Tribunals. It is indeed worth highlighting that the ICJ, in enquiring on the Serbia/Montenegro's responsibility for genocide, essentially relied on the assessments by the ICTY jurisprudence of the *actus reus* and *mens rea* of Serbian and Bosnian/Serbian agents on trial. In this respect, (i) the general identity of the individuals who were killed directly, (ii) the fact that the leadership of a targeted group was selected for elimination at first, (iii) the ideological dehumanisation of the "other", as well as (iv) the fact that not only individual members of the group were eliminated, but also religious and cultural institutions of the community were destroyed: All these factors were considered of great relevance by those criminal Tribunals, when dealing with the deliberate destruction in whole or in part of a group in Rwanda and former-Yugoslavia. The ICJ also resorted to these factors in the case concerning the situation in former-Yugoslavia.

[46]See above, fn. 24.

3.1.1 The Killings of Armenian Military and Civilians

We do not know the exact number of Armenians (directly) killed in the 1915–1916 massacres and deportations.[47] However, as has been stressed in the jurisprudence of the ICTY, a numeric assessment of the number of people killed is not required for determining the destruction of a group in whole or in part.[48] Indeed, other acts are relevant—and may even be more relevant—for such a determination. We shall borrow the same criterion here.

What is certain is that sometime after WWI had broken out in 1914, the Armenians soldiers, in the first place, were submitted in the Ottoman Army to a very discriminatory treatment. They were disarmed and only utilised in labour battalions, where they were also constantly humiliated, ill-treated, even starved. Then, starting from February 1915, these soldiers were systematically killed. The killings lasted until their almost complete elimination, except for those soldiers who had accepted the Muslim faith and assimilation into the Turkish culture in order to save their lives.[49] This modality of elimination of Armenians is similar to what occurred in the Srebrenica genocide, where the able-bodied Bosniak men—soldiers or civilians—were all killed in less than a week through a planned and organised military operation. These killings prevented the reproduction for generations in the

[47]On the issue of the number of victims I will not participate to "the war of numbers", which is ongoing between some historians and Turkish rulers from the end of WWI. I will only recall that an official Ottoman statistic calculated 800,000 Armenians' losses between 1915 and 1917–18 (Ottoman Gazette, No. 3909, 21 July 1920). Even if concerning a period of at least one year longer, this number is by far sufficient to consider that a substantial part of Armenians disappeared in 1915–16. Indeed, the actual victims to consider are not only those who died and even less who were directly killed (on the notion of victims see Donat Cattin, in this Volume). On the calculation of the number of the Armenian losses, I refer to a recent essay even though it considers the period of 1915–1923: Bijak and Lubman (2016). The Authors resort to the same demographic methodologies the Chambers were confronted with in the ICTY cases when they had to calculate the losses of Bosniaks, Croats and Serbs in the former Yugoslavia conflict.

[48]ICTY, Trial Chamber Judgment, *Karadžić*, 24 March 2016, vol. 1, p. 205.

[49]This is how Morgenthau describes the Armenian soldiers' situation in the Army at the beginning of the war: "In the early 1915, the Armenian soldiers in the Turkish army were reduced to a new *status*. Up to that time most of them had been combatants, but now they were all stripped of their arms and transformed into workmen […] road labourers and pack animals. Army supplies of all kinds were loaded on their backs, and, stumbling under the burdens and driven by the whips and bayonets of the Turks, they were forced to drag their weary bodies into the mountains of the Caucasus […]. They had to spend practically all their time in the open, sleeping on the bare ground whenever the ceaseless prodding of their taskmasters gave them an occasional opportunity to sleep. They were given only scraps of food; if they fell sick they were left where they had dropped, their Turkish oppressors perhaps stopping long enough to rob them of all their possessions even of their clothes. If any stragglers succeeded in reaching their destinations, they were not infrequently massacred […]. In almost all cases the procedure was the same. Here and there squads of 50 or 100 men would be taken, bound together in groups of four, and then marched out to a secluded spot a short distance from the village. Suddenly the sound of rifle shots would fill the air… In cases that came to my attention, the murderers had added a refinement to their victims' sufferings by compelling them to dig their graves before being shot […]": Morgenthau (1918), pp. 302–303.

Muslim community of the region, as it was clearly underlined in the *Karadzic* case.[50]

Killing almost all the able-bodied male members of a community means indeed the destruction of the future of that community, in particular if this conduct is also accompanied, as mentioned, by the provoked deaths of women and children, the forced religious conversion of women with consequent marriage with men of the dominant group, and, as we will see, the appropriation of children by families of this group. The impact on the composition of the targeted group and on the birth-rate of future generations appears in its full drama. This is what also occurred to Armenians in 1915–16.[51]

A way of killing Armenian soldiers and other able-bodied men by giving this conduct a semblance of legality was to hang them following verdicts by Martial Courts, which were "not based on any of the established laws of the Empire", as James Bryce described the situation in reporting the "hanging of 20 Huntchakists at Constantinople."[52] The following event of 1915 illustrated by Amb. Morgenthau confirms Bryce's view about using Martial Courts for hanging innocent Armenians. Seven Armenians of Smyrna had been sentenced by hanging for allegedly committing "some rather vague political offense in 1909", while "neither Rahmi Bey, the Governor General of Smyrna, nor the Military Commander believed that they were guilty". Indeed, these authorities "wired Constantinople that under the Ottoman law the accused had the right to appeal for clemency to the Sultan", but Enver Pasha replied: "Technically, you are right; hang them first and send the

[50]In the part concerning Srebrenica of the *Karadžić* TC Judgement is stated: "The Chamber notes that the operation, which was carried out by the Bosnian Serb Forces who vigorously pursued the Bosnian Muslim males in the column, encompassed the killing of all Bosnian Muslim men in Bosnian Serb custody, irrespective of whether they were combatants or civilians and regardless of whether they were captured or had surrendered. The Chamber considers that this, combined with the manner as well as the systematic and highly organised nature of the killings, demonstrates a clear intent to kill every able-bodied Bosnian Muslim male from Srebrenica. Noting that killing every able-bodied male of a group results in severe procreative implications that may lead to the group's extinction, the Chamber finds that the only reasonable inference on the basis of such evidence is that members of the Bosnian Serb Forces orchestrating this operation intended to destroy the Bosnian Muslims in Srebrenica as such." ICTY, Trial Chamber Judgment, *Karadžić*, 24 March 2016, vol. 1, para. 5669.

[51]This also is what Morgenthau underlines: "These massacres were not isolated happenings; I could detail many more episodes just as horrible as the one related above; throughout the Turkish Empire a systematic attempt was made to kill all able-bodied men, not only for the purpose of removing all males who might propagate a new generation of Armenians, but for the purpose of rendering the weaker part of the population an easy prey.": Morgenthau (1918), p. 304.

[52]The same author then went on to say: "The same day twelve Armenians were hanged at Kaisaria, on the charge of having obeyed instructions received from the secret conference held at Bukarest by the Runtchakists and Droshakists. Besides these hangings, 32 persons have been sentenced at Kaisaria to terms of hard labour, ranging from ten to fifteen years. Most of them are honest merchants who are in no sort of relation with the political parties", Bryce and Toynbee (1916) p. 10 of the General Description.

petition for pardon afterward." The seven Armenians were eventually spared, but thanks only to the personal intervention of Morgenthau with Enver Pasha.[53]

While documents and testimonies reveal the circumstances of killings of Armenian able-bodied men, I have not found any evidence on rebels—insurgent soldiers or civilians—killed in combat activities in a civil war against the Ottoman government.[54] I have only read or heard categorical assertions on such deaths by some scholars, who, however, bring contradictory or no evidence at all to support their assertions.

The other most significant method to target Armenian community consisted in the elimination of its leadership. Over two thousand members of the religious, intellectual, political, military, professional, financial leadership of the Armenian community were quickly arrested the 24 April 1915 in Constantinople and later in other Ottoman cities. They were then moved out of cities and near all eventually killed, while some of them were deported with other civilians.[55] From the available documentation, it appears that the Armenian dignitaries deported and massacred were peaceful Ottoman citizens concerned with their business, professional and intellectual activities and not at all with revolutionary or separatist activities.[56] Amongst them, the poet Daniel Varujan, journalists and priests, as Soghomon Gevorki Soghomonyan (the so called Komitas, who survived the deportation and emigrated to the US thanks to the intervention of Amb. Morgenthau with the Triumvirate.[57]) Amongst the deportees, who were then massacred, there were even some Armenians who had been "accused" by some "countrymen" of collaborating with the Ottoman rulers, rather than caring for the interest of the community, in particular of its less privileged members.[58]

In the situation of the Tutsi genocide in Rwanda before the ICTR, as well as in the ethnic cleansing of the territories of former Yugoslavia—a criminal behaviour that was qualified as genocide of the Bosniak community in a few ICTY cases—we have witnessed to the same phenomenon: attacks against the community-leaders as determinants of its destruction. This was indeed a particularly effective criminal means for completely disorienting the victimized community and preventing its ability to organize an effective defence capable of preventing genocide.

In the context of 1915–16, attacks against the leadership were particularly significant, given the way in which the Ottoman *Millet* rule operated. In fact, individual members of a Jewish or Christian *Millet* did not have direct relations with the Ottoman Administration. Such relations were mediated by the leaders of the Millet,

---

[53]Morgenthau (1918), p. 352–353.

[54]See below, Sect. 3.1.6 the different context of the Van events.

[55]See, among several others, Bloxham (2007), p. 70.

[56]Some of them avoided killing and deportation only because the Turks needed them on ground of their particular profession. See on such situation Davis (1918), p. 71.

[57]However, he could not psychologically survive the horrors he had suffered and witnessed and he died in an American psychiatric hospital.

[58]See, for instance, above fn. 8 about Andranik.

who administrated the whole life of the community. Thus, the elimination in Constantinople of the Armenian leadership was the first signal of the intent to disarticulate and dismember the entire community in view of depriving it of any possibility to organise resistance and defence.

As already noted, in addition to the killings of the members of a group, the elimination of a national/religious group as such can be attained by other criminal means, which can turn out to be even more determinant than the killing proper. I shall now move on to discuss these other means.

3.1.2 Causing Serious Bodily or Mental Harm to Armenians

After the elimination of soldiers, able-bodied men and the community-leaders, other civilians were targeted. Besides direct killings, the use of torture's techniques and imposition of inhuman living conditions in the villages led to the death of the few men who had been exempted from military enrolment,[59] while elders, women and children were deported through the so called death-marches.[60] As Morghenthau underlines

---

[59]Some of these unimaginable tortures are described by direct victims and eyewitnesses, as reported by Davis (1918), particularly p. 66.

[60]Bryce and Toynbee report the deportations of Armenians as follows: "The exiles from each centre were broken up into several convoys, which varied in size from two or three hundred to three or four thousand members. A detachment of gendarmerie was assigned to every convoy, to guard them on the way, and the civil authorities hired or requisitioned a certain number of ox-carts (arabas), usually one to a family, which they placed at their disposal; and so the convoy started out. The mental misery of exile was sufficiently acute, but it was soon ousted by more material cares. A few days, or even a few hours, after the start, the carters would refuse to drive them further, and the gendarmes, as fellow Moslems, would connive at their mutinousness. So the carts turned back, and the exiles had to go forward on foot. This was the beginning of their physical torments, for they were not travelling over soft country or graded roads, but by mule-tracks across some of the roughest country in the world. It was the hot season, the wells and springs were sometimes many hours' journey apart, and the gendarmes often amused themselves by forbidding their fainting victims to drink. It would have been an arduous march for soldiers on active service, but the members of these convoys were none of them fitted or trained for physical hardship. They were the women and children, the old and the sick. Some of the women had been delicately brought up and lived in comfort all their lives some had to carry children in their arms too young to walk; others had been sent off with the convoy when they were far gone with child, and gave birth on the road. None of these latter survived, for they were forced to march on again after a few hours' respite; they died on the road, and the new-born babies perished with them. Many others died of hunger and thirst, sunstroke, apoplexy or sheer exhaustion [...]." Bryce and Toynbee (1916), p. 642. See also below, fn. 62.

> …the Armenian proceedings of 1915 and 1916 evidenced an entirely new mentality. This new conception was that of deportation.[61]

Deportation is not an act envisaged as such among acts of genocide in the 1948 Convention and the ICTY and ICTR Statutes. However, deportation is first of all relevant, in the optic of the objective element of a conduct aimed at the destruction in whole or in part of a community, to the conduct causing serious bodily or mental harm to the members of the group. It is indeed indisputable that any expulsion or deportation or even relocation of members of a community causes serious bodily or mental harm to them as well as harm to the entire community as such, especially to its identity. Harm results from the simple circumstance that the members of the community are eradicated from their territory, their centuries-old cultural and religious references, their homes and families that the criminals use to separate at the beginning of the criminal transaction—the men on one side, the women and children on the other, on a different path but usually toward the same tragic fate.

However, the deportations of the Armenian population did not only constitute eradication from homeland, forced transfer from a territory to another, from a locality to another, as often happened in Bosnia-Herzegovina, where expelled populations managed to start another life elsewhere, outside the cleansed territory (hence victims of other crimes against humanity, but not of genocide, except in Srebrenica). In the case of deportations of Armenians, after being violently taken from their homes, deprived of their properties, totally eradicated from their centuries-old homeland, victims were forced to tread a footpath toward the Anatolian and Mesopotamic deserts. In these "death marches", without sufficient water and food and under the violent control by the Ottoman gendarmes, who beat and tortured them whenever they simply asked to rest, Armenians died in hundreds of thousands on account of starvation or attacks, as the available photos clearly

[61]Morgenthau (1918), p. 365. And: "As a matter of fact, the Turks never had the slightest idea of reestablishing the Armenians in this new country. They knew that the great majority would never reach their destination and that those who did would either die of thirst and starvation, or be murdered… The real purpose of the deportation was robbery and destruction; it really represented a new method of massacre." Morgenthau (1918), p. 115 f. And further: "When the Turkish authorities gave the orders for these deportations, they were merely giving the death warrant to a whole race; they understood this well, and, in their conversations with me, they made no particular attempt to conceal the fact." A protestant missionary, in describing deportations in his diary, writes: "for most of the women and children was reserved the long and lingering suffering that made massacre seem to them a merciful fate – suffering such as was foreseen and planned by the perpetrators of this horror": Riggs (1997), Chap. XV, entitled "The Turkish Idea of Deportation", p. 140.

reveal showing the remains, in particular of the weakest members of the community, lying on the road.[62]

In short, deportations were never evacuations for military necessity and temporary resettlements, as the Turkish authorities and some commentators claimed and still claim. The deportations of Armenians were organised and carried out in view of a fate of death.

The fact that, instead being relocations, these deportations aimed at provoking a fate of non-return and death, is further confirmed by the general destruction of the Armenian cultural and religious buildings,[63] as well as by the Decrees of confiscation and expropriation of the Armenian properties, assets and other goods. As has been significantly pointed out,

> The seizure of the Armenian property was not just a byproduct of the CUP's genocidal policies, but an integral part of the murder process, reinforcing and accelerating the intended destruction. The expropriation and plunder of deported Armenians' movable and immovable properties was an essential component of the destruction process of Armenians.[64]

In addition to starvation and maltreatments, women and children were also often submitted to sexual abuses, rape in particular, by the guards, before often being eventually killed. Even if some of them survived, it is worth noting that sexual abuses, besides causing serious bodily and mental harm, are the best weapon for destroying a community. Indeed, systematic sexual abuses render it very difficult for the victims to go back to a normal life or even to be re-accepted in the community, often because of prejudices born out of ignorance. This is particularly frequent for women, who often prefer even to commit suicide than go back to their

---

[62]On some terrible deportations accounts see Davis (1918), Bryce and Toynbee (1916), in particular pp. 98 ff. G. Gorrini, the Italian Consul-General in Trebizond gave this account to his government when back to Italy: "The passing of gangs of Armenian exiles beneath the windows and before the door of the Consulate; their prayers for help, when neither I nor any other could do anything to answer them; the city in a state of siege, guarded at every point by 15,000 troops in complete war equipment, by thousands of police agents, by bands of volunteers and by the members of the 'Committee of Union and Progress'; the lamentations, the tears, the abandonments, the imprecations, the many suicides, the instantaneous deaths from sheer terror, the sudden unhinging of men's reason, the conflagrations, the shooting of victims in the city, the ruthless searches through the houses in the countryside; the hundreds of corpses found every day along the exile road; the young women converted by force to Islam or exiled like the rest; the children torn away from their families or from the Christian schools, and handed over by force to Moslem families, or else placed by hundreds on board ship in nothing but their shirts, and then capsized and drowned in the Black Sea and the River Deyirmen Dere – these are my last ineffaceable memories of Trebizond, memories which still, at a month's distance, torment my soul and almost drive me frantic", quoted and translated from Italian by Hovannisian (1994), p. 125.

[63]As L. Basso has significantly pointed out: "Destroying or tainting a culture means destroying the dialectic between the individual and social features, which is the rhythm of the human life, it means to depersonalize, anonymize, throw into the vacuum of a pure material existence deprived of the warmth of life, deprived of human dimension" (quoted in Monina (2016), p. 387. The translation is mine).

[64]Kurt (24 April 2015) and Kurt (2016).

community. Therefore, massive and systematic sexual abuses of women and children destroy the future not only of the individual victims, but of a community as such. After all, in the Armenian deportations, abused women and children no longer had a community or a village to go back to.

In addition to the massive and systematic sexual abuses of women, in Causing Serious Bodily or Mental Harm to Armenians one must equally include the forced assimilation of Armenian women in the Muslim community through imposed marriages with men of this community. It has indeed to be taken into account that the Muslim ritual that was followed could not be considered a real marriage by a Christian woman. This practice often also led to women's suicides or, in any case, to causing them serious mental harm.[65]

3.1.3 Deliberately Inflicting on the Armenian Community Conditions of Life Calculated to Bring About Its Physical Destruction in Whole or in Part

Deportations, rather than killings, were the most relevant determinant of the deliberate destruction of the Armenian community. As clarified in the previous Sections, deportations of Armenians not only caused them serious bodily or mental harm, but brought to their physical destruction because of the horrendous conditions under which the deportations were organized and carried out, including the localities chosen for the new "fake destinations". Thus, in my view, such deportations should rather be qualified as acts deliberately inflicting on the group conditions of life calculated to bring about its physical destruction in whole or in part, a behaviour that contains in itself the specific intent of the destruction of a group.

Even if a small percentage of each group of deportees was able to reach the "fake destination"—nothing else than an open-air concentration camp in the desert—, here the majority of them died of starvation, or on account of torrid climate conditions, typhus and acts of violence by the guards.[66] The open-air concentration camp of Deirez-Zor in eastern Syria is emblematic for understanding the living conditions in these destinations. Among the survivors of the death marches towards the Syrian desert, 200,000 more Armenians died in that camp of starvation, epidemics and killed by guards, under the cruel supervision of the Governor of the Region, Zeki Bey.[67]

Therefore, only few of each group of deportees could survive and thanks only to the help from compassionate local populations or relief organisations.[68]

---

[65]See, inter alios, Kurt (2015).

[66]Consul Leslie Davis, entered one of these camps and described it as follows: "the most horrible scene I have ever witnessed, one not surpassed by any in Dante's Inferno": Davis (1918), p. 76.

[67]Walker (1990), pp. 223, 229.

[68]See Jacobsen (2001), Riggs (1997) and Atkinson (2001). See also the *Study for the League of Nations* by the British Historian C. A. Macartney, 1930, quoted by Shirinian (2016).

3.1.4 Imposing Measures Intended to Prevent Births Within the Armenian Community

This act is in part overlapping with the *killings* of able-bodied men and in part with the deportations of Armenian women and children under terrible *conditions of life, calculated to bring about their physical destruction*. Indeed, both series of acts had severe procreative implications that might have led to the extinction of the Armenian community and that certainly drastically reduced its procreative capacity.[69] The fact that by these acts the CUP also intended to prevent births within the Armenian community is proved by a message of Minister of Interior Talât Pasha to the local Government of Aleppo, in which he says that "the feeding of [...] children or any attempt to prolong their lives" is regarded "as an act entirely opposed to/the/ purpose" of the Turkish government and "the survival of these children as detrimental."[70]

3.1.5 Forcibly Transferring Armenian Christian Children to the Muslim Community

Some children who were not directly killed, or did not die as a consequence of the living conditions imposed on them, and were given in custody to the Ottoman authorities by their parents that so hoped to save their lives, were put in Muslim orphanages and/or taken by Muslim families and often even utilised as slaves or servants.[71] In all these situations, they grew up in Islamic belief and culture.[72] Especially many girls survived as they were taken—when not kidnapped during the night—by Turkish or Kurdish men to become their wives.[73] This clearly constitutes

---

[69]See on this the messages about children destined by him to a fate of death, which were sent by the Minister Talât Pasha to the Government of Aleppo, referred to in Sect. 3.2.3.

[70]Telegram of 14 January 2016, in Andonian (1965), p. 56. This book was translated into English from the Original written in Armenian in 1919. It collected the telegrams sent by Talât and given to Andonian by an Ottoman official. Turkish authorities contest the authenticity of this correspondence, which is instead affirmed by researchers such as Yves Ternon, Vahakn N. Dadrian, Taner Akçam. See in particular Ternon (1989), Chapter II of Part I.

[71]On this, see the witness-survivor account in Davis (1918), p. 71. The American Consul at Trebizond, Oscar S. Heizer, so describes this situation in a message of 7 July 1915 to Ambassador Morgenthau: "The city of Trebizond and surrounding villages is estimated at 10,000 Armenians. Of this later number 5200 have already been sent away. The children, when the parents so desired, were left behind and placed in large houses in different parts of the city. There are approximately three thousand such children retained in these houses called by the Turks 'Orphanages'. Girls up to 15 years of age inclusive, and boys to 10 years of age inclusive are accepted; those over these ages are compelled to go with their parents [...]. The institutions are guarded by gendarmes and each institution has a Turkish Mudir or Director." See http://www.wbarrow.co.uk/rememberarmenia/pdfs_in_chapters/06_armenia2_reports.pdf, p. 90.

[72]Shirinian (2016), Davis (1918), p. 106 ff.

[73]See the testimonies on this situation in Davis (1918), p. 97 ff., in particular p. 101.

an act of forcibly transferring children of the Armenian Christian community to the Muslim community.

It is true that some Muslim families took Armenian children to save them, but this charitable behaviour was not so frequent, since Turks, Kurds and Circassians who were ready to save Armenians, even children, risked serious sanctions by the Ottoman authorities, including executions.[74]

3.1.6 Reading the Facts Explored Pursuant to the Official Turkish Positions and that of Some Historians

While after WWI the Sublime Porte acknowledged the massacres and deportations, ceasing to claim both the justification of an Armenian uprising and the death of hundreds of thousands of civilians on account of war as well as misdeeds of bandits, after the Turkish "revolution" the new State started again by invoking these justifications, as it still does.

However, not many historians maintain the thesis of an Armenian uprising as a defence for the tragic events. At any rate, those who do refer to both the activities of (some) Armenian revolutionists, who were attracted by the socialist ideals coming from the pre-revolutionary Tsarist Empire, and the Armenian rebellion of Van. While these historians omit to underline the very sporadic character of Armenian revolutionist activities, the local rebellion of Van is qualified by them as an uprising that would have escalated to a civil war.[75] However, neither an uprising nor a civil war have been demonstrated with factual evidence: they are just categorically asserted.

Perhaps the advocates of this thesis did not have the opportunity to see the photographs taken by Armin Wegner, the military paramedic of the German Army fighting in the Ottoman Empire against the Entente Powers and other photographs

---

[74]See the testimonies about the charitable conduct of some Turkish women in Davis (1918), p. 106. James Bryce notices: "The Turkish officials are usually heartless and callous. But here and there we see one of a finer temper, who refuses to carry out the orders given him and is sometimes dismissed for his refusal. The Moslem rabble is usually pitiless. It pillages the houses and robs the persons of the hapless exiles. But now and then there appear pious and compassionate Moslems who try to save the lives or alleviate the miseries of their Christian neighbours." (Preface to Bryce and Toynbee (1916)).

[75]The new Ottoman Minister of Interior Mustafa Arif Bey stated on 13 December 1918: "Surely a few Armenians aided and abetted our enemy, and a few Armenian Deputies committed crimes against the Turkish nation… it is incumbent upon a government to pursue the guilty ones. Unfortunately, our wartime leaders, imbued with a spirit of brigandage, carried out the law of deportation in a manner that could surpass the proclivities of the most bloodthirsty bandits. They decided to exterminate the Armenians, and they did exterminate them. This decision was taken by the Central Committee of the Young Turks and was implemented by the government" (quoted by Dadrian (1991), p. 110).

showing the tragedy of the deportations.[76] Do these images really show a police/military repression of a rebellion or do they instead portray columns of mainly elders, women and children marching in horrible living conditions and the remains of skeletal civilians lying on the road sides, who clearly appear to have suffered from starvation, torture, other inhuman acts, when not of direct killing?[77]

Furthermore, do those pictures reveal the "unfortunate result of civil war, famine and epidemics", as also alleged by Turkey and some historians? During a civil war, civilians die of famine and epidemics in their homes, villages, in hospitals if any, and not in columns of forced marches, as photographs show and eye-witnesses—survivors, diplomats and honest Turks and Kurds—have often testified before abandoning this world.

I cannot believe that one can still argue for a general "Haik rebellion" and the "unfortunate result of civil war, famine and epidemics", having seen those photos, read the reports about the massacres and deportations written by the consulates or religious missions as well as the statements of the Ottoman rulers when planning and deciding those misconducts. As mentioned, consulates and religious missions were present across the Ottoman territory and witnessed the tragic events, while the statements of the Turkish rulers were reported even by diplomats of Powers in friendly relations with the Porte, such as the US, which was not in war with the Ottoman Empire, and Germany, the best ally of that Empire.

Of course, I cannot but recognize that the Armenian community claimed for a long time an autonomy that would have permitted an equal *status* between its members and Muslims in enjoying political and civil rights, given that the reforms introduced for this purpose had never become effective.[78] The position of Armenians in the Ottoman Empire worsened as the nationalistic "ideals" of

---

[76]See above, fn. 11. The Turkish historian Halil Berktay gives his impression when showing these pictures: "Everywhere in the Western world, there are photographs of these incidents which we can't bear to look at. The first time I encountered these visual records, I cried and could hardly breathe for several minutes. They are no different from the images of the concentration camps, or the massacres in Africa. For there are huge numbers of people in these pictures." (supra, fn. 3).

[77]This is what Morgenthau writes on 10 July to the US Secretary of State Bryan "[…] persecution of Armenians assuming unprecedented proportions. Reports from widely scattered districts indicate systematic attempt to uproot peaceful Armenian populations and through arbitrary arrests, terrible tortures, wholesale expulsions and deportations from one end of the Empire to the other accompanied by frequent instances of rape, pillage, and murder, turning into massacre, to bring destruction and destitution on them. These measures are not in response to popular or fanatical demand, but are purely arbitrary and directed from Constantinople in the name of military necessity, often in districts where no military operations are likely to take place […]", in Papers Relating to the Foreign Relations of the United States, 1915 Supplement, The World War, Section "Efforts in behalf of Armenians and Jews in Turkey", p. 983.

[78]Some of these rights were indeed formally conferred first through the tanzimat and then, in 1914, by the new reform, but both reforms remained on paper.

turkification and islamization of the country developed. I cannot but also recognize that in 1915 the Armenians were of course opponents of the radicalization of those ideals by the Triumvirate. Yet, this opposition arose precisely because, rather than protecting Armenians pursuant to the San Stefano and Berlin Treaties, those nationalistic and racist "ideals" implied the elimination of a nation with a very defined secular identity. That nation was also the most numerous and territorially extended and integrated in the economic life of the Empire among the Christian nations of the Empire. How could the "Young Turks" turkify and islamize the few remaining Ottoman territories without eliminating the Armenians? In fact, they could not be simply expelled towards an independent Armenian State, as it had been done for the Ottoman Christian Greeks, who were expelled to Greece.

The revolt of the Armenian population in the Van Villajet, which was located near the Caucasus battle front, broke out in this context in April/May 1915,[79] when the massacres were already under way and the city of Van had been besieged by the Turkish Army, in order to cleansing it from Armenians, as this results from researches and analyses of several historians and diplomats. Ambassador Morgenthau, who was at all times in contact with the US Consul in the Van District, so described the situation:

> The Turks' army turned aside and invaded their own territory of Van. Instead of fighting the trained Russian army of men, they turned their rifles, machine guns, and other weapons upon the Armenian women, children, and old men in the villages of Van… On April 15, about 500 young Armenian men of Akantz were mustered to hear an order of the Sultan; at sunset they were marched outside the town and every man shot in cold blood. This procedure was repeated in about eighty Armenian villages in the district north of Lake Van, and in three days 24,000 Armenians were murdered in this atrocious fashion.[80]

[79]Amb. Morghenthau describes the previous situation in Van in the following way: "Its Turkish governor, Tahsin Pasha, was one of the more enlightened type of Turkish officials. Relations between the Armenians, who lived in the better section of the city, and the Turks and the Kurds, who occupied the mud huts in the Moslem quarter, had been tolerably agreeable for many years": Morgenthau (1918), p. 110.

[80]Morgenthau (1918), p. 297. The protestant missionary already quoted writes: "The loss of Van to the Russians, through the activity and bravery of the Armenians, produced a tremendous impression. Of course it was not then generally known that the Armenians had only acted in self-defense after the Turks had massacred many of them. Outbreaks were reported in various places, and some of these, notably in the region of Diarbekir, were real enough, though the Armenians were the victims not the aggressors in these disturbances." (Riggs 1997, p. 50).

Therefore, rather than an uprising, this revolt can be considered a strong resistance and a form of self-defense by a desperate community under Turkish attack,[81] analogous to the Warsaw ghetto revolt during WWII.[82] Of course, Armenians hoped to receive Russian support.[83] However, it is significant that, before the arrival of the Russian army, in an attempt to peacefully resolve a situation at risk of becoming tragic for them, the Armenians were also seeking the support and assistance from Germany to mediate with the Ottoman authorities the end of the serious misdeeds against them. As the war ally of the Porte, Germany was indeed military present in the Van District! This desperate attempt failed as the Germans

[81]Morgenthau writes: "these events [the Van revolt] are always brought forward by the Turks as a justification of their subsequent crimes. As I shall relate, Enver, Talât, and the rest, when I appealed to them in behalf of the Armenians, invariably instanced the 'revolutionists' of Van as a sample of Armenian treachery. The famous "Revolution", as this recital shows, was merely the determination of the Armenians to save their women's honour and their own lives, after the Turks, by massacring thousands of their neighbours, had shown them the fate that awaited them." (Morgenthau 1918, p. 227). The Austrian Military Attaché and Military Plenipotentiary to the Ottoman Empire said "The Van uprising certainly was an act of desperation. The local Armenians realized that general massacres against the Armenians had already started and they would be the next target. In the course of the summer 1915 the Turkish government with inexorable consequence brought its bloody task of extermination of an entire nation to an end." (quoted by Dadrian (1994), p. 116. See also Akçam (2006), p. 200. On the contrary, in McCarthy et al. (2006), these events are described as following: '[t]he slaughter of Muslims that accompanied the Armenian revolt in Van Province inexorably led first to Kurdish reprisals on the Armenian, then to a general and mutual massacre of the people of the East. The Armenian revolt began an intercommunal war, in which both sides, fearing their own survival, killed those who, given the chance, would have killed them. The result was unprecedented horror. History records few examples of mortality as great as that suffered in Van Province." (p. 265).

[82]And, *mutatis mutandis*, nobody is attempting to use this revolt as a justification of the massacre of Polish Jews by the Nazi!

[83]The U.S. Secretary of State Bryan so writes to the Ambassador Morgenthau, on 27 April 1915: "Russian Ambassador has brought to our attention an appeal made by the Catholicos of the Armenian Church that this Government use its good offices with the Turkish Government to prevent the massacre of non-combatant Armenians in Turkish territory. You will please bring the matter to the attention of the government, urging upon it the use of effective means for the protection of Armenians from violence at the hands of those of other religions. The Russian Ambassador calls attention to the fact that there are many Mussulmans in Russian territory and that these enjoy immunity from religious persecution." (Papers quoted supra, fn. 77).

refused to interfere owing to political reasons and in order not to displease (*sic*!) the Ottoman rulers.[84]

This said about the facts, we will later return to the argument of the civil war as an alleged legal justification, if any, of the massacres in light of the law applicable at that time (Sect. 4.2 below).

3.1.7 The Sublime Porte Destroyed in Substantial Part the Ottoman Armenian Community

The evidence analysed above shows that all relevant means were resorted to by the Turkish rulers of the Ottoman Empire in order to destroy the Armenian community living for centuries in that Empire. It also shows that some Armenians could survive for different reasons. Some Armenians survived deportation and the horrible conditions of life in the camps, or succeeded to escape and, in some cases, leave the Ottoman territory, thanks only to help by relief organisations or religious missions. Some others, in particular women and very young children, were able to survive losing their Armenian identity and Christian faith. Some children, in particular when sold as slaves instead of being treated as children, also succeeded to escape. Therefore, the fact that some Armenians survived deportation does not imply—as claimed by some commentators and Turkey's authorities—that they simply suffered evacuation from their villages for security reasons or military necessity and consequent relocation under difficult war conditions and attacks by bandits. It does not imply that they did not suffer violent eradication from their homeland and elimination by means of cruel deportations on the ground of being Armenians and Christians. I consider that conclusive evidence of the destruction of the Ottoman Armenian community in its substantial part is overwhelming.

[84]The German Ambassador in Constantinople, Wangenheim, replied to an attempt by Amb. Morgenthau to obtain his support in favour of the Armenians as follows: "The United States is apparently the only country that takes much interest in the Armenians. Your missionaries are their friends and your people have constituted themselves their guardians [...]. Mr. Bryan has just published his note, saying that it would be unnatural not to sell munitions to England and France. As long as your government maintains that attitude we can do nothing for the Armenians." (Morgenthau 1918, p. 139). However, not all German Diplomats had such an approach. For instance, according to Amb. Morgenthau, the indignation of Neurath, the Conseiller of the German Embassy had "reached such a point that his language to Talât and Enver became almost undiplomatic", but "he had failed to influence them". Neurath told Morgenthau that "They [were] immovable and [were] determined to pursue their [...] course" (p. 140).

3.2 *The Specific Moral Element*

3.2.1 A Short Preliminary Clarification

As stated in the first genocide case before the ICTR and then repeated in all ICTR and ICTY cases, as well as by the ICJ in the *Genocide* case,

> Genocide is distinct from other crimes inasmuch as it embodies a special intent or *dolus specialis*... The special intent in the crime of genocide lies in the intent to destroy, in whole or in part, a national, ethnical, racial or religious group, as such.[85]

As noted before, my analysis is essentially functional to verifying whether the massacres and deportations of Armenians may or may not be labelled as a destruction of the Christian Armenian community by the Ottoman Empire rather than by individuals. This means that there is no need—and it would be impossible—to enquire about the intent of the Turks, Kurds and Circassians who carried out the destructive acts in the field. However, the State is a collective entity and thus the intent of a State is the intent of its agents. In the genocide case the ICJ stressed indeed that: "it has jurisdiction under Article IX to find a State responsible if genocide or other acts enumerated in Article III are committed by its organs, or persons or groups whose acts are attributable to it."[86] Therefore, especially the intent of CUP members should be enquired. And this can be done, as already underlined, independently of any criminal procedure against the individual agents.[87]

Before discussing evidence of the intent requirement, I need to briefly take in consideration the positions of Turkey and some commentators on this issue.

3.2.2 Turkey's Claim that the Intent to Destroy the Armenian Community Is Lacking

Turkey and some supporters of its denialist positions claim that the requirement of the "intent to destroy" the Armenian community for a qualification of genocide is

---

[85] ICTR, Trial Chamber Judgment, *Akayesu*, 2 September 1998, para. 498. As to the jurisprudence of the ICJ, see the *Genocide case*, para. 242 ff.

[86] The question of the attribution to a State of the acts of its agents was largely discussed by ICJ in the *Genocide* case from the perspective of the possibility to attribute to it the acts of both *de iure* organs and other entities or individuals under their control: ICJ, *Genocide case*, paras. 385–395. This latter aspect is also relevant here insofar it concerns the activities of the semi-secret *Special Organisation,* which, as already noted, acted as *de facto* (if not *de iure)* organ of the Ottoman State (see above fn. 30).

[87] As ICJ, *Genocide case*, para. 182 stressed, "State responsibility can arise under the Convention for genocide and complicity, without an individual being convicted of the crime or an associated one".

not met.[88] Pursuant to those positions, intent would be lacking for a political reason, the Armenian soldiers being killed in a civil war and Armenian civilians having died on account of the difficult war conditions or being massacred for vengeance by bandits outside of the Ottoman control.[89] In sum, massacres and deportations did not occur in view of the destruction of a community as such, but only on a political ground—the civil war—, which is not envisaged by the Genocide Convention.

On the other hand, some denialists claim that the destructive intent requirement is not met because massacres and deportations were not planned, while planning would be a constitutive component of genocide.

Massacres and Deportations Occurred on a Political Ground

The first argument is not well posed, either factually or legally. If it is true that the 1948 Convention does not contemplate *political* genocide, however, in the above-mentioned argument there is not only a confusion between a potential political purpose and the criminal means of pursuing it by targeting a specific group. There is also a misrepresentation of the facts. Who resorts to the "political ground", rather than denying the genocidal intent, denies indeed the facts that occurred, as they result from my analysis and, above all, from the analysis of authoritative historians. One alleges that other facts happened, which instead are largely contested, including by me, hopefully with some success.[90]

Moreover, when claiming a political ground in an attempt to justify massacres (as they are indeed labelled even by some supporters of their legality), one cannot take into account facts that occurred after the outbreak of the atrocities and just as a reaction to them (as the Van rebellion) and ignore the previous overall political situation and the very critical situation on the ground. Political reasons are indeed behind the massacres and deportations, but certainly not a civil war that would have broken at the initiative of revolutionist Armenians. As we will see in Sect. 3.2.4, (b) (ii), these political reasons can rather help to ascertain the intent to destroy the

---

[88]See Lewy (2005b). See also the Conference of Prof. McCarthy in the Canadian Parliament (see the video of 26 February 2015, https://www.youtube.com/watch?v=gQw_dLdV_zA, 2 March 2015). Yet his interpretation of the 1915–1916 events also appears in his other works quoted supra fn. 16.

[89]During a talk with Enver Pasha, Amb. Morgenthau said: "Of course I know that the Cabinet would never order such terrible things as have taken place. You and Talât and the rest of the Committee can hardly be held responsible. Undoubtedly your subordinates have gone much further than you have ever intended. I realize that it is not always easy to control your underlings." Enver answered: "You are greatly mistaken [...]. We have this country absolutely under our control. I have no desire to shift the blame on to our underlings and I am entirely willing to accept the responsibility myself for everything that has taken place. The Cabinet itself has ordered the deportations. I am convinced that we are completely justified in doing this owing to the hostile attitude of the Armenians toward the Ottoman Government, but we are the real rulers of Turkey, and no underling would dare proceed in a matter of this kind without our orders." Morgenthau (1918), p. 351–352.

[90]In any case, as convincingly Travis (2016) shows, the war, in particular a civil war situation is perfectly compatible with the destructive intent of the authors in adopting suppressive measures against the insurgents and the civilians belonging to the insurgents' community.

Armenian Christian community as such and also show how the argument of Armenian uprising is unfounded.

Admittedly, Hitler as well had the political project of a "pure" society, which was not criminalized as such in Nuremberg. However, the elimination of the "other" (Jew *versus* Aryan), without which this project could not be pursued, was criminalized both in the Nuremberg Statute (although only through the crimes against humanity of extermination and persecution) and in the Genocide Convention as a specific and separate crime against humanity. This means that in no case political goals may be pursued by criminal means.

Likewise, the argument against labelling the behaviour of the Serbs in Srebrenica as genocide because of the existence of a political goal—the construction of Great Serbia—was also developed by Karadzic in his self-defence during trial before the ICTY. By this argument, he attempted to contest the aim of the destruction of the Bosniak community. However, the ICTY Chambers rejected it. Rather, the evidence relative to the construction of a "pure" Great Serbia helped to assess the context and intent of crimes against humanity, as well as the specific intent of Srebrenica genocide. The Project of Great Serbia was certainly political, as political was the project of turkification of the Ottoman Empire, which in any case arose before the Van rebellion. However, the means for carrying out both these projects were criminal. In the first case, the expulsion of all the Bosnian Muslims (the so-called Bosniaks) from the all Bosnian municipalities and their elimination from Srebrenica and the surrounding zone, abandoned by thousands of them when seeking refuge in the enclave, wrongly relying on international protection; in the second case, the cleansing of Anatolia from the overall Armenian community—and not only from the alleged rebels—, in view of its destruction in whole or in part. The means were therefore criminal even if used—hypothetically—for the purported political goal of repressing an uprising.

Therefore, irrespective of the circumstance that the uprising justification misrepresents the real facts occurred in 1915–16, the possibility of labelling or not the Armenian massacres and deportations of 1915–16 as deliberate destruction of a community only depends on the existence or lack in the facts occurred of the determinants of a deliberate destruction of a group as such on racial, national, ethnical or religious ground. To put it simply, one cannot decide and organize massacres and "death marches" against members of a protected groups and then say that this conduct cannot be qualified as destruction of the group because it was carried out for political reasons![91]

[91]For an opposite view see McCarthy et al. (2006), p. 265. Concerning the arguments put forward by those authors, I also reject the argument of the combat victims on both sides. Leaving aside elderly and women, I am wondering whether the hundreds (or thousands) of children killed at Van were also combatants.

Massacres and Deportations Were not Planned

I need to clear the field of the further objection coming from Turkey and some commentators, both claiming that the genocidal intent is not met because the alleged planning requirement is lacking.[92]

Actually, planning is not considered by the ICTR and ICTY or ICJ jurisprudence to be a constitutive element of genocide, as it is not for any crime of international concern. When dealing with genocide cases, the ICTY and ICTR Appeal Chamber, in confirming or rejecting the views of ICTR and ICTY Trial Chambers, categorically stated:

> the existence of a plan or policy is not a legal ingredient of the crime.[93]

Yet the ICTR and ICTY Appeal and Trial Chambers have expressed the view that, when in fact a plan is proven, the ascertainment of the intent to destroy in whole or in part the targeted group is facilitated. So, the Appeal Chamber in an ICTR case expressed itself as follows: "[The Trial Chamber] further opined (and the Appeals Chamber agrees) that even though a genocidal plan is not a constituent element of the crime of genocide, the existence of such a plan would be strong evidence of the specific intent requirement for the crime of genocide."[94] By this statement, the Appeal Chamber indicated the possibility of resorting to the proof of planning of genocide as one of the strongest circumstantial evidence for proving the specific intent. Therefore, even though planning is not a constitutive element of genocide, the assessment of planning, if any, may turn out to be functional to the determination of the intent to destroy in whole or in part the Christian Armenian community as such as indirect evidence to use *ad abundantiam* or even if direct evidence is lacking.

---

[92]An Ambassador of Israel, Rivka Kohen, has also declared that "the 1915 events couldn't be considered genocide because the main killings in these events were not planned and the Ottoman government had no intention to destroy a nation or a group of people as such" (Press conference, Yerevan, 7 February 2002, quoted in European Journal of International Law, 2012, fn. 21). This is the official view of Israel, which can thus claim the Shoah to be a unique case and support Turkey – its only Muslim ally – in the "Armenian question". I would expect a more impartial attitude with respect to the Armenian tragedy from a State representing millions of victims of Holocaust.

[93]See, inter alia, ICTY, Appeals Chamber Judgment, *Jelisic*, 5 July 2001, para. 48. Planning is, in the ICTY and ICTR Statutes, a mode of responsibility, often alleged by the Prosecutor with regard to the top rulers of the State involved in genocide, crimes against humanity, war crimes. Policy is instead required as constitutive component of crimes against humanity other than genocide pursuant to the Statute of the International Criminal Court (ICC).

[94]ICTR, Appeals Chamber Judgement, *Kayishema and Ruzindana*, 1 June 2001, para. 138.

3.2.3 The Direct Evidence of the Specific Intent to Destroy the Armenian Nation as Such

Some messages sent by the members of the Triumvirate, or their collaborators, to local Ottoman authorities can validly be considered direct evidence of the real intent of the Ottoman rulers towards the Armenian community.

In a message of 9 March 1915, the Minister of Interior Talât Pasha informs the Government of Aleppo that

> All rights of the Armenians to live and work on Turkish soil have been completely cancelled, and with regard to this the Government takes all responsibility on itself, and has commanded that even babies in the cradle are not to be spared. The results of carrying out this order have been seen in some provinces.

However, Talât is concerned over the fact that, in spite of his orders, some local authorities, in particular in the Aleppo Province, are reluctant to implement the decisions of the "Young Turks". So, he continues in this message by noting that

> for reasons unknown to us, exceptional measures are taken with 'certain people', and those people instead of being sent straight to the place of exile are left in Aleppo, whereby the Government is involved in an additional difficulty.

He thus orders that the Government of Aleppo,

> without listening to any of their reasoning, remove them - women or children, whatever they may be, even if they are incapable of moving....do not let the people protect them, because, through their ignorance, they place material gains higher than patriotic feelings, and cannot appreciate the great policy of the Government in insisting upon this.

Furthermore, he suggests that

> instead of the indirect measures of extermination used in other places – such as severity, haste (in carrying out the deportations), difficulties of traveling and misery – direct measures can safely be used there, so work heartily.

He concludes his message informing the government of Aleppo that

> General Orders have been communicated from the War Office to all the Commanders of the Army that they are not to interfere in the work of deportation,

ordering the local government to

> tell the officials that are to be appointed for that purpose that they must work to put into execution our real intent, without being afraid of responsibility

and asking that cipher reports be sent to him every week on the results of the activities on which he had given instructions.[95]

[95] 9 March 1915, http://www.christianity.com/church/church-history/timeline/1901-2000/turkish-order-to-murder-armenians-at-aleppo-11630707.html.

In a further message of 25 March 1915, signed as The Djemiet (the Executive Committee of the "Young Turks"), sent to Djemal Bey, the CUP Delegate at Adana, Talât, President of The Djemiet, writes:

> the duty of everyone is to effect on the broadest lines possible the realization of the noble project of wiping out of existence the well-known elements who for centuries have been the barrier to the empire's progress in civilization.

Apart from the reference to the "noble project" of annihilation of the Armenians, which is very relevant from the perspective of intent, it is also noteworthy that, through his words, the Minister gives an ideological reason for "wiping out of existence" the Armenians, and this in order to reinforce the pledge of everyone to "this action no matter what happens". Even clearer is the incitement to

> work so that the means used may lead to the desired end.

In addition, in order to strengthen his instructions, the President evokes a decision of the Djemiet

> "to uproot and annihilate the different forces which for centuries have been a hindrance", adding that "for this purpose [the Djemiet] is forced to resort to very bloody methods".

And, in order to avoid any perplexity on resorting to these methods, he concludes:

> certainly the contemplation of these methods horrified us, but the Djemiet saw no other way of insuring the stability of its work.[96]

Furthermore, what could be clearer than the following words contained in a message sent on 16 September 1915 by Talât to the Prefecture of Aleppo?

> You have already been advised that the Government, by order of the Djemiet has decided to destroy completely all the indicated persons living in Turkey… Their existence must come to an end, however tragic the means may be; and no regard must be paid to either age or sex, or to conscientious scruples.[97]

The intent to efficiently work for a rapid annihilation of the Armenian community without being disrupted by foreign interventions is apparent from another message to the Prefecture of Aleppo, where Talât expresses his concern about Americans who

> remain unconvinced, despite our assurance that the deportations will be accomplished in safety and comfort.

Indeed, he suspects

---

[96]Horne (1923), p. 174. Almost all documents mentioned can also be found in *Armenian Genocide Turkish Documents,* https://www.Google.It/#Q=Uacla and at http://www.firstworldwar.com/source/armenia_Talâtorders.htm. Further numerous relevant documents proving the specific intent can be found in Dadrian (1991).

[97]Horne (1923), p. 174.

> that the American Consuls are obtaining information by some secret means.

Thus, he recommends the need to

> "be careful that events which attract attention shall not occur in connection with those who are near cities and other centres", since "it is necessary that a show of gentle dealing shall be made for a while, and the usual measures be taken in suitable places." At the end, he gives the order "recommended as very important" that "all persons who have given information to the contrary shall be arrested and handed over to the military authorities for trial by court-martial."[98]

At the beginning of 1916, a substantial part of the Armenian community had already been eliminated. However, notwithstanding the orders given by Talât to the Prefecture of Aleppo on the 3 September 1915 to

> "include the woman and children also in the orders which have been previously prescribed as to be applied to the males of the intended persons" and to "select employees of confidence for these duties,"

the Minister is informed on January 1916

> that certain orphanages [...] have been opened to receive also the children of the Armenians.

This was occurring, he writes,

> through ignorance of our real purpose, or through contempt of it.

He thus alerts the authorities of Aleppo that

> the Government will regard the feeding of such children or any attempt to prolong their lives as an act entirely opposed to its purpose, since it considers the survival of these children as detrimental.

He concludes his message by recommending

> that such children shall not be received into the orphanages, and no attempts are to be made to establish special orphanages for them.[99]

This message, apart from implicitly referring to the destructive purpose of the Government, also clearly expresses the decision to condemn Armenian children to death in the desert camps, a condemnation which means the destruction of the future of the community in the Ottoman Empire.

In the meantime, Morgenthau frequently went to meet Talât and Enver, the Minister of War, with the additional purpose of intervening on behalf of the Armenians. From Talât he received the following response, which shows the destructive intent of one of the most powerful member of CUP:

---

[98] 18 November 1915, Horne (1923), p. 175.

[99] 15 January 1916, Horne (1923), p. 176. See Kelly (2008), p. 151–152.

> We have already disposed of three quarters of the Armenians; there are none left in Bitlis, Van and Erzerum. The hatred between the Turks and the Armenians is now so intense that we have got to finish with them. If we don't, they will plan their revenge.[100]

Even if accepting that the Triumvirate only intended to free the Ottoman Empire from Armenians plotting with the enemy, the following response of Enver Pasha, given in the occasion of a further intervention by the US Ambassador on behalf of Armenians, reveals the deliberate indiscriminate attack against the entire Armenian community:

> We have no time to separate the innocent from the guilty.[101]

As to the last talk with Enver and Talât before leaving office in Constantinople in 1916, in which he was asking guarantees about the treatment of US, Britain and French citizens and missions in the Empire (still at war with UK and France), Amb. Morgenthau reports that, having also asked

> 'How about the Armenians?', Talât's geniality disappeared in an instant. His face hardened and the fire of the beast lighted up his eyes once more. 'What's the use of speaking about them?' he said, waving his hand. 'We are through with them. That's all over'.[102]

These messages avoid any doubt about the real nature of the deportations: They were deliberately organized as measures of destruction of the community.

Also relevant insofar as the intent is concerned are the decisions taken by the Triumvirate in 1915–16 in order to give a semblance of legality to its wrongdoing. These decisions, far from providing a legal framework, clearly show the pursuit of the purpose of eliminating the Armenian presence in the Ottoman Empire. I refer here to only three significant examples: 1. The Law of 10 June 1915, followed by and others laws with analogous contents, declared the goods of deportees "abandoned properties" ("emvali metruke"), hence subject to confiscation and relocation; already in June 1915, this clearly reveals the actual fate of the deportees. 2. The Government also issued public edicts through which Armenians were banished from the different Ottoman provinces; see in particular the edict concerning the Harput Province of the 26 June 1915, about which an eyes witness, the U.S. Consul at Harput, Leslie A. Davis, refers in his Report to US authorities.[103] 3. On 1 January 1916, the Minister of Commerce directed banks to transfer Armenian assets—land,

---

[100]Morgenthau (1918), p. 126.

[101]Morgenthau (1918), p. 127.

[102]Morgenthau (1918), p. 148.

[103]Davis (1918), p. 52.

bank deposits, etc.—to State commissions, since the fate of the Armenians was close to the final solution.[104]

We could confine ourselves to the reported words and to the above-mentioned decisions taken by the Ottoman rulers in order to conclude that the intent of the Ottoman State to destroy the Armenian community as such is largely proven pursuant to the standard of proof applied by ICJ, ICTY and ICTR in the genocide cases. However, Turkey contests both the authenticity of the messages that I have analysed above and the reliability of the *Story* of the American Ambassador, as well as the interpretation of the governmental decisions given here, which is indeed corroborated by the vast majority of historians and lawyers. Therefore, I will further enquire, only *ad abundantiam* from my point of view, on the circumstantial evidence resulting from both the facts of 1915–16 and the evidence relative to the policy and planning of the destruction in question, if any. For this exercise I will be guided, as usually, by the jurisprudence of the ICJ and the two *ad hoc* Tribunals.

3.2.4 The Circumstantial Evidence of the Specific Intent to Destroy the Armenian Nation as Such

The Factors Proving the Destructive Intent in the light of International Jurisprudence

The ICTR and ICTY Trial Chambers have observed that "in the absence of a confession it is difficult to prove /the genocidal/intention".[105] This explains why they considered that specific intent as requirement under the Genocide Convention "can be inferred from a number of other factors,"[106] which these Tribunals have often resorted to, on a case by case basis.[107] In particular, the ICTY and ICTR Chambers consider that the genocidal intent

> may be inferred from a number of facts such as the general political doctrine which gave rise to the acts possibly covered by the definition [of genocide], or the repetition of

[104]Some disputes concerning these confiscations were brought by heirs of victims before U.S. Courts, pursuant to the California legislature that extended the statute of limitations for actions seeking the recovery of "looted assets" by any "Armenian Genocide victim" or any "heir or beneficiary of an Armenian Genocide victim" who resides in California. Indeed, the statute provides that such actions could be brought on or before 31 December 2016. See, for instance, *Varoujan Deirmenjian* v. *Deutsche Bank US District Court*, California (Judge Morrow) 11 September 2006, https://www.courtlistener.com/opinion/2415413/deirmenjian-v-deutsche-bank-ag/.

[105]ICTY, Trial Chamber Decision on *Consideration of the Indictment within the framework of Rule 61 of the Rules of Procedure and Evidence*, *Karadzic and Mladic*, 11 July 1996, para. 94, fn. 102. See in the same vein, ICTR, Trial Chamber Judgment, *Akayesu*, 2 September 1998, para. 523.

[106]Inter alia, *Akayesu*, confirmed on appeal and ICJ, *Genocide case*, para. 370 ff. See Cassese (2008), p. 143.

[107]See, inter alia, ICTR, Trial Chamber Judgment, *Rutaganda*, 6 December 1999, para. 61–63. See also ICTR, Trial Chamber Judgment, *Musema*, 27 January 2000, para. 167.

> destructive and discriminatory acts…, the perpetration of acts which violate, or which the perpetrators themselves consider to violate the very foundation of the group – acts which are not in themselves covered by the list [of acts of genocide], but which are committed as part of the same pattern of conduct.[108]

The same Chambers consider that it is also possible to deduce the genocidal intent

> from the general context of the perpetration of other culpable acts systematically directed against that same group, whether these acts were committed by the same offender or by others.[109]

The ICTY and ICTR have also resorted to factors such as

> the scale of atrocities committed, their general nature, in a region or a country, or furthermore, the fact of deliberately and systematically targeting victims on account of their membership of a particular group, while excluding the members of other groups.[110]

They also considered the following factors as proving the genocidal intent: the number of victims, the expropriation of their properties, the use of insulting expressions towards the members of the community targeted, the destruction of its cultural and religious buildings and, as already noted, the planning of genocide by the top rulers of the State involved as well as the overall policy.[111] The same factors were considered by the ICJ in the Genocide case.

The Application of the same Factors to the Armenian Case

The factors this international jurisprudence relies on are all present in the case of the Armenian massacres and deportations. Almost all plainly result from the analysis of the material element of the criminal acts perpetrated in 1915–16 against members of the Armenian community. I will therefore refer to these factors very briefly, while I will discuss more in detail the issue of the general policy and the planning, both as strong circumstantial factors.

The Circumstantial Evidence Resulting from the Facts Assessed

The evidence on the high scale of killings of disarmed and weakened soldiers regularly enrolled in the Ottoman Army and thousands of innocent civilians, in particular able-bodied men, reveals the necessity for the perpetrators "to kill outright all men who were in their prime and thus capable of propagating the accursed species".[112]

---

[108]ICTY, Trial Chamber Decision on *Consideration of the Indictment*, quoted supra, fn. 104, para. 95. See also ICTR, Trial Chamber Judgment, *Semanza*, 15 May 2003, para. 313. ICTR, Trial Chamber Judgment, *Bagilishema*, 7 June 2001, para. 63.

[109]See, inter alia, ICTR, *Akayesu*, para. 523 and *Musema*, para. 166.

[110]See, inter alia, ICTR, *Akayesu*, para. 523 and *Musema*, para. 166.

[111]See in this vein ICTR, *Bagilishema*, para. 63.

[112]Morgenthau (1918), p. 109.

From the evidence of direct killings of other civilians, such as women, children and elders, as well as the evidence of their massive deaths on account of the horrendous conditions of life to which they were submitted can clearly be inferred the intent to destroy the all Armenian community inhabiting the Empire. Indeed, the fact that few Armenians survived deportations thanks only to some courageous and compassionate individuals and some relief organizations proves that deportations were not meant to be relocations or expulsions. They consisted in marches towards the desert without hope for return, without hope for a new life. The return of Armenians to their homeland was not envisaged at all. Rather, not only their physical, but also their "objective" existence in Ottoman villages and cities needed to be erased. Deportations equalized to death sentences.

The destructive intent is also indirectly proved by the Ottoman Decrees on "The Abandoned Properties". They were indeed Decrees of confiscation and appropriation of Armenians' properties, insofar properties were not taken in custody by the Ottoman State in order to be given back to the Armenians once the (false) military necessities were over. The fact that all their valuables—e.g. money, rings, watches, and jewelry—were taken to the police stations for (false) "safe keeping, pending their return", "and then were parceled out among the Turks" renders the real intent of the Ottoman rulers apparent.[113] The economy of the Empire needed to be rebuilt as a "pure" Turkish economy.

We find the same logic in the elimination or reconversion of the Armenians' educational and cultural institutions, religious symbols and buildings. Every footprint of the community was intended to be destroyed.

Another clear sign of the destructive intent of the actors of the 1915–16 events is that targeting civilians started with the arrest, deportation and subsequent killing of the entire Armenian leadership in the most important cities of the Empire. This was done in the genocidal logic that a snake needs to be eliminated by squashing its head, as some witnesses who testified in the ICTR genocide cases interpreted the killing of Tutsi leaders. The fact that not only Armenian dignitaries allegedly sympathizing with revolutionist ideals were slaughtered, but also any other community-leader was targeted with the same deadly means, is telling of the destructive intent of the members of the CUP.

The specific intent under discussion is also revealed by the extended and coordinated manner in which massacres and deportations occurred in all the Provinces where the Armenians were present all over the Ottoman territory.

Finally, I refer to another circumstantial factor referred to by a direct witness. This factor proves the malicious intent of the Ottoman rulers to destroy the Ottoman community without risking foreign interference:

---

[113]Morgenthau (1918), p. 116. Jesse K Jackson, the U.S. diplomat who served as consul in Aleppo, 1915–16, described in his dispatches the local towns and districts "where Armenians have already been practically exterminated" and called the Turkish government's confiscation scheme "a gigantic plundering scheme as well as a final blow to extinguish the [Armenian] race", quoted by Robertson (2016), para. 38.

> the Ottoman Government did its utmost to prevent the news of what it was doing to the Armenians from leaking through to the outer world. A stringent censorship was established at all the frontiers, private communication was severed between Constantinople and the provinces, and the provinces themselves were isolated from one another.[114]

These precautions are also confirmed by two messages of Minister of the Interior Talât to the Prefecture of Aleppo. In the first one he says:

> We are informed that some correspondents of Armenian journals are acquiring photographs and letters which depict tragic events, and these they give to the American Consul at Aleppo. Dangerous people of this kind must be arrested and suppressed.[115]

Some days after that message he again alerts the Prefecture of Aleppo writing:

> We are informed that foreign officers are finding along the roads the corpses of the indicated persons, and are photographing them. Have these corpses buried at once and do not allow them to be left near the roads. This order is recommended as very important.[116]

Even if several other factors concerning the facts occurred in 1915–16 could be referred to in order to indirectly show the specific intent to destroy the Armenian community, I consider that there is no need to provide further evidence of this kind. I will instead move to briefly discussing "the general political doctrine" behind the destruction of the Armenian community, as well as the planning of its destruction. Both factors are indeed of primary importance especially when enquiring on the State responsibility rather than on the criminal responsibility of the individual perpetrators of the atrocities of 1915–16.

The Armenian Nation as Such an Obstacle to the Turkification of the Ottoman Empire

It is undisputed among historians that in 1909, the radical nationalistic policy of turkification and islamisation of the remaining Ottoman territories commenced at the initiative of the "Young Turks". This policy was also accompanied by the so-called Pan-Turkism, i.e. the project of unification of all Turks under the same rule, the dreamed State of Turkestan, or even the project of Pan-Turanism.[117] This meant that all the Christians should be eliminated from these territories. Indeed, the Christian Assyrians, as the Greeks-Orthodox, also suffered extermination, although to a lesser extent than the Armenians. Greeks-Orthodox, in particular, suffered

[114] Bryce and Toynbee (1916), General description.

[115] 11 December 1915, http://www.firstworldwar.com/source/armenia_Talâtorders.htm.

[116] 29 December 1915, http://www.firstworldwar.com/source/armenia_Talâtorders.htm.

[117] Lothrop Stoddard (1917).

mainly expulsions to an existing independent Greek State, which the Armenians instead lacked.[118]

Further factors made the situation of the Armenian community different with respect to other Christian communities of the Empire. First, this community, inhabiting mostly, for centuries, the strategic territory of East Anatolia and Cilicia, was not only the oldest but also the largest among the Christian communities living there. The arrival in these regions of Muslim refugees, coming from the Balkan and Caucasian territories, which had been lost by the Ottoman Empire during previous wars, did not only reduce the Armenian community from one third to one fourth of the total population of those territories, but also led to a difficult coexistence between the Muslim and the Christian communities, in particular the Armenian one. After all the defeats suffered in the Balkan wars and the independence acquired by many peoples of the Empire, the Armenian community was perceived as a serious obstacle to the turkification and islamization of the few territories that remained under Ottoman rule.[119]

These difficulties were also provoked by the rise of liberal and democratic ideals in the Ottoman Empire, under the influence of Europe and America. Especially among the Armenians the awareness was growing of their different religious and ethnic secular identity. Furthermore, this awareness had naturally increased after the pogroms suffered at the end of XIX and the beginning of the XX centuries. As mentioned, this led them to seek a larger autonomy in the context of the Ottoman rule in view of benefiting from more extensive civil and political rights and, above all, equality with Muslim citizens.[120]

Moreover, as we will see, the Sublime Porte had undertaken, under the San Stefano and Berlin Treaties, the obligation to enact reforms that the Armenians were locally asking, but had never complied with this obligation, as had never complied with the obligation to protect Armenians from Circassians and Kurds.[121]

---

[118]The difference between the two situations also appears evident by the fact that Greeks under expulsions were requested to sign documents certifying that they were voluntarily abandoning their lands and houses. This same occurred with the Bosniaks who were forced to abandon their houses and villages and to sign a declaration certifying their consent (indeed, the assessment of these facts, together with killings, tortures etc., in other Municipalities than Srebrenica, brought in the *Karadzic* and *Mladić* ICTY cases to the assessment of many crimes against humanity, but not of genocide).

[119]Morgenthau reports a talk with a representative of the National police, which thus explained the decision of the Ottoman authorities to massacre and deport Armenians: "the profound moral reason why we must, as statesmen, show ourselves indifferent to the sufferings of the Christian peoples of Turkey, however painful that may be to our human feelings [...]. That is our duty, which we must recognize and confess before God and before man. If for this reason we now maintain the existence of the Turkish state, we do it in our own self-interest, because what we have in mind is our great future": Morgenthau (1918), p. 139.

[120]Autonomy does not mean independence. A *status* of autonomy is an internal notion, in the context of the constitutional and administrative organization of a state, while independence marks the existence of a *State superiorem non recognoscens*.

[121]See Sect. 4.1.1.

Such a non-compliance led some "revolutionists" among the Armenians to dream of independence in an Armenian State.[122] The large majority of them did not follow the revolutionist ideals and, in any case, were not ready to start a civil war to claim their rights. As results also from the provisions of those Treaties, the Armenians, being fully integrated into the professional and economic life of the Ottoman Empire, but sensible to the Christian ideals driving Europe, were indeed seeking to reach a new, more liberal *status* by peaceful means and with the support of European countries, as specifically provided by the Berlin Treaty.[123] However, for the Ottoman Empire, which had fallen into the obsession of Pan-Turkism, Anatolia, considered to be its heartland, could not be a territory where a *status* of larger autonomy could be recognized to a Christian community that was strongly aware of its religious and ethnic identity. It is because of these reasons that the Ottoman rulers targeted the Christian Armenian community as such for destruction.

Planning the Destruction of the Armenian Nation

As in the case of the direct evidence of intent, I will refer here to the actual words of the members of the Triumvirate or their delegates, as well as to some statements and comments of direct witnesses.

During a meeting with Amb. Morgenthau, who was intervening in favour of Armenians, the Minister of War Enver Pasha said:

> As I told you once before, I warned the Armenian Patriarch that if the Armenians attacked us while we were engaged in a foreign war, that we Turks would hit back and that we would hit back indiscriminately.

If this is not evidence of the Armenian rebellion, it is certainly a confession of the existence of a plan of indiscriminate deportations. In the same vein, after a long discussion about the Armenian uprising and plotting with the Russian enemy, the Minister of War Enver Pasha so concluded:

---

[122]The recognition by Turkey of Armenia as independent State and the possible transfer of some Ottoman "Armenian" Provinces under the sovereignty of this new State were provided for by the Sèvres Treaty. It was indeed evident that the events of 1915–16 – in a minor extent still unfolding when the Treaty was adopted – rendered almost impossible for the remaining part of the community to coexist with Muslim Turks in the Ottoman Empire.

[123]The following editorial, which appeared in June 1898 in the Armenian Revue *Droschak*, is particularly revealing as to this approach: "Nous avons toujours été favorables à l'idée de solidarité. [...] S'il existe aujourd'hui un certain antagonisme national entre Turcs et Arméniens ottomans, c'est pour l'essentiel à cause du gouvernement. Et nous sommes persuadés qu'à l'avenir, lorsque des conditions politiques acceptables auront été instaurées en Turquie, les deux nations continueront à vivre en paix et dans la sérénité et se dirigeront, dans un effort général, vers la plus haute civilisation. [...] Peu importe que certains représentants décrépits de la Jeune Turquie, qui ignorent tout de notre action, répandent des insinuations contre nous, présentant à la face de toute l'Europe les comités arméniens comme 'les destructeurs de villages turcs' et jetant à la figure des révolutionnaires arméniens le qualificatif de 'séparatiste'" (the original French version, p. 59–60, quoted in Kévorkian and Ternon (2014), p. 24).

> If two hundred Turks could overturn the Government, then a few hundred bright, educated Armenians could do the same thing. We have therefore deliberately adopted the plan of scattering them so that they can do us no harm.

Apart from the alleged justification, which is not relevant now, what is important here is the direct reference to the adoption of a plan. Furthermore, it is noteworthy that the content of this plan is blatantly described, with no caution, by the word "scattering," rather than by the word "relocating", habitually maliciously used by the Turkish authorities in referring to the Armenians' deportations without return. Considering, in addition, that the plan was not that of "scattering" just a few hundred "bright, educated Armenians", but hundreds of thousands of them of any social condition, sex and age, the word "scattering" gives the clear image of an overall plan apt to dismember, disarticulate, destroy that community in whole.[124]

Also relevant from the viewpoint of the existence of a plan is the fact that, as reported by, inter alios, Morgenthau with regard to one of the modalities of deportations without return,

> scarcely had the former possessors left the village, when Mohammedan mohadjirs – immigrants from other parts of Turkey – would be moved into the Armenian quarters.[125]

The following instruction of 10 January 1916 by Abdullahad Nouri, the Commissioner for deportations to the "General Committee for settling the deportees" also shows the existence of an overall plan that involved Ottoman officials, on different level of the governmental organization:

> Enquiries having been made, it is understood that hardly ten percent of the Armenians subjected to the general deportation have reached the places destined for them; the rest have died from natural causes, such as hunger and sickness. We inform you that we are working to bring about the same result with regard to those who are still alive, by using severe measures.

Furthermore, the simple existence of such a Committee reveals how the CUP planned and organized everything in order to efficiently and rapidly carrying out mass-killings and deportations. Even torture was meticulously planned, as Morgenthau reveals:

> One day I was discussing these proceedings with a responsible Turkish official, who was describing the tortures inflicted… This official told me that all these details were matters of nightly discussion at the headquarters of the Union and Progress Committee. Each new method of inflicting pain was hailed as a splendid discovery, and the regular attendants were constantly ransacking their brains in the effort to devise some new torment. He told me that they even delved into the records of the Spanish Inquisition and other historic institutions of torture and adopted all the suggestions found there. He made no secret of the fact that the Government had instigated them, and, like a Turk of the official classes, he enthusiastically approved this treatment of the detested race.[126]

---

[124]Morgenthau (1918), p. 115–116.

[125]Morgenthau (1918), p. 116.

[126]Morgenthau (1918), p. 114.

It is noteworthy that the Ottoman Martial Courts ascertained the planning of the destruction of the Armenian community too. For instance, a Court stressed in one case how the CUP and a local governor had planned "the massacre and annihilation of the Armenians" by employing criminals released from prison "to act as their guards but with directions to kill the men and to drown the children." This, in addition to revealing a precise plan as circumstantial evidence of intent, is also direct evidence of the intent to arrive to a "final solution", as the same Courts further pointed out.[127]

Moreover, the fact-finding mission undertaken by a team led by General Harbord in September 1919, concluded that the massacres and deportations were carried out pursuant to a "definite system". In particular, the team had verified that soldiers were going from town to town, summoning all Armenian men, aged 15–45, to government offices and then marching them off, to execution.[128] This system included the removal of "untrustworthy" public servants and their replacement by men who were regarded as "more reliable".[129] So, a significant instance of this approach is the following one illustrated by Amb. Morgenthau: when the war started,

> the Central Government recalled Tahsin Pasha, the conciliatory governor of Van, and replaced him with Djevdet Bey, a brother-in-law of Enver Pasha [...]. He hated the Armenians and cordially sympathized with the long-established Turkish plan of solving the Armenian problem. There is little question that he came to Van with definite instructions to exterminate all Armenians in this province.[130]

The circumstantial evidence of the specific intent to destroy the Armenian community in whole is in my view overwhelming on the basis of the planning factor as well.

---

[127]Horne (1923).

[128]Quoted by Robertson (2009), para. 42. Even if the press is at times unreliable, it is also true that it has first hands information. If such information is compatible with other kinds of information, it can be cautiously utilized even in a criminal proceeding. So allow me to report the following dispatch from Henry Wood, correspondent of the American "United Press" at Constantinople, published in the American Press on 14th August 1915: "sealed orders were sent to the police of the entire Empire. These were to be opened on a specified date that would ensure the orders being in the hands of every department at the moment they were to be opened. Once opened, they provided for a simultaneous descent at practically the same moment on the Armenian population of the entire Empire."

[129]"Turkish officialdom has always contained a minority of men who do not believe in massacre as a state policy and cannot be depended upon to carry out strictly the most bloody orders of the Central Government." (Morgenthau 1918, p. 111).

[130]Morgenthau (1918), p. 111.

3.2.5 The Intent to Destroy in a Substantial Part the Armenian Nation as Such Is Proven

The planners—State agents, and thus the Ottoman Empire—intended to cancel all footprints of the Armenian identity and culture from a territory where this identity and culture had been essential components of a multicultural Empire for centuries.

None, except who completely shuts her or his eyes to what happened and denies everything or knows what happened but intentionally denies it, could contest all those tragic, large scale, systematic and all-around coordinated events—and not single random episodes—suffered by the members of the Christian Armenian community and aimed by the Ottoman rulers to a specific intended end: the elimination of that community in whole.[131]

While the evidence concerning intent reveals that the target was the destruction of the Armenian community in whole, on the basis of the facts assessed we can only conclude on its destruction in substantial part on the ground of its Christian and ethnic identity.

4 The Applicable Law

4.1 The San Stefano and Berlin Treaties

4.1.1 Obligations of the Ottoman Empire

Pursuant to the principle of *lex specialis derogat generali*, I will first consider the conventional rules applicable to the relations between the Sublime Porte and some European States, concerning Non-Muslim Minorities in the Ottoman territories, especially the Armenian one.

Stipulated at the end of the Russian–Ottoman war (1877–1878), the Peace Treaty of San Stefano imposed to the Sublime Porte an obligation vis-à-vis Russia

[131]In holding this view I am in good company. Even diplomats of a friend and allied Power, as the German Ambassador to Istanbul, Count Wolf-Metternich, reported to its government that "the CUP demands the extirpation of the last remnants of Armenians [...]" and commented that "Turkification means licence to expel, to kill or destroy everything that is not Turkish, and to violently take possession of the goods of others". The German Vice-Consul in Erzurum reported that the CUP members "are bluntly admitting that the purpose of their actions is the total obliteration of the Armenians". He also mentioned that an authoritative person would have "word-for-word declared" that "we will have in Turkey no more Armenians after the war" (quoted by Robertson 1999, para. 38). Another German who was opposed to the atrocities was Neurath, the Counselor of the German Embassy. Morgenthau says about him: "His indignation reached such a point that his language to Talât and Enver became almost undiplomatic. He told me, however, that he had failed to influence them. They are immovable and are determined to pursue their present course" (Morgenthau, 1918, p. 140).

> to carry into effect, without further delay, the improvements and reforms demanded by local requirements in the provinces inhabited by Armenians, and to guarantee their security from Kurds and Circassians (Article XVI).

This Treaty was partially modified by the Berlin Treaty of 1878. The latter imposed on the Ottoman Empire *vis-à-vis* the then Great European Powers—United Kingdom, Austria-Hungary, France, Germany, Italy, Russia—an analogous obligation, but also added a provision on compliance with it by means of supervision by the Powers. Indeed, according to Article LXI of the Treaty, The Sublime Porte undertook

> to carry out, without further delay, the improvements and reforms demanded by local requirements in the provinces inhabited by Armenians, and to guarantee their security against the Circassians and Kurds. It will periodically make known the steps taken to this effect to the powers, who will superintend their application.

Furthermore, Article LXII of this Treaty had a broader scope. It dealt with the rights of any religious minority, but in a softer way, as it referred to a declaration by the Sublime Porte rather than to its "commitment", in a logic of respect due to "domestic jurisdiction":

> The Sublime Porte having expressed the intention to maintain the principle of religious liberty, and give it the widest scope, the Contracting Parties took note of this spontaneous declaration. In no part of the Ottoman Empire shall difference of religion be alleged against any person as a ground for exclusion or incapacity in matters relating to the enjoyment of civil or political rights, admission to public employments, functions, and honors, or the exercise of the various professions and industries, in any locality whatsoever [...]. The right of official protection by the Diplomatic and Consular Agents of the Powers in Turkey is recognized both as regards the above-mentioned persons and their religious, charitable, and other establishments in the Holy Places and elsewhere.[132]

In short, in the Berlin Treaty, the Ottoman Empire had unilaterally promised to guarantee to the members of whatever religion parity with Muslim citizens in the enjoyment of civil and political rights and access to any profession. With regard to Armenians, the obligations of the San Stefano Treaty to carry out the reforms they locally demanded—which also implicitly meant a *status* of large autonomy of their community—and to protect them from Kurds and Circassians were reiterated. Moreover, while the more general unilateral promise was subject to the traditional institute of diplomatic protection, the obligations concerning Armenians were exposed in the Treaty of Berlin to a more intrusive monitoring procedure by the European Powers.

All these provisions clearly prove that even at that time, international (conventional) law considered it necessary to protect certain groups as such due to their

---

[132]It needs however to be underlined that the formula "shall" referred to the exclusion of any discrimination on religious grounds, contained in the Porte declaration, clearly shows that a unilateral promise by a Party to a Treaty attested by the other Parties had a binding effect. Such effect is further proved by the provision envisaging the diplomatic protection of persons claiming religious liberty and civil and political rights without discrimination. On unilateral declarations as binding instrument in international law see Eckart (2012).

characteristics: in general, for their religious belief, in particular—and in addition, where appropriate, for the distinctive trait of the specific group, as the Armenian one.[133] However, at that time, international law did not specifically prohibit the destruction of a national, religious or ethnic group as such, although, certainly, protection of a religious and ethnic minority implicitly meant prohibition of its destruction in whole or in part.

All the obligations contained in the mentioned provisions were breached. First, the State did fail to guarantee civil and political rights to all Ottoman citizens without discrimination and to specifically protect the Armenian community from Kurds and Circassians. Thus, even if we could hypothetically accept, among the different and contradictory claims of the current Turkish authorities, that "suffering" was caused to Armenians "by bandits"—meant to be Kurds, Circassians (but also Turks)—the Ottoman Empire still violated the obligations taken on pursuant to the above-mentioned treaty provisions.

Furthermore, as the assessed evidence shows, the Ottoman State, instead of protecting that community from Kurds and Circassians, employed some members of these two communities for carrying out this destruction across the all territory. The Sublime Porte also directly committed the atrocities through its top rulers, who planned, decided, organized, ordered, instigated and led the destruction of the community for its being Christian and Armenian. The Ottoman rulers even resorted to and instigated especially nationalistic Turks against Armenians, fabricating their traitorous conduct.[134]

4.1.2 Obligations of European States Parties

As already noted, not only Turkey, but also the European Powers failed to abide by the San Stefano and Berlin Treaties. Too concerned with dividing the territories of the disintegrating Empire among themselves, they failed to oversee the application of the Ottoman obligations concerning Armenians. This inaction is incompatible with the Berlin Treaty, which specifically provides a monitoring procedure by those Powers.

The joint Declaration of 24 May 1915 of Russia, the United Kingdom and France, which labelled the first massacres as "crimes against humanity and against

[133]The Treaty of Sèvres referred to "race" too. Race as the ground for targeting the Armenians is also referred to by Amb. Morgenthau mainly in telegrams to the US Secretary of State, which are mentioned in the present paper. Indeed, Armenians and Turks are not considered of the same race. But, at that time, the term race was used in a broader sense than currently.

[134]How can the Turks, Kurds and Circassians as such take on their shoulders all the responsibility for the destruction of the Armenian community and not react to the false interpretation of these tragic events that the Turkish authorities continue to give? Were there thousands of bandits in the Ottoman Empire in 1915–16? No, besides some bandits used by the top rulers for the commission of the most dreadful crimes, there were mostly "unsophisticated" people instigated and ordered by political and religious Muslim authorities to eliminate the alleged traitors members of a Christian Nation and take their properties.

civilization" and called for the individual criminal responsibility of the Ottoman agents before the jurisdiction of any of these Powers, cannot indeed be considered an effective supervision of the Ottoman conduct. It remains, as we will see later, a significant document meant to assess crimes against humanity and the states' *opinio iuris in fieri* concerning the legal consequences of such crimes. However, it was not followed by any effective measure, although only for political reasons.[135] European Powers, as the U.S., confined themselves to receiving extensive diplomatic, consular and missionary correspondence on the beginning, continuation and progression of the massacres and deportations.[136] At best, they reacted by condemning the horrors, while local populations and missions were prevented by the Ottoman authorities from assisting Armenians or in any case were powerless in efficiently relieving them, given the enormous entity of the tragedy. Private citizens and religious institutions, in particular in the US, collected money in view of helping a population that was doomed to elimination.

It is true, as we should see, that during the Paris Peace Conference the massacres and deportations of Armenians also ended up on the table. The victorious powers made indeed every possible effort to establish the State and individual Ottoman responsibilities through the Peace Treaty with Turkey. However, subsequently, concerned about their own interests in the face of the difficulties which arose with the new Turkish rulers, the European Powers, not only did abandon the project of an independent Armenian State, which should have incorporated a part of the Ottoman territory inhabited by Armenians, but also abandoned Armenians to their fate, included the few survivors who had remained in Turkey. This 'U-turn' allowed the crimes against Armenians to continue undisturbed in Turkey until 1923.

It would be important, when national, European and international institutions, or even States, recognize the Armenian massacres or "genocide", that they also recall the then Great Powers' complicity, by omission, with the Ottoman Empire.

4.2 *The Applicability of the* Martens Clause *to the Alleged Armenian Uprising*

I will now move on by assuming that the atrocities of 1915–16 took place in a situation of civil war that would have broken out because of the Armenians' uprising against the Empire and their fighting with the Russian enemy. The aim is to show that the issue of the responsibility of the Ottoman State and its successor State

[135] See below, Sect. 4.5.3.

[136] Italy, for instance, received alarming messages on the situation from its Consul-General in Trebisonda, Giacomo Gorrini. The Consul, after ending his mandate in the Ottoman Empire when Italy entered into war, also gave a dramatic interview to the Newspaper "Il Messaggero". Yet, the Italian rulers preferred to look the other way too.

would still remain on the table. In this case, this responsibility would be for violations of international law applicable to armed conflicts.

Although I personally believe that at that time, some fundamental customs of war applicable to international conflicts were also applicable to civil war—as it emerges from the *Lieber* Code, which some scholars consider a domestic codification of international law of war[137]—the existence in 1915 of established customs of war applicable to the civil war context may be disputable. Thus, leaving aside customs of war, I consider that a situation of civil war was still covered by the *Martens clause*. This clause stated:

> Until a more complete code of the laws of war is issued, the High Contracting Parties think it's right to declare that in cases not included in the Regulations adopted by them, populations and belligerents remain under the protection and empire of the principles of international law, as they result from the usages established between civilized nations, from the laws of humanity and the requirements of the public conscience.[138]

This clause was originally proposed by the Russian delegate Martens at The Hague Conference of 1899. It was then included in the 1899 and 1907 Conventions concerning the laws and customs of war on land, the former having been ratified also by The Sublime Porte. Notwithstanding the different—strict and broad—interpretations of this clause given by States and scholars, the majority seem correctly to be in favour of its literal reading. Accordingly, as the ILC put it

> even in cases not covered by specific international agreements, civilians and combatants remain under the protection and authority of the principles of international law derived from established custom, from the principles of humanity and from the dictates of public conscience.[139]

Civil wars as well had to be included among such cases. Although the issue of regulating civil warfare was, already at that time, on the agenda of the international community, no international convention had been stipulated in this matter as yet. Thus, if not customs of war, at least "the usages established between civilized nations", the "laws of humanity" and the "requirements of the public conscience" of the *Martens clause* were the legal standards applicable at that time to a civil war context as well.

This said, I consider quite obvious, in the light also of the facts occurred in 1915–16, that, as a party to the 1899 Hague Convention, even though it carried out

---

[137]During the American civil war, in 1865, Henry Wirz, a Major of the Confederate Army, accused by a US war Commission of violations of the laws of war against enemy prisoners in a camp under his control, was tried and sentenced to death. Apart from the question that later arose about the unfair proceedings that led to this conviction, this trial clearly shows that some laws of war applied even in civil war, as after all the *Lieber* Code, promulgated as General Order No. 100 by President Lincoln on 24 April 1863, provided. Its Articles 149–157 applied to insurrection, civil war and rebellion. See the interesting observations on *Lieber* Code by the European Court of Human Rights (Grand Chamber), *Komonov* v. *Latvia*, 17 May 2010, paras. 63–77 and 207.

[138]See Ticehurst (1997).

[139]Report of the International Law Commission on the Work of its Forty-sixth Session, 2 May/22 July 1994, GAOR A/49/10, p. 317.

military operations aiming at repressing an uprising, the Ottoman Empire seriously violated the principles of international law as derived by the above-mentioned legal standards, which were referred to in broadly accepted multilateral Conventions. Moreover, that State was a party to one of those Conventions.

Even assuming hypothetically that the "massacres" were not violations of international law, they were certainly criminal under Ottoman law, as it clearly emerges from the trials of 1919–20, in which the rebellion justification was rejected.[140] It is thus certain that the repression of a rebellion did not allow for the elimination of elders, women and children.[141]

At the same time, we cannot forget that, from the analysis conducted on the facts, it becomes quite evident that the acts committed against both the Armenian leadership and the Armenian elderly, women and children were absolutely unrelated to a police or military repression of an uprising, as the killings of Armenian soldiers enrolled in the Ottoman Army were also carried out outside of any military operation against insurgents.

4.3 The Applicability of the Laws of Humanity to the Events of 1915–16

I am firmly convinced that both peoples and States have always been, and certainly were in 1915–16, strongly disturbed by dreadful massive violations of the laws of humanity, in whatever circumstance they had been committed, in particular when affecting elderly, women, children. The history of human and interstates relations proves it. For instance, nobody would presently deny the massacres committed by crusaders during the eight/nine Christian "religious wars". The dispute is on the number of victims among Muslims—and Jews—rather than on the massacres themselves. How could one discuss about such misdeeds without a reference to universal humanitarian values? It is evident that even if they occurred in the XI-XIII centuries, the crusaders' conduct was and is considered incompatible with the laws

[140] See some of the Excerpts from the proceedings of the Courts Martials held in Istanbul from April to July 1919 against the leaders of the CUP – published in the Ottoman Official Journal *Takvim I Vekai*, n. 3571 – reprinted in Libaridian (2007), p. 130 ff. From these Excerpts the ideology of the CUP leaders that inspired their deeds reveals apparent and they clearly do not show any repression of an uprising.

[141] In the propagandist conferences and in other symposiums of prof. McCarthy I did not hear any reference to elders, women, children. It seems that the Armenian community was only composed of combatants killing Turkish combatants and civilians. See, for instance, the Australian Turkish Advocacy Alliance Symposium of 7 December 2013, where that professor embarks, inter alia, in a completely wrong definition of genocide.

of humanity and "the requirements of the public conscience", be it Christian, Muslim or Jewish.[142]

It is true that human rights were codified in international law only after WWII as outcome of the tragic events of that war and under the influence of some liberal Constitutions of XIX and XX centuries. However, the English *Magna Carta Libertatum* of 1215, the English Bill of Rights of 1689, the US Bill of Rights of 1789, the French Declaration of the Rights of Man and of the Citizen of 1789 had already spread their ideals of freedom and humanity around the world. Thus, fundamental humanitarian values had already influenced the codification of international law, including the law of armed conflicts.[143] The laws of humanity and the requirements of public conscience were indeed considered principles of international law, as expressly affirmed in the *Martens clause*. It is *in re ipsa* that, as principles of international law, they were and are of general application and know no frontiers. It would thus be absolutely illogic to consider them applicable in a war context and not in a context of peace or widespread hatred against a minority. Humanitarian values as such are indeed universal *ratione temporis*, *ratione loci*, *ratione personae* and applicable in any context.[144] The universality of some fundamental humanitarian values is confirmed by the title itself of the Universal Declaration on Human Rights adopted in 1948 by UNGA. It was indeed possible to adopt this international instrument in 1948 as a *Declaration* only insofar some fundamental human rights were already a legacy of international law. In any case, if not every right recognized in the Declaration existed in 1915–16, the right of innocent persons to life and the right to not be submitted to torture[145] were certainly part of the humanitarian principles in force at that time and were applicable irrespective of any conventional obligation.

A confirmation of the existence at that time of international humanitarian principles can be found in the intervention by the U.S. with the Ottoman authorities in defence of the Armenians, even though that State was not party to the San Stefano and Berlin Treaties. By a telegram of the 11 August 1915, Ambassador Morgenthau makes some suggestions to the US Secretary of State, Bryan, for such

[142]Christian Europe and above all the Catholic Church would need to recognize that Crusades were not Holy wars, just as all Islamic States and all Islamic religious authorities would need to recognize that the Jihad against Christians is not a Holy war.

[143]For instance, the *Declaration Renouncing the Use, in Time of War, of Explosive Projectiles Under 400 Grammes Weight*, Saint Petersburg, 29 November/11 December 1868, in its Preamble referred to the requirements of humanity such as limits to the necessities of war.

[144]In 165 B.C., in one of his theatrical works, Publius Terentius Afer expressed a clear concept of *Humanitas*: "Homo sum, humani nihil a me alienum puto" (*Heautontimorùmenos*, verse 77)!

[145]Torture against a person for obtaining information or confession was perhaps still legal at that time, but torture against innocent children, women and elders was certainly not. Yet, already in 1764, Cesare Beccaria pleaded against the use of judicial torture to extract confessions: "Dei delitti e delle pene", Ch. XVI "Della tortura", a cura di Renato Fabietti, Mursia, Milano 1973.

intervention.[146] The Ottoman Minister of the Interior did not claim the illegality of an intervention in favor of Ottoman citizens as intervention in the Porte's "internal affairs". Amb. Morgenthau reported to Bryan on his steps and the assurances received by the Minister "that orders were telegraphed to provinces exempting from deportation all Protestant and Catholic Armenians."[147] Of course, these assurances were not genuine. Mass-killing and deportations continued, as another telegram sent in the same period by the Ambassador to Bryan reveals.[148] However, violations of international norms do not prove that those norms do not exist. Rather, their existence is proved by the fact that the State author of the violations manifests its availability to put an end to them or provides (false) justifications for its wrongdoing, as Turkey does nowadays.

It is finally noteworthy that the Ottoman authorities themselves were convinced of the existence of universal laws of humanity and civilization, as it appears evident from the illustration given by a Turkish historian. He reports that when introducing a motion in the Parliament for the purpose of launching an investigation of crimes committed against Armenians during the war, deputy Fuad, referring to the atrocities, invoked "the rules of humanity" (*kavaidi insaniye*). A senator, Damad Ferit, who became Grand Vizier, i.e., Prime Minister, four months later, on that same day, described the massacres as a type of atrocity which makes "humanity and the civilized world shudder, and shudder forever." Furthermore, in his speech in the Senate on 21 November 1918, the preeminent Turkish statesman, Reşit Akif, the first post-war president of the Council of State, a supreme Ottoman judicial organ, invoked "the world's sense of humanity" (*cihani insaniyeti*) when decrying the crimes perpetrated against the Armenians. And the Final Report of the investigating Special Committee created at the end of 1918 by the Senate evoked "the basic principle of the laws of humanity" (*insanligin esas hukuk kaidelerine*), which, it said, "the targeted perpetrators had violated".[149]

---

[146]Here the suggestions: "(1) that the United States Government on behalf of humanity urgently requests the Turkish Government to cease at once the present campaign and to permit the survivors to return to their homes if not in the war zones, or else to receive proper treatment; (2) that if our present relations permit, an official appeal be made to the Emperor of Germany to insist on Turkey, his ally, stopping this annihilation of a Christian race; (3) that a vigorous official demand be made without delay for the granting of every facility to Americans and others to visit and render pecuniary and other assistance they may desire to Armenians already affected by Government deportation." The U.S. Secretary of state agreed on these suggestions.

[147]Telegram of 18 August 1915. The US Ambassador also reports on his steps in favor of the Armenians working in U.S. Consulates, religious missions and Colleges, in order to allow them to leave the Ottoman territory. He wrote to Bryan in these terms: "Minister of War has promised to permit departure of such Armenians to the United States whose emigration I vouch for as *bona fide*".

[148]In the same telegram mentioned above he adds: "Destruction of Armenian race in Turkey is progressing rapidly".

[149]V. Dadrian (2010), pp. 61 and 64. As mentioned Sect. 3.2.3, even a member of the Triumvirate confessed: "certainly the contemplation of these methods horrified us, but the Djemiet saw no other way of insuring the stability of its work."

The qualification of the Armenian massacres and deportations as violations of principles of humanity is also confirmed, as we will see, by the works of the Commission created by the Paris Peace Conference for an initial enquire on the responsibility of the Authors of WWI (see below, Sect. 4.4).

In conclusion, in my opinion, given that even the crusades were and are discussed with reference to fundamental humanitarian principles, surely by 1915–16, when liberal and socialist ideals had for a long time began to inspire the conscience of people and some illuminate rulers, principles of international law derived from the laws of humanity and requirements of the public conscience were applicable in view of the protection of members of minority groups as well as individuals as such.

The Christian Armenian community benefited thus from a twofold protection: by the conventional rules of San Stefano and Berlin Treaties and by the laws of humanity as principles of general international law, recognized by the whole civilized world, of which the Ottoman Empire was an important member.[150]

4.4 *The Laws of Humanity at the Paris Peace Conference*

Thanks to an Armenian Memorandum received by the States' delegates, and the Memorandum of 14 November 1918 of the Italian Consul-General in Trebizond, Giacomo Gorrini, the massacres and deportations of Armenians came in 1919 on the table of the Paris Conference. The International "Commission on the Responsibility of the Authors of the War and on Enforcement of Penalties" received the mandate to also enquiry on the violations committed during the war. The above-mentioned Armenian Memorandum was among the documentation that constituted the basis for the Commission's enquiry and Report to the Conference.[151] The atrocities committed against Armenians felt therefore within its competence.

Concerning the applicable law, the Commission considered included in its mandate the violations of the "laws of humanity" committed by the defeated States and their agents. As it will be discussed later, the U.S. representatives dissented on the applicability of those laws in the context of criminal proceedings. They however agreed to their application to the responsibility of the defeated States. This twofold

[150]Article 38 of the Statute of the Permanent Court of International Justice, as later of the Statute of the ICJ, also implicitly refers to those principles in indicating the applicable law. Indeed, in addition to international conventions and customary rules it contemplates the general principles of law recognized by civilized nations, among which are also included humanitarian principles. Thus, these latter were also in force in the Ottoman Empire, as the 1919–20 trials showed.

[151]See the Commission Report: Commission on the Responsibility of the Authors of the War and on Enforcement of Penalties, in The American Journal of International Law, 1920, Vol. 14, No. 1/2, p. 113. On the works of this Commission see also the comments made by Marchesi, in this volume.

approach emerges clearly from the following statement made by US representatives in the final part of their Memorandum:

> With [the] reservation as to the invocation of the principles of humanity, the American are in substantial accord with the conclusions reached by the Commission on this head that: 1. The war was carried on by the Central Empires, together with their Allies, Turkey and Bulgaria, by barbarous or illegitimate methods in violation of the established laws and customs of war and the elementary principles of humanity. 2. A Commission should be created for the purpose of collecting and classifying systematically all the information already had or to be obtained, in order to prepare as complete a list of facts as possible concerning the violations of the laws and customs of war committed by the forces of the German Empire and its allies, on land, on sea, and in the air, in the course of the present war.[152]

The selective approach with regard to laws of humanity is after all coherent with the fact that the U.S., when becoming party to both 1899 and 1907 Hague Conventions containing the *Martens Clause*, introduced no reservation to this clause. And, indeed, those Conventions impose obligations only on States and not on individuals, nor do they deal with individual criminal responsibility.

Given that we are now discussing the Sublime Porte's responsibility, the arguments put forward for the US dissent are irrelevant here. I will come back to this in Sect. 4.5.2, when dealing with the law applicable at that time to the individual criminal responsibility for violations of the laws of humanity. What is relevant here is that in its Report, the Commission unanimously applied "the laws of humanity" to the responsibility of the States Authors of war. As noteworthy is the fact that, most likely, the Commission resorted to the "laws of humanity" only with respect to the Armenian massacres and deportations, as the crimes committed by the defeated States against the enemy combatants and civilians resulted in violations of the law and customs of war, in particular the Hague regulations, which were not applicable to the crimes against Armenians.[153]

We do not know the specific views of the said Commission on the "Armenian question". In particular, we do not know whether it considered the tragic events of 1915–16 as massacres and deportations of members of an innocent community or as a military operation exceeding the limits of a repressive violence against a seditious community. I am however inclined to rule out that the Commission, after having read the Armenian Memorandum and heard the speech held on 11 July 1915 at the Paris Conference by one of the Ottoman delegates who confessed the massacres, could have accepted to the second interpretation of the events. My view appears confirmed by the Entente Powers Declaration of 15 May 1915, which referred to crimes committed against "inoffensive [harmless] Armenian population" by "Kurd and Turkish populations.... with the connivance and often assistance of Ottoman authorities". Thus, it is most likely that the Commission, although referring to the "laws of humanity", did so independently from the *Martens clause*, which was applicable to the narrower context of the conduct of hostilities rather

---

[152] Commission on the Responsibility of the Authors of the War and on Enforcement of Penalties, in The American Journal of International Law, 1920, Vol. 14, No. 1/2, p. 134.

[153] On this point see Marchesi, in this volume.

than the context involving mass-killings and deportations of innocent civilians and soldiers of the Ottoman Army.

4.5 *Crimes Against Humanity and the Issue of Competent Jurisdiction*

The individual criminal responsibility notably of the Ottoman high and lower officials who avoided it—and they were actually the large majority—, can no longer be implemented. However, it still retains relevance here for being linked to both the Ottoman Empire's potential responsibility for failing to effectively prosecute the culprits of the massacres and deportations, and the potential responsibility of Turkey for having, inter alia, elevated some of those officials to the rank of national heroes. This aspect deserves therefore a specific analysis.

4.5.1 A Preliminary Comparison with the Individual Criminal Responsibility for War Crimes

As a matter of fact, although the notion of war crime was for long time a legacy of international law before WWII,[154] no international Convention envisaged the criminal responsibility of individuals—state agents or private citizens—for these crimes. International conventional rules only imposed obligations on States. They did not deal with individual criminal responsibility for war crimes not even as object of a State obligation.[155] This approach was coherent with the fact that the punishment of war criminals was still a prerogative of national jurisdictions according to the jurisdictional links provided by their military codes. These jurisdictions prosecuted, during the war, enemy criminals of war and, rather after the war, the members of their national Army responsible for war crimes towards the members of the enemy Army.

Although individual criminal responsibility was then brought into effect only according to internal military codes, international law was still involved in this matter by allowing the punishment of war crimes committed by the enemy. In particular, it allowed—as it still allows—the attribution not only to a state but also to a state-agent of the responsibility for violations of the law of war committed by the latter in his official capacity. Furthermore, international law also needed—as it still needs—to allow for exceptions to the general rules of international immunities

[154]See above fn. 137 about the Henry Wirz trial, to which also the post WWI Commission referred in its Report (p. 142).

[155]Only in 1949, shocked by the horrendous crimes of WWII, which for a long time had remained unpunished, states first undertook the obligation to pursue certain war crimes – the grave breaches of the four Geneva Conventions – according to the principle of universal jurisdiction.

of some top leaders accused of war crimes, in view of their prosecution by a foreign jurisdiction. Unfortunately, these exceptions are disputed even nowadays, save before international criminal jurisdictions.

Like the notion of customs of war, the notion of war crime was not widely accepted in the context of civil war, even if instances of trials held before WWII against military officers responsible of war crimes committed in such a context are not lacking. At any rate, this latter category indisputably entered into international law applicable to non-international conflicts only after WWII. Therefore, even if we were to accept the unlikely hypothesis that the massacres originated from an Armenian uprising, the relevant category of crime applicable to those events would still be that of crimes against humanity as violations of the laws of humanity.[156]

4.5.2 Crimes Against Humanity at the Paris Peace Conference and in the Sèvres Treaty

The novelty of this Conference was in particular the decision to abandon the practice of general amnesty clauses that were habitually contained in previous peace treaties and to deal with the individual criminal responsibility for the dreadful crimes that were committed during the war. As already noted, massacres and deportations of Armenians were therefore put on the table of the Paris Conference in 1919 also from the viewpoint of individual criminal responsibility and were thus dealt with by the above-mentioned Commission.

Certainly, these crimes were not of the same kind of crimes as those committed by the defeated combatants against soldiers and civilians of the enemy winning Powers, i.e. war crimes. The acts of 1915–16 against Armenians were, rather, crimes committed by Ottoman agents and private citizens against their co-citizens, although members of a minority and/or, according to Turkey and some historians, members of an insurgent minority group flanking the enemy.

It is because of their specificity in respect to war crimes that, although unanimously voting the Commission Report as a whole and accepting the applicability of the laws of humanity to the States violations, the US members of the Commission —two out of 15, representing 1 out of 10 States—reserved their position on the applicability of the "laws of humanity" in judicial criminal proceedings. They argued that, while

> the laws and customs of war are a standard certain, to be found in books of authority and in the practice of nations … the laws and principles of humanity vary with the individual, which, if for no other reason, should exclude them from consideration in a court of justice, especially one charged with the administration of criminal justice.[157]

---

[156]Allow me to quote myself: Lattanzi (2014). Currently, the crimes committed during a civil war, if linked with the conduct of hostilities are also labelled as war crimes rather than crimes against humanity. It is indeed by now indisputable that the conducts in the context of this kind of war are also covered by the "laws and customs of war".

[157]Report of the Commission created by the Paris Peace Conference, p. 134.

Yet the US representatives' reservation was weakened not only by the different approach of the largest majority of the members of the Commission—13 out of a total of 15, representing 9 States out of a total of 10. It was also weakened by the fact that, as it becomes evident from their Memorandum, the US representatives were particularly concerned about potential criminal proceedings against Heads of States; for them they were claiming only moral and political responsibility. Thus, they could not agree to consider them responsible on the basis of the laws of humanity.[158]

However, not only did the Commission, in its Report, consider the laws of humanity applicable to the facts falling within its enquiry, but it also categorically concluded on individual criminal responsibility by stating:

> All persons belonging to enemy countries, however high their position may have been, without distinction of rank, including Chiefs of States, who have been guilty of offences against the laws and customs of war or the laws of humanity, are liable to criminal prosecution.[159]

The Report of the Commission confirms, as I have tried to demonstrate, that the "laws of humanity" were a legacy of international law before WWI—and the traditional State responsibility for their violations was universally accepted, including by the US. It also shows the general awareness, emerging amongst many difficulties and political obstacles, as witnessed by the reductive US positions, of the need to couple such a collective responsibility with individual criminal responsibility—irrespective of the official qualification of the individual accused.[160] All this occurred in connection with the massacres and deportations of Armenians in 1915–16, as witnessed by the position of the European Powers, which emerges from the 25 May 1915 Declaration.[161]

Indeed, the Nuremberg and Tokyo Tribunals applied crimes against humanity considering them a legacy of international law before the adoption of the two

[158] Report of the Commission created by the Paris Peace Conference, p. 135–136.

[159] Report of the Commission created by the Paris Peace Conference, p. 117.

[160] It is worth noting that the States who led to the Commission's conclusion concerning individual criminal responsibility were important Powers such as UK, France, Japan and Italy (this latter certainly less important than the first two in absolute terms, but not from the point of view of it being the cradle of law).

[161] As reported by Dadrian (2010), p. 61, "In the immediate aftermath of the war, the highest authorities identified with the post-war Turkish Government, raised their voices to severely condemn the wartime treatment of the Armenians. In doing so, they remarkably used the term "crimes against humanity." The Sultan, the highest authority, for example, used exactly these words when denouncing the crimes (Kanuni insaniyete karşi ika edilen ceraim).

respective Statutes that provided this category of crimes.[162] And the existence, since 1899, of the *Martens clause* demonstrates that the foundation of this kind of responsibility already existed in 1915–16 at least with respect to crimes against humanity committed in a general war context of war, as it was the case in the IMTs' Statutes.

4.5.3 The Issue of Jurisdiction on Crimes Against Humanity

The above-mentioned Commission of the Paris Peace Conference also proposed a common system of repression by the winning Powers of any violation of the laws and customs of war and laws of humanity committed during the war.

We know that the Declaration of 1915 had already envisaged the intention of the Entente Powers to "hold personally responsible [for] these crimes all members of the Ottoman government and those of their agents who are implicated in such massacres." But this intention never became effective. It could thus be assumed that, at that time, the individual criminal responsibility for violations of the laws of humanity might have been only pleaded before the jurisdiction of the concerned State. Arguably, this view could be also based on the fact that some authors of the Armenian massacres were prosecuted by Ottoman Martial Courts and not by the jurisdictions of the Entente Powers as envisaged in the 1915 Declaration. Furthermore, when some of the architects of the massacres were arrested and transferred to Malta under the British jurisdiction, together with some authors of war crimes committed against the Entente's prisoners of war, this jurisdiction was not eventually exercised towards anybody. This signifies that suspects of war crimes against British prisoners of war were not prosecuted either in Malta, although the notion of war crime, as its prosecution by the enemy jurisdiction, was without question accepted for a long time.

Actually, even if some perplexities about the applicable law and competent jurisdiction for the accused of Armenian massacres and deportations could have arisen, Britain's decision to send back to the Ottoman territories all the suspects of crimes arrested and transferred to Malta was indeed due to other reasons. First, the Ottoman State did not render available—as promised—the relevant evidentiary documentation concerning the crimes. Further, and even more importantly,

---

162See above fn. 37. C. Tomuschat, a very authoritative German international law scholar, discussing on the principle *nullum crimen sine lege* in connection with the Nuremberg IMT trials, writes: "crimes against humanity have deep roots in the minds of all human beings. The Martens clause that refers to 'the laws of humanity and the dictates of the public conscience' may be referred to in this connection. There cannot be the slightest doubt that all the offences set out under the title 'crimes against humanity' are not only morally objectionable, but deserve to be punished and must be punished because of their abhorrent character if peaceful coexistence in human society is to be maintained. Nobody can legitimately claim that he believed that such actions in which he participated and that are to be classified as 'crimes against humanity' were perfectly lawful. The scope *ratione materiae* of the *nullum crimen* rule must accordingly be reduced." Tomuschat (2006), p. 835.

a political reason led to release the suspects, i.e. the exchange between the more than 100 of them and 22 British prisoners of war, including some important personalities, taken hostage by the new Turkish leaders.[163] In my view, a political decision of this kind cannot be considered evidence of the inexistence, at that time, of the category of crimes against humanity or of the incompetence of a foreign jurisdiction for their prosecution. Rather, the Malta episode shows how the international community was concerned about the need to not leave in the hands of the State directly involved the punishment of individuals responsible both of war crimes and crimes against humanity—at least if they were committed in a general war context. This need strongly emerged at the Paris Peace Conference, first of all in the works of the above-mentioned Commission. In its conclusions on this issue, the Commission considered two different solutions: the jurisdiction of a national court on the persons who committed

> outrages against civilians or soldiers of *several* Allied nations or whose orders affected the conduct of operations against *several* of the Allied armies,

and the jurisdiction of a high tribunal on other persons

> against whom it may be considered advisable not to proceed before a national court.

According to another contributor to this volume, this

> residual category... includes... the authors of the Armenian massacres.[164]

I agree with this assumption, especially as the Sèvres Peace Treaty just envisaged for those massacres this latter solution.[165] At the end of the Paris Conference, in addition to the Versailles Peace Treaty with Germany, additional Peace Treaties were indeed stipulated with the other defeated States. So, the Sèvres Peace Treaty was signed by Turkey, the Allied Powers—UK, France, Italy, Japan—and the other so-called Allied Associated Powers, among which the newly independent State of Armenia, destined for a very short life (1918–1922). In its Article 230, this Treaty first provided for the Turkish commitment to hand over to the Allied Powers the persons whose surrender might be required by the latter as being responsible for massacres and deportations committed "during the continuance of the state of war on territory which formed part of the Turkish Empire on August 1, 1914". Furthermore, "the right to designate the tribunal" to try "the persons so accused" was also reserved to the Powers. Turkey would have had to recognize such a special tribunal representing the winning Powers or a League of Nations tribunal to be established in order to deal with the said massacres.

These commitments certainly represented new forms of reparation specific to the gravity of the violations committed, which Turkey was ready to undertake

---

[163]About this exchange the British Foreign Office declared: "It is in a measure yielding to blackmail, but seems justified by present conditions." (quoted by Bass (2000), p. 142).

[164]Marchesi, in this Volume.

[165]On this Treaty and its relevance see below, Sect. 4.6.1.

voluntarily. Therefore, in my view, the reference to "crime against humanity and civilization" and the intention to bring the individuals responsible before the Entente Countries jurisdictions contained in the Declaration of 1915 was not purely rhetoric or symbolic. On the contrary, it represented a first expression of an *opinio iuris in fieri* on this category of individual crimes. It also showed the conviction that the individual criminal responsibility of states agents for those crimes could be pleaded not only before the jurisdictions of the State involved, but also before foreign or international jurisdictions.[166]

The fact that the Sublime Porte organized internal martial court proceedings in 1918–19, in order to avoid that its rulers should appear before the jurisdictions of the Entente Powers as envisaged by the 1915 Declaration, can be read in the logic of a sort of principle of complementarity—as nowadays operating with respect to the ICC proceedings.[167] This would be a clue, if not yet a conclusive proof, that

[166]Something analogous to this form of individual criminal responsibility has for a long time been a part of international law in the matter of piracy, in order to protect, in this case too, a universal value (freedom of navigation). Most certainly, a perpetrator of a crime against humanity is, like as a pirate, *hostis humani generis*.

[167]This complementarity in favour of Ottoman jurisdictions could not work as that justice proved to be ineffective. This is the reason why the Sèvres Treaty envisaged a different solution. However, according to some deniers of the deliberate massacres and deportations, these proceedings would have been carried out under the "pressure" of the Entente Powers and this would prove that they were not genuine; furthermore, according to the nationalistic feeling of the Turkish people against these proceedings these would have been nothing but pure vengeance; in any case, they would have been conducted in violation of fair trial principles and in absentia; therefore the motivations contained in the records of these trials, as regarding the intent element in particular, would not be reliable: see in this vein the arguments developed by Lewy (2005b), p. 3 ff. First of all it is noteworthy that those who affirm the annihilation of the Armenian community do not base themselves only on the Courts Martials' findings, as Lewy seems to assume. Furthermore, the arguments concerning the Courts Martials proceedings show how the historic truth can be distorted. The first argument is entirely false, given that any Ottoman tribunal should have needed to ascertain what happened: whether deliberate massacres organized by Ottoman agents or only criminal acts of private citizens – bandits, as alleged by Turkey - out of the police control. The second argument is equally false, in the first place because the people "feelings" also were instigated by the new rulers and, further, amongst such people there were at least a few hundred suspects of the massacres, who had "founded" reasons to be concerned about criminal proceedings, including because they feared being dispossessed of Armenian properties robbed or obtained *gratis et amore Dei*. Third, the fair trial argument, including the reference to the fact that some trials were conducted in absentia, is also ridiculous. The proceedings were certainly not conducted pursuant to the fair trials rules as presently in force and referred to in the Lewy "Revisiting" paper (he refers among other things to common law procedural rules, while in the Ottoman Empire civil law was in force!). But, according to an authoritative Author as Cassese (2009), "if appraised in light of the available translations and by the procedural standards of that period, those trials may be held to have been conducted in a sufficiently fair manner" (p. 250); furthermore, some trials were held in absentia because the accused had fled with the assistance of the Turkish rulers. Apart from this fact, it is noteworthy that such trials are still allowed – with certain guarantees of course that at that time did not yet exist - in some democratic civil law systems, as the Italian one, for instance. Why does Lewy not mention that some accused escaped justice with the complicity of the Turkish rulers instead of trying to discredit the truth ascertained by the Martial Courts through the vengeance argument? Finally, when underlining that "the British high commissioner in Turkey

these Powers were entitled, already at that time, either to prosecute the Ottoman agents for the violations of the laws of humanity in their own courts or to create a common jurisdiction for that purpose, as envisaged in the Sèvres Treaty. This means that already a long time before the Nuremberg and Tokyo Statutes, the belief had arisen among States that individual criminal responsibility, not only for war crimes but also for crimes against humanity in a context of war, was to be recognized in addition to the international responsibility of the State concerned.[168] The awareness that individual criminal responsibility for crimes against humanity could be also brought before both foreign and international jurisdictions had been growing equally long before the adoption of those Statutes.

More than one century after those tragic events, when all the planners, organizers, civil and military commanders, instigators, executors have left this world, the individual criminal responsibility for the Armenian massacres and deportations is no longer under discussion. This however means that, whatever approach we take on the qualification of the situation in which the massacres and deportations of

---

reported popular perception that "regard[ed] executions as necessary concessions to entente rather than as punishment justly meted out to criminals", what does Lewy mean? That the British Commissioner shared the people perception *(vox populi vox dei?)*? Was not the Commissioner rather noting that people did not recognize what these proceedings were in fact, i.e. the "punishment justly meted out to criminals"? Otherwise why resort to the word "criminals"? Furthermore, if no witness was heard during the trials, as he alleges, why does he refer to lost *depositions*? And why does he not raise questions about "this loss"? And why should the deposition of General Vehib Pasha not be a proof of guilt if it was also present in the *verdict* of the Harput trial and not only in the indictment? How can he say that "The regime also used the Special Organization to suppress "subversion" and "possible collaboration" with the external enemy and then say that this Organization "played no role in the Armenian deportations", when Turkey does not deny that deportations were used as a measure of suppression of the "subversion"? On the last pillar of his "Revisiting the Armenian Genocide" – the criticism towards The Memoirs of NaimBey –, on whose reliability I am totally unprepared, I can only note that the criminal orders given by Talât Pasha are not only referred to in these Memoirs. Rather, The Memoirs are corroborated on these orders by other sources, such as Morgenthau's account and not only. As for the willingness of Talât Pasha – also evoked by Lewy - to consider interventions in favor of some Armenians by U.S. diplomats and missionaries this is confirmed also in Morgenthau's accounts, where we even find an explanation for Talât's attitude (the falsity of this attitude is revealing in the message quoted above, fn. 146). In any case, this is not an argument which can dismiss the numerous proofs of Talât's involvement in the massacres and deportations. In conclusion, the Lewy's "Revisiting" fails, in my view.

[168]Indeed, the Nuremberg and Tokyo Statutes only envisaged crimes against humanity connected with war crimes, i.e. with warfare. We had to wait until the ICTR Statute for a provision affirming the *vindicatio in libertatem* of crimes against humanity from warfare, even though relied to an extended discrimination context. While the conflict context still remained in the ICTY Statute. And in order to obtain an absolute and definitive *vindicatio in libertatem* we had to wait for the ICC Statute, which provides crimes against humanity also in a peace context. This was not the case in 1915–16. Thus the factual and legal link of the Armenian massacres and deportations with WWI is very relevant in view of the applicability of such category of crimes. This is a further reason for not confusing here the Armenian massacres of the end of the XIX and the beginning of the XX centuries, as well as the crimes committed after the war, with the massacres and deportations of 1915–16, at the peak of the war.

Armenians were carried out—destruction of an innocent community or excessive repression of a civil war caused by the alleged Hayk rebellion—, what continues to retain legal relevance and importance is the issue of State responsibility.

4.6 The Reparation Obligations

4.6.1 The Measures of Reparation in the Treaty of Sèvres

Not only did the Sèvres Treaty refer, in its Part IV—"Protection of Minorities"—to "the terrorist regime which has existed in Turkey since November 1, 1914," as well as to "the massacres perpetrated in Turkey during the war" and to the "deportations" of the same period, but it also contained numerous provisions imposing on the Porte several kinds of reparations for those wrongdoings.[169]

First, Turkey had

> to afford all the assistance in its power or in that of the Turkish authorities in the search for and deliverance of all persons, of whatever race or religion, who have disappeared, been carried off, interned or placed in captivity since November 1, 1914.

The Treaty further contemplated for Turkey other traditional reparation commitments, namely: the recognition of "the injustice of the law of 1915 relating to Abandoned Properties *(Emval-i-Metroukeh)*", the declaration of its retroactive nullity and the commitment

> to facilitate to the greatest possible extent the return to their homes and re-establishment in their businesses of the Turkish subjects of non-Turkish race who have been forcibly driven from their homes by fear of massacre or any other form of pressure since January 1, 1914,

and the recognition

> that any immovable or movable property of the said Turkish subjects or of the communities to which they belong, which can be recovered, must be restored to them as soon as possible, in whatever hands it may be found.

The arbitral commission envisaged by the Treaty for the implementation of all these commitments would have had a very large competence, inter alia, in the following matters:

> "the removal of any person who, after enquiry, shall be recognised as having taken an active part in massacres or deportations or as having provoked them", "the measures to be taken with regard to such person's possessions...", "the cancellation of all acts of sale or any acts creating rights over immovable property concluded after January 1, I914", "the disposal of property belonging to members of a community who have died or disappeared since January 1, 1914, without leaving heirs".

[169]Even if it did not contain a clear reference to the substantial applicable law, the title of Part IV seems to indicate that according to the negotiators, the Ottoman wrongdoing amounted to a violation of the specific minority protective regime created by the San Stefano and Berlin Treaties.

A very modern form of reparation was also envisaged for this latter situation:

such property may be handed over to the community instead of to the State.

In short, all possible forms of reparation were provided for, including *restitutio in integrum ante* the massacres, which in 1920 was still partially possible, although the destruction of the community, even in part, could never be redressed. By providing for all those commitments, the Treaty did nothing else than specify and describe in detail, as it is usual by conventional rules, reparations for wrongful acts as already regulated by general international law. It also provided a modern form of reparation, which is the provision on the jurisdiction of an international criminal tribunal (see above, Sect. 4.5.2).

Unfortunately, due to the lack of ratification by the new Parliament in place in Ankara, this Agreement never entered into force.[170] This was the outcome, first of all, of the ambitious efforts of Greece, supported by UK, to extend its territories at the expenses of what remained of the dismembered Ottoman Empire. The Greek-Turkish war broke out in 1920. At first, Greece succeeded in occupying a large part of the western third of Anatolia and in approaching to the Turkish capital of Ankara. But, in 1922, Turkey regained its territories. This reinforced its nationalistic ideals and led the military commander of that victory, Mustafa Kemal, to become the hero of the Country and its new supreme ruler. Furthermore, the new political and economic interests of the European Powers in their relations with the new successor Turkish State led, in 1923, to replace the Sèvres Treaty with the Lausanne Treaty. The latter Treaty completely ignored the Armenians and only contained some provisions on the (future) protection of religious minorities in Turkey, as if nothing had happened in 1915–16. Rather, it contained a Declaration of Amnesty, in total contradiction with the decisions taken at the Paris Peace Conference and more or less implemented against Germany according to the Versailles Treaty.

Had either the Sèvres Treaty been ratified and then implemented in its Part IV, or had at least this Part been integrated in the Lausanne Treaty as such, this would have permitted to definitively establish the truth, to keep the memory alive, to partially repair the damages and restore the life of survivors in their villages and ancestral homeland. It might also have allowed for the prevention of the further attacks that the few remaining Armenians continued to suffer in Turkey until 1923.

However, even though the Sèvres Treaty has never entered into force, it still retains some relevance in discussing the Armenian massacres and deportations.

[170]The Ottoman Parliament was dissolved on the 5 April 1920 under the pressure of the occupying Entente Powers and the majority of its members were arrested and transferred to Malta for being accused of war crimes and Armenian massacres. The new Grand National Assembly started its first session on the 13 April 1920 in Ankara under the Turkish National Movement rule (the party of Mustafa Kemal). The Treaty of Sèvres was signed the 10 August 1920 by the delegation representing the Sultan, who was heading the "Constantinople government". In fact, a revolution was under way.

Indeed, in my view, if all these wrongdoings had not been committed or only some "excessive" military operations had been undertaken in repressing a rebellion, the European States parties and Turkey would have never evoked in that Treaty the "massacre" and "deportations", nor resorted to the expression "a terrorist regime" in qualifying the responsible government. Nor would Turkey have undertaken the obligations to restore and repair the serious wrongful acts of 1915–16 which were confirmed in this Treaty, or the obligation to accept a special jurisdiction in relation to these acts. Is it imaginable that all the signatory States, including the one directly involved in the massacres, simply fabricated, during the 15 months of negotiations, all these tragic events evoked in this Treaty? After all, the atrocities committed against Armenians had already been the object of a confession, on the 11th of July of 1919, by the Ottoman delegate at the Paris Conference, the Grand Vizier Damat Ferid Pasha.[171]

Actually, the new Turkey's rulers, with the complicity of European major and minor Powers, prevented the entry into force of the Sèvres Treaty for political and economic egoistic interests. They did so not because the Treaty's assessment of what happened in 1915–16 was wrong or unfair. Admittedly, the further dismembering of the Ottoman Empire envisaged by that Treaty and driven by the ambitions of the European Powers was unfair.[172] Conversely, the general acknowledgement of the massacres and deportations of Armenians even by Turkey itself was certainly neither wrong nor unfair, as it was not unfair to envisage the reparations for these serious violations of International Law.

In sum, in my view, the changed political situation which led to new negotiations with Turkey in 1923 does not nullify the Ottoman acknowledgement, in a public document signed by the all negotiators and which was assumed to become the binding international Treaty of Sèvres, of an historical truth: the massacres and deportations carried out by a "terrorist" regime. This historical truth as partially attested in that text, alongside the reparation obligations under general international law, which were there only confirmed and detailed, cannot be ignored or, even less,

[171]See Heinsohn (1998), p. 80. This book is a compilation of genocide lexicon following an alphabetical order, starting from A (Abdul Hamid II) until Z (Zwangssterilisation: forced sterilization).

[172]Those amputations were also based, in my view, on the wrong belief in the superiority of the Christian culture over the Muslim one. I am convinced that a lot of human tragedies have occurred also because Europeans and Americans believe that their culture – the Christian culture – is superior to others, as, after all, the Muslim-Turks also believed about their culture and religion at the time in which the massacres took place. It is significant that, when discussing about the exchange between more than 100 Turks with 22 Europeans, a member of the British Parliament expressed himself in the following terms: "I had to explain [to Parliament] why we released the Turkish deportees from Malta, skating over thin ice as quickly as I could … The staunch belief among Members [of Parliament] is that one British prisoner is worth a shipload of Turks, and so the exchange was excused" (quoted by Bonello (19 April 2012)).

denied.[173] Moreover, these provisions remain a model for what Turkey would still need to do, although many reparations applicable in 1920 are materially inapplicable nowadays.

This is why I have discussed some of the Sèvres provisions.

4.6.2 The Reparation Obligations of the Ottoman Empire and the Republic of Turkey: Some Brief Remarks

As mentioned, immediately after WWI, the Ottoman Empire has not only recognized, at the internal and international level, the Armenian massacres and deportations as serious violations of both the conventional rules on the protection of minorities and the laws of humanity. It was also ready to repair those misdeeds. The situation changed drastically with the take-over by the new rulers, who decided to continue along the way of the Turkish nationalism, although by a more modern and liberal approach. In any case, they needed to deny the truth on the Armenian partial destruction, thus reparation obligations could not even arise. This means that those obligations both for the Ottoman Empire and Turkey as its successor—but also of Turkey as such—are still open for discussion in the debate about the atrocities committed against Armenians.[174] I will therefore move on towards brief observations on certain general aspects. The topic of reparations is indeed analyzed in detail in the essays of Latino and Donat Cattin, in this volume.

Let me first consider the identification of the states towards which this responsibility has arisen.

As already determined, the Empire has violated the provisions of the San Stefano and Berlin Treaties towards the Great Powers that were parties to them. These parties could claim the consequences of violations not only of those specific conventional rules, but also of principles of international law deriving from the laws of humanity. Could the violations of these laws and requirements as part of general international law also be pleaded by all the states of the then international society? This is strongly disputable in my view. The *opinio iuris* on *erga omnes* obligations has only arisen after WWII. Thus, the responsibility for violations by the Sublime Porte of principles of general international law as derived by the laws of humanity, outside the sphere of the mentioned Treaties, might only be pleaded by the Christian Powers that had a specific interest in the compliance with these principles towards Christian communities.[175]

---

[173]For the same approach to the Treaty of Sèvres see Verhoeven (1984), p. 277.

[174]The UNGA Res. 60/147 on the Basic Principles and Guidelines on the Right to Remedy and Reparation for Victims of Gross Violations of Human Rights Law and Serious Violations of International Humanitarian Law codifies international customary rules – at least insofar as the basic principles are concerned – on obligations/rights in the matter of reparation. See on this Resolution Latino, in this volume.

[175]These Countries were not only European. This is clearly confirmed by the intervention of US in favor of Armenians.

According to general international law, the state international responsibility for commission subsists alongside the responsibility by omission to prevent and/or repress conducts contrary to international law. The obligation to repress is thus a substantial one before being a reparation obligation, in particular the form of the so called satisfaction.[176] The obligations to prevent and punish the massacres and deportations of 1915–16 also stemmed from the specific obligation of the San Stefano and Berlin Treaties to protect Armenians from Kurds and Circassians. The Sublime Porte has therefore violated both kinds of obligations, even if the Turkish claim of Armenians as victims of criminal bands would be acceptable, view that, as proudly affirmed by Enver Pasha, the CUP had the overall control of the situation.[177] Yet the Turkish claim is indeed in contradiction with the Enver affirmation.

A further relevant argument of the Turkish authorities in the attempt to close the "Armenian question" is that the criminal trials held after WWI in Turkey against certain individuals (in particular against certain members of the Ottoman Turkish leadership) represent a definitive solution of the question of the overall responsibility of the Sublime Porte and thus also of Turkey as its successor State. The relation between internal criminal proceedings and state responsibility entails indeed a different evaluation depending on the position of the individuals whose conducts have led to a State responsibility. In the case of private citizens, their effective punishment might even exclude the occurrence of a state responsibility if the obligation to prevent their conduct was not violated. Conversely, the wrongful conduct of state agents is directly attributable to the state, which will thus also be responsible for its commission.[178] Therefore, the punishment of states agents does not exhaust the state responsibility even where the obligation to prevent the crimes was not violated. Their repression would only be one of the modes of responsibility applicable, in particular a form of "satisfaction", besides being a substantial obligation *per se*, as noted before. In any case, the punishment of individual-state

[176]Indeed, the obligations to prevent and repress any act in violation of international law on the territory under the States' control is an expression of their sovereignty, which involves powers, but also obligations. And without doubt, these obligations existed at that time at least with respect to minority rights if not with respect to the rights of individuals as such. But, in my view, insofar as the violations of the laws of humanity are concerned, the obligations of their prevention and repression protected anybody.

[177]See supra, fn. 89.

[178]ICTY, Appeal Judgment, *Tadic*, 15 July 1999, para 131: "In order to attribute the acts of a military or paramilitary group to a State, it must be proved that the State wields overall control over the group, not only by equipping and financing the group, but also by coordinating or helping in the general planning of its military activity. Only then can the State be held internationally accountable for any misconduct of the group. However, it is not necessary that, in addition, the State should also issue, either to the head or to members of the group, instructions for the commission of specific acts contrary to international law." From this point of view, it is relevant what Morgenthau was told by Enver Pasha about the control of CUP on the atrocities against Armenians. The commission of wrongful acts in violation of international law resulting from acts of its civil and military servants – who were at the top of a state-level organization or acted at the provincial and district levels -, who planned, ordered, instigated, led, aided and abetted, and executed the massacres was thus attributable to the Ottoman State.

agents needs to have been effectively and impartially implemented, which was not the case with regard to the activity of the Ottoman Martial Courts of 1919–1920 and its follow-up.

Other important forms of "satisfaction" are the recognition of violations of international law, as the Sublime Porte did during the Paris Peace Conference and through the Sèvres Treaty, and the demand of an apology, as the Ottoman delegate did at the Paris Peace Conference.

Other forms of reparation for moral and material damage incurred during violations by commission and/or omission would also be applicable, such as the *restitutio in integrum* as far as possible, a monetary indemnity etc.[179] Both of those forms of reparation were envisaged, as we have seen, in the Sèvres Treaty. None of those reparation obligations, which existed independently of any conventional rule, were complied with either by the Ottoman Empire or by its successor State, except, to a very limited extent, by way of the restoration of some Armenian religious sites in Eastern Turkey.[180] Yet, the reconstruction of Armenian Churches and cultural institutions is still possible. It would be a partial *restitutio in integrum* ante 1915–16.

Finally, another relevant question concerns the responsibility of Turkey for the continuing non-compliance with several obligations as consequences of its own violations of the right of Armenians to truth, memory and apologies.[181] The condolences expressed by Erdogan in April 2014 to the descendants of the Armenian victims cannot be considered a form of apology in so far as they could be expressed for any death, independently on any direct involvement in it. Apologies, instead, show the awareness of one's own involvement in the events. Thus, even less can those condolences be considered a recognition of the atrocities committed by the Ottoman Empire or the subsequent violations committed at the detriment of Armenians by Turkey itself.

Moreover, having adopted, inter alia, the Law of 27 June 1926 and the follow-up Regulation of 1928 concerning the Armenian properties seized during the tragic events of 1915–16, the Republic of Turkey did not only violate its obligations to repair the wrongdoings of that period, but became directly involved in an act strictly inherent to those events, as it appears evident from the analysis of the facts carried out in this essay. Indeed, pursuant to that Law, Turkish governmental officials, politicians, and bureaucrats who were executed as a result of their roles in the Armenian deportations or who were unfortunately murdered by an Armenia terrorist group were declared "national heroes" and their families received in reward the so-called "Abandoned Properties of Armenians". The 1928 Regulation granted Muslim refugees who were using Armenian properties the right to have the title

[179]On the broad range of reparations in the "Armenian question" see Guibert and Kim (2016).

[180]So, for instance, the Holy Cross Armenian Church of Akhtamar Island (Lake of Van), erected between 915 and 921, looted during the Armenian massacres, as the monastic buildings then destroyed, have been restored in 2006.

[181]See on this, David Donat Cattin, in this volume.

deeds of those properties, which included houses, lands, field crops, and shops.[182] Hence, through that Law and Regulation, Turkey carries responsibility both for the partial destruction of the Armenian community as well as for the violation of its obligation to return those properties—the *restitutio in integrum* obligation—to Armenian survivors who had suffered those events and were still alive, or to theirs heirs.[183]

A more detailed discussion of Turkey's responsibilities certainly deserves great attention, but it goes beyond my task.[184]

5 Final Remarks

It is not my intention, in these final remarks, to provide an overview of all the elements characterizing the *Metz Yeghern*[185] from an essentially legal perspective, as they emerge from the above analysis. I shall confine myself to few remarks from a rather political perspective. In doing so, my point of departure is the following statement by the British government about the destruction of the Armenian community:

> In the absence of unequivocal evidence to show that the Ottoman Administration took a specific decision to eliminate the Armenians under their control at the time, British governments have not recognised the events of 1915 and 1916 as genocide.[186]

Apart from the question of the evocation of a strange standard of evidence—unequivocal! (in any case, it is indeed unequivocal!)—, *specific* clear decisions were taken by the Turkish rulers to eliminate the Ottoman Armenian community. At any rate, even if documentation on such decisions were not available—what is not the case—, following the criteria set up by international criminal tribunals and ICJ concerning the intent of destroying a substantial part of a community protected by the Genocide Convention, this specific subjective element can be inferred from other elements, as shown in Sect. 3.2. All these elements are in fact present in the *Metz Yeghern* case: the nature of the wrongful acts committed; their massive, systematic and simultaneous occurrence in the concerned territory; the specificity of "deportations", intentionally aimed to avoiding the return of Armenians in their century-old homeland; the appropriation of the Armenians' properties and the

[182]On this, see the interview with Ümit Kurt by Ketsemanian (23 September 2013). See also Akçam and Kurt (2015) p. 172.

[183]Avedian (2012).

[184]As mentioned, for some details on the remedies to the partial destruction of Ottoman Armenians I refer to the contributions in this volume of Latino and Donat Cattin.

[185]In my final remarks I prefer to refer to the partial destruction of the Armenian community in 1915–16 by using the same expression used by the Armenians themselves, as a timid form of recognition of their reasons: Metz Yeghern (The Great Evil).

[186]Quoted in Robertson (2009).

destruction of Armenian cultural and religious buildings etc., from which it clearly results that a return was excluded.

What more could the British Government, like others Governments and several national Parliaments, need in order to recognize the Ottoman decision to destroy the Armenian community? Would it require a written document of the Ottoman government urging all Muslims to go and kill any Armenian living in the Ottoman territory?[187]

As in 1915–16, current political and diplomatic expedience prevails not only over justice, but, unfortunately, over law as well. It is however shameful that, instead of saying *mea culpa* for the past complicity in the Armenian massacres, the former Entente Powers continue with an approach which is absolutely incompatible with the rule of law. At least today, this rule should prevail, as these same Countries repeatedly and rhetorically plead.

I do not mean that States should recognize the Armenian *genocide*, i.e. that they should resort to this term for labelling the massacres of 1915–16. However, they should state the correct reason in refusing to use it, namely that the term *genocide* did not exist at that time (as it did not exist at the time of the holocaust). And they should not stop here. Above all, they should not label the destruction of a community as a "terrible episode". It was not an *epeisodos*, which means, in ancient Greek, a secondary unexpected arrival in a drama representation. It was the drama, the tragedy, of hundreds thousands—perhaps 1.200.000/1.500.000—members of the community. It was the destruction of a very substantial part of it. Therefore, it would be correct and fair, in particular for European countries and the US, even if not using the term genocide, to recognize and attest that the massacres and deportations of Armenians resulted in the partial destruction of their community under the Ottoman control, which the European Powers and the US have witnessed from the beginning until the final solution. Especially the former European Powers, including Germany, the Military Allied of the Sublime Porte, would need to say *mea culpa* for failing to stop massacres and deportations when they were

[187]The present UK rulers should remember that David Lloyd George, the British Prime Minister during the Paris Peace Conference, referring to the Armenian massacres, wrote in 1939: "By these atrocities, almost unparalleled in the black record of Turkish rule, the Armenian population was reduced in numbers by well over one million … If we succeeded in defeating this inhuman empire, one essential condition of the peace we should impose was the redemption of the Armenian valleys forever from the bloody misrule with which they had been stained by the infamies of the Turk." (Loyd George, Memoirs of the Peace Conference, Vol 2, New Haven: Yale University Press, 1939, p. 811)." In 1929, Winston Churchill, the then former War Minister, wrote: "In 1915 the Turkish government began and ruthlessly carried out the infamous general massacre and deportation of Armenians in Asia Minor … whole districts were blotted out in one administrative holocaust" (Winston Churchill, The World Crisis: The Aftermath, London 1929, p. 405).

underway.[188] Indeed, they had the military power and the obligation to stop them, instead of just being concerned about territorial conquests to the detriment of the Ottoman Empire, as the UK did by engaging in the ruinous Dardanelles campaign.[189] Especially UK would need to say *mea culpa* for having allowed the Sèvres acknowledgements of the massacres and deportations to be erased from the history of international relations, making the destruction of the Armenian community slip into oblivion for decades; an oblivion that even gave a *génocidaire* like Hitler the opportunity to say, in his famous speech on the eve of his invasion of Poland,

> Who, after all, speaks today of the annihilation of the Armenians?[190]

and thus take that annihilation as model for the same annihilation of European Jews. Therefore, the former European Powers, in particular the former victorious WWI Powers, should also recognize that if they had done what was needed concerning the *Metz Yeghern*, the Shoah might perhaps have been prevented.

I am not in full agreement with the insistence of Armenians community that Turkey and the whole international community should term the *Metz Yeghern* as genocide. This approach allows both of them to resort to an argument—the non-retroactivity of the Genocide Convention—that ends up being a pretext for not recognizing the massacres and deportations and their destructive characteristics.[191] If Turkey was to agree to renounce the denial of the partial destruction of the Armenian community or its justification, why could not the Armenian community and the Republic of Armenia renounce their claim to the qualification of these atrocities as genocide? Having put that question in a conciliatory spirit (certainly

[188]As reported by Morgenthau (1918), p. 128, Dr. Lepsius, a German missionary in the Ottoman Empire expressed to him "the humiliation which he felt, as a German, that the Turks should set about to exterminate their Christian subjects, while Germany, which called itself a Christian country, was making no endeavours to prevent it." Morgenthau explains this German attitude, considering the meeting he had with the German Ambassador at Constantinople, in the following way: "Wangenheim pretended to regard the Armenian question as a matter that chiefly affected the United States. My constant intercession in their behalf apparently created the impression, in his Germanic mind, that any mercy shown this people would be a concession to the American Government. And at that moment he was not disposed to do anything that would please the American people." (Morgenthau 1918, p. 142). Germany indeed had intervened at the beginning, albeit weakly, on a diplomatic level, under pressure by the US (but especially with the aim of objecting "to statements made by Turks throughout the interior that the anti-Armenian measures originated with the Germans": see the correspondence on this *démarche* between Amb. Morgenthau and the US Secretary of State of 12 August 1915, *Papers* quoted supra fn. 77). Later, although being present with its Army on the Ottoman territory as a Power allied with the Empire, Germany witnessed massacres and deportations without lifting a finger to save the Armenians.

[189]This campaign was conducted from the 25 April 1915, when the news about the first massacres had already reached Europe and the U.S., until 9 January when the British Navy was definitively defeated at Gallipoli: see on the impact of this campaign Flores, in this Volume.

[190]Hitler speech on 22 August 1939.

[191]On the impact of external pressures on the dialogue between Turks and Armenians as well as on the Turkish democratisation process see the view of Açar and Rüma (2007).

easier for me than for an Armenian), I must however recognize that, if there was a deliberate partial destruction of the Armenian community, as it was, I do not see why a new term by which we now indicate a crime presenting the same determinants of a past crime should not be used for more appropriately describing a crime of the past, as the same Genocide Convention does in its Preamble.[192] As Amb. Morgenthau already indicated in 1916, the Armenian massacres and deportations were surely a "murder of a nation", i.e. a genocide—using a modern term which was not yet in use at that time.

This said, I am convinced that the key question continues to be the following: was the Armenian community under Ottoman control destroyed in whole or in part or not? In the opinion of many historians, political scientists, jurists, diplomats, including Turks, and in my own opinion too, all the determinants of the 1915–16 events prove that the substantial part of the Armenian community was destroyed. Denying this is incorrect—not to say offensive to the Armenian community first, but also to humanity as a whole. If, even without resorting to the term genocide, Turkey were to acknowledge this historic truth and cease to claim the Armenian uprising as justification for its actions, and if it did something towards making repairs, would I be Armenian, I would be satisfied.

The following question would however be: did the destruction of the Armenian nation occur in a legal vacuum? If we impartially evaluate the content of International Law at that time, could anyone answer in the negative?

Yet another question would be: do the consequences of this wrongdoing by The Sublime Porte and the further wrongdoing by its successor Turkish State still affect the Republic of Turkey? Notwithstanding the short and superficial discussion of an aspect that deserves further legal analysis, I hope that I have been able to show that this question also needs to be answered in the affirmative.

Further questions would be as follows. What necessary steps should Turkey adopt in order to remedy the wrongdoing of the Ottoman Empire and its own? The response is that Turkey should, above all, cease hiding the truth and hiding its archival documents,[193] as this leads towards shielding, at least to some extent, the

[192]See above, footnote 26.

[193]Given that they are partially accessible in ancient Turkish language, Turkey would need to organize their translation for rendering them available to a vaster public.

truth. It could only then negotiate the applicable forms of reparation with the Armenian community and/or the Armenian State now representing it.[194]

And what steps should European States take towards remedying the complicity of the former Entente Powers in the events of 1915–16 by not intervening, in breach of their obligations under the Berlin Treaty, and by having canceled the *Metz Yeghern* in the negotiations of the Lausanne Treaty as during the following years when every effort was made for it to fall into oblivion?

In my view, the European Countries would need to do everything possible to facilitate negotiations by preliminarily recognizing their responsibility in the violent disintegration of the Ottoman Empire, which facilitated massacres and deportation of Armenians. This could be a further means of obtaining Turkey's availability to recognize the historical truth.

However, it would be perhaps better that Armenians and the civil society of good will abandon the authorities to their falsities, to their diplomatic expediencies and focus on the relations between the two communities, the Turkish and the Armenian. As a forceful supporter of the genocide claim has written in 2004, "A paradigm shift is necessary that includes new aspects of the conflict, the aspects that have never previously been considered. We must re-conceptualize the problem and put both societies at the center of our analysis. This paradigm shift should focus on the creation of a new cultural space in which this new approach can develop. One way of doing this is to encourage direct interaction between the two communities, so that each party can develop a realistic image of the other."[195]

The two communities must finally realize that the dispute between the two opposite narratives of the partial destruction of the Armenian nation is indeed a dispute between the Turkish authorities and the Armenian community and not between the Turkish and the Armenian communities *inter se*. The two communities must understand that they are both the victims of the Turkish denialist attitude. Only a direct transnational dialogue between the two communities, without the States' mediation, could erase for Armenians the false image of "Turks as barbaric

---

[194]I have to confess that I cannot understand the denialist attitude of the Republic of Turkey (see on this attitude the observations of Chorbajian (2016)). Why don't the Turkish authorities understand that such an attitude will only lead more and more experts to discuss these events and conclude that there was in fact an Armenian genocide? That this attitude will spread more and more increasing among people the awareness about the massacres and deportations, gradually leading every man, woman and child in the world, starting from the Turkish citizens, to know what in fact happened? For the truth this is fantastic, but the credibility of Turkey at the international level will gradually be lost, which is not in the interest of its government and its people. Why are honest Turks to feel uncomfortable in discussing about these events, as my personal experience has taught in discussing with a Turkish friend? Why don't the Turkish authorities understand that by their attitude they harm their people? The doubt arises that they don't care. They care more about hiding wrongdoings for which above and first of all the members of previous Turkish governments rather than the present ones - in any case not the Turkish people as such - are personally responsible. However, denying past Ottoman and Turkish authorities' wrongdoings is a new violation of international law, as already noted.

[195]Akçam (2004), p. 252. Even if they were written in 2004, the quoted affirmations are still needed.

criminals" and for the Turks the false image of "Armenians as traitors and terrorist criminals".[196]

Post scriptum

My paper is very long. This requires an explanation. When I started studying the "Armenian question", I knew very little about it. Hence, no prior knowledge of facts influenced my analysis. I am a jurist, not an historian, and, therefore, I could not carry out a historical and documentary research myself. However, I needed to base my legal reasoning on some essential historical facts. I thus had to borrow data coming from available historical research with the ambition to be comprehensive. Given the enormous volume of materials that have been written on this controversial issue, I tried to make a balanced selection within the enormous amount of the historical and legal literature of both sides of the dispute. I needed to often refer to what I had read and to clarify why I found one position more reliable than another. This explains the length of the paper.

References

Acquaviva G (2011) At the origins of crimes against humanity: clues to a proper understanding of the *nullum crimen* principle in the Nuremberg Judgment. J Int Crim Justice 9:881–903

Açar DA, Rüma İ (2007) External pressure and Turkish discourse on 'Recognition of the Armenian Genocide'. Southeast Eur Black Sea Stud 7:449–465

Akçam T (2004) From Empire to Republic: Turkish nationalism and the Armenian genocide. Zed Books Ltd, London, New York

Akçam T (2006) A shameful act: The Armenian genocide and the question of Turkish responsibility. Metropolitan Books, New York

Akçam T (2008) Review essay: Guenter Lewy's The Armenian Massacres in Ottoman Turkey. Genocide Stud Prev 3:111–145

Akçam T (2012) The Young Turk's crime against humanity: The Armenian genocide and the ethnic cleansing in the Ottoman Empire. Princeton University Press, Princeton

Akçam T, Kurt Ü (2015) The spirit of the laws: the plunder of wealth in the Armenian genocide. Berghahn, New York, Oxford

Andonian A (1965) The memoirs of Naim Bey: the Turkish Armenocide. Historical Research Association, Documentary Series, vol 2, second reprinting. University of Pennsylvania Printing Office, Philadelphia

[196] Furthermore, the Armenian community needs to strongly condemn the acts of terrorist vengeance followed by some members of ASALA against Turkey's representatives, just as the Turkish people has to take the courage, as some Turkish intellectuals do, to oppose the denialist attitude of their authorities.

Atkinson T (2001) The German, the Turk and the devil made a triple alliance: Harpoot Diaries, 1908–1917. Taderon Press, London
Avedian V (2012) State identity, continuity, and responsibility: The Ottoman Empire, the Republic of Turkey and the Armenian genocide. Eur J Int Law 23:797–820
Bass G (2000) Stay the hand of vengeance. Princeton University Press, Princeton
Bijak J, Lubman S (2016) The disputed numbers: in search of the demographic basis for studies of Armenian population losses, 1915–1923. In: Demirdjian A (ed) The Armenian genocide legacy, pp 26–43. Palgrave Macmillan, London
Bloxham D (2007) The great game of genocide: imperialism, nationalism, and the destruction of the Ottoman Armenians. Oxford University Press, Oxford
Bruneteau B (2006) Il secolo dei genocidi. Il Mulino, Bologna
Bonello G (19 April 2012) Turkey's EU Minister, Judge Giovanni Bonello and the Armenian genocide—'Claim about Malta Trials is nonsense'. The Malta Independent
Bryce J, Toynbee A (1916) The treatment of Armenians in the Ottoman Empire, 1915–16: documents presented to viscount grey of Falloden by Viscount Bryce (aka The Blue Book). HM Stationery Office, London
Cassese A (2008) International criminal law. Oxford University Press, Oxford
Cassese A (2009) The Massacres of Armenians. In: Cassese A (ed) The Oxford companion to international criminal justice. Oxford University Press, New York, pp 248–250
Chorbajian L (2016) They brought it on themselves and it never happened: Denial to 1939. In: Demirdjian A (ed) The Armenian genocide legacy, 167–182. Palgrave Macmillan, London
Churchill WS (1929) The world crisis: the aftermath. Thornton Butterworth Limited, London
Dadrian VN (1989) Genocide as a problem of national and international law: The World War I Armenian case and its contemporary legal ramifications. Yale J Int Law 14:221–334
Dadrian VN (1991) Documentation of the Armenian genocide in Turkish sources. In: Charny I (ed) Genocide: a critical bibliographic review, vol 2. Mansell, London; Facts on File, New York, pp 86–138
Dadrian VN (1994) Documentation of the Armenian genocide in German and Austrian sources. In: Charny I (ed) The widening circle of genocide (Genocide: a critical bibliographic review, vol 3). Transaction Publishers, Rutgers, New Brunswick
Dadrian VN (1995) The history of the Armenian genocide: ethnic conflict from the Balkans to Anatolia to the Caucasus. Berghahn Books, Providence, USA, and Oxford, United Kingdom
Dadrian VN (1997) The Turkish Military Tribunal's prosecution of the authors of the Armenian genocide: four major court-martial series. Holocaust Genocide Stud 11:28–59
Dadrian VN (2010) The Armenian genocide as a dual problem of national and international law. Univ St. Thomas J Law Public Policy 4:60–82
Davis LA (1918) The slaughterhouse province: an American diplomat's report on the Armenian genocide of 1915–1917. In: Blair S (ed) (1988). Aristide D. Caratzas, New York
de Zayas A (2010) The genocide against the Armenians 1915–1923 and the relevance of the 1948 genocide convention. Haigazian University, Beirut
Eckart C (2012) Promises of States under international law (Translated from the original in German). Hart Publishing, Oxford and Portland, Oregon
Flores M (2015) Il genocidio degli armeni. Bologna: Il Mulino
Guibert N, Kim S (2016) Compensation for the Armenian genocide: a study of recognition and reparations. In: Demirdjian A (ed) The Armenian genocide legacy. Palgrave Macmillan, London, pp 102–117
Gürün K (1985) The Armenian file: the Myth of innocence exposed. K. Rustem and Bro. and Weidenfeld & Nicolson, London, Nicosia, Istanbul
Gürün K (2001) The Armenian file: the Myth of innocence exposed. K. Rustem and Bro. and Weidenfeld & Nicolson, London, Nicosia, Istanbul
Heinsohn G (1998) Lexikon der Völkermorde. Rowohlt Taschenbuch Verlag, Reinbek
Horne, CF (ed) (1923) Source records of the Great War, Vol. III (1915). National Alumni, New York

Horne J, Kramer A (2001) German atrocities 1914: a history of Denial. Yale University Press, New Haven CT

Hovannisian RJ (1994) Etiology and sequelae of the Armenian genocide. In: Andreopoulos GJ (ed) Genocide: conceptual and historical dimensions. University of Pennsylvania Press, Philadelphia, pp 111–140

Jacobsen M (2001) Diaries of a Danish Missionary: Harpoot, 1907–1919. Taderon Pr, United Kingdom

Kelly MJ (2008) Genocide—The power of a label. Case West Reserv J Int Law 40:147–162

Ketsemanian V (23 September 2013) The confiscation of Armenian properties: an interview to Ümit Kurt. The Armenian Weekly

Kévorkian R, Ternon Y (eds) (2014) Mémorial du génocide des Arméniens. Éditions du Seuil, Paris

Kieser H-L, Oktem K, Reinkowski M (eds) (2015) World War I and the end of the Ottomans: from the Balkan Wars to the Armenian genocide. I.B.Tauris, London

Kurt Ü (24 April 2015) The Armenian genocide and the law. https://www.opendemocracy.net/north-africa-west-asia/umit-kurt/armenian-genocide-and-law

Kurt Ü (2015) Cultural erasure: the absorption and forced conversion of Armenian women and children, 1915–1916. Études Arméniennes Contemp 7:71–82

Kurt Ü (2016) The plunder of wealth through abandoned properties laws in the Armenian genocide. Genocide Stud Int 10:37–51

Lattanzi F (2014) The distinction between war crimes and crimes against humanity. In: Cortese B (ed) Studi in onore di Laura Picchio Forlati – Essays in Honour of Laura Picchio Forlati – Etudes en l'honneur de Laura Picchio Forlati – Festschruft Laura Picchio Forlati. Giappichelli, Torino, pp 67–82

Lemkin R (1933) Acts constituting a general (Transnational) danger considered as offences against the law of nations. In: Additional explications to the special report presented to the 5th conference for the unification of penal law in Madrid, 14–20 October 1933. http://www.preventgenocide.org/lemkin/madrid1933-english.htm

Lemkin R (1944) Axis rule in occupied Europe. Laws of occupation, analysis of government, proposals for redress. Carnegie Endowment for International Peace, Washington

Lewy G (2005a) The Armenian Massacres in Ottoman Turkey: a disputed genocide. The University of Utah Press, Utah

Lewy G (2005b) Revisiting the Armenian genocide. Middle East Q 12:3–12

Libaridian GJ (2007) Modern Armenia: people, nation, state. New Transaction, New Brunswick and London

Lloyd George D (1939) Memoirs of the Peace Conference, vol 2. Yale University Press, New Haven

Lothrop Stoddard T (1917) Pan-Turanism. Am Political Sci Rev 11:12–23. https://www.jstor.org/stable/pdf/1944138.pdf?acceptTC=true

McCarthy J (2015) Turks and Armenians: nationalism and conflict in the Ottoman Empire. Turko-Tatar Press, Madison, Wisconsin

McCarthy J (2006) The Armenian Rebellion at Van, Utah Series in Turkish and Islamic Studies

McCarthy J, Arslan E, Taşkiran C, Turan Ö (2006) The Armenian Rebellion at Van. Salt Lake City. The University of Utah Press, Utah

Metz HC (ed) (1995) Turkey: a country study. GPO for the library of congress, Washington

Monina G (2016) Lelio Basso, leader globale. Un socialista nel secondo Novecento. Carocci, Roma

Morgenthau HI (1918) Ambassador Morgenthau's story. Doubleday, Page & Company, Garden City, New York

Naar DE (2016) Sephardim since Birth: reconfiguring Jewish identity in America. In: Soomekh S (ed) Sephardi and Mizrahi Jews in America. Purdue University Press, West Lafayette, Indiana, pp 75–104

Niepage M (1917) The Horrors of Aleppo seen by a German eyewitness. A word to Germany's accredited representatives. T. Fisher Unwin Ltd, London

Payaslian S (2006) The destruction of the Armenian Church during the genocide. Genocide Stud Prev: Int J 1:149–172
Phillips DL (2015) Centennial of the Armenian genocide: recognition and reconciliation. The Huffington Post
Riggs HR (1997) Days of tragedy in Armenia: personal experiences in Harpoot, 1915–1917. Ann Arbor Gomidas Institute, Michigan
Robertson G (2009) Was there an Armenian genocide? Geoffrey Robertson Qc's opinion with reference to Foreign and Commonwealth Office documents which show how British Ministers, Parliament and people have been misled, 9 October 2009. Policy Memorandum, Foreign and Commonwealth Office to Minister, London
Robertson G (2016) Armenia and the G-word: the law and the politics. In: Demirdjian A (ed) The Armenian genocide legacy. Palgrave Macmillan, London, pp 69–83
Sarafian A (1999) The Ottoman archives debate and the Armenian genocide. Armenian Forum 2, n 1. https://www.scribd.com/document/152956068/The-Ottoman-Archives-Debate
Schabas WA (2011) Crimes against humanity as a paradigm for international atrocity crimes. Middle East Crit 20:253–269
Shaw SJ, Shaw EK (1977) History of the Ottoman Empire and modern Turkey, vol. II: Reform, revolution and republic. The rise of modern Turkey, 1808–1975. Cambridge University Press, New York
Shirinian L (2016) Orphans of the Armenian genocide with special reference to the Georgetown Boys and Girls in Canada. In: Demirdjian A (ed) The Armenian genocide legacy. Palgrave Macmillan, London, pp 44–66
Tacar P, Gauin M (2012) State identity, continuity, and responsibility: The Ottoman Empire, the Republic of Turkey and the Armenian genocide: a reply to Vahagn Avedian. Eur J Int Law 23:821–835
Ternon Y (1989) Enquête sur la négation d'un genocide. Editions Parenthèses, Marseille
Ticehurst R (1997) The *Martens Clause* and the laws of armed conflict. Int Rev Red Cross 37:125–134
Tomuschat C (2006) The legacy of Nuremberg. J Int Crim Justice 4:830–844
Travis H (2016) Counterinsurgency as genocidal intent: from the Ottoman Christians to the Bosnian Muslims. In: Demirdjian A (ed) The Armenian genocide legacy. Palgrave Macmillan, London, pp 149–164
Üngör UÜ (2016) The Armenian genocide in the context of 20th century paramilitarism. In: Demirdjian A (ed) The Armenian genocide legacy. Palgrave Macmillan, London, pp 11–25
Van Hear N (1998) New diasporas: the mass exodus, dispersal and regrouping of migrant communities. Taylor & Francis, London
Verhoeven J (1984) Le peuple arménien et le droit international. In: Chaliand G (ed) Le crime de silence: le génocide des Arméniens. Champs Flammarion, Paris, pp 257–287
Walker CJ (1990) The survival of a nation. Routledge, London
Weitz ED (2015) A century of genocide: Utopias of race and nation. Princeton University Press, Princeton and Oxford

On the Applicability of the Genocide Convention to the Armenian Massacres

Chiara Cipolletti

Contents

1 Introduction 106
2 States' Obligation to Prevent and to not Perform Acts of Genocide Under the Genocide Convention 107
3 The Non-retroactivity of Treaties 112
 3.1 Is There Room for Exceptions to the Principle of Non-retroactivity in the Genocide Convention? 114
 3.2 The Effects of *jus cogens* on the Principle of Non-retroactivity 117
 3.3 The Nineteenth-Century Treaties for the Protection of Minorities 120
4 Concluding Remarks 121
References 122

Abstract The paper deals with the relationship between State responsibility for acts of genocide and the Armenian events of 1915. The author explores the question of the temporal applicability of the Genocide Convention of 1948, specifically concerning the issue of State responsibility for the commission of acts of genocide. As "Metz Yeghern" happened long time before the entry into force of the Genocide Convention, these treaty provisions could be applied only if they were found to be retroactive. Through an analysis of the text of the Convention, its preparatory works and the case law of the International Court of Justice, the author demonstrates that no exceptions can be established for the general rule of non-retroactivity of conventional rules; therefore, it is not possible to hold Turkey responsible for those events under the Genocide Convention.

C. Cipolletti (✉)
University of Teramo, Teramo, Italy
e-mail: chiara.cip@hotmail.it

F. Lattanzi and E. Pistoia (eds.), *The Armenian Massacres of 1915–1916 a Hundred Years Later*, Studies in the History of Law and Justice 15,
https://doi.org/10.1007/978-3-319-78169-3_4

1 Introduction

In the early twentieth century, the Ottoman Empire was the scene of a terrible massacre of Armenians. The responsibility of Turkey for this event has long been discussed, especially after the entry into force of the Convention on the Prevention and Punishment of the Crime of Genocide (hereinafter the Genocide Convention),[1] since its acts may be qualified as acts of genocide in the light of the Genocide Convention.

This paper intends to offer some reflections upon the issue of the temporal scope of the Genocide Convention, in order to determine whether it may be applied to events which occurred in Armenia between 1915 and 1916.

The attention given to the issue by scholars[2] and the recent involvement of the International Court of Justice in the interpretation of the Convention[3] testify the complexity of the topic.[4]

The subject also has a pivotal role in the current relations between Turkey and Armenia, as evidenced by the request of an opinion on the applicability of the Genocide Convention to events that took place in the twentieth century by the Turkish-Armenian Reconciliation Commission (TARC)[5] to the International Centre for Transitional Justice.[6]

The first section of this article will deal with States' obligations under the Convention. While much attention has been continuously paid to the constituent elements of the crime of genocide[7] and to the responsibility of individuals, the issue of State responsibility for genocide had, for many years, not been the object of the same interest.

The debate concerning State responsibility has gained more visibility in connection with the gradual disappearance of individuals, accused of acts of genocide, and the recent decision by the International Court of Justice in the *Bosnia and*

---

[1]Convention on the Prevention and Punishment of the Crime of Genocide, Paris, 9 December 1948, in United Nations Treaty Series, vol. 78, p. 277.

[2]Schabas (2000, 2010); De Zayas (2010); Robertson (2010).

[3]International Court of Justice, *Application of the Convention on the Prevention and Punishment of the Crime of Genocide (Croatia v. Serbia)*, Judgment, 3 February 2015, ICJ Reports 2015.

[4]The issue is further complicated by the current problem of denial of genocide, recently addressed by the European Court of Human Rights in the case *Perinçek c. Switzerland*, Court (Grand Chamber), 15 October 2015, No. 27510/08; for an analysis of the case see Della Morte (2016) and Leotta, in this volume; for the position of the European Court of Human Rights on the genocide denial see Lobba (2015).

[5]The Turkish-Armenian Reconciliation Commission was established in July 2001 by civil society representatives with the aim to improve the relationship between Armenia and Turkey.

[6]According to the International Centre for Transitional Justice, the Genocide Convention can not be applied retroactively and does not constitute a basis for establishing the responsibility of Turkey with regard to any events happened before the entry into force of the Convention. The opinion is available at http://www1.american.edu/cgp/TARC/ICTJ%20Memorandum%20Feb.%2003.pdf.

[7]See, for example, the analysis by Simon (1996).

Herzegovina v. Serbia and Montenegro case, on the suitability of the Convention to establish States' obligation not only to prevent genocide, but also not to commit acts of genocide.[8] Even though today this idea is almost universally accepted,[9] the nature of such State obligation is still not straightforward. For this reason, it is here worth considering more precisely which obligations States are bound by the Genocide Convention and what kind of responsibility derives from their violation.

The second section will discuss the *ratione temporis* application of the Genocide Convention and address why it is difficult to maintain that Turkey is today internationally responsible for violating the obligations imposed by that Convention, with regard to the massacre of 1.5 million Armenians in the Ottoman Empire.[10] While the nearly forty years elapsed between these terrible events and the entry into force of the Convention would seem, at first sight, to prevent altogether the application of the Convention, a different conclusion could be reached, if the retroactive application of the Convention could be demonstrated. I will first consider the obligations imposed on States by the Genocide Convention, and then focus on the interpretation of the intertemporal regime of treaties and on the application of this regime to the Genocide Convention.

2 States' Obligation to Prevent and to not Perform Acts of Genocide Under the Genocide Convention

The term genocide was first used by the Jewish jurist Raphael Lemkin in 1944[11]; the topic captured the attention of United Nations shortly afterwards. The General Assembly employed the expression in Resolution 96(I) of 11 December 1946, which requested the Economic and Social Council to "undertake the necessary studies, with a view to drawing up a draft convention on the crime of genocide to be submitted to the next regular session of the General Assembly".[12] After two years, in 1948, the United Nations Convention on the Prevention and Punishment of the Crime of Genocide was adopted unanimously and entered into force in 1951.

Article I of the Genocide Convention establishes States' obligations to prevent and to punish the crime of genocide, providing that "genocide, whether committed in time of peace or in time of war, is a crime under international law which they undertake to prevent and to punish".

[8]International Court of Justice, *Application of the Convention on the Prevention and Punishmentof the Crime of Genocide (Bosnia and Herzegovina* v. *Serbia and Montenegro)*, Judgment, 26 February 2007, ICJ Reports 2007, p. 43, paras. 173–179.

[9]Shabas (2000), p. 434.

[10]This paper does not deal with the transmissibility of responsibility from the Ottoman Empire to Turkey; on this point see Paddeu (2015); Dumberry (2014).

[11]Lemkin (1944).

[12]The resolution is available at http://www.un.org/ga/search/view_doc.asp?symbol=A/res/96(I).

The express inclusion of obligations to prevent and to punish genocide leaves the question open about the existence of an obligation upon States not to commit genocide.

The reference of Article IX of the Genocide Convention to the responsibility of a State for genocide is unhelpful. The article concerns the settlement of disputes among contracting States and mentions, among other hypothesis, disputes "relating to the responsibility of a State for genocide".[13]

This reference does not clarify which substantive obligations the Convention imposes upon the contracting parties; as highlighted by the International Court of Justice in the *Case concerning Application of the Convention on the Prevention and Punishment of the Crime of Genocide (Bosnia and Herzegovina v. Serbia and Montenegro)*: "Article IX is essentially a jurisdictional provision".[14]

According to the ICJ, the Convention imposes upon States not only the obligation to prevent and repress acts of genocide committed by individuals, but also the obligation not to commit themselves acts of genocide. In fact, through a teleological interpretation of Article I, in the light of the "humanitarian and civilizing" purpose of the Convention, the Court considers that, notwithstanding the lack of any express reference in the text of the Convention to an obligation prohibiting States from committing genocide,

> It would be paradoxical if States were … under an obligation to prevent, so far as within their power, the commission of genocide by persons over whom they have a certain influence, but were not forbidden to commit such acts through their own organs, or persons over whom they have such firm control that their conduct is attributable to the State concerned under international law. In short, the obligation to prevent genocide necessarily implies the prohibition of the commission of genocide.[15]

---

[13]Article IX of the UN Genocide Convention. There are 15 reservations to this article by contracting States (The reservations are available at https://treaties.un.org.). These reservations have been highly controversial due to their debatable consistency with the object and the purpose of the treaty. The International Court of Justice in *Reservations to the Convention on the Prevention and Punishment of the Crime of Genocide*, Advisory Opinion, 28 May 1951, ICJ Reports 1951, p. 24 made it clear that reservations to the Genocide Convention are not as such inadmissible, but it is "the compatibility of a reservation with the object and purpose of the Convention that must furnish the criterion for the attitude of a State in making the reservation on accession as well as for the appraisal by a State in objecting to the reservation." The joint separate opinion of Judges Higgins, Kooijmans, Elaraby, Owada and Simma to the Judgment of the International Court of Justice, *Armed Activities on the Territory of the Congo (New Application: 2002) (Democratic Republic of the Congo v. Rwanda)*, Judgment, 3 February 2006, ICJ Reports 2006, p. 6 demanded the International Court of Justice (which deemed the Rwanda's reservation to Article IX compatible with the object and purpose of the Genocide Convention) to revisit its position on the compatibility of reservations to Article IX.

[14]International Court of Justice, *Application of the Convention on the Prevention and Punishment of the Crime of Genocide (Bosnia and Herzegovina v. Serbia and Montenegro)*, Judgment, 26 February 2007, ICJ Reports 2007, para. 166.

[15]Ibidem. On the legal obligation to prevent genocide and its interpretation in the *Bosnia v. Serbia* judgment of the International Court of Justice see Forlati (2011). The reasoning of the Court has been criticized by Gaeta (2007), p. 633 et seqq., who argued that the Court applied principles of treaty interpretation in order to infer from the treaty new obligations rather than to clarify its

The Court went so far as to recognise explicitly that nothing in the Convention allows to conclude that the existence of conventional provision imposing obligations upon individuals excludes that the contracting parties are also subject to such obligations and responsibilities for their violation.[16]

It should be noted that State responsibility is different and separate from that of individuals, notwithstanding the circumstance that both cases arise from the breach of the same conventional rules.[17] As the International Court of Justice held:

> State responsibility and individual criminal responsibility are governed by different legal regimes and pursue different aims. The former concerns the consequences of the breach by a State of the obligations imposed upon it by international law, whereas the latter is concerned with the responsibility of an individual as established under the rules of international and domestic criminal law.[18]

With regard to the responsibility of States, arising from the breach of the Convention, the ICJ stressed that this responsibility is not of a criminal nature, but is responsibility under international law. In fact, according to the Court neither the concept of criminal responsibility of States exists in international law, nor the Genocide Convention is a means for the introduction of such responsibility.[19]

The issue of State responsibility was addressed during the preparatory works of the Genocide Convention, because of an amendment proposed by the United Kingdom[20] and supported by Belgium.[21] Sir Gerald Fitzmaurice, the British representative, considered it necessary to provide for international State responsibility,

meaning. In her opinion, the obligation on States not to commit genocide does not descend from the treaty, but from customary international law. Spinedi (2002), p. 899 agrees with the Court's view on the paradoxical consequences of denying State responsibility for its own acts of genocide.

[16]International Court of Justice, *Application of the Convention on the Prevention and Punishment of the Crime of Genocide (Bosnia and Herzegovina v. Serbia and Montenegro)*, Judgment, 26 February 2007, ICJ Reports 2007, para. 174.

[17]As noted by Nollkaemper (2003) this responsibility can also be concurrent. The author includes genocide among the few acts which can lead both to individual responsibility and State responsibility and mentions as an example the concurrent responsibility for acts of genocide in the former Yugoslavia of Slobodan Milosevic.

[18]International Court of Justice, *Application of the Convention on the Prevention and Punishment of the Crime of Genocide (Croatia v. Serbia)*, Judgment, 3 February 2015, ICJ Reports 2015, para. 129.

[19]Ibidem, para. 170.

[20]As underlined by Mr. Fitzmaurice, during the Sixth Committee of the General Assembly, Summary records of meeting, UN Doc. A/C.6/SR.95, p. 344: "his delegation had proposed that amendment in order that the convention might contain a direct reference to the type of genocide which was most likely to occur, i.e. genocide committed by a State or a Government. Since it was to be assumed that individuals acting on behalf of the State would not be punished by the courts of that State, it was essential to insert into the convention provisions to the effect that such acts would constitute a violation of the convention".

[21]Position expressed by Belgium during the Sixth Committee of the General Assembly, Summary records of meeting, UN Doc. A/C.6/SR.95, p. 345.

in order to give effect to the Genocide Convention,[22] while other States opposed this amendment because of the reference to criminal responsibility of State, an inconceivable idea, at least in their opinion.[23] Consequently, the whole debate concerned the nature of such responsibility.[24] In the end, the United Kingdom amendment was not adopted[25] and the only reference to State responsibility left is the one in Article IX.

Since the Genocide Convention does not provide a specific regime of State responsibility for the violation of the obligations therein spelled out,[26] it is necessary to refer to general international law in order to identify the consequences arising from the breach of primary rules on genocide. This approach greatly helps in understanding concerns about the retroative application of the Genocide Convention.

The responsibility of States for genocide was expressly considered by the International Law Commission (ILC) Special Rapporteur, Roberto Ago. During the preparatory works of the Draft articles on Responsibility of States for Internationally Wrongful Acts (hereinafter Draft Articles on States Responsibility),[27] Ago advocated the prohibition of genocide as an example of obligation so "grave and injurious" as to give rise to an aggravated regime of responsibility. In fact, the perpetration by a State of acts of genocide was encompassed among those serious breaches of obligations established by peremptory norms of general international

[22]Position expressed by the United Kingdom during the Sixth Committee of the General Assembly, Summary records of meeting, UN Doc. A/C.6/SR.104, p. 444.

[23]Position expressed by the French representative during the Sixth Committee of the General Assembly, Summary records of meeting, UN Doc. A/C.6/SR.95, p. 348; position expressed by the Philippine representative during the Sixth Committee of the General Assembly, Summary records of meeting, UN Doc. A/C.6/SR.130, p. 433 and UN Doc. A/C.6/SR.104, p. 441–442. The debate on the criminal responsibility of States has brought forward the discussion of the ILC on the incorporation of the notion of "international crime" into the Draft Articles on Responsibility of States for Internationally Wrongful Acts.

[24]See Robinson (1960). State responsibility should not be considered criminal, as Professor Spinedi exhaustively explained with reference to Article 19 of the Draft Articles on Responsibility of States for Internationally Wrongful Acts: "This does not mean, however, that the Commission had the intention to attach to these acts forms of responsibility similar to those provided in the penal law of modern domestic legal system", Spinedi (1989), p. 52. In the First Report on State Responsibility, by Mr James Crawford, Special Rapporteur, UN Doc. A/CN.4/490 and Add.1-7, paras. 52–54 French and Czech Republic representatives emphasized that: "the law of international responsibility is neither civil nor criminal, and that it is purely and simply international".

[25]Summary records of meeting, UN Doc. A/C.6/SR.96, p. 355.

[26]Report of the International Law Commission on the work of its fifty-third session, UN Doc. A/56/10, in Yearbook of the International Law Commission 2001, vol. II, Part Two.

[27]The Draft Articles on Responsibility of States for Internationally Wrongful Acts, with commentaries, in Yearbook of the International Law Commission, 2001, vol. II, Part Two.

law, which Ago proposed to call crimes of States.[28] Arangio-Ruiz, Fourth Special Rapporteur of the ILC on the matter, went even further: assuming genocide as an example of breaches recognized as crime on the basis of the law in force,[29] he proposed to establish institutional mechanism for the assessment of an aggravated responsibility of States.[30]

It is well known that the obligations imposed by peremptory norms are owed towards the international community as a whole. Such obligations were acknowledged for the first time by the International Court of Justice in the *Barcelona Traction, Light and Power Company, Limited* case. Here, the ICJ distinguished the obligation of a State vis-à-vis another State and: "obligations of a State towards the international community as a whole"[31] deriving, for example, in the Court's view "from the outlawing of acts of … of genocide".[32]

It is accepted today that the peremptory nature of the international law rule on the prohibition of genocide[33] gives rise, in case of violation, to a regime of State responsibility,[34] which can not be defined as criminal, but merely as aggravated, due to the peremptory nature of the obligations breached.

The specificity of this regime is that every other State is obliged not to recognize as lawful the situation derived from the violation, not to render aid or assistance in maintaining that situation, and to cooperate to bring to an end through lawful means the breach (Article 41 of the Draft Articles on State Responsibility). Also, as the obligation is owed towards the international community as a whole, every State may ask the wrongdoer for the cessation of the serious wrongful act, assurances of non-repetition and a full reparation for the injury caused to the beneficiaries of the prohibition of genocide, that is, the individuals concerned (Article 48).

---

[28]Third Report on State responsibility, by Mr. Roberto Ago, Special Rapporteur, the internationally wrongful act of the State, source of international responsibility, UN Doc. A/CN.4/246 and Add.1-3 in Yearbook of the International Law Commission, 1971, vol. II (1), p. 210. The proposal to distinguish international crimes of States and delictes was dismissed and the Draft Articles on State Responsibility only refers to serious breaches of obligations provided by peremptory norms of international law.

[29]Sixth Report on State responsibility, by Mr. Gaetano Arangio-Ruiz, Special Rapporteur, UN Doc. A/CN.4/461 and Add.1-3 & Add.2/Corr.1, in Yearbook of the International Law Commission 1994, vol. II(1), p. 19.

[30]Seventh Report on State responsibility, by Mr. Gaetano Arangio-Ruiz, Special Rapporteur, UN Doc. A/CN.4/469 and Add.1-2, in Yearbook of the International Law Commission 1995, vol. II (1).

[31]International Court of Justice, *Barcelona Traction, Light and Power Company, Limited (Belgium v. Spain)*, Judgment, 5 February 1970, ICJ Reports 1970, p. 3, paras. 33–34.

[32]Ibidem.

[33]International Court of Justice, *Case Concerning Armed Activities On the Territory of the Congo (Democratic Republic of the Congo v. Rwanda)*, Jurisdiction of the Court and Admissibility of the Application, Judgment, 3 February 2006, ICJ Reports 2006, para. 64. Milanovic (2006), p. 563.

[34]In the case of genocide, the seriousness of the breach is "substantive" and not "circumstantial", due to the impossibility to distinguish individual circumstances essential to qualify the act as a serious breach of obligation under article 40 of the Draft Articles on State Responsibility. See Palmisano (1994). See infra, par. 3.3.

3 The Non-retroactivity of Treaties

The rules on temporal application of treaties are codified in the United Nations Vienna Convention on the Law of Treaties (VCLT) of 1969.[35] The VCLT provides in Article 28 for the non-retroactivity of treaties and, specifically, that treaty rules:

> do not bind a party in relation to any act or fact which took place or any situation which ceased to exist before the date of the entry into force of the treaty with respect to that party.

This means that every treaty is binding for the parties only after it has entered into force and that it does not extend its effects to facts that have occurred before the treaty entered into force.[36]

This rule is an application to treaties of the well-established international law principle of non-retroactivity. In the field of State responsibility, this principle is codified in Article 13 of the Draft Articles on State Responsibility, which states:

> An act of a State does not constitute a breach of an international obligation unless the State is bound by the obligation in question at the time the act occurs.

Apart from being both a customary and a conventional rule, as well as perhaps a general principle of international law, the principle of non-retroactivity has a complex nature.[37] It embraces two mainstays of public international law: State consent and the rule of law.[38] Allowing for the retroactive effect of a treaty norm means to overlook the fact that there is consent only when a State agrees to be bound by a conventional rule, through ratification or signature of a treaty. On the other hand, the principle of non-retroactivity guarantees the respect of the rule of law, in that it assures certainty and foreseeability of the legal consequences of conducts.[39]

It is worth recalling that, although Article 28 of the Vienna Convention entered into force in 1980, it can easily be considered a codification of earlier customary international law. This is shown by the fact that already in 1952, in the *Ambatielos* case,[40] the International Court of Justice recognised the principle of

---

[35] Vienna Convention on the Law of Treaties, Vienna, 23 May 1969, in United Nations Treaty Series, vol. 1155, p. 331.

[36] Kotzur (2014), p. 164 distinguishes between "true retroactivity" and "material retroactivity": the first refers to the application of a rule to a situation already settled in the past, the second to cases where the rule is applied to the current effects of an event that happened before its entry into force.

[37] Rodas (1973).

[38] Kotzur (2014), p. 154.

[39] According to Kotzur (2008) legal stability is an aspect of the legal certainty, which itself constitutes an element of the rule of law.

[40] International Court of Justice, *Ambatielos case (Greece v. United Kingdom)*, Judgment (preliminary objection), 1 July 1952, ICJ Reports 1952, p. 40.

non-retroactivity and, on this basis, declined its jurisdiction under a Treaty of 1926,[41] with regard to facts that had taken place in 1922 and 1923.[42] The Court argued that accepting the Greek claim of Court jurisdiction on events happened before the entry into force of the Treaty, would mean to give retroactive effects to the jurisdiction clause (Article 29) of the Treaty.[43]

This authoritative recognition of the principle of non-retroactivity confirms that Article 28 of the Vienna Convention of the Law of the Treaties has codified a rule, that was already a part of customary international law, at least in (but very likely much before) 1952. The Genocide Convention entered into force in 1951. It can therefore be maintained without much doubt that the principle of non-retroactivity also applies to the Genocide Convention.

This is however not the last word on the subject. The non-peremptory nature of the non-retroactivity principle leads to reflect upon possible exceptions and their potential application to the Genocide Convention. Under Article 28, the principle of non-retroactivity shall apply

> unless a different intention appears from the treaty or is otherwise established.

Indeed, it is possible to resort to such an exception in cases where an intention of the contracting parties can be inferred, even if not explicily spelled out in the text of the treaty.[44]

---

[41]Treaty of Commerce and Navigation between Greece and United Kingdom signed at London on 16 July 1926.

[42]The Greek Government used the "similar clauses theory" in order to justify its claim: "The theory is that where in the 1926 Treaty there are substantive provisions similar to substantive provisions of the 1886 Treaty, then under Article 29 of the 1926 Treaty this Court can adjudicate upon the validity of a claim based on an alleged breach of any of these similar provisions, even if the alleged breach took place wholly before the new treaty came into force". The Court rejected this theory due to the absence of a special clause or special object requiring retroactive interpretation. This special object was instead recognised by the Permanent Court of International Justice, *Mavrommatis Palestine Concession* case, Judgment, 30 August 1924, in Serie A- No 2 (1924), p. 34, where it holds that the Protocol XII to the Treaty of Lausanne "was drawn up in order to fix the conditions governing the recognition and treatment by the contracting Parties of certain concessions granted by the Ottoman authorities before the conclusion of the Protocol. An essential characteristic therefore of Protocol XII is that its effects extend to legal situations dating from a time previous to its own existence. If provision were not made in the clauses of the Protocol for the protection of the rights recognized therein as against infringements before the coming into force of that instrument, the Protocol would be ineffective as regards the very period at which the rights in question are most in need of protection. The Court therefore considers that the Protocol guarantees the rights recognized in it against any violation, regardless of the date on which it may have taken place".

[43]International Court of Justice, *Ambatielos case* (*Greece v. United Kingdom*), Judgment (preliminary objection), 1 July 1952, ICJ Reports 1952, p. 40.

[44]For instance, it has been pointed out that in the Sevres Treaty the intention of parties to give retroactive enforcement to it was made clear from the reference to the need to prosecute crimes committed during the war.

3.1 Is There Room for Exceptions to the Principle of Non-retroactivity in the Genocide Convention?

The text of the Genocide Convention provides elements neither for its retroactive enforcement, nor for the prohibition of its retroactive application[45]; moreover, it is hard to deduce from the treaty the intention of the Contracting Parties to ascribe a retroactive effect to the Convention.

The preparatory works do not easily lend themselves to support an intention of the parties to give to the Convention a retroactive application. This is due to various elements.

First of all, the Convention provides for its entry into force

> on the ninetieth day following the date of deposit of the twentieth instrument of ratification or accession.[46]

Moreover, during the negotiations the Czechoslovakian delegation proposed to add in the Convention

> express provisions asserting the peoples' desire to punish all those who, *in the future*, might be tempted to repeat the appalling crimes which had been committed.[47]

Likewise, the Philippine delegation, speaking about the opportunity to provide for the punishment of acts of genocide *in the future*, stated that

> any individual guilty of genocide should be punished, whoever he might be. In the recent past, as at various periods in history, it was generally the heads of State who had committed genocide. It was therefore essential to provide for their punishment in future.[48]

The Peruvian delegation described the Convention as a means

> for the punishment of those who would be guilty of violating its provisions *in the future*.[49]

---

[45]Contrary to other treaties where the prohibition to apply their rules retroactively is clearly established.

[46]Article XIII of the Genocide Convention.

[47]Position expressed by the Czechoslovakian representative during the Sixth Committee of the General Assembly, Summary records of meeting, UN Doc. A/C.6/SR. 66, p. 30.

[48]Position expressed by the Philippine government during the Sixth Committee of the General Assembly, Summary records of meeting, UN Doc. A/C.6/SR.95, p. 340.

[49]Position expressed by the Peruvian government during the Sixth Committee of the General Assembly, Summary records of meeting, UN Doc. A/C.6/SR. 110, p. 498.

The Dominican delegation emphasized the novelty of the concept of genocide[50] and the representative of the United Kingdom the fact that "the aim of the Convention was to establish the concept of a new crime".[51]

This is all evidence showing that the parties did not intend to give retroactive application to the Convention.[52]

On the other hand, there are elements which could reveal a different purpose: for instance, Article I states that

> The Contracting Parties *confirm* that genocide … is a crime under international law,[53]

instead of using the verb "declare". The same approach might be inferred from the preamble, where it is recognized that

> at all periods of history genocide has inflicted great losses on humanity.

Moreover, arguments in favour of the retroactive application of the Convention are previous cases of retroactive application of treaties, such as the London Agreement of 1945. With regard to the London Agreement, Kelsen stated that, even if the principle of non-retroactivity is a principle of justice, it is hard to consider the retroactivity of the law—applied to individuals responsible for illegal acts during the Second World War—as absolutely incompatible with justice. In fact, in Kelsen's opinion, when two different postulates of justice are in conflict, the higher should prevail; indeed, punishing individuals responsible for international crimes committed during the war was of greater importance than complying with the principle of non-retroactivity, also considering the numerous exceptions to it.[54]

Applying Kelsen reasoning to the Armenian massacres would mean to balance State responsibility with the principle of non-retroactivity. As in the case of individual responsibility, the principle of legality guarantees that State responsibility arises only for the breach of an international obligation in force when the conduct was taking place.

The main difference with individual responsibility lies in the fact that State responsibility is grounded on the principle of consent to the obligation involved,

---

[50]Position expressed by the Dominican Republic during the Sixth Committee of the General Assembly, Summary records of meeting, UN Doc. A/C.6/SR.76, p. 126 and by the Philippines, UN Doc. A/C.6/SR.71, p. 79.

[51]Position expressed by the United Kingdom during the Sixth Committee of the General Assembly, Summary records of meeting, UN Doc. A/C.6/SR.76, p. 127.

[52]International Centre for Transitional Justice, The Applicability of the United Nations Convention on the Prevention and Punishment of the Crime of Genocide to Events Which Occurred During the Early Twentieth Century, February 2003, available at http://www.armenian-genocide.org/files/ICTJ_Memorandum.pdf.

[53]Article I of the Genocide Convention.

[54]Kelsen (1947).

a basic principle of international law.[55] The principle of non-retroactivity itself descends from the rule of consent. To deny application of the former means to introduce an exception to a fundamental principle of international law. For this reason, a retroactive application of a treaty is coinceivable only when there is a clear intent of the Contracting Parties in this direction. The contradictory nature of the elements contained in the Convention and in its preparatory works do not allow to reach this conclusion.[56]

The International Court of Justice has recently reached the same conclusion in the case *Croatia v. Serbia*. The Serbian Government had argued that Croatia complained about events which had taken place before the then Republic of Yugoslavia became party to the Genocide Convention. Therefore, the Convention could not be applied. On the other hand, Croatia asserted that there was a presumption of favour of the retroactive application of, at least, some rules of the Convention and that the Genocide Convention was "capable of encompassing genocide whenever occurring, rather than only genocide occurring in the future after the Convention enters into force for a particular State".[57] In addressing this claim, the Court clarified that:

> Logic, as well as the presumption against retroactivity of treaty obligations enshrined in Article 28 of the Vienna Convention on the Law of Treaties, thus points clearly to the conclusion that the obligation to prevent genocide can be applicable only to acts that might occur after the Convention has entered into force for the State in question. Nothing in the text of the Genocide Convention or the *travaux préparatoires* suggests a different conclusion.[58]

The Court noticed that in numerous treaties the intention to apply the treaty retroactively was directly stated in the text of the treaty; it recalled, for instance, Article 1 of the 1968 Convention on the non-applicability of Statutory Limitations

[55]Crawford (2008), p. 5 recalls as, at its origin, "international law was entirely dependent on the consent - express or implied- of States"; Jennings QC and Watts (2008), p. 14 said that "'common consent' could be said to be the basis of international law as a legal system", the authors refer to the express or tacit consent of States to the rules of international law; Brownlie (1973), p. 2; Aust (2005), p. 4; see also Permanent Court of International Justice, *S. S. Lotus (France v. Turkey)*, Judgment, 7 September 1927, in Series A No. 10, p. 18.

[56]Does not conflict with these conclusions, the fact that some scholars deduce from the text of the Convention the existence of individual crime of genocide in general international law before the entry into force of the Convention. In fact, the same author confirms that the existence of genocide as a crime does not extend its effetcs to the additional obligations imposed on the parties by the Treaty. From this, they derive a limited retroactivity of the Convention, see Tams (2014). See also Schabas (2010), p. 41–42 who argued that, as shown by the experiences of the Treaties of Versailles, Sèvres and the Rome Statute, in these cases the exception becomes the rule, i.e. "the general rule for treaties dealing with international criminal liability for atrocity crimes actually seems to favor retrospective application".

[57]International Court of Justice, *Application of the Convention on the Prevention and Punishment of the Crime of Genocide (Croatia v. Serbia)*, Judgment, 3 February 2015, ICJ Reports 2015, para. 94.

[58]Ibidem, para. 95.

to War Crimes and Crimes against Humanity[59] or Article 2(2) of the 1974 European Convention on the Non-Applicability of Statutory Limitations to Crimes against Humanity and War Crimes.[60] In both these cases, the application of the Convention to acts committed prior to entry into force is expressly established.

In the end, the Court referred to its previous case law, *Belgium v. Senegal, Questions relating to the Obligation to Prosecute or Extradite*.[61] Here, the Convention against Torture and Other Cruel, Inhuman or Degrading Treatment or Punishment[62] was applied only to acts committed after its entry into force, although acts qualified by the Convention as crimes were most likely already part of customary law.

In light of this earlier position, the Court denied the retroactive applicability of the Genocide Convention and concluded that considering the rules of the Convention as the basis of obligations related to acts committed before its ratification would contrast with Article 28 of the Vienna Convention.[63]

3.2 *The Effects of* jus cogens *on the Principle of Non-retroactivity*

Another issue concerns the relationship between the principle of non-retroactivity and *jus cogens*.

The doctrine has highlighted how *jus cogens* interfers with the strict application of intertemporal rules.[64] The need to connect the *application* of a treaty with the subsequent developments of the law—a need clearly stated with regard to *interpretation* of the treaties in Article 31(3)(c) of the 1969 Vienna Convention—is especially challenged by the evolution of *jus cogens*. Indeed, when a rule of *jus*

[59]Convention on the Non-Applicability of Statutory Limitations to War Crimes and Crimes Against Humanity, New York, 26 November 1968, in United Nations Treaty Series, vol. 754, p. 73; Article 1 provides: "No statutory limitation shall apply to the following crimes, irrespective of the date of their commission […]".

[60]European Convention on the Non-Applicability of Statutory Limitations to Crimes against Humanity and War Crimes, Strasbourg, 25 January 1974, in European Treaty Series, No. 82; Article 2 provides: "1. The present Convention applies to offences committed after its entry into force in respect of the Contracting State concerned. 2. It applies also to offences committed before such entry into force in those cases where the statutory limitation period had not expired at that time".

[61]International Court of Justice, *Questions relating to the Obligation to Prosecute or Extradite (Belgium v. Senegal)*, Judgment, 20 July 2012, ICJ Reports 2012, p. 422 et seq.

[62]Convention against Torture and Other Cruel, Inhuman or Degrading Treatment or Punishment, New York, 10 December 1984, in United Nations Treaty Series, vol. 1465 p. 85.

[63]For a critical anlysis of the judgment, see Akhavan (2015).

[64]Kotzur (2008), who interprets intertemporal law as an issue of temporal scope of application of law.

cogens is involved, the stability of a rule should be revaluated in favour of the current concept of law and justice.[65]

In light of these assumptions, it is worth considering whether a norm of *jus cogens* may restrict the principle of non-retroactivity, determine exceptions to the latter or, even, exclude its application.

In fact, one could argue that the prohibition of genocide might, as a norm of *jus cogens*, exclude the application of the principle of non-retroactivity and, therefore, entail the retroactive application of the Genocide Convention to events that occurred before its entry into force.

With regard to the rule(s) concerning genocide, the elements in favour of its peremptory nature are manifold.[66]

The ILC addressed the issue of the interaction between a norm of *jus cogens superveniens* and a treaty in the VCLT. According to the VCLT, in case of conflict

---

[65] *Ibidem*, who referred to the case of International Court of Justice, *South West Africa (Ethiopia v. South Africa; Liberia v. South Africa)*, Second Phase, Judgment, 18 July 1966, ICJ Reports 1966, p. 6 as an example of cases where there has been a change in the intertemporal rule with the aim to protect human dignity.

[66] The Draft Articles on the Law of Treaties with commentaries, in Yearbook of the International Law Commission, 1966, vol. II, p. 248, enumerated genocide, among other examples, as "one of the most obvious and best settled rules of jus cogens" in order to better explain the nature and aim of article 50. More than thirty years later, the ILC mentioned again the prohibition of genocide as an example of *jus cogens* in the commentary to article 40 of its Draft Articles on States' Responsibility, which disciplines serious breach by a State of obligations arising under peremptory norms of general international law. As evident by the contest, this article, as well as the commentary, concerns State responsibility and not individual responsibility. With specific regard to the peremptory character of this norm, the Draft Articles, p. 112–113 stressed the support of a "number of decisions by national and international courts" and the commentary to Article 26 of the same Draft Articles refers to the prohibition of genocide as one of the few examples of *jus cogens* norm clearly accepted and recognized (Ivi, p. 85). Moreover, the *jus cogens* nature of the prohibition has been famously upheld by the International Court of Justice. In *Congo v. Rwanda, Case Concerning Armed Activities On the Territory of the Congo (Democratic Republic of the Congo v. Rwanda)*, Jurisdiction of the Court and Admissibility of the Application, Judgment, 3 February 2006, ICJ Reports 2006, para. 64 the Court first underlined the *erga omnes* nature of principles enshrined by the Convention and then stressed – in an *obiter dictum* – the *jus cogens* character of the prohibition of genocide. Furthermore, the International Court of Justice in its *Reservations to the Convention* on *Genocide, Advisory Opinion*, 28 May 1951, ICJ Reports 1951, p. 23 already emphasized: "the universal character both of the condemnation of genocide and of the co-operation required 'in order to liberate mankind from such an odious scourge' (Preamble to the Convention)". Although this is a common opinion among scholars (Wouters and Verhoeven 2005), the recognition of this nature by the International Court of Justice is especially relevant if one considers the caution shown by the Court in explicitly qualifying rules as norms of *jus cogens*; as underlined by Bianchi (2008), the International Court of justice refers in this case for the first time to the notion of *jus cogens*, precisely with regard to the prohibition of genocide. Finally, according to the ICJ State responsibility for genocide refers not only to the obligation to prevent and repress acts of genocide, but also to the obligation not to commit acts of genocide (*Application of the Convention on the Prevention and Punishment of the Crime of Genocide (Bosnia and Herzegovina v. Serbia and Montenegro)*, Judgment, 26 February 2007, ICJ Reports 2007) and it would be "paradoxical" to exclude the obligation not to commit acts of genocide from the content of the norm.

between a new peremptory norm and a treaty, the last is terminated *ex nunc.*[67] Thus, effects *ex tunc* of the new norm are excluded: even if the new norm is peremptory, it does not have retroactive effect. In the commentary to the Draft Article on the Law of Treaties, the ILC emphasized several times that "a rule of *jus cogens* does not have retroactive effects".[68] Peremptory rules, therefore, do not give rise to an exception to the application of the rule of non-retroactivity.

If this is true for the effects of a treaty, it is more so for a State's responsibility to arise. In this area, the principle *tempus regit actum* is clearly established and, as already mentioned, may be considered an expression of both the necessity of the State consent and the certainty of the law. Moreover, if a State could be held responsible for an act considered lawful at the time it was carried out, because of the later formation of a new norm of *jus cogens*, this may seriously threaten the stability of international relations and increase the number of disputes for past events.

As stressed by the arbitrator Max Huber in the *Island of Palmas* case,

> a juridical fact must be appreciated in the light of the law contemporary with it, and not of the law in force at the time when a dispute in regard to it arises or fails to be settled.[69]

While the progressive development of the law is an essential element to fulfill the changing needs of the society, and should lead the evolutionary interpretation of treaties, this evolution cannot entail a retroactive application of the law, even in case of *jus cogens* norms.

The legality of an act must be evaluated in the light of the law in force when the act was committed. It follows that States' obligation not to commit genocide, notwithstanding the peremptory nature of the rule, cannot imply retroactive application of the Genocide Convention.[70]

This conclusion leaves aside every discussion about the nature of *jus cogens* as a concept based on natural law, existing from time immemorial. Following this approach, the responsability of Turkey would be based on the breach of a peremptory norm on the prohibition of genocide in force during the Armenian massacres, and not on an exception to the principle of non-retroactivity of the Genocide Convention because of the peremptory nature of the rule involved.

---

[67]Article 64 of Vienna Convention provides "If a new peremptory norm of general international law emerges, any existing treaty which is in conflict with that norm becomes void and terminates."

[68]Draft Articles on the Law of Treaties with commentaries, p. 261. The Commission reaffirmed this principle in the commentary to articles 50, 61 and 67: "in the view of the Commission, there is no question of the present article having retroactive effects."

[69]Permanent Court of Arbitration, *Island of Palmas case (United States v. Netherlands)*, 4 April 1928, in Reports of International Arbitral Awards, vol. II, p. 845.

[70]Draft Articles on Responsibility of States for Internationally Wrongful Acts, with commentaries 2001, in Yearbook of the International Law Commission, 2001, vol. II, Part Two, p. 58.

3.3 The Nineteenth-Century Treaties for the Protection of Minorities

A different argument used to endorse the retroactive application of the Genocide Convention is its declaratory nature of pre-existing international law.[71] Such an argument relies on the fact that in 1969 the UN Commission on Human Rights clarified that the Genocide Convention was a codification of general international law. The same view was shared by the International Court of Justice in the *Reservations to the Genocide Convention* case,[72] as well as by eminent scholars.[73]

Under the *tempus regit actum* principle, enshrined in Article 13 of the Draft Articles on State Responsibility, it would be necessary to verify whether a rule imposing upon States the obligation not to commit acts of genocide was already in force in 1915.[74] It is beyond the scope of this paper to analyse the existence of a rule of general international law[75] in force in that period, but some elements can be inferred from the conventional rules provided for in nineteenth-century treaties.

A number of bilateral and multilateral treaties on the protection of minorities bound States and particularly the Ottoman Empire. Among them, one can recall the Treaty of San Stefano between Russia and the Ottoman Empire of 1878;[76] the Cyprus Convention between Britain and Turkey of the same year;[77] the Treaty of

[71]De Zayas (2010), p. 13. This argument was dismissed by the International Court of Justice in the case *Application of the Convention on the Prevention and Punishment of the Crime of Genocide (Croatia v. Serbia)*, Judgment, 3 February 2015, ICJ Reports 2015, para. 95.

[72]International Court of Justice, *Reservations to the Convention on the Prevention of Genocide*, Advisory Opinion, 28 May 1951, ICJ Reports 1951, p. 23.

[73]Robinson (1960); Kuper (1984); Jescheck (2000). However, they refer to the crime of genocide and not to State responsibility for genocide. With regard to State responsibility De Zayas (2010), p. 39 specified that: "What the Genocide Convention added to the existing body of international law was an affirmative obligation on States parties to make provision for effective penalties for all acts punishable under the Convention (article V), a duty to prosecute (article VI) by a competent national tribunal or by an international criminal court to be established".

[74]The same view was shared thereafter by the Institute de Droit International in its resolution The Intertemporal Problem in Public International Law, 1975, according to which "Unless otherwise indicated, the temporal sphere of application of any norm of public international law shall be determined in accordance with the general principle of law by which any fact, action or situation must be assessed in the light of the rules of law that are contemporaneous with it".

[75]Lattanzi, in this book.

[76]Article XVI of the Treaty of San Stefano stated that: "the Sublime Porte engages to carry into effect, without further delay, the improvements and reforms demanded by local requirements in the provinces inhabited by Armenians, and to guarantee their security from Kurds and Circassians".

[77]In Article I of the Cyprus Convention the Ottoman Empire promised to "introduce necessary reforms, to be agreed upon later between the two Powers, into the government, and for the protection of the Christian and other subjects of the Porte in these territories".

Berlin of 1878.[78] This last treaty provided, at Article LXI, that the Ottoman Empire, also known as the Sublime Porte, had the responsibility to protect the security of the Armenian minority against Kurdish and Circassian threats.

The express reference to Armenians in some of these treaties bears testimony to the fact that the issue was already acknowledged at the international level, and that there was an obligation upon the Ottoman Empire to protect this minority. The aim to protect minority somehow anticipated the content of the prohibition of genocide, which, according to the Genocide Convention, refers to

> acts committed with intent to destroy, in whole or in part, a national, ethnical, racial or religious group.[79]

Some have proposed to interpret the provisions of the treaties concerning the protection of minorities in the light of the argument used by the International Court of Justice in the *Bosnia and Herzegovina v. Serbia and Montenegro* case, i.e. that it would be paradoxical to recognize the Turkish obligation to protect the Armenians and not to recognize a duty of the latter not to commit acts of genocide against them.[80] Moreover, according to this opinion, the perpetration of acts of genocide would be at variance with the purpose of the conventions mentioned.

This interpretation could facilitate the recognition of the international responsibility of Turkey towards other States parties to the relevant treaties. However, the responsibility of Turkey, in this case, does not descend from the retroactive application of the Genocide Convention, but directly from treaties in force at this time or from the breach of corresponding rules of general international law.

4 Concluding Remarks

The question of the applicability of the Genocide Convention to the Armenian massacres requires an evaluation of the temporal scope of the Convention, as well as of the nature of the obligation for States not to commit acts of genocide. The International Court of Justice has recognized the peremptory nature of the prohibition of genocide, and the present inquiry has taken such an assessment as authoritative.

The *ratione temporis* application of treaties in international law is governed by the principle of non-retroactivity, which only admits exceptions in cases where a different intention appears from the treaty or is otherwise established. With regard to the Genocide Convention, neither the text of the Convention, nor the preparatory

[78]Article LXI of the Berlin Treaty provided for the obligation upon the Ottoman Empire to "carry out, without further delay, the improvements and reforms demanded by local requirements in the provinces inhabited by the Armenians, and to guarantee their security against the Circassians and Kurds".

[79]Article II of the Genocide Convention.

[80]Roscini (2014).

works allow for the conclusion that the there is such an exception to non-retroactivity. Furthermore, the well-established principle of *tempus regit actum*, together with the fundamental aim to guarantee the stability of international relations and the certainty of law, excludes any exceptions to the rule of non-retroactivity, even when the norm at issue is a peremptory one.

The Genocide Convention cannot be applied retroactively at the time of the Armenian "massacres"; thus, the international responsibility of Turkey cannot be established on the ground of the Genocide Convention. However, as aforesaid, the exclusion of Turkey responsibility under the Genocide Convention does not affect its possible responsibility for breach of other conventional obligations, such as those arising from treaties for the protection of minorities.

It seems appropriate to conclude the present remarks by quoting the answer given by Schabas to Jean-Paul Sartre, in an imaginary dialogue:

> 'The fact of genocide is as old as humanity' wrote Jean-Paul Sartre. The law, however, is considerably younger.

References

Akhavan P (2015) Balkanizing jurisdiction reflections on Article IX of the genocide convention in Croatia v. Serbia. Leiden J Int Law 28:893–897

Aust A (2005) Handbook of international law. Cambridge University Press, Cambridge

Aust A (2006) Vienna convention on the law of treaties (1969). Max Planck Encyclopedia of Public International Law. https://doi.org/10.1093/law/epil/9780199231690/law-9780199231690-e1498

Bianchi A (2008) Human rights and the magic of *Jus Cogens*. Eur J Int Law 19:491–508

Bonafè B (2015) Responsabilità dello Stato e dell'individuo per crimine di genocidio: persistenti incertezze nella giurisprudenza della Corte internazionale di Giustizia. http://www.sidiblog.org. Accessed 3 May 2017

Brownlie I (1973) Principles of public international law. Clarendon Press, Oxford

Crawford J (2008) Brownlie's principles of public international law. Oxford University Press, Oxford

Della Morte G (2016) Bilanciamentro tra libertà di espressione e tutela della dignità del popolo armeno nella sentenza *Perinçek c. Svizzera* della Corte europea dei diritti umani. Rivista di diritto internazionale 99:183–189

De Zayas AJD (2010) The genocide against the Armenians 1915–1923 and the relevance of the 1948 genocide convention. Haigazian University, Beirut

Dumberry P (2014) The consequences of Turkey being the 'Continuing' state of the Ottoman Empire in terms of international responsibility for internationally wrongful acts. Int Crim Law Rev 14:261–273

Forlati S (2011) The legal obligation to prevent genocide: Bosnia v. Serbia and beyond. Polish Yearbook Int Law 31:189–205

Gaeta P (2007) On what conditions can a state be held responsible for genocide? Eur J Int Law 18:631–648

Jescheck H (2000) Genocide. In: Bernhardt R (ed) Encyclopaedia of public international law, vol 4. North Holland Publishing Company, North Holland, pp 541–544

Jennings QC R, Watts A (2008) Oppenheim's international law. Oxford University Press, Oxford

Kelsen H (1947) Will the judgment in the Nuremberg trial constitute a precedent in international law? Int Law Q 2:153–171

Kotzur M (2008) Intertemporal law. Max Planck Encyclopedia of Public International Law. https://doi.org/10.1093/law:epil/9780199231690/law-9780199231690-e1433?prd=epil
Kotzur M (2014) The temporal dimension: non-retroactivity and its discontents. In: Tams CJ, Tzanakopoulos A, Zimmermann A (eds) Research handbook on the law of treaties. Edward Elgar Publishing, Cheltenham, pp 153–186
Kuper L (1984) International action against genocide. Minority Rights Group, London
Lattanzi F (1983) Garanzie dei diritti dell'uomo nel diritto internazionale generale. Giuffrè, Milano
Lemkin R (1944) Axis rule in occupied Europe laws of occupation, analysis of government, proposals for redress, laws of occupation, analysis of government, proposals for redress. Carnegie Endowment for International Peace, Washington
Lobba P (2015) Holocaust denial before the European Court of human rights: evolution of an exceptional regime. Eur J Int Law 26:237–253
Milanovic M (2006) State responsibility for genocide. Eur J Int Law 17:553–604
Nollkaemper A (2003) Concurrence between individual responsibility and state responsibility in international law. Int Comp Law Q 52:615–640
Paddeu F (2015) Ghosts of genocides past? State responsibility for genocide in the former Yugoslavia. Camb Law J 74:198–201
Palmisano G (1994) Les causes d'aggravation de la responsabilité des États et la distinction entre 'crimes' et 'délits' internationaux. Revue Générale de Droit International Public 98:629–674
Robertson G (2010) Was there an Armenian genocide? Univ St. Thomas J Law Public Policy 4:83–126
Robinson N (1960) The genocide convention. A commentary. Institute of Jewish Affairs, New York
Rodas JG (1973) The doctrine of non-retroactivity of international treaties. Revista da Faculdade de Direito 68:341–360
Roscini M (2014) Establishing state responsibility for historical injustices: the Armenian case. Int Crim Law Rev 14:291–316
Ronzitti N (1978) La disciplina dello *jus cogens* nella convenzione di Vienna sul diritto dei trattati. Comunicazioni e studi 15:241–299
Rosenne S (1970) The temporal application of the Vienna convention of the law of treaties. Cornell Int Law J 4:1–24
Schabas WA (2000) Genocide in international law: the crimes of crimes. Cambridge University Press, Cambridge
Schabas WA (2010) Retroactive application of the genocide convention. Univ St. Thomas J Law Public Policy 4:36–59
Simon TW (1996) Defining genocide. Wis Int Law J 15:243–256
Spinedi M (1989) International crimes of state: the legislative history. In: Weiler J, Cassese A, Spinedi M (eds) International crimes of state: a critical analysis of the ILC's draft Article 19 on state responsibility. De Gruyter, Berlin, pp 7–138
Spinedi M (2002) State responsibility v. individual responsibility for international crimes: Tertium non Datur? Eur J Int Law 13:895–899
Tams JC (2014) Article I. In: Tams C, Berster L, Schiffbauer B (eds) Convention on the prevention and punishment of the crime of genocide, commentary. Verlag C. H. Beck oHG, Munich, pp 33–79
Wouters J, Verhoeven S (2005) The prohibition of genocide as a norm of Ius Cogens and its implications for the enforcement of the law of genocide. Int Crim Law Rev 5:401–416

Is Customary Law on the Prohibition to States to Commit Acts of Genocide Applicable to the Armenian Massacres?

Alessandra Gianelli

Contents

1 Introduction 126
2 The Prohibition for States to Commit Acts of Genocide 127
3 The Behavior of the Different States Involved During and After Metz Yeghern 134
4 Non Retroactivity of the Peremptory Rule 137
5 The Effects of the Peremptory Rule upon States' Contemporary Conduct 138
6 Conclusions 139
References 140

Abstract At the time of the massacres commonly known as *Metz Yeghern*, did some international unwritten rule exist regarding what is later defined as genocide? If not, does the subsequent coming into being of a customary, peremptory rule have any effect today for Turkey and for all the other contemporary States? The absence of a customary rule prohibiting States from committing genocides at the time of *Metz Yeghern* is demonstrated through the analysis of rulings of the International Court of Justice, the preparatory works of the International Law Commission's Articles on the Law of the Treaties and on State Responsibility, the preparatory works of the 1948 Genocide Convention and the behavior of the different States involved during and after 1915–1916 massacres. The current peremptory rule on the prohibition of genocide is neither retroactive nor applicable to many of the current behaviors of modern Turkey vis-à-vis Armenians and/or those past events, whose illegality is often questioned on different grounds.

A. Gianelli (✉)
University of Teramo, Teramo, Italy
e-mail: agianelli@unite.it

F. Lattanzi and E. Pistoia (eds.), *The Armenian Massacres of 1915–1916 a Hundred Years Later*, Studies in the History of Law and Justice 15,
https://doi.org/10.1007/978-3-319-78169-3_5

1 Introduction

The main facts commonly known as *Metz Yeghern* took place more than one hundred years ago, between 1915 and 1916, although massacres of Armenian in the Ottoman Empire had occurred, at various times, well before those years. A common argument among those who support the application of the prohibition against genocide to those events, is that, while not explicitly qualified as such at the time, genocide was already acknowledged as a violation of fundamental tenets among Nations.[1] According to this view, the subsequent Convention for the Prevention and Suppression of Genocide (1948) only confirmed, as it indeed declares,[2] prior rules. Thus, Turkey should be held responsible—at the time and up to today—for the breach of such an international obligation.

Turkey does not dispute that massacres took place. Apart from the issue of identity/continuity between the Ottoman Empire under the Young Turks Government and the new Republic,[3] Turkey has rather contested the figures of victims usually quoted and, above all, the planning of a concerted action by the government then in power with the distinct intent to eliminate altogether an Armenian presence in the country.[4] It is therefore the qualification of genocide applied to the massacres, which is challenged, both on the historical and on the international law level.

Also, Turkey maintains that, because it subjected, after the war, persons accused of the massacres to criminal trials, it cannot still be held responsible for those events.[5] Turkey ratified the Genocide Convention in 1950, without attaching any reservation.

The present short essay will not discuss whether what happened in the Ottoman Empire can be described as genocide, according to the definition in use since 1944. I will only mention that many believe that it can, also in the light of the vast amount of documents unearthed up to today.[6] For the purpose of the following observations, I will simply assume that a genocide did occur. I will rather try to consider whether, at the time those facts occurred, some international unwritten rule existed regarding what is later defined as genocide and, if not, whether the subsequent

[1]De Zayas (2010).

[2]Convention of 9 December 1948, 78 U.N.T.S. 277, Article I.

[3]It is here assumed that the Ottoman Empire and Turkey share the same international personality, a much debated conclusion. A different conclusion is reached, for example, by the European Parliament, Resolution on a Political Solution to the Armenian Question, A2-33/87 No. 10.

The issue is not analyzed here in order to concentrate on the object of the present essay, as spelled out in the title of the contribution. For a review of the different positions, see the debate between Avedian (2012) and Tacar and Gauin (2012)

[4]For example, Tacar and Gauin (2012). On the evidence of the genocidal intent by Ottoman officials in *Metz Yeghern* see extensively Lattanzi, in this volume.

[5]Tacar and Gauin, 2012; see Rosanò, in this volume.

[6]In this volume, see Flores, Lattanzi.

coming into being of a customary, peremptory rule has any effect today for Turkey and for all the other States.

2 The Prohibition for States to Commit Acts of Genocide

A customary rule has, by definition, no precise date of coming into force. A quick, not unfailing but still reliable way to consider the rule in existence is to rely on such a finding authoritatively expressed by courts, mostly international but also national, and/or by codification works of the subject. A widespread treaty practice is also often considered an element proving the existence of the rule.[7] Any interpreter, whether a court, a Government's advisor or a scholar, will most likely indicate that at a certain time the rule is—or is not—in existence, without trying to set a specific moment for its entry into force. Peremptory norms are defined as customary norms[8]; their ascertainment is, in principle, subject to these rules of thumb.

Among unwritten rules, principles of various nature, not only recognized by civilized nations (Article 38(c) of the International Court of Justice (ICJ) Statute) but also of international law, are today evoked both by the ICJ case-law and by the doctrine. What seems to distinguish principles from rules, is the absence of a need to prove the existence of the former.[9] Principles appear to include norms of various content and determinacy, ranging from self-determination—considered, however, also a peremptory norm—to proportionality.

The prohibition of genocide includes more than one rule. The 1948 Convention expressly deals with the obligations to prevent and suppress conducts, which fall under the definition of genocide as a crime carried out by individuals.[10] However, the Convention has long been interpreted as implying also a prohibition for States against committing acts of genocide.[11] The ICJ has adopted this reading. In *Bosnia v. Serbia* (2007), the Court relied both on logical arguments, as well as on the "established purpose" of the Convention, the wording of Article IX and its *travaux préparatoires*, to conclude that

---

[7]The International Law Commission (ILC) has recently (2016) adopted on first reading sixteen Draft Conclusions on the Identification of customary international law (A/71/10, Chapter V). The ILC has followed the mainstream approach in defining what is customary international law and how we can ascertain it.

[8]Articles 53 and 64, Vienna Convention on the Law of Treaties (1969).

[9]Gaja (2013), para. 18.

[10]See the contribution of Marchesi, in this book.

[11]Lattanzi (1983), p. 225. However, criticisms about the notion of genocide as a wrongful act of State persisted until the judgments of the ICJ mentioned in the text: see, for ex., Schabas (2000), pp. 418 ff.

> the obligation to prevent genocide necessarily implies the prohibition of the commission of genocide[12]

and that the

> State is not exempted from its own responsibility for internationally wrongful conduct by the prosecution and punishment of the State officials who carried it out.[13]

More recently, in *Croatia v. Serbia* (2015), the Court identified Croatia's claim as the invocation of Serbia's responsibility for the commission of acts of genocide[14]; and went on to deny that the Convention, even if confirming obligations *already* existing in international law, could be resorted to as a basis for its jurisdiction with regard to facts, which had occurred before the entry into force of the Convention for one party.[15]

Earlier on, in its 1951 Opinion, the Court had stated that "the principles underlying the Convention are principles which are recognized by civilized nations as binding on States, even without any conventional obligation".[16] The Court then added that the object of the Convention in safeguarding certain human groups is

> to confirm and endorse the most elementary principles of morality.[17]

In its later case-law, the Court has repeatedly referred to these passages as a recognition of the general international law character of rules prohibiting genocide.[18] Furthermore, in *Congo v. Rwanda* (2006), it was with regard to the prohibition of genocide that the Court first clearly endorsed the notion of peremptory norm.[19] In these various decisions, the ICJ has thus used both the term principle and the expression customary law in referring to the prohibition(s) of genocide. At one time, the Court has also declared that

> the Convention embodies principles that are part of customary international law.[20]

---

[12]ICJ Reports, 2007, p. 110 ff., para. 166.

[13]ICJ Reports, 2007, para. 173. The International Law Commission noticed, in its commentary to draft Article 19 adopted on first reading of the Draft Articles on State Responsibility, that "Punishment of those in charge of the State machinery who have [...] organized an act of genocide does not *per se* release the State itself from its own international responsibility for such acts". Yearbook of the International Law Commission 1976, Vol. II, Part Two, p. 104.

[14]ICJ Reports 2015, para. 99.

[15]ICJ Reports 2015, para. 99.

[16]ICJ Reports 1951, Reservations to the Convention on the Prevention and Punishment of the Crime of Genocide, p. 23.

[17]Ibidem. As evidence of this conclusion, the Court mentioned General Assembly res. 96 (I), where it is affirmed the intention of the United Nations to condemn and punish the crime of genocide. The resolution addresses only the crime of individuals.

[18]Barcelona Traction, ICJ Reports (1970), p. 33.

[19]ICJ Reports 2006, p. 31.

[20]Croatia v. Serbia, ICJ Reports 2015, para. 87.

The customary and peremptory nature of the prohibition for States to commit genocide had been first acknowledged by the International Law Commission (ILC). When the ILC introduced in its draft Articles on the Law of Treaties the notion of *jus cogens*, it mentioned in its commentary to the provision, which was to become Article 53 of the 1969 Vienna Convention, a treaty "contemplating [...] genocide" as an example of treaty that is void, because in conflict with a peremptory norm.[21] In the same provision, the ILC defined *jus cogens* as rules of general international law, dealing with a particular nature of subject-matter.[22] The Commission specified that the

> emergence of rules having the character of *jus cogens* is comparatively recent, while international law is in the midst of rapid development.[23]

The ILC mentioned again genocide among the examples of rules, the breach of which would give rise to international crimes of States, when working on the first reading of the State Responsibility draft Articles (1976).[24] On this occasion also, the ILC stressed the subject-matter of the obligations involved, and traced to the time following the Second World War the emergence of the view about a distinct regime of State responsibility for breaches of obligations of fundamental importance to the international community as a whole. When the ILC concluded the codification of State responsibility in 2001, the controversial definition of international crimes of States had disappeared. However, the commission of genocide was once more one of the examples of a serious breach of an obligation arising under a peremptory norm of general international law, which the ILC noted in its commentary to Article 40. The ILC added that such a conclusion about genocide was supported by national and international courts.[25] Those violations entail the consequences spelled out in Article 41, that is, obligations for all the States not to recognize as lawful situations created by such violations, nor to render aid or assistance in maintaining those situations. It is a well-supported idea, that *jus cogens* norms also give rise to *erga omnes* obligations. In this respect, their violations include the right of all the States involved to invoke the responsibility of the wrongdoing State (Articles 48, 54 of the ILC 2001 Draft Articles).

The 1948 Genocide Convention is today ratified by 147 States, thus enjoying wide support. The original signatory States between 1948 and 1949 were 41, the great majority of the international persons then in existence. During the preparatory works, it was frequently said that, apart from the Holocaust, genocides had repeatedly happened throughout history. The idea that genocide was already illegal, and that a future Convention would not introduce it *ex novo* was often voiced;

---

[21]Yearbook of the International Law Commission 1966, Vol. II, p. 248, para. 3.

[22]Ibidem, para. 2.

[23]Ibidem, para. 3.

[24]Yearbook of the International Law Commission 1976, Vol. II, Part Two, p. 95 ff., 101.

[25]Report of the International Law Commission on the work of its fifty-third session, 2001, p. 112–113.

mostly, it was a generic statement, which cannot be specifically referred to States' rather than to individuals' conduct.[26] Some declarations, though, were more precise, affirming for example that

> the obligation to ensure national suppression existed prior to any discussion of the convention on genocide.[27]

At the same time, the notion was also repeatedly shared that, aside from individuals, it was Governments, or collectivities, which committed genocide.[28] It was debated whether the Convention should address the conduct of States, in addition to the conduct of individuals. France proposed an amendment to the definition contained in Article II, according to which genocide

> is committed, encouraged or tolerated by the heads of a State.[29]

According to the French delegate,

> When the crime of genocide was committed, it was committed either directly by the Governments themselves or at their behest ... the Government's responsibility was in all cases implicated.[30]

The amendment was rejected, on the basis of the argument that there had been cases of genocide committed by military groups with no connection to Governments.[31] There is no record of States maintaining, at this point, that genocide could not be carried out by States. Rather, it was the possible exclusion of private parties from those responsible for genocide, which was the reason given for the vote against the French proposal. Some States admitted that

> the most serious cases [of genocide were those] where it was committed with the complicity of governments.[32]

The United States made a difference between the case in which organs of the State

> were themselves ready to commit the crime of genocide

---

[26]See, for instance, A/C.6/SR. 63, 30 September 1948, and the debate in A/C.6/SR. 67, 5 October 1948, A/C.6/SR.68, 6 October 1948, in particular United Kingdom, USSR, Yugoslavia, Uruguay; Cuba, A/C.6/SR. 73, 13 October 1948.

[27]France, A/C.6/SR. 80, 21 October 1948.

[28]South Africa, A/C.6/SR. 64, 1 October 1948; United Kingdom, A/C.6/SR. 64, 1 October 1948 and A/C.6/SR.68, 5 October 1948, A/C.6/SR. 69, 7 October 1948; Belgium, A/C.6/SR. 65, 2 October 1948 and A/C.6/SR.68, 6 October 1948; Lebanon, A/C.6/SR. 66, 4 October 1948; Panama, A/C.6/SR. 69, 7 October 1948; Belgium, A/C.6/SR. 73, 13 October 1948; Haiti, A/C.6/SR. 75, 15 October 1948; United States, A/C.6/SR. 78, 19 October 1948; France, A/C.6/SR. 80, 21 October 1948.

[29]A/C.6/224, 8 October 1948.

[30]A/C.6/SR. 78, 19 October 1948; in the same sense Philippines, A/C.6/SR.97, 9 November 1948.

[31]A/C.6/SR. 79, 20 October 1948; A/C.6/SR. 80, 21st October 1948.

[32]Ibidem, Iran; United Kingdom. See also Yugoslavia, A/C.6/SR. 80, 21 October 1948.

and that in which

> the State was incapable of protecting the victims. In the first case, the Government should be held responsible for the crime on the ground that it had participated in it directly; but in the second case, if the Government had been unable to prevent or suppress genocide, although it had taken all appropriate measures to do so, the question of international rather than State responsibility might arise […] On the other hand, if a State had not done all it could to prevent or punish the crime, international responsibility would come under consideration[33]

Such an approach was shared by the United Kingdom.[34]

This State proposed, with no success, to modify what would become Article III, in order to use a term more appropriate to States than "punishable". The United Kingdom observed that genocide was

> a crime which was customarily committed by States, Governments or government institutions.[35]

Later during the preparatory works, the United Kingdom submitted another amendment, this time to the future Article IV, which provided for States and governments' responsibility for breach of the Convention. In his role of delegate from that State, Fitzmaurice explained that

> when a head of State was guilty of genocide, it was in reality the State itself or the Government which committed the crime.[36]

This amendment too was rejected,[37] because of the difficulty for many delegates to conceive of a distinct State's responsibility while addressing the criminal responsibility of individuals, who could very well be heads of States or Governments.[38] The arguments given were that only physical, and not legal, entities

[33]USA, A/C.6/SR. 79, 20 October 1948.

[34]Ibidem.

[35]A/C.6/SR.84, 26 October 1948 (Fitzmaurice).

[36]A/C.6/SR.92, 5 November 1948; A/C.6/SR.93, 6 November 1948.

[37]A/C.6/SR.96, 9 November 1948.

[38]For example, the United States declared that it "did not share the opinion of the United Kingdom representative that genocide could be committed by juridical entities such as the State or the Government; in reality genocide was always committed by individuals. It was one of the aims of the convention on genocide to organize the punishment of that crime. It was necessary to punish perpetrators of acts of genocide, and not to envisage measures such as the cessation of imputed acts or payment of compensation". A/C.6/SR.93, 6 November 1948. Later, the United States stressed again "the necessity of remaining within realistic bounds. The aim of the convention was to ensure the suppression of genocide and the punishment of the culprits. It should therefore not contain provisions regarding the payment of reparations to the victims; that question belonged to another branch of the law". A/C.6/95, 8 November 1948. See, in the same vein, the statement by France, ibidem. See also Venezuela, A/C.6/95, 8 November 1948.

could commit acts of genocide, and that States could not be subjected to criminal sanctions.[39]

As is well-known, the amendment providing for the jurisdiction of the International Court of Justice in cases of States responsibility, presented again by the United Kingdom together with Belgium,[40] was instead approved.[41] The argument of the proponents was the same, i.e. that individuals'

> crimes were insignificant […] in comparison with the crimes committed by Governments, which involved millions of human beings, and nothing in the text before them permitted action to be taken against Governments". According to Belgium, the ICJ's jurisdiction would cover "all disputes relating to the direct responsibility of a State for the commission of such acts"[42]

Some States understood the provision as establishing the ICJ's jurisdiction in cases of responsibility arising from the breach of the obligations to prevent and repress the crime of genocide.[43] Many others, however, shared the view that it was

> obvious that if a State committed crimes of genocide, after having signed the convention, such an act would constitute a breach of the convention.[44]

It is interesting to note that the consequences of the violation of the Convention, which an international court might "order" in such a case, were for Fitzmaurice "cessation of those acts",[45] as well as reparation.[46] Other States too considered that a responsibility of a State would involve "reparations to be paid to victims".[47]

---

[39]In its explanation of vote, Turkey stated that it "had voted against the United Kingdom amendment […] because he had felt that … the amendment to article V was superfluous".

[40]A/C.6/SR. 100, 11 November 1948. The amendment, A/C.6/258, read: "Any dispute between the High Contracting Parties relating to the interpretation, application or fulfilment of the present Convention, including disputes relating to the responsibility of the State for any of the acts enumerated in articles II and IV, shall be submitted to the International Court of Justice, at the request of any of the High Contracting parties".

[41]A/C.6/SR.95, 8 November 1948; A/C.6/SR.104, 13 November 1948.

[42]Belgium, A/C.6/SR.95, 8 November 1948; United Kingdom, A/C.6/SR.96, 9 November 1948.

[43]Uruguay, A/C.6/SR.97, 9 November 1948.

[44]India, Cuba, A/C.6/SR.95, 8 November 1948. See also the statements given by Luxembourg, Ecuador, A/C.6/SR.96, 9 November 1948; Egypt, A/C.6/97, 9 November 1948; Netherlands, ibidem; Philippines, ibidem; Cuba, ibidem; Bolivia, ibidem; Poland, A/C.6/98, 10 November 1948. Such a responsibility was also the reason for some delegations (India) to vote against the amendment, A/C.6/SR.103, 12 November 1948.

[45]A/C.6/SR.92, 5 November 1948.

[46]A/C.6/SR.93, 6 November 1948; A/C.6/97, 9 November 1948. However, later in the debate, in answering to the Iranian statement, Fitzmaurice pointed out that "The cases of reparation mentioned by the Iranian representative did not occur in acts of genocide, because the offences were generally committed by the State against its nationals". A/C.6/SR.104, 13 November 1948.

[47]Sweden, A/C.6/SR.92, 5 November 1948; Belgium, A/C.6/SR.93, 6 November 1948, A/C./SR95, 8 November 1948. On the other hand, Luxembourg's representative, Mr. Pescatore, maintained that "Such responsibility would thus arise whenever genocide was committed by a State in the territory of another State. In that case, the State which had suffered damage would have a right to reparation": A/C.6/SR.103, 12 November 1948. Along the same line, the representative

But some States were very critical about the possibility that a State should be obliged to pay reparations for damages incurred by its own subjects.[48]

An insider's chronicle of the preparatory works, such as the one provided by Lemkin's papers, throws light on the political reasons for the many, contrasting positions the various States held during the debates, and on the multiple issues they were concerned about; they appear to have little to do with State's responsibility itself.[49]

As already mentioned, the ICJ has also considered these *travaux préparatoires* in its judgment *Bosnia v. Serbia* (2007), although only with reference to Article IX. The Court concluded, as noted, that

> Contracting Parties to the Convention are bound not to commit genocide, through the actions of their organs or persons or groups whose acts are attributable to them.[50]

Summing up, the case-law of the ICJ, the ILC codification works on the Law of Treaties as well as on State responsibility and the preparatory works of the 1948 Convention point out that: the prohibition against committing genocide applies to States; the rule is customary; it is today surely peremptory; the breach of the obligation not to commit genocide involves special consequences; these were spelled out by the ILC in Article 41 of the Draft Articles on State responsibility.

As for the crucial point of understanding *when* the prohibition came about, it has certainly been in existence since the aftermath of the Second World War. The universal condemnation which was expressed during the preparatory works of the Convention leaves little doubt about a customary counterpart of States' treaty obligations, and the responsibility for their breach. However, as the very idea of State's responsibility was emerging, its content was still the object of much uncertainty. It was probably only with the codification of the law of responsibility that the consequences of the breach of the prohibition to commit genocide—aside from obligations concerning individual criminal responsibility—became clearer.

---

of Iran noted that "In international law, a State asked for reparation of damages inflicted on its nationals by another State: but in the case of genocide, it was a question of injuries inflicted on citizens by citizens of the same State […] if a State were not directly but indirectly concerned, merely as signatory to the convention. If each State party to the convention were entitled to reparations, such a provision would obviously lead to abuse". A/C.6/SR.104, 13 November 1948.

[48]The U.S. delegate, upon voting in favour of the adoption of the Convention, declared with regard to Article IX: "If the words "responsibility of a State" were taken in their traditional meaning of responsibility towards another State for damages inflicted, in violation of the principles of international law, to the subjects of the plaintiff State; and if, similarly, the words "disputes […] relating to the […] fulfilment" referred to disputes concerning the interests of subjects of the plaintiff State, than those words would give rise to no objection. But if, on the other hand, the expression "responsibility of a State" were not used in the traditional meaning, and if it signified that a State could be sued for damages in respect of injury inflicted by it on its own subjects, then there would be serious objections to that provision". A/C.6/133, 2 December 1948.

[49]Cooper (2008).

[50]ICJ Reports, 2007, paras. 167, 175–179.

The 1948 Convention has a direct connection with other, former treaties. As the delegate of Greece put it during the preparatory works,

> The protection of groups was not a new idea. Treaties had already assured the protection of minorities. The convention on genocide was an extension of that protection to certain groups; that instrument would define genocide and would determine the degree to which its protection should be extended to cover minorities.[51]

The Ottoman Empire was party to various treaties, which included provisions on the protection of minorities and specifically of Armenians, at the time of *Metz Yeghern*,[52] although they might have been denounced at the break of the war.[53] A significant reaction by other States at that time to a perceived violation not only of a treaty, but also of a customary international obligation, or maybe an international principle, would be good evidence of the existence or emergence of a customary prohibition of (what would be later termed) genocide.

3 The Behavior of the Different States Involved During and After Metz Yeghern

The general outrage and condemnation, which accompanied *Metz Yeghern*, should be considered keeping in mind all of the above considerations. What strikes the present writer is that no mention was made, during the preparatory works of the 1948 Convention, of *Metz Yeghern* itself as a relevant precedent both for the definition of genocide and for its consequences.[54] Political considerations with regard to Turkey, one of the original Member States of the United Nations, might have been relevant.[55] However, the general impression is that many delegates had the feeling they were finally coming to legal terms with a long-lived, morally unspeakable but still only partially regulated conduct. State acts, which many

[51] A/C.6/SR. 74, 14 October 1948.

[52] On the treaties which contained provisions on the protection of minorities in force at the time of *Metz Yeghern*, see the paper by Lattanzi, in this volume.

[53] See Dadrian (1989), p. 221 ff., who argues that the Ottoman Empire might have justifiably invoked the break of the war as a cause of termination of those treaties.

[54] So much more in light of the works of Lemkin, who made proposals concerning a specific crime of killings of a specific racial or religious group to be persecuted on the international level, after having studied the trial of Soghomon Tehlirian for the assassination of the former Ottoman Interior Minister Talaat Pasha in Germany. Lemkin publicized these proposals already in 1933: Acts Constituting a General (Transnational) Danger Considered as Offences Against the Law of Nations, 5th Conference for the Unification of Penal Law, Madrid. http://preventgenocideinternational.org.

[55] As the US delegate noted with regard to the text of the preamble of the Convention, "It was to be hoped that all countries would eventually sign the convention and it would be easier for them to do so if no mention of the past activities of any particular country were included". A/C.6/SR.110, 18 November 1948.

delegates found even difficult to contemplate, appear among those aspects not formerly disciplined.

The various careful historical reconstructions available today about the conduct and positions of the different actors of *Metz Yeghern* are based, among other things, on the acts of the criminal proceedings, which took place in Turkey after World War I, as well as on diplomatic correspondence, military, political and intelligence files of the Ottoman Empire, the European Powers, and the United States. Besides, newspapers articles and book chronicles of the time shed further light on what happened. Evidence from this wealth of material toward the emergence of the notion of genocide as a crime of individuals is not straightforward, even in the presence of the common Entente Powers Declaration of 24 May 1915, which labeled *Metz Yeghern* as crimes against humanity and against civilization.[56]

Concerning the qualification of the behavior of the Ottoman Empire itself, as well as its consequences, the conduct of the various States is even more ambiguous. Certainly the public condemnations of the massacres were directed at the Turkish Government. In their joint Declaration of 24 May 1915, France, the British Empire and Russia declared all members of the Turkish government responsible. The US Ambassador went so far as to define the massacres "a campaign of race extermination", although in his communications with the State Department and not publicly.[57] However, it is not clear whether the Powers were addressing only the members of the Government as individually and criminally liable, or also the State as a whole as responsible on the international law level.

More significant for the focus of the present enquiry is the fact that the victorious Powers tried, through the Treaty of Sévres, to impose upon the defeated State, not only the trial of the individuals accused of crimes by the Powers themselves or a third body, but also reparations and restoration into their property for the victims of the massacres or delocation,[58] as well as obligations concerning the protection of the rights of minorities in the future.

However, later on these requests were foregone: the British Empire decided to exchange Ottoman prisoners charged with the crimes with its own war prisoners[59]; a general amnesty was declared by the Treaty of Lausanne, the only one ratified by Turkey with the Allied Powers[60]; mention of reparations to the victims of massacres

---

[56]See again Marchesi, in this volume.

[57]Such was the wording of a telegram from Henry Morgenthau Jr. to the Secretary of State on 16 July 1915. The telegram went on stating: "I believe nothing short of actual force which obviously United States are not in a position to exert would adequately meet the situation".

[58]The Treaty of Sévres (Article 144) contained detailed provisions about the restoration of property to "Turkish subjects of non-Turkish race who have been forcibly driven by their homes by fear of massacre or any other form of pressure". The Treaty was never ratified by Turkey.

[59]The other Powers may have desisted from similar intentions even before the British Empire: Robertson 2009–2010, p. 87.

[60]Amnesty Declaration attached to the Lausanne Treaty. Other treaties concluded by Turkey (Treaty of Kars (1921) with Armenia, Azerbaijan and Georgia; Treaty of Ankara (1921) concluded by Turkey and France) included general amnesties for facts subsequent to *Metz Yeghern*.

or delocation completely disappeared within such Treaty. Only the protection of minorities remained. But some historians maintain that, when the Treaty of Lausanne was concluded, minorities had practically disappeared from the territory of the Republic of Turkey.[61]

Once again, political considerations concerning the future and specifically individual relations with Turkey were the significant factor in the decisions of other States to cease from seeking something from the new Republic or doing something themselves concerning the Armenian massacre.[62] This is no particularly special or new case in the framework of international relations. For the purpose of the present observations, though, such practice offers no element towards the identification of a peremptory rule, whose violation, as the ILC spelled out, *requires* States to adopt certain conducts.

But the inconsistency of the conduct carried out by the Allied Powers is an obstacle even toward the identification of an emerging, ordinary customary rule, which by definition requires some common patterns of behavior. Because the conduct prescribed is one of abstention, there is no other chance for third States to implement a prohibition rule than at times of its violation. With regard to *Metz Yeghern*, instead, the mixed reaction by the Allied Powers did not go, in the end, much further than the official condemnations. One could argue that, given the common *opinio*, not much else was needed: the regime of consequences could have been the ordinary responsibility system, as today is clearly spelled out in Article 55 of the 2001 ILC Draft Articles. But it is precisely at that "grey" moment between a common awareness and the establishment of a customary norm, that something more than verbal condemnations is needed, in order to define a proper rule. Otherwise, an easy objection is that those condemnations are merely moral.[63]

Another possible ground for invoking the responsibility of the Sublime Porte for its own conduct could have been the appeal to humanitarian principles. The applicability of such principles, on the basis of the Martens clause, is maintained elsewhere in this volume.[64] The sparse action, if not inaction, of the victorious Powers in this context, on a proper legal basis, is all the more telling about the identification of a specific obligation.

The only element which remains relevant about the Armenian massacres, in view of the emergence of an unwritten rule, is the general outcry which accompanied and followed it, as well as the recognition of the seriousness of those facts, at

---

[61] Avedian (2012), p. 809.

[62] As Avedian (2012), p. 804, puts it, "the major power policies of securing economic and political interests simply outweighed the issue of pursuing the question of punishment for Armenian massacres". See extensively Dadrian (1989), p. 221 ff. On the other hand, Tacar and Gauin (2012), p. 828, maintain that the reason for the release of the Ottoman officials imprisoned in Malta by British forces in 1919–1921 was the absence of any evidence of their involvement in the massacres.

[63] Schabas (2010), p. 57, reaches this conclusion too.

[64] See the contribution by Lattanzi.

least at one time, by Turkey itself.[65] Because there was no specific invocation of treaties, and because Armenians were Ottoman subjects, the condemnation discloses a relatively new international concern for the times. This concern would, in part, influence the customary rule prohibiting States from committing genocide in later years.[66] When genocide appeared again in Europe just about two decades later, the international community was ready for embracing proper rules.

The (embarrassed?) silence about *Metz Yeghern* during the preparatory works of the Genocide Convention seems then justified. The Armenian massacres could not be identified as a relevant precedent towards the emergence of a legal regime of consequences for what was being termed in 1948 as genocide, with regard to State responsibility.

4 Non Retroactivity of the Peremptory Rule

The highly moral content of the prohibition of genocide by States may give rise to the question, whether the customary and peremptory rule in force nowadays has any retroactive effect. If such were the case, and all the requirements of genocide were found to have occurred, Turkey could be responsible today for what happened one century ago.[67]

Peremptory rules are not retroactive. This clearly emerges already from the Vienna Convention on the Law of Treaties, which introduced the notion of *jus cogens*. In the Convention, the conflict of a treaty with an existing peremptory rule is a ground for its invalidity (Article 53), while the contrast with a supervening peremptory rule (Article 64) is a cause of termination of the treaty, which precludes any effects only *ex nunc*. The Vienna Convention deals with a conflict of rules, a question different from the one examined here. However, it is clear that the solution given by Article 64 is based upon the non-retroactivity of *jus cogens*.

Such is also the opinion of the ILC, as spelled out in the commentary to Article 13 of the Draft Articles on State Responsibility. The Article requires that an international obligation be in force at the time the act occurs, for it to be a breach. The provision does not foresee any exception. The commentary explains that

---

[65]As illustrated by Lattanzi, above, in interpreting Articles 142 ff. of the Treaty of Sèvres. Also, the exercise of Turkish jurisdiction and the sentencing of public officials immediately at the end of WWI may be taken as an establishment and recognition of what happened.

[66]Dadrian (1989), p. 322, puts it as "the Armenian experience of noble talk without substantive action". De Zayas (2010), p. 34 ff., reaches a different conclusion, regrettably with not much evidence to his avail. Schabas (2010), p. 47–48, appears to reason along the lines here exposed, with regard to the crime of individuals.

[67]On the different question of the retroactive application of the Genocide Convention, see Cipolletti, in this volume.

> even when a new peremptory norm of general international law comes into existence … this does not entail any retrospective assumption of responsibility.[68]

It cannot, thus, be maintained that the imperative nature of the prohibition of genocide allows for its application to facts, which occurred some decades before its coming into being. This also implies, that one cannot invoke the obligations of third States, spelled out in Article 41 of the 2001 Draft Articles on State Responsibility. Those obligations follow the serious breach of obligations deriving from peremptory norms. As *Metz Yeghern* did not involve a breach of an obligation arising from a peremptory rule of its time, those consequences are not applicable.[69]

5 The Effects of the Peremptory Rule upon States' Contemporary Conduct

A different matter is the question, whether the rule in force today involves obligations concerning Turkey and other States with regard to their contemporary conduct. In other words, the question which remains to be addressed here, is whether the *historical* qualification of genocide of *Metz Yeghern* involves international legal consequences.

Because other contributions deal specifically with the various issues, it is here offered only a general framework of reference. As for the denial of genocide,[70] the peremptory norm may require States to adopt certain criminal rules in their internal legal systems, in view of the prevention or punishment of genocide. A right/obligation to remember might be connected to that norm too.[71] As already mentioned, this is however a different rule from the one that prohibits States from committing genocide.

As for the possible international law bases for reparations to the heirs of the victims of the massacres,[72] it is interesting to note that a quasi-official Turkish position admits that, when a claim for restitution or reparation connected to the Armenian massacres is presented with adequate evidence, Turkish courts will uphold it, even after a century.[73] Such position does not rest upon the qualification

---

[68]Report of the International Law Commission, 53rd session (2001), A/56/10, at 135.

[69]De Zayas (2010) thinks otherwise.

[70]See the papers by Spatti, Leotta, Latino.

[71]I leave it to other authors to consider, whether the denial of an historically proven genocide is a breach of the obligation to prevent genocide.

[72]On this aspect, see the paper by Donat-Cattin in this volume.

[73]Tacar and Gauin (2012), p. 832–833. The European Parliament Resolution on a Political Solution to the Armenian Question, 1987, declares at point 2 that "the present Turkey cannot be held responsible for the tragedy experienced by the Armenians of the Ottoman Empire and stresses that neither political nor legal or material claims against present-day Turkey can be derived from the recognition of this historical event as an act of genocide".

of genocide of the massacres; however, it seems to imply that the passing of time has not affected the individual claims arising from those events. This approach calls to mind that there is no statute of limitations for international crimes, as clearly established in various instruments and, lately, in Article 29 of the Statute of the International Criminal Court. More to the point, such a solution is maintained by various instruments concerning reparations to victims of gross violations of human and humanitarian rights.[74] For the purpose of the present remarks, the Turkish position—if clearly established—might be considered an admission of the gravity of the massacres and of the necessity to provide for reparations, notwithstanding the time passed.

The present rule on the prohibition of genocide could be applied, if it were demonstrated that the genocide was continuing today. Certainly, no acts like those described in Articles II or III of the Genocide Convention are being carried out nowadays by Turkey. Rather, one should consider whether a notion of "cultural genocide" could be applied, on the basis of the historical qualification of *Metz Yeghern*, to that treatment of the Armenian cultural heritage, under form of destruction or reconversion of churches and properties, which is denounced by the Armenian communities as going on up to today. The inquiry should also address, whether a rule on the prohibition of cultural genocide would have the same nature and imply the same consequences as those provided today for genocide.[75]

6 Conclusions

The conclusion about the absence of a customary rule prohibiting States from committing genocides at the time of *Metz Yeghern* may appear a rather somber one. This, however, does not amount to denying that other rules might be applicable to the massacres.[76] Also, it does not imply that what happened may not be qualified as genocide.

Justice Cardozo once borrowed Lauterpacht's expression in observing how difficult it was to clearly identify when international law emerges from

> a twilight existence during which it is hardly distinguishable from morality or justice.[77]

[74]See, for example, Basic Principles and Guidelines on the Right to a Remedy and Reparation for Victims of Gross violations of International Human Rights Law and Serious Violations of International Humanitarian Law, UN General Assembly resolution 60/147, 16 December 2005.

[75]See Mucci's contribution in the present volume.

[76]As maintained by Lattanzi, in this volume.

[77]The words are Justice Cardozo's, in *New Jersey v. Delaware*, 1934, U.S. Supreme Court Report, vol. 291, 361 ff., at 383, quoting Lauterpacht, The Function of Law in the International Community, 1933. 110, 255.

All of the few, unchallenged *jus cogens* norms and most certainly the prohibition of genocide, have a very strong ethical content; here, twilight may indeed be very hardly distinguishable from daylight. At the same time, because of such a strong foundation, unwritten rules of this sort may be quicker to emerge than other rules, and may be easily assumed as principles. If *Metz Yeghern* does not involve Turkey's responsibility under the head of commission of genocide, it certainly greatly contributed to raising a universally shared opinion, which not too many years later, in the aftermath of yet another genocide, brought to the emergence of a customary, peremptory norm.

References

Avedian V (2012) State identity, continuity, and responsibility: The Ottoman Empire, the Republic of Turkey and the Armenian genocide. Eur J Int Law 23:797–820
Cooper J (2008) Raphael Lemkin and the struggle for the genocide convention. Palgrave Macmillan, London
Dadrian VN (1989) Genocide as a problem of national and international law: The World War I Armenian case and its contemporary legal ramifications. Yale J Int Law 14:221–334
de Zayas AJD (2010) The genocide against the Armenians 1915–1923 and the relevance of the 1948 genocide convention. Haigazian University, Beirut
Dumberry P (2014) The consequences of Turkey being the 'Continuing' state of the Ottoman Empire in terms of international responsibility for internationally wrongful acts. Int Crim Law Rev 14:261–273
Flores M (2015) Il genocidio degli Armeni. Il Mulino, Bologna
Gaeta P (2007) On what conditions can a state be held responsible for genocide? Eur J Int Law 18:631–648
Gaja G (last updated May 2013) General principles of law. Max Planck Encyclopedia of Public International Law
Lattanzi F (1983) Garanzie dei diritti dell'uomo nel diritto internazionale generale. Giuffrè, Milano
Robertson G (2009–2010). Was there an Armenian genocide? Univ St. Thomas J Law Public Policy 4:83–127
Roscini M (2014) Establishing state responsibility for historical injustices: the Armenian case. Int Crim Law Rev 14:291–316
Schabas WA (2000) Genocide in international law: the crime of crimes. Cambridge University Press, Cambridge
Schabas WA (2010) Retroactive application of the genocide convention. Univ St. Thomas J Law Public Policy 4:36–59
Tacar P, Gauin M (2012) State identity, continuity, and responsibility: The Ottoman Empire, the Republic of Turkey and the Armenian genocide: a reply to Vahagn Avedian. Eur J Int Law 23:821–835
Winter J (2003) America and the Armenian genocide of 1915. Cambridge University Press, Cambridge
Symposium: State Responsibility (1999) Eur J Int Law 10:339–460

Part II
Which Possible Legal Consequences?

Metz Yeghern and the Origin of International Norms on the Punishment of Crimes

Antonio Marchesi

Contents

1 Introduction 144
2 The Start of Metz Yeghern and the Declaration of 24 April 1915 145
3 The Deportations to Syria and the Second Phase of Metz Yeghern 147
4 Post-war Developments at National Level: The Commissions of Enquiry and the Domestic Trials 148
5 The International Reactions: The "Commission on Responsibility of Authors of the War and on Enforcement of Penalties" and the "Dissenting Opinion" by Its American Members 151
5.1 Applicable Law 152
5.2 Personal Responsibility 153
5.3 Jurisdiction and Appropriate Tribunal 153
5.4 The "Dissenting Opinion" by the American Members 155
6 Continued: The Provisions on "Penalties" in the Treaty of Sèvres and Their Subsequent Abandonment 157
7 Concluding Remarks 159
References 160

Abstract This essay does not specifically address the issue of the Armenian massacres of 1915–1916 as genocide. Rather, it considers whether and to what extent the international reactions caused by those events represent an advancement towards the development of the broader notion of international crimes and, perhaps more interestingly, of a special legal regime applicable to the punishment of crimes falling within that notion. For this purpose, after briefly considering the domestic reactions to the 1915–1916 massacres—i.e. the establishment of commissions of enquiry and the celebration of trials—it moves on to examine the reactions they triggered at the international level, including: the Joint Declaration by the Allied Powers of 24 May 1915; the proposals on applicable law, personal responsibility

A. Marchesi (✉)
University of Teramo, Teramo, Italy
e-mail: a.marchesi@mclink.it

F. Lattanzi and E. Pistoia (eds.), *The Armenian Massacres of 1915–1916 a Hundred Years Later*, Studies in the History of Law and Justice 15,
https://doi.org/10.1007/978-3-319-78169-3_6

and appropriate tribunal made by the Commission on Responsibility of Authors of the War and on Enforcement of Penalties (the so-called "Commission of the Fifteen"), set up in the context of the Paris Peace Conference; the provisions in part VII, and in Article 230 in particular, of the Peace Treaty of Sévres. The fact that the prevailing interests of the victors of World War I, together with the strong resistance of the new Turkish leadership, prevented the promises contained in those documents from becoming reality does not mean that these did not lay the ground for the construction of a truly innovative legal framework which was to become reality, sadly, only after the end of another world war.

1 Introduction

The fact that the Armenian massacres of 1915 and 1916 occurred several years before the notion of genocide came into existence has given rise to the well-known debate on the applicability of that specific notion—and of international norms on genocide—to those events. While it is now broadly accepted that the facts known as *Metz Yeghern* present all the constitutive elements of genocide and that there is no reason not to describe them as such (i.e. to use new language to describe facts occurred before that language came into being),[1] the question of whether the specific obligations provided for under the Genocide Convention of 1948 or other international norms dependant on the qualification of given events as genocide are applicable retroactively to those facts is more problematic.[2]

Having said this, while the issue of their qualification as genocide is the most politically charged among all issues concerning the Armenian massacres, the latter are of relevance to international legal studies for reasons which go beyond that specific point. One of the questions which arises in relation to the 1915–1916 events is whether and to what extent the reactions they provoked internationally represent an advancement towards the development of the broader notion of international crimes—and of a special legal regime applicable to crimes falling within that category—several decades before it received a decisive impulse through the establishment of the two post-World War II tribunals in Nuremberg and Tokyo. Indeed, whatever opinion one may have concerning their *ex post* qualification as acts of genocide, it is quite clear that the Armenian Massacres were considered, during and in the aftermath of the events themselves, to be particularly egregious crimes, worthy as such of a response on behalf of the international community.

[1]This point is thoroughly discussed in Lattanzi, in this volume.

[2]Applicability of the Genocide Convention and/or other legal norms specifically referred to genocide to the Armenian massacres is discussed in Cipolletti and in Gianelli, in this volume.

In the following pages, we will discuss whether and how the way in which the issue of individual responsibility for *Metz Yeghern* was approached after World War I is a step towards the development of an international regime for the punishment of crimes of international concern.

2 The Start of Metz Yeghern and the Declaration of 24 April 1915

The start of *Metz Yeghern*, which was preceded by a number of attacks on the Armenian population carried out between the end of the nineteenth and the beginning of the twentieth century, is generally set by historians at 24 April 1915, when over 2000 members of the Armenian élite were arrested in Constantinople. This operation, apparently aimed at depriving the Armenians of their political and intellectual leadership, was followed, soon after, by the first deportations of Armenians in a number of provinces of the Ottoman Empire. The deportations of Armenians continued throughout the summer of 1915 to the point that by the end of July a large part of Cilicia had been "cleaned up".[3] The initial steps of *Metz Yeghern* met with a rather forceful international reaction which took the form of a joint declaration by the Allied powers—France, Great Britain and Russia—made public on 24 May 1915.

The initiative to produce a statement was taken by Russia, which proposed a text to the governments of France and Great Britain. In the course of the negotiations which took place between the three governments two changes were made to the initial draft. First, the expression "crimes against Christianity and civilization" was replaced with "crimes against humanity and civilization". The reference to Christianity, while probably addressed to the authorities and to the public in neutral countries such as Italy or the United States and possibly to a part of the German population as well, would have given the impression that the three countries were acting exclusively on religious grounds, with a view to protecting Christian populations only.

The second amendment to the text proposed by Russia is the replacement of the final words "in the massacres of the Armenians" with the words "in such massacres" with a view to conveying a more general scope to the statement.

The wording of the final text of the declaration is as follows:

> For about a month the Kurd and Turkish populations of Armenia has been massacring [killing]Armenians with the connivance [approval] and often assistance of Ottoman authorities. Such massacres took place in middle April at Erzerum, Dertchun, Eguine, Akn, Bitlis, Mush, Sassun, Zeitun, and throughout Cilicia. Inhabitants of about one hundred

[3]For a more detailed account of the facts and historical context of *Metz Yeghern*, which are only briefly mentioned in this essay, see *inter alia* Dadrian (1995); Bloxham (2007); Kévorkian (2006); Akçam (2012); Flores (2015).

> villages near Van were all murdered. In that city [the] Armenian quarter is besieged by Kurds. At the same time in Constantinople Ottoman Government ill-treats inoffensive [harmless] Armenian population. In view of those new crimes of Turkey against humanity and civilization, the Allied governments announce publicly to the Sublime-Porte that they will hold personally responsible [for] these crimes all members of the Ottoman government and those of their agents who are implicated [involved] in such massacres.

The Declaration of 24 May 1915 deserves attention for a number of reasons, beginning with the description of the Armenian massacres as "crimes [of Turkey] against humanity and civilization". It is apparently the first time in which the expression "crimes against humanity", later to become part of the Nuremberg triad, is used in an international law context.[4] It indicates, as a minimum, that the Allied Powers consider those crimes to be a matter of international concern, a circumstance which, if the statement is to be more than purely rhetorical, implies legal consequences.

The other notable element in the Declaration is, indeed, the indication of the possible legal effects which its authors attach to the qualification of the events as "crimes against humanity". These are set out in the last sentence of the Declaration, in which the Allies affirm their intention to "hold personally responsible" the individual authors of those crimes—meaning that they intend bringing them to justice or, at least, to ensure that they are brought to justice. This part of the statement has in fact implications with respect to two different aspects: on the one hand, jurisdiction, on the other, immunities and personal responsibility of State organs. Insofar as jurisdiction is concerned, it should be pointed out that a group of states without a direct connection with the crimes—on account either of territory or of the nationality of those involved—are stating their intention to take action in view of the punishment of the authors of those crimes. As for immunities and personal responsibility, by clarifying that they intend to bring to justice state organs at all levels, including both members of Government and their agents, the authors of the Declaration are saying that they will not consider immunity, functional immunity in particular, as being applicable in the case in question.

In short, the Declaration includes a combination of elements which suggest a move towards the development of special rules which are considered to be justified by the egregious nature and the international relevance of the crimes committed by Turkey against the Armenian population in 1915.

[4]Schabas (2000), p. 16–17. On the Joint Declaration of 24 May 1915 see also Leotta (2013), p. 39–40.

3 The Deportations to Syria and the Second Phase of Metz Yeghern

The reaction of the Allied Powers to the beginning of the massacres did not, unfortunately, prevent these from continuing. Actually, according to some historians the Declaration of 24 May is likely to have contributed to the continuation of *Metz Yeghern*.[5] It is a fact that only a few days after the Declaration was made public a "temporary" law on deportation was adopted, providing a legal basis, at the domestic level, for the conduct of those involved—apparently in response, inter alia, to the fear that the Declaration, by referring to the responsibility of all the agents implicated, could have caused in some of those taking part in the actions against the Armenians.

From August 1915 to July 1916, for almost a year, the plan to eradicate the Armenian presence from within the boundaries of the Ottoman Empire was carried out. Hundreds of thousands were deported and transferred to detention camps, mainly in the region of Aleppo in Syria. The legal framework provided by the law on deportation was supplemented by other acts including another "temporary" law, the law on expropriation and confiscation, which is important to the extent that, on the one hand, it undermines the argument of military necessity used by the Ottoman authorities to justify the deportations while, on the other, it contributes to render those deportations definitive, thus shedding more light on the nature and meaning of overall operation.

At this stage all Armenians, without distinction, came to be considered enemies to get rid of and were targeted by the "Special Organization" set up by the *Ittihad* party, by the army and by Kurdish and other armed bands and forcibly transferred to inhospitable areas. During the journey they were subjected to violence of all sorts, including torture and rape. The Minister of Interior's authorization to kill anyone who attempted to escape amounted to a blanket authorization to take life.

In the end only a part of the deportees eventually reached Syria, all the others having died as a result either of violence or of illness and lack of food. Thus, even if one were to accept the idea that the decision to deport the Armenian population was, initially, a decision simply to eliminate their presence within the Empire by carrying out a plan of ethnic cleansing, it nonetheless resulted in the physical elimination of the majority of the population concerned. Historians vary, in fact, in attributing this result to the different ways in which the plan was carried out in practice—the death toll varying depending on time and place—, and/or to elements

[5]Two main reasons are given for this: first, the circumstance that the Allies had already taken a clear position and passed judgment over the facts may have led to the belief that there was no longer any advantage in stopping or slowing down the implementation of the plan; second, the fact that the Declaration was viewed as an interference in the domestic affairs of the Ottoman Empire meant that, according to the Ottoman Government, it deserved to be both rejected and ignored in practice.

of the plan itself, such as the rule according to which the deportees could not amount to more than 10% of the population of the territory of destination.

By the end of 1915 about 900.000 Armenians had reached their destination in Syria (another 800.000 having died, while approximately 300.000 succeeded in avoiding deportation or in escaping before reaching the camps). This is where what is usually referred to as the second phase of the genocide took place. Starting in March 1916 and continuing throughout the year, it produced another 600.000 victims, 200.000 of which in the camp of Zor alone. The above-mentioned "10% rule" and the fear of what could have happened after the end of the war following the defeat of the Ottoman Empire are likely to have played a role in the decision to continue in the implementation of what—whether or not it was limited to deportation in the first phase—had by then become a plan of extermination proper.[6]

4 Post-war Developments at National Level: The Commissions of Enquiry and the Domestic Trials

A detailed description of the historical facts relating to *Metz Yeghern* is beyond the scope of this essay, as is any attempt to summarize the complex political and diplomatic issues which accompanied the final stages of World War I and the defeat and subsequent demise of the Ottoman Empire. Let us just mention that on 1 November 1918, shortly after an armistice was signed in Mudros, a German ship rescued the principal masterminds behind the genocide, allowing them to escape; and recall that, during the further twenty months which it took to sign the Treaty of Sèvres, on 10 August 1920, the massacre of the Armenians was the object of significant developments within the Empire: a lengthy and heated debate in the Ottoman parliament, followed by the establishment of commissions of enquiry and of military courts, in view of the celebration of trials against a number of individuals on account of the role they played in the events.

The Ottoman authorities were in fact well aware of the intention of the Allied Powers to address, in continuity with the approach adopted with the Declaration of 24 May 1915, the issue of punishment for the Armenian massacres in the context of the Peace Treaties, and were clearly anxious to divert any international move in this direction by dealing with it domestically as soon as possible. And while the lively debate which took place in Parliament towards the end of 1918 reflected the entire spectrum of positions on *Metz Yeghern*, ranging from full recognition to complete denial of the events, the main thrust, on which there appears to be common ground, was to attribute responsibility to specific individuals, thus avoiding the collective responsibility of Turkey and its population as a whole.

---

[6]This was confirmed during the main trial which took place in Istanbul against the leaders of the *Ittihad* party. See below.

Two different commissions of enquiry were set up in this context: the so-called Fifth Commission, established by Parliament, and the so-called Mazhar Commission, appointed by the Sultan. The Fifth Commission is interesting to the extent that its work suggests that all decisions concerning the massacres were in fact concentrated in the hands of three ministers, the involvement of the Ottoman Government as such being rather limited. In other words, emphasis was placed on the personal responsibility of few individuals.

However, the work of the Mazhar Commission turned out to be the more effective of the two. Its far-reaching powers of interrogation and arrest and its ability to collect a considerable amount of evidence from state officials helped to prepare the ground for the military trials that followed.

The first court martial to be set up, which became known as War Tribunal n.1, was established by the Sultan on 14 December 1918 with, as mentioned, the stated aim of anticipating efforts by the Allies to deal with the crimes committed during World War I internationally. This tribunal was soon complemented by the creation of other martial courts, both in Istanbul and in the provinces, which were subsequently the object of a number of decrees aimed at increasing their powers and improving their organization. Several trials were conducted before these courts in the period ranging from early 1919 to the middle of 1920. Trials against local officials were celebrated in different cities and death sentences were handed down and carried out against those defendants who were not at large. The execution of Mehmet Kemal, local governor in Yozgat, was met by a vast public reaction on the occasion of his funeral—a clear indication of the strong support that the forces behind the genocide still enjoyed among the population and the difficulties of acceptance met by the trials.

As for the main trial, celebrated against the high level leaders of the *Ittihad* party, it began in Istanbul on 28 April 1919 and lasted slightly over two months. The defendants were accused, among other things, of having created the "Special Organization" with the task of carrying out the deportation of the Armenian population. In fact, during the trial ample evidence emerged indicating that the term "deportation" was to be considered equivalent to "liquidation" and that an actual decision to carry out a genocide proper, albeit *ante litteram*, had in fact been taken. The general coordinator of the plan was the Minister of Interior Talat Pasha, under whom a clear chain of command was set up for the purpose of implementing it. On 5 July 1919 the verdict was issued and Talat Pasha, together with other four defendants, all of which had escaped, was sentenced to death, while other defendants in the trial were either sentenced to prison terms or acquitted.

The domestic trials against those accused of planning, organizing and supervising the implementation of the massacre of the Armenians—in addition to establishing facts that indicate that the events which took place fall within what, a few years later, was to be described as genocide—are interesting for other aspects which are relevant to this essay.

First, as mentioned, they were celebrated with the aim of dealing with the events of 1915–1916 at the national level and, thus, to divert the plan of the Allies to set up, in line with the Declaration of 24 May 1915, criminal proceedings of an international nature of some sort. The trials, however, were also influenced by the national situation. The political climate in the country was not favorable. Not only had the reaction to the execution of Mehmet Kemal revealed the feelings of a large part of the population, but the nationalist sentiment (which was fuelled by the Greek occupation of Izmir, carried out with British and French support) and the increasing influence of the nationalist movement of Mustafa Kemal contributed to discouraging a more assertive judicial action. In the end, what actually occurred—the celebration of a number of trials but with less commitment to doing justice than what would have ideally been required—appears to have been the result of the opposing pressure by foreign powers (and, more specifically, of the threat that judicial action would be taken by foreign powers), on the one hand, and domestic forces, on the other.

Second, the domestic trials served the purpose of focusing on the responsibility of individuals, as opposed to the international responsibility of the Ottoman Empire. This is confirmed by the fact that the main culprits were considered as leaders of a political group, the *Ittihad* party, rather than as members of the Government. This element implies that attribution of responsibility for those facts to the State was out of order and, consequently, that the possibility of granting the defendants immunity *ratione materiae* was ruled out not so much on account of the special nature of the crimes—and thus of a possible exception to the rule on immunity of state organs—, but simply because the massacres were treated as a criminal plan by a group of individuals who were not acting in their capacity as organs of the State.

In short, the judicial action against those accused of taking part in *Metz Yeghern* which was brought at national level in 1919–1920 ran counter to both innovative elements of the Allied Declaration of 24 May 1915: (a) the possibility for states other than the territorial state to exercise criminal jurisdiction and (b) the affirmation of an exception to the rule on immunity of State organs. More specifically, the effort to try those accused of the Armenian Massacres swiftly at national level served the purpose of avoiding "international" or foreign trials, which would have been unacceptable to the nationalistic sentiment prevalent in the country; and the treatment of the whole affair as a "private", albeit politically motivated, plan of the *Ittihad* party, rendered irrelevant the discussion around possible exceptions to the immunity (and personal responsibility) of State organs on account of the special nature of the crimes concerned.

5 The International Reactions: The "Commission on Responsibility of Authors of the War and on Enforcement of Penalties" and the "Dissenting Opinion" by Its American Members

In parallel with developments occurring at national level, the issue of individual responsibility for crimes committed during World War I by Germany and its Allies, including the Ottoman Empire, was also on the agenda of the Peace Conference in Paris. On 25 January 1919, the Conference adopted a British proposal to establish a "Commission on Responsibility of Authors of the War and on Enforcement of Penalties" with a view to punishing those responsible for initiating the war, on the one hand, and those who had committed violations of the "laws and customs of war", on the other.

The points which the so-called "Commission of the Fifteen" was charged to investigate include:

> (a) [t]he facts as to breaches of the laws and customs of war committed by the forces of the German Empire and their Allies, on land, on sea, and in the air during the present war;
> (b) [t]he degree of responsibility for these offences attaching to particular members of the enemy forces, including members of the General Staffs, and other individuals, however highly placed;
> (c) [t]he constitution and procedure of a tribunal appropriate for the trial of these offences.[7]

In order to perform its role it divided into three Sub-Commissions: Sub-Commission I, on Criminal Acts, "to discover and collect the evidence necessary to establish the facts relating to culpable conduct which (a) brought about the World War and accompanied its inception, and (b) took place in the course of hostilities"; Sub-Commissions II and III, respectively on "the Responsibility for the War" and on "the Responsibility for the Violation of the Laws and Customs of War", "to consider whether, on the facts established by the Sub-Commission on Criminal Acts" with respect to the crimes falling respectively under (a) and (b), "prosecutions could be instituted, and if [they] decided that prosecutions could be undertaken, to prepare a report indicating the individual or individuals who were, in [their] opinion, guilty, and the court before which prosecutions should proceed".[8]

---

[7]Report presented to the Preliminary Peace Conference, in American Journal of International Law 1920, vol. 14, p. 95.

[8]Ibidem, p. 97–8.

5.1 Applicable Law

The work of Sub-Commission I, on "facts", as reflected in the relevant part of the Commission's report to the Conference of 29 March 1919, is indeed very thorough, based as it is on a large number of sources, including the "Armenian memoranda". These sources

> supply abundant evidence of outrages of every description committed on land, at sea, and in the air, against the laws and customs of war and of the laws of humanity. In spite of the explicit regulations, of established customs, and of the clear dictates of humanity, Germany and her allies have piled outrage upon outrage.[9]

The Commission's general conclusion is that

> 1. The war was carried on by the Central Empires together with their allies, Turkey and Bulgaria, by barbarous or illegitimate methods in violation of the established laws and customs of war and the elementary laws of humanity....[10]

What is especially interesting and deserves to be highlighted is that Sub-Commission I (or, rather, the majority of its members), even though the Commission of the Fifteen was set up by the Paris Conference with a view to punishing—in addition to those who had initiated the war itself—those who had committed violations of the "laws and customs of war" during the conflict, broadens the scope of its investigation to cover those who had committed violations of the elementary laws of humanity as well. This inclusion, which turned out to be highly controversial (to the extent that it provoked, as we will see, the dissent of the American members of the Commission), is crucial with respect to the object of this essay. While violations of "laws and customs of war" amount to crimes against enemy soldiers, violations of the "laws of humanity" include crimes against one's own citizens, such as those committed by the Ottoman authorities against the Armenian population of the Empire. The legal basis for the punishment of those responsible for violations of this kind is to be found in the so-called Martens clause, as included in the Hague Convention of 1907 on the Laws and Customs of War on Land, according to which

> Until a more complete code of the laws of war has been issued, the High Contracting Parties deem it expedient to declare that, in cases not included in the Regulations adopted by them, the inhabitants and the belligerents remain under the protection and the rule of the principles of the law of nations, as they result from the usages established among civilized peoples, from the laws of humanity, and the dictates of the public conscience.

[9]Ibidem, p. 113.

[10]Ibidem, p. 115.

5.2 *Personal Responsibility*

The Commission's report to the Peace Conference is interesting also in the parts concerning "Personal responsibility" and "Constitution and procedure of an appropriate tribunal", covered respectively in Chapters III and IV.

On the first issue, the Commission states expressly that "in the hierarchy of persons in authority, there is no reason why rank, however exalted, should in any circumstances protect the holder of it from responsibility when that responsibility has been established before a properly constituted tribunal".[11] After elaborating on the position of Heads of State, a point which is specifically relevant with respect to the role of the German Kaiser,[12] the Commission also addresses the issue of superior orders, on which it states that

> civil and military authorities cannot be relieved from responsibility by the mere fact that a higher authority might have been convicted of the same offence. It will be for the court to decide whether a plea of superior orders is sufficient to acquit the person charged from responsibility.[13]

The Commission concludes this section by affirming the principle of personal responsibility of state organs in general terms:

> All persons belonging to enemy countries, however high their position may have been, without distinction of rank, including Chiefs of States, who have been guilty of offences against the laws and customs of war or the laws of humanity, are liable to criminal prosecution.[14]

5.3 *Jurisdiction and Appropriate Tribunal*

As for the "appropriate tribunal" issue, Chapter IV approaches it separately in relation to the offences which "brought about the War and accompanied its inception" and those in violation of "the laws and customs of war and the laws of humanity". With respect to the latter, a further distinction is made. Insofar as

---

[11]Ibidem, p. 116.

[12]On this point the Commission states that "even if, in some countries, a sovereign is exempt from being prosecuted in a national court of his own country the position from an international point of view is quite different" and concludes, in a rather forceful manner, that "laying down the principle that the greatest outrages against the laws and customs of war and the laws of humanity, if proved against him [a head of state], could in no circumstances be punished […] would shock the conscience of civilized mankind" (Report presented to the Preliminary Peace Conference, in American Journal of International Law 1920, vol. 14, p. 116).

[13]Report presented to the Preliminary Peace Conference, in American Journal of International Law 1920, vol. 14, p. 117.

[14]Ibidem.

> individuals alleged to be guilty of the crimes of which an enumeration has been given in Chapter II,

and who have been taken prisoners or otherwise fallen into the power of another belligerent, are concerned, the Commission states that

> Every belligerent has, according to international law, the power and authority to try [them] [...]

and

> [...] has, or has power to set up, pursuant to its own legislation, an appropriate tribunal, military or civil, for the trial of such cases.[15]

However, while the option according to which each belligerent is responsible for trying persons belonging to enemy countries fallen within its power is deemed to be simpler and less time consuming than its possible alternatives, there are, nonetheless, certain special situations which require a different solution. The Commission lists four cases, concerning primarily persons who have committed outrages against civilians or soldiers of *several* Allied nations or whose orders affected the conduct of operations against *several* of the Allied armies. It also considers, among the special cases requiring a different solution, that of other persons "against whom it may be considered advisable not to proceed before a national court", a residual category which includes, in our view, the authors of the Armenian massacres (as violations of the laws of humanity against one's own citizens are not included in any of the other categories of crimes envisaged with respect to the most suitable adjudicating body).For all these special situations,

> the Commission is of opinion that a high tribunal is essential.[16]

Plans for setting up such a "high tribunal"—i.e. an international tribunal as opposed to the courts of each belligerent—are spelt out in some detail in the Commission's report which deals with composition, applicable law,[17] penalties,[18]

[15]Ibidem, p. 121.

[16]Ibidem, p. 121–2.

[17]"The law to be applied by the tribunal shall be 'the principles of the law of nations as they result from the usages established among civilized peoples, from the laws of humanity and from the dictates of public conscience'" (Report presented to the Preliminary Peace Conference, in American Journal of International Law 1920, vol. 14, p. 122).

[18]"When the accused is found by the tribunal to be guilty, the tribunal shall have the power to sentence him to such punishment or punishments as may be imposed for such an offence or offences by any court in any country represented on the tribunal or in the country of the convicted person" (Report presented to the Preliminary Peace Conference, in American Journal of International Law 1920, vol. 14, p. 122).

procedure (including referral to national courts),[19] the role of the "Prosecuting Commission" and *ne bis in idem.*[20]

The Commission's final recommendations to the Peace Conference include the following:

> 1. That a high tribunal be constituted as above set out.
>
> 2. That it shall be provided by the treaty of peace: (a) That the enemy governments shall, notwithstanding that peace may have been declared, recognize the jurisdiction of the national tribunals and the high tribunal, that all enemy persons alleged to have been guilty of offences against the laws and customs of war and the laws of humanity shall be excluded from any amnesty to which the belligerents may agree, and that the governments of such persons shall undertake to surrender them to be tried. …
>
> 3. That each Allied and Associated Government adopt such legislation as may be necessary to support the jurisdiction of the international court, and to assure the carrying out of its sentences […].[21]

The proposals of the "Commission of the Fifteen" to the Peace Conference are innovative and far reaching. Insofar as personal responsibility for *Metz Yeghern*—i.e. for crimes committed by members of the Ottoman leadership against citizens of the Ottoman Empire itself—is concerned, the applicable law consists, as mentioned, in the "laws of humanity" as referred to in the "Martens clause". As for "appropriate tribunal", jurisdiction belongs either the courts of one of the Allied countries, if the accused have fallen under its power, or, in alternative, to the "high tribunal".

5.4 *The "Dissenting Opinion" by the American Members*

Although they did, as we will see, contribute to the inclusion of a specific chapter on "penalties" in the Peace Treaty of Sèvres between the Ottoman Empire and the Allied Powers, neither the proposals by the Commission of the Fifteen on applicable law or on personal responsibility, or its plan to set up a "high tribunal" were ever implemented. The Commission's proposals faced manifold political obstacles.

[19] "The tribunal shall determine its own procedure. It shall have power to sit in divisions of not less than five members and to request any national court to assume jurisdiction for the purpose of inquiry or for trial and judgment" (Report presented to the Preliminary Peace Conference, in American Journal of International Law 1920, vol. 14, p. 122).

[20] "No person shall be liable to be tried by a national court for an offence in respect of which charges have been preferred before the tribunal, but no trial or sentence by a court of an enemy country shall bar trial and sentence by the tribunal or by a national court belonging to one of the Allied or Associated States" (Report presented to the Preliminary Peace Conference, in American Journal of International Law 1920, vol. 14, p. 123).

[21] Ibidem.

In legal terms, they were met with the critical position adopted by the delegation of the United States, which is the object of a rather lengthy memorandum.[22]

The first reason of dissent refers to applicable law. According to the American members

> there were two classes of responsibilities, those of a legal nature and those of a moral nature, [...] legal offences were justiciable and liable to trial and punishment by appropriate tribunals, but ... moral offences, however iniquitous and infamous and however terrible in their results, were beyond the reach of judicial procedure, and subject only to moral sanctions.[23]

The majority of the Commission, however, was apparently unwilling to follow this approach. According to its American members:

> The duty of the Commission was [...] to determine whether the facts found were violations of the laws and customs of war. It was not asked whether these facts were violations of the laws or of the principles of humanity. Nevertheless, the report of the Commission does not, as in the opinion of the American representatives it should, confine itself to the ascertainment of the facts and to their violation of the laws and customs of war, but, going beyond the terms of the mandate, declares that the facts found and acts committed were in violation of the laws and of the elementary principles of humanity. The laws and customs of war are a standard certain, to be found in books of authority and in the practice of nations. The laws and principles of humanity vary with the individual, which, if for no other reason, should exclude them from consideration in a court of justice, especially one charged with the administration of criminal law.[24]

For these reasons, the American representatives were

> [...] unable to agree with th[e] conclusion [by the majority of the Commission], in so far as it subjects to criminal, and, therefore, to legal prosecution, persons accused of offences against 'the laws of humanity'.[25]

The difference of opinion with the majority extended to the Commission's recommendations on "appropriate tribunal". On this point

> the American representatives believed that the nations should use the machinery at hand, which had been tried and found competent, with a law and a procedure framed and therefore known in advance, rather than to create an international tribunal with a criminal jurisdiction for which there is no precedent, precept, practice, or procedure. They further believed that, if an act violating the laws and customs of war committed by the enemy

---

[22]Report presented to the Preliminary Peace Conference, Annex II, Memorandum of Reservations presented by the Representatives of the United States to the Report of the Commission on Responsibilities, 4 April 1919, in American Journal of International Law 1920, vol. 14, p. 127.

[23]Ibidem, p. 128.

[24]Ibidem, p. 133–4.

[25]Ibidem, p. 135. The other substantive issue on which the American members of the Commission do not share the position of the majority – an issue which is not directly relevant to the punishment of those responsible for the massacre of the Armenians – concerns responsibility of heads of State. According to them the Commission's report "subjects chiefs of states to a degree of responsibility hitherto unknown to municipal or international law, for which no precedents are to be found in the modern practice of nations".

> affected more than one country, a tribunal could be formed of the countries affected by uniting the national commissions or courts thereof, in which event the tribunal would be formed by the mere assemblage of the members, bringing with them the law to be applied, namely, the laws and customs of war, and the procedure, namely, the procedure of the national commissions or courts.[26]

In the end,

> the uncertainty of the law to be administered, in that liability is made to depend not only upon violations of the laws and customs of war, but also upon violations of 'the laws of humanity'

on the one hand, and the lack of "precedent, precept, practice, or procedure" for the envisaged "high tribunal" on the other, were for the American delegates insurmountable obstacles which prevented them from joining in the Commission's conclusions and recommendations.

6 Continued: The Provisions on "Penalties" in the Treaty of Sèvres and Their Subsequent Abandonment

The Treaty of Sèvres between the Allied Powers and Turkey, signed by Great Britain, Italy and France—not by the United States—on 10 August 1920, several months after the end of the Paris Conference, includes, as mentioned, a section devoted to criminal justice: Part VII of the Treaty, on "Penalties". Articles 226 and 227 deal with those responsible for violations of the laws and customs of war, against nationals of either one or more Allied powers. Article 226 recognizes to the Allies a right to try them,

> notwithstanding any proceedings or prosecution before a tribunal in Turkey or in the territory of her allies,

and imposes on the Turkish Government an obligation to hand over all those accused of such crimes. Article 227 distinguishes the case of

> [p]ersons guilty of criminal acts against the nationals of one of the Allied Powers

from that of

> [p]ersons guilty of criminal acts against the nationals of more than one of the Allied Powers.

[26]Report presented to the Preliminary Peace Conference, Annex II, Memorandum of Reservations presented by the Representatives of the United States to the Report of the Commission on Responsibilities, 4 April 1919, in American Journal of International Law 1920, vol. 14, p. 141–2.

The former shall be brought before the military tribunals of the power concerned, while the latter shall be tried by military tribunals composed of members of the military tribunals of the Powers concerned.[27]

The most significant provision is, however, article 230, dealing with those

> responsible for the massacres committed during the continuance of the state of war on territory which formed part of the Turkish Empire on August 1, 1914,

a broad formulation covering *Metz Yeghern*. The Turkish Government is under an obligation to hand these persons over to the Allied Powers. The Allies, in turn,

> "reserve themselves the right to designate the tribunal which shall try the persons so accused", while "the Turkish Government undertakes to recognize such tribunal".

The second part of the provision is particularly noteworthy. It establishes that:

> In the event of the League of Nations having created in sufficient time a tribunal competent to deal with the said massacres, the Allied powers reserve themselves the right to bring the accused persons mentioned above before such tribunal, and the Turkish Government undertakes equally to recognise such tribunal. [...].

Article 230 thus envisages two options insofar as the issue of "appropriate tribunal" is concerned, assigning to the Allied Powers the right to choose between the two. The first option is to bring those responsible for the Armenian massacres before their own courts, after the Turkish authorities have fulfilled their obligation to hand them over; the second is to renounce national jurisdiction over those crimes in favor of a tribunal to be set up by the League of Nations.

Both options, to the extent that Article 230 deals not with crimes against the enemy but with outrageous acts carried out by leaders against their own population, are innovative. On the one hand, the accused of these acts, which are considered to be in violation of the *laws of humanity*, can be brought before courts of states other than the territorial state or the state of nationality of the victim (i.e. before the courts of states which, unlike the case of violations of laws and customs of war committed against members of their armed forces, have no direct link, either territorial or personal, with the events concerned). On the other hand, the qualification of those acts also justifies, according to Article 230, the jurisdiction of an international tribunal to be established by the League of Nations. The latter could be either a permanent tribunal or a tribunal set up *ad hoc*, as per the "high tribunal" envisaged by the Commission of the fifteen—the provision does not address this alternative. Both cases—universal state jurisdiction and jurisdiction by an international tribunal —represent attempts, albeit different in many respects, to create a system aimed at administering criminal justice, and at implementing the principle of personal criminal responsibility of state organs, on behalf of the international community.

---

[27]The other provisions in the section on "penalties" are Article 228, which imposes an obligation to provide documents and information, and Article 229, which partially extends the regime imposed on Turkey to "the Governments of the States to which territory belonging to the former Turkish Empire has been or may be assigned".

The Treaty of Sèvres was never ratified. The Grand Vizier of the Ottoman Empire, Ahmed Pasha, intended ratifying it, but the victorious rebellion by the nationalist leader Mustafa Kemal, who viewed the Treaty as unacceptable, prevented this from happening. In fact, the issue of punishment of the authors of the atrocities committed during World War I—and specifically of those who planned, organized and carried out *Metz Yeghern*—gradually lost ground, not only on account of developments within Turkey, but also due to the attitude of the Allied Powers. Even the United Kingdom, who had at one stage been the strongest supporter of an international trial, changed its priorities when the issue of territorial settlement clearly became prevalent over that of criminal justice.

In this new domestic and international context the Allies and the Turkish authorities resumed negotiations. The Treaty of Sèvres, which had become obsolete, was eventually replaced by the Treaty of Lausanne, signed in 1923, which entirely overruled the provisions on criminal justice included in the former peace treaty. In an "Amnesty Declaration" annexed to the Treaty of Lausanne the decision not to carry out proceedings aimed at punishing those responsible for *Metz Yeghern* and to render null and void all judicial rulings already taken in this respect—a decision which had already been adopted by the new Turkish leadership at national level—was confirmed internationally. And a specific provision of the Treaty, Article 119, affirmed the agreement by the parties to

> repatriate at once the prisoners of war and interned civilians who are still in their hands

(an exchange between Turkish prisoners detained in Malta and British prisoners of war having already been accepted by the United Kingdom in 1921).[28] The issue of international justice for the crimes committed in the context of the massacre of the Armenians was, therefore, from this moment onwards, off the agenda.

7 Concluding Remarks

The fact that the prevailing interests of the victors of World War I, together with the strong resistance of the new Turkish leadership, prevented the promises contained in the Declaration of 24 May 1915 and the innovative proposals of the Commission of the Fifteen, as well as Part VII of the Treaty of Sèvres, from becoming reality, while they clearly reflected the momentous obstacles faced by the attempt to ensure justice for international crimes, should not lead us to believe that the international reactions to *Metz Yeghern* did not have any impact. On the contrary, the fact that a new approach to the issue of punishment for acts which "shock the conscience of mankind" was laid down and discussed at length, not only by jurists but also by diplomats representing states (with the expectation—at least until 1920—that it

[28]See, inter alia, Flores (2015), pp. 250–253.

would actually be acted upon), is a development which should not be underestimated.

Even though they were not judicially implemented, the proposals which formed the reaction to *Metz Yeghern*, i.e. to particularly unacceptable behavior of those in power within a state against their own citizens (well beyond the traditional notion of violations of the laws and customs of war against enemy soldiers or the enemy population and independently—we should add—of whether or not that behavior falls within the specific notion of genocide), did lay the ground for the construction of a truly innovative legal framework. Sadly, this framework was to be translated into judicial action only after the tragedy of another World War. The reaction to the second global armed conflict of the twentieth century was undoubtedly prepared by the discussions and plans which emerged after the first: to the point that the provision in Article 230 of the Treaty of Sèvres is expressly acknowledged in 1948 by the United Nations War Crimes Commission, as a model for the establishment of the international tribunals in Nuremberg and Tokyo.[29] It is in fact open to question whether those tribunals, without that model, would have been the same (or would have come into existence at all).

Thus, it can safely be said that the long journey of international criminal justice, which today—seventy years after Nuremberg and Tokyo and twenty after the establishment of the International Criminal Court—is still short of completion, began in the aftermath of the massacre of the Armenians, in relation to which, as early as 1915, the expression "crimes against humanity" was for the first time not only used but also given a legal meaning.

References

Akçam T (2012) The Young Turk's crime against humanity: the Armenian genocide and the ethnic cleansing in the Ottoman Empire. Princeton University Press, Princeton

Bloxham D (2007) The great game of genocide. Imperialism, nationalism, and the destruction of the Ottoman Armenians. Oxford University Press, Oxford

Dadrian VN (1995) The history of the Armenian genocide. Ethnic conflict from the Balkans to Anatolia to the Caucasus. Berghahn Books, Providence, USA, and Oxford, United Kingdom

Flores M (2015) Il genocidio degli armeni. Il Mulino, Bologna

Kévorkian RH (2006) Le Génocide des Arméniens. Odile Jacob, Paris

Leotta CD (2013) Il genocidio nel diritto penale internazionale. Giappichelli, Torino

Schabas WA (2000) Genocide in international law. The crime of crimes. Cambridge University Press, Cambridge

[29]UN Commission on Human Rights, Information Concerning Human Rights Arising From Trials of War Criminals: Report Prepared by The United Nations War Crimes Commission in accordance with the request received from the United Nations, 28 May 1948, UN Doc. E/CN.4/W.20/Corr.1.

Armenian Cultural Properties and Cultural Heritage: What Protection under International Law One Hundred Years Later?

Federica Mucci

Contents

1 The "'G' Word" Was Coined Bearing in Mind the Deportations and Massacres of the Armenians and Holding the Cultural Factor in Great Consideration 162
2 Massive Destruction and Loss of Armenian Cultural Properties During World War I: A History yet to Be Fully Traced, Told and Recognised, to Be Read in the Framework of the Laws and Customs of War on Land 164
3 Would the Destruction of Armenian Cultural Properties by the Territorial State Fall Today Under a Prohibition in International Law? 167
4 The Fate of Armenian Exported and Confiscated Cultural Properties, the First Legal Cases and Recent Virtuous International Practices 172
5 Today for Yesterday and Tomorrow: Armenian Cultural Heritage Internationally Protected as a Sign of Shared Recognition 175
References 178

Abstract "Cultural genocide" is not *per se* covered by the 1948 UN Convention. However it was very carefully taken into consideration in works of the most prominent scholars immediately after the Armenian massacres of 1915–17. The fact that violent acts of cultural destruction and other similar actions directed at annihilating the distinctive culture of a group are usual precursors of massive killings and of other serious violations of human rights was evident before and during WWII and is even more evident today. Consequently the few limited, albeit significant, international legal rules concerning the protection of cultural heritage that were in force in 1915 have considerably developed and are still evolving, within the protection of human rights and peace. Today, States are under the duty to protect cultural heritage whatever its origin, both in time of peace and in time of war, and

F. Mucci (✉)
University of Rome "Tor Vergata", Rome, Italy
e-mail: federica.mucci@uniroma2.it

F. Lattanzi and E. Pistoia (eds.), *The Armenian Massacres of 1915–1916 a Hundred Years Later*, Studies in the History of Law and Justice 15,
https://doi.org/10.1007/978-3-319-78169-3_7

the UN Security Council itself endorses UNESCO's efforts, addressing not only the unlawful destruction and looting and smuggling in the event of armed conflicts, but also "the attempt to deny historical roots and cultural diversity" because it "can fuel and exacerbate conflict and hamper post-conflict national reconciliation". In this context, the recent attention paid by Turkey to the protection of certain specific Armenian sites is an undoubtedly positive sign, and it is essential that involvement of all relevant stakeholders in the management of the properties is ensured.

1 The "'G' Word" Was Coined Bearing in Mind the Deportations and Massacres of the Armenians and Holding the Cultural Factor in Great Consideration

Coining a new word to describe an event is indicative of the need to stigmatise it, to single it out of the realm of what until then were apparently similar events, underlining its peculiar features. The term 'genocide' was coined by Raphael Lemkin when facing the Nazis' exterminatory intentions towards European Jews during World War II, bearing in mind the Armenian massacres which had occurred during World War I. The new word was clearly created to highlight the seriousness of specific massive criminal acts with dramatically huge human and socio-cultural consequences.[1]

Though Lemkin first used and explained the meaning of 'genocide' in his "Axis Rule in Occupied Europe", completed in 1943 and published in 1944, he was working since the 1920s on the idea that some acts constituted grave threats to public international order and in the 1930s he was elaborating on the

> general (transnational) danger [that] threatens the interests of several States and their inhabitants.

In this context, he proposed delineating a set of offences relating to

> acts so harmful and dangerous to the international community that their character as offences against the law of nations would be considered by tone as indicated and necessary and could not raise any objection.

Together with the provocation of catastrophes in—and the intentional interruption of—international communications and the propagation of human, animal or

[1]Since the legal concept of genocide had not been conceived yet at the time of the Armenian events and modern Turkey does not recognise them as genocide, the "'g' word" is not indisputably applied to the Armenian deportations and massacres. For instance, it is not employed in the U.S. Turkey Christian Churches Accountability Act (H.R. 4347) of 18 July 2014, but it is explicitly employed by the European Parliament in its resolution of 18 June 1987 on a political solution to the Armenian question. However most historians consider the killings the first genocide of the twentieth century (see Cooper (2005), p. 81–93).

vegetable contagions, these offences comprised specifically "acts of barbarity" and "acts of vandalism".[2]

These last two categories of general (transnational) threats share a common reasoning: they focus on group protection. The most recent historic event that had drawn attention to the need for new rules protecting from such threats was the Armenian genocide. While acts of barbarity are attacks carried out against an individual as a member of a collectivity, acts of vandalism produce collective damage through systematic and organized destruction of the art and cultural heritage in which the unique genius and achievement of a collectivity are revealed in the fields of science, arts and literature.

Lemkin noted that the contribution of any particular collectivity to "world culture" forms the wealth of all humanity, hence vandalism is tantamount to an assault on "world culture", necessarily conceived as a general ('transnational', in the contemporary acception of 'international') threat, since it doesn't only affect a separate interest of the directly affected group. The emergence of a collective interest of the international community in the protection of cultural heritage "belonging to any people whatsoever" was then clearly confirmed through the conclusion of the 1954 Hague Convention for the Protection of Cultural Property in the Event of Armed Conflict.[3]

It is fundamental that we capture the real significance of this attention to culture, which has been further explored in Lemkin's subsequent works and still today is so full of meaning. This attention must in no way be conducive to misleading prioritizations. No monstrous contest of seriousness is suggested between attacks physically directed at human beings and attacks directed at their cultural heritage: on the contrary, they are believed by Lemkin—and perceived today by the international community—to be two facets of the same crime, the violent actions directed at cultural heritage usually preceding (and then also accompanying and following) in time violent actions directed at the physical integrity of people.

In Lemkin's words:

> Physical and biological genocide are always preceded by cultural genocide or by an attack on the symbols of the group or by violent interference with religious or cultural activities. In order to deal effectively with the crime of genocide one must intervene at the very inception of the crime.

It must be stressed that, since "the crime" is genocide, "cultural genocide" as its usual "inception" is here pointed at as a clear sign that the aggression to the human dignity of the group has already escalated, reaching the 'level' of genocide. With respect to Nazi mass murder, Lemkin stressed that it could not be separated from their attack on culture:

---

[2]See Lemkin (1933); Kebranian (2016). Lemkin did not succeed in having either offence juridically codified, but "if we take Lemkin's writings from the 1930s and 1940s together, then we learn that (his idea of) 'genocide' names the crime (as both barbarian and vandal" (see Kazanjian (2011)).

[3]Quotation from the Preamble of the Convention.

> side by side with the extermination of 'undesirables' went a systematic looting of artworks, books, the closing of universities and other places of learning, the destruction of national monuments.[4]

Recalling Lemkin's thought when studying the international legal protection of cultural heritage in situations of aggression against the individual and collective human rights of a group is particularly appropriate, since—as is already clear from the few words that have been quoted—the "father" of the Convention against genocide was convinced of the relevance of the cultural factor. In the end, though, after having made two attempts, a pragmatic approach to the dynamics of the negotiation induced him to renounce his efforts to advocate the inclusion of "cultural genocide" in the Convention.[5]

The Convention itself is subsequent in time and not relevant when studying which international law rules could be applied to the facts which occurred from 1915 to 1917 to the Armenian people. It is certainly relevant, though, that in the most prominent scholar's elaborations before and after WWII on these themes, violent acts of cultural destruction and other similar actions directed at annihilating the distinctive culture of a group were pointed at as the usual precursors of massive killings and the other "main" acts constituting genocide.

2 Massive Destruction and Loss of Armenian Cultural Properties During World War I: A History yet to Be Fully Traced, Told and Recognised, to Be Read in the Framework of the Laws and Customs of War on Land

One of the most striking features that indicate the difference between the Armenian genocide during WWI and the Shoah during WWII—apart from the, nonetheless relevant, different dimensions, historical circumstances, intents and

---

[4]See Moses (2010). In his analysis of how genocide was perpetrated during WWII, Lemkin identifies several techniques of genocide in the political, social, cultural, economic, biological, physical, religious and moral field, mass killings being only the most evident of the physical techniques of genocide. As for the cultural techniques of genocide, they touch, on the one hand, on government control of the programs taught in schools and on limiting the freedom of artistic expression, on the other hand on depriving the population "of inspiration from the existing cultural and artistic values. Thus, especially in Poland, national monuments were destroyed and libraries, archives, museums, and galleries of art carried away" (see Lemkin (2008-Second Edition), p. 84).

[5]For the sake of compromise, Lemkin accepted that "for the purposes of international legislation the definition must be limited to more basic elements, such as killings, mayhem, and biological devices, as, for example, sterilization", as he saw that cultural genocide would encounter strong objections from many UN delegates, for whom only mass murder "shocked the conscience of mankind", even though he had written that "cultural genocide is the most important part of the Convention" (see Moses (2008), p. 12).

methods—pertains to the lack of recognition of what happened. While Germany has abundantly recognised and condemned what happened during WWII, Turkey does not recognise the Armenian genocide, despite the resolute position by Europe requesting recognition.[6] The position maintained by Turkey has significant consequences for the assessment of damages and loss of cultural properties also.

The determination not to recognize the facts of 1915–17 by the State on whose territory they occurred, in conjunction with the lack of an international institution entrusted with the task of ascertaining what really happened, makes it impossible to have available official data not only concerning the massacres, but also concerning the destruction of cultural properties. If we refer to the numbers referred to by scholars, one third of the almost 3000 Armenian religious structures (churches and monasteries) were

> leveled to the ground

between 1915 and 1923 and 700 other religious constructs were partially destroyed through

> willful destruction by fire or explosives.

Many other sacred sites were converted into

> mosques, museums, prisons, sporting centers, granaries, stables, and farms.[7]

These distressing counts call to mind similar—"official"—numbers evoked during the trials at the International Criminal Tribunal for the Former Yugoslavia. The Tribunal could rely on two experts' reports that were prepared in 2002 for the Office of the Prosecutor of ICTY on destruction of cultural property.[8] Religious heritage was sistematically attacked during the Balkan conflict. It has been calculated that 92% of the surveyed mosques and 57% of the surveyed Catholic churches located in Bosnia and Herzegovina were destroyed or heavily damaged from March 1992 to November 1995.[9] Though not all the religious buildings destroyed were ancient and relevant as cultural heritage, the cultural loss was huge.

The Armenian cultural sites that were damaged or destroyed during and immediately after WWI not only have not been assessed officially, they were also very probably not protected under international law since they were not damaged by violent action of the enemy but by intentional action of the territorial State. A "self-damaging attitude" of this kind was not explicitly taken into consideration in the 1899 II Hague Convention. Its two concise rules that can be applied to the protection of cultural properties were shaped bearing in mind the most common risks to which cultural properties were exposed during armed conflicts: destruction and seizure at the hands of the enemy. The territorial State is not explicitly

---

[6]On the position of the European Union see infra, Part III.

[7]See Kebranian (2016).

[8]See Walasek (2015).

[9]See Riedlmayer (2002).

prohibited from carrying out this same behaviour with reference to "its own" cultural properties. The Convention prohibits

> to destroy or seize the enemy's property [...]

and imposes that

> all necessary steps

be taken to spare edifices devoted to the arts in the course of sieges and bombardments,

> provided that they are not used at the same time for military purposes.

The besieged are under the obligation to

> indicate these buildings or places by some particular and visible signs, which should previously be notified to the assailants,

but they are not obliged not to use them for military purposes, as would later be stated in the 1954 Hague Convention.[10]

It is at least very doubtful that destruction at the hands of the territorial State could be considered as being prohibited by the general Martens clause included in the Preamble, since the common interest of the international community for the protection of cultural heritage was definitely regulated and accepted by States at the universal level only in the 1954 Hague Convention. In fact, though there were several signs of the diffused need for better international rules against acts of barbarity and vandalism, such rules were certainly not yet in existence in 1915 under general international law as they were for the barbarity physically inflicted on human beings. It would be preposterous to maintain that they definitely existed also for acts of vandalism on the State's own cultural heritage.[11]

---

[10]See in particular Articles 23(g) and 27 of the Regulations annexed to the Convention (Law and Customs of War on Land). Turkey ratified the 1899 II Hague Convention in 1907, while it has never ratified the subsequent 1907 Hague Convention.

[11]This also leads one to think that obligations of respect in 1915 did not yet bind territorial States with reference to "their own" cultural properties, in contrast with the subsequent regime established in the 1954 Hague Convention. The label "crimes against humanity" was first used for a category of international crimes in 1915, when the governments of France, Great Britain and Russia issued a joint declaration denouncing the Turkish government's massacre of the Armenian population. Nothing, though, came out of this pronouncement and in the end the Treaty of Lausanne did not include provisions for the prosecution of Turkish nationals and consequently the potential prosecution of those charged with violations of the "laws of humanity" for crimes against the Armenians of Turkey was removed. It can be agreed that "such a clearly politically motivated decision did not, however, alter the fact that criminal responsibility had been recognised" (see Bassiouni (2011), p. 94), hence the WWI facts have influenced subsequent developments in general international law, without being covered by those subsequent rules.

One must add to the damage and destruction of Armenian immovable cultural sites, the loss of an unknown number of movable cultural properties, including ancient Armenian manuscripts, with their distinctive "illuminations".[12] It is even more difficult to calculate the consequences of the genocide on the Armenian intangible cultural heritage, though the resilience of cultural roots in living human groups is perhaps even stronger when groups have been forcibly removed from their original dwelling places.[13]

3 Would the Destruction of Armenian Cultural Properties by the Territorial State Fall Today Under a Prohibition in International Law?

The intentional destruction of its own cultural properties by Turkey in 1915–1923 escapes the qualification of war crime and cannot be concretely qualified as a crime against humanity, since this category of crimes did not yet exist, despite the attempts to affirm it after WWI. However the protection of cultural heritage in international law is considerably higher today. Several treaties covering different aspects of cultural heritage protection have been concluded at the universal level, under the auspices of UNESCO, and also at the regional level, particularly in the Council of Europe. It could seem a meagre consolation for the Armenian grievances; it is not if we consider that the protection of remaining Armenian cultural sites is all the more important now, in the light of the wilful destruction that took place in the past.

The effort directed at cultural annihilation is seen by today's scholars—and, more important, by States—as an aspect of the violation of fundamental collective rights that deserves careful attention and response through international initiatives.[14] Beginning with the Hague 1954 Convention, the protection of cultural heritage and cultural diversity has been highlighted as a common fundamental interest of the international community, both in times of war and in peacetime. In

[12]See infra, § 4. Manuscript illumination is a crucial element in the strong Armenian tradition of providing sacred texts with beautiful, authentic and meaningful physical forms.

[13]Fortunately, the resilience of cultural heritage (immovable, movable and living) is great and, in the long run, usually stronger than the violence used by criminals pursuing cultural cleansing policies. It descends from the vital identitary role of culture and from the interconnections among cultures. As Ghandi observed, "No culture can live if it attempts to be exclusive".

[14]Cultural annihilation is pursued through different kinds of action, including the destruction and expropriation of properties, but also the defacement of sacred sites converted into sites for menial functions, such as stables (taking example from the distant past of the Armenian events at the beginning of the XX century) or parkings (as happened, instead, at the end of the XX century, during the conflict in former Yugoslavia).

these last years, the international community has reacted taking a plurality of initiatives when confronted with the more recent and contemporary attacks on both cultural heritage sites and the human right to life, particularly during the conflict in former Yugoslavia and, today, in reaction to the attacks by islamic fundamentalist groups in the Middle East and Africa.

The request, by the European Parliament,

> to take the necessary steps, in collaboration with UNESCO and the International Criminal Court, to extend the international law category of crimes against humanity so that it encompasses acts which wilfully damage or destroy the cultural heritage of mankind on a large scale

calls for a directly 'normative' approach to these issues at the level of individual criminal responsibility.[15] The response of the international community to cultural collective offences, though, is more complex than this, recently growing and taking various forms, particularly through the obligations imposed by the UN Security Council to facilitate the safe return of cultural properties to Iraq and Syria and the enhancement of peacekeeping international forces thanks to integrated "tasks forces" specialised in the protection of cultural heritage.[16]

Administering criminal justice is a particularly relevant, thorny and delicate issue in post-conflict situations. These other recent actions of the international community are also explicitly presented as instrumental to restoring peace in conflict and transition situations.[17] It would be essential today to study the century-old Armenian "cultural genocide", not only to learn a lesson from the past in order to prevent

---

[15]See European Parliament Resolution of 30 April 2015 on the Destruction of Cultural Sites Perpetrated by ISIS/Da'esh (2015/2649(RSP)), para. 17.

[16]Massive intentional destruction of cultural heritage has been condemned by the international community by recognising individual criminal responsibility as a war crime, since probably a better charge under the crimes against humanity, at least for the most recent events by ISIS and its affiliates, is lacking at the moment (on recent developments in State practice and *opinio juris* about these issues after the 2003 UNESCO Declaration of principles concerning the Intentional Destruction of Cultural Heritage see Mucci (2016).

[17]See UNESCO General Conference, Reinforcement of UNESCO's Action for the Protection of Culture and the Promotion of Cultural Pluralism in the Event of Armed Conflict (Doc. 38 C/49, of 2 November 2015), particularly paragraphs 8–10, recalling also UN Security Council Resolution 2199(2015), linked to previous Resolution 1483(2003). In Resolution 2347(2017), adopted on 24 March 2017, the Security Council has recalled its previous resolutions condemning again the illicit traffic and wilful destruction of cultural properties, but emphasizing that also "the attempt to deny historical roots and cultural diversity […] can fuel and exacerbate conflict and hamper post-conflict national reconciliation, thereby undermining the security, stability, governance, social, economic and cultural development of affected States".

similar events in the future,[18] but also to focus on the perspective of building opportunities for stronger dialogue and peace in the region through the 'revitalization' of damaged cultural sites that have not been properly managed until now.

It has been noted that in Turkey in the last decade efforts have been mobilized in order to pursue reparative justice and reconciliation through attempts at reclaiming and restoring Armenian damaged properties and that renovations at three sites in particular have become nodes of socio-political discussion. Two of them (the Church of the Holy Cross, on Aktamar island in Lake Van, and Saint Giragos church in Diyarbakir) were directly involved in the events of the Armenian 'cultural genocide' in 1915 and the following years, while the decline of the archaeological site of Ani began with the Mongol invasions and an earthquake long before the Ottomans and WWI.[19]

These three sites could be seen as examples of the complex issues raised by such a revitalization effort. The political reasons behind these choices and some of the adopted solutions have been object of debate.[20] Nevertheless, though rare and debated, these efforts are undoubtedly better than total inaction resulting in leaving the sites in a state of abandon that could lead to oblivion. Each State Party of the 1972 UNESCO World Heritage Convention (almost all States, including Turkey) is bound to do its best

> to ensure that effective and active measures are taken for the protection, conservation and presentation of the cultural and natural heritage situated on its territory,

i.e. of all the sites corresponding to the definitions given in the Convention (general protection regime) and not only of those that have been inscribed in the List (special protection regime).[21]

---

[18]Lemkin regretted that his proposal for the introduction of acts of barbarism and vandalism and of the complementary "principle of universal repression" had not been accepted by the Madrid Conference on the Unification of Penal Law in 1933 because "an international convention, duly signed and ratified by the countries there represented in 1933, would have made it possible, as early as that date, to indict persons who had been found guilty of such criminal acts whenever they appeared on the territory of one of the signatory countries" (see Lemkin (2008), p. 92.) An enhanced attention to the "cultural precursors" could be usefully considered as an element to be taken into consideration in the perspective of the prevention of genocide, under an acception, though, far more extended than Lemkin's and applicable also to actions directed at indigenous peoples (see the idea of "the emergence of synergies between cultural rights, cultural heritage and genocide prevention" in Novic (2016)).

[19]See Kebranian (2016), p. 247.

[20]The Holy Cross was reopened in 2007, but as a museum, while the Armenian community wanted it to be returned to its original function (see Ekmanian (2010)); the inscription, in 2016, of the site of Ani by Turkey in the World Heritage List was cherished by most of the Armenian community, stressing, though, that it was an Armenian, not a Turkish site (see Armenpress (July 2016)). As for Saint Giragos, it was renovated and reopened in 2011 as part of a reconciliation process begun by the government, but it has been seized in April 2016, together with a number of other churches and other properties in the city of Diyarbakir (see Yeginsu (2016)).

[21]Cf. Article 5 of the Convention.

Though it should not be construed as an obligation of result (not even for those sites that have been included in the List, since the UNESCO World Heritage Committee can only direct recommendations to the territorial State concerning the management of the sites), this treaty obligation to ensure proper protection and management of cultural sites has been interpreted by eminent scholars as certainly banning intentional destruction, considering that destruction is just the opposite of protection.[22]

Hence, under treaty law, this could be the contemporary answer to the question of whether the destruction of Armenian cultural properties by the territorial State would fall today under a prohibition also in peacetime. As for—specifically—the time of conflict, Turkey is a Party to the Hague 1954 Convention, imposing both safeguard and respect obligations on the territorial State towards its own cultural properties, though not to its Second Additional Protocol, devised to enhance the effectiveness of the protection regime. It could also be inferred that prohibition of the intentional destruction of cultural heritage is developing under general international law, imposing both individual and State responsibility for acts of intentional destruction when conducting peacetime activities and in the event of armed conflict, including the case of occupation, as stated in the 2003 UNESCO Declaration Concerning the Intentional Destruction of Cultural Heritage.[23]

This development of general international law has been triggered by several acts of intentional destruction that have shocked the international community (*in primis* the destruction of the Buddhas of Bamjian by the Talibans in 2001, but also previous events during the Balkan war, including the destruction of the old bridge of Mostar and the bombing of the old city of Dubrovnik).[24] It is not easy to assess what stage of development general international law has reached by now on these issues. Territorial sovereignty should always be adequately taken into account and the most innovative ways of prevention and reaction that have been envisaged—namely the UNESCO "task forces" to be put at the disposal of UN peacekeeping forces through operative

[22]See Francioni and Lenzerini (2003); on the difference between obligations of means and of result in the works of the International Law Commission see Dupuy (1999).

[23]The Declaration was adopted "Mindful of the development of rules of customary international law" (see Preamble).

[24]The destruction of the Buddhas of Bamiyan could not be considered a war crime, since the giant statues were not destroyed in the course of fighting and, at that time, the Bamiyan Valley and the rest of the country were free of hostilities and held securely under the Taliban government control. Their demolition was in no way facilitated or motivated by the conflict, while a legal state of belligerent occupation is not indisputably applicable to non-international armed conflicts (see O'Keefe (2014), p. 516). Not to mention the difficulty of categorizing contemporary conflicts under the "classic" distinction of international and non-international conflicts (see Akande (2011)). At the same time, it was not easy, under those circumstances, to clearly assess a specific violation of the obligations of the State for the protection of cultural heritage in time of peace, apart from the already-mentioned general obligation of protection under the World Heritage Convention. While the moral condemnation of the wilful act of destruction by a shocked international community (that had fruitlessly tried to make the Talibans recede from their intent) was strong and immediate, the answer provided by the international legal order was not clear. This uncertainty of the rules was unacceptable, thus the Member States of UNESCO adopted the 2003 Declaration of principles.

mechanisms yet to be developed,[25] together with the possible revision of the ICC Statute to include the intentional large scale destruction of outstanding cultural properties as a crime against humanity—are still to be completed. As for the deployment of UNESCO experts on the ground (the so-called UNESCO task forces) in the framework of the activities for the implementation of the Strategy for the reinforcement of UNESCO's action for the protection of culture and the promotion of cultural pluralism in the event of armed conflict and its proposed action plan, it is to be noted that in November 2016 the Executive Board of UNESCO explicitly requested the Director-general of the Organization to ensure that such activities are carried out with the express consent of the territorial States concerned.[26]

The extreme complexities to be faced and the imperative of the protection of State sovereignty make it in fact impossible to develop a strong protection regime, with a preventive potential effect, in absence of cooperation by the territorial State. A disputed case of wilful destruction that has recently happened with reference to the Armenian cultural heritage concerns the Djulfa cemetery, in Azerbajian. The cemetery, situated in a remote frontier area and in use from the early Middle Ages until the destruction of the town in 1605, was an outstanding testimony of Armenian culture because it hosted thousands of traditionally carved tombstones, mostly from the 15th and 16th century, in the shape of so-called khatchkars. According to ICOMOS reports, the destruction process began in 1998 when 800 khatchkars were removed; it was then temporarily halted, following protests from UNESCO, but was taken up again in 2002. By January 2003 the destruction was completed. In 2005 all that remained of the khatchkars on the site was crushed into pieces and in March 2006 the site was turned into a military zone.[27]

The destruction took place in the context of the suspended conflict between Armenia and Azerbaijan in the territory of Nagorno-Karabach and was part of a broader practice of ethnic cleansing conducted by both Armenia and Azerbaijan, as stated by the European Parliament, who condemned any action seeking to destroy

[25]To be absolutely clear on the issue of necessary coordination with the UN, the General Conference of UNESCO has introduced an amendment to the draft resolution which states that it has adopted the Strategy for Reinforcing UNESCO's Action for the Protection of Culture and the Promotion of Cultural Pluralism in the Event of Armed Conflict "with the understanding that its implementation will be carried out in full coordination and collaboration with concerned Member States and within the framework of United Nations bodies and their mandate" Cfr. UNESCO Doc. 38 C/Resolution 48 cit., § 1.

[26]See UNESCO Doc 200 EX/Decisions, Paris, 18 November 2016, Decision 5.I.F.2. at §7. Curiously, and in a less imperative way, in this Decision the Executive Board "Recalls that activities foreseen in the Strategy for the reinforcement of UNESCO's action for the protection of culture and the promotion of cultural pluralism in the event of armed conflict and its proposed action plan should be conducted in accordance with relevant United Nations rules and decisions and in full respect of the prerogatives of the competent United Nations bodies", while these two requirements (express consent of the territorial States concerned and compliance with relevant UN normative framework) were placed at exactly the same level in the previous Resolution of the General Conference (see supra, at note 25).

[27]See ICOMOS World Reports on Monuments and Sites in Danger, 2002/2003 and 2006/2007, http://www.icomos.org/risk/.

cultural heritage and tried, without success, to send a delegation to visit the archaeological site at Djulfa.[28] According to the European Parliament, the destruction of the Djulfa cemetery is just one of the several destructions of sites of historical importance that have taken place on both Armenian and Azerbaijani territory, despite the fact that both States are Parties to the 1954 Hague Convention and to its Second Additional Protocol.

4 The Fate of Armenian Exported and Confiscated Cultural Properties, the First Legal Cases and Recent Virtuous International Practices

In addition to incidental damage and intentional destruction, the other main issue when considering the international protection of cultural heritage is the exit of movable cultural properties out of the State in violation of relevant domestic and international regulations. International cooperation rules to combat the illicit import, export and transfer of ownership of cultural properties are not very effective and private international law complexities have to be taken into account when tackling with return/restitution requests.[29] As for the time of conflict, the ban of seizure extended to cultural properties irrespective of their private or public ownership, was already codified in the The Hague 1899 Convention though, as has already been mentioned, it was conceived to be applied only if it occurred at the hands of the enemy.[30] It must also be considered that the codification of the ban unfortunately does not automatically imply that effective ways of preventing the uncontrolled removal of cultural properties are provided for, and violations continue to occur.

Despite the serious and internationally recognised massive illicit removal of movable cultural properties during WWII,[31] it has not been possible to agree on an international overall framework to regulate the issues relating to restitution requests since, in fact, no agreement exists on the fundamental question as to whether successor states must be held responsible for internationally wrongful acts against

[28]See European Parliament Resolution on Cultural Heritage in Azerbaijjan, PT6_TA(2006)0069.

[29]See the UNESCO 1970 Convention on the Means of Prohibiting and Preventing the Illicit Import, Export and Transfer of Ownership of Cultural Property and the Unidroit Convention on Stolen or Illegally Exported Cultural Objects, Rome, 1995.

[30]See Article 47 of Convention (II) with Respect to the Laws and Customs of War on Land and its annex: Regulations concerning the Laws and Customs of War on Land. The Hague, 29 July 1899. See also supra, at § 2.

[31]The Nuremberg Tribunal condemned Alfred Rosenberg, inter alia, for the activities of the Einsatzstab Rosenberg, an organisation which planned and directed the looting of the cultural treasures of nearly all Europe (see Nowlan (1993)). At the trial Colonel Storey compared these activities to those of a horde of vandals forcing a treasure house and proved "the execution of the policy to strip the occupied countries of the accumulated product of centuries of devotion to art and the pursuit of learning".

cultural heritage committed by their predecessor states during WWII. The negotiations undertaken by UNESCO on the text of the Draft Declaration of Principles Relating to Cultural Objects Displaced in Connection with the Second World War were greatly affected by the conflicting interests of states and the final text, presented in 2007, could not be adopted.[32]

The absence of an effective overall regulatory framework leaves each restitution request to its own destiny, in consideration of the peculiar circumstances of each case. If this is true for cultural properties displaced during WWII, it is all the more so for cultural properties displaced during WWI. Whereas several restitution claims concerning Nazi-looted art have been resolved in recent years, other cases relating to looted cultural objects, in particular during the Armenian massacres, have emerged only recently.[33]

The first case concerning the restitution of movable cultural properties dating from the Armenian genocide was settled through an agreed compromise solution in 2015, after five years of legal battle in the USA between the California-based Armenian Apostolic Church and the J. Paul Getty Museum in Los Angeles. The dispute was over the ownership of eight brilliantly illustrated manuscript pages, the Canon Tables, comprising the table of contents of the Zeyt'un Gospels, the earliest signed work of Toros Roslin, the most celebrated scribe in Armenia in the 13th century. The Getty bought the pages from an Armenian-American family in 1994 but their proper ownership has been in question since 2010 when a lawsuit was brought against the Getty Museum. The lawsuit was finally settled last year when the Getty Museum acknowledged the church as the rightful owner and the church agreed to donate the pages to the museum.[34]

The conclusion of this settlement in itself significantly confirms that a new vision, acknowledging both the rightful specific titles of origin/ownership and the common general interest of the whole international community in each cultural property, can effectively be embraced today on the basis of a common commitment to protection. It is, in fact, remarkable that this first legal case concerning the restitution of cultural objects displaced during the Armenian genocide could be settled through an agreement that recognised rightful titles but physically left the objects elsewhere. Another outstanding example of a similarly innovative practice can be found in the 2006 agreement between Italy and the Metropolitan Museum of New York for the restitution to Italy of the Euphronios Krater and other objects (though in this case in the end the krater was loaned, not donated, to the

[32]Scholars think that "arguably, the stormy negotiations on the text of the Draft Declaration and its final rejection have put an end to the debate on the existence of legal regime of the succession to responsibility for internationally wrongful acts against cultural heritage committed in the second world war" (see Jakubowski (2015), p. 198).

[33]Peters (2012), p. 141.

[34]See Halperin (2015); Finkel (2016).

Metropolitan Museum, and the return of other works of art of equivalent beauty and importance, which were also the object of long-term loans, was planned).[35]

The Zeyt'un Gospel, from which these eight pages had been taken during its wanderings after the Armenian genocide,[36] is now preserved in the Mashtots Matenadaran Ancient Manuscripts Collection, near Yerevan. It is the largest and most valuable collection of Armenian manuscripts (approximately 17.000) and was inscribed by UNESCO in the Memory of the World Register in 1997.[37] Over the years, the manuscripts were often buried, hidden in the forests or taken to the mountains to be saved from foreign vandalism. For instance the largest of the manuscripts in the collection was completed in 1204 (and weighs over 32 kg). 600 calf hides were used to make the parchment for it. It was kept in the library of the Monastery of the Holy Apostles in Mush when, during the tragic events of 1915, it was split into two parts in order to divide the weight, and taken away by two Armenian women who escaped from a massacre. After long wanderings, the two parts were finally brought separately to the Matenadaran archives and reunited; though many pages are missing and many are ruined, they are preserved and studied in the Institute at the foot of Mount Ararat.[38]

Another domestic—and possibly also international—"first Armenian case", pertaining to the return of expropriated immovable properties, touches also importantly on cultural heritage. In this case, too, the plaintiff is an Armenian religious institution, but the action is against Turkey.

On 15 June 2016, the Constitutional Court of Turkey rejected, on procedural grounds, an application by the Armenian Catholicosate of Cilicia demanding the return of the former headquarters of the Catholicosate in Sis (today Kozan, in Turkey); the Court stated that the Catholicosate had not first exhausted administrative and judicial ways of application. Hence, the Catholicosate announced that it

---

[35]The Euphronios Krater was acquired by the Metropolitan Museum in 1972; the krater had probably been illicitly excavated in Italy in 1971. On the necessity of developing alternative means to traditional treaties, confirmed by recent cases regarding the illicit traffic of archeological relics, see Casini (2011). It is certainly true that "this is happening, in part, because, in most cases, actual control and effective restitution can only take place after a specific agreement between the actors involved is reached". "In part", though, these settlements are also the proof of a new approach, trying to reconcile opposite stands in the interest of public access to cultural properties and to encourage more accurate and transparent acquisition policies by the museums.

[36]All the movements of the book have been traced and are referred to in Aleksanyan et al. (2016).

[37]UNESCO established the Memory of the World Programme in 1992. Impetus came originally from a growing awareness of the parlous state of preservation of, and access to, documentary heritage in various parts of the world An International Advisory Committee (IAC) first met in Pultusk, Poland, in 1993. It produced an action plan which affirmed UNESCO's role as coordinator and catalyst to sensitize governments, international organizations and foundations, and foster partnerships for the implementation of projects. The Memory of the World Register was founded on the 1995 General Guidelines and has grown through accessions approved by successive IAC meetings. The full list of registered heritage is available on UNESCO website at http://www.unesco.org/new/en/communication-and-information/memory-of-the-world/register/full-list-of-registered-heritage/registered-heritage-page-1/.

[38]As noted by Fiks (1973), many of the Matenadaran's manuscripts have had an adventurous life.

was ready for the first time to take legal action against Turkey, submitting its request to the European Court of Human Rights.[39] The Catholicosate, i.e. the administrative center of the church, was moved from Armenia to Cilicia in the 10th century and, after changing a few locations, was finally established in Sis in the year 1295. It remained in Sis till 1921. The Sis Catholicosate was progressively destroyed, starting in September 1915, and then confiscated.[40] It is of great interest for Armenian cultural identity, and that was precisely the reason for its destruction, as attested by a telegram of the Interior Minister Talat Pasha dated 30 April 1916 where it is stated that:

> Basically the goal of the abolition of the Sis Catholicosate and, at the first opportunity, the expulsion of the Catholicos from there, is the complete removal of the existence of this place which possesses very great historical and national value in Cilicia for Armenians.[41]

5 Today for Yesterday and Tomorrow: Armenian Cultural Heritage Internationally Protected as a Sign of Shared Recognition

Having taken into consideration some outstanding cases pertaining to the destruction, loss, recovery and revitalization of specific Armenian cultural properties within the framework of international law, I would like to draw a future-oriented conclusion concerning Armenian cultural heritage globally considered, built also on the awareness of past events.

Today, unlike a hundred years ago, not only the intentional destruction of cultural properties by the State in its territory is likely to be prohibited by a rule of general international law which wasn't yet complete at the time of the adoption of the 2003 Declaration by UNESCO but has progressed as a consequence of the

[39]See Armenpress (December 2016). Catholicos Aram I of the Great House of Cilicia has affirmed that the lawsuit demanding the return of the Armenian Catholicosate of Cilicia in Sis will be formally submitted to the European Court of Human Rights and that this will be the first legal action taken against Turkey after the Armenian Genocide of 1915. He stated also that this legal action is the result of long and serious reflection, consultation, and study, and is based on the provisions of international law, including the decisions of the Lausanne Conference of 1932 pertaining to the minorities living within the boundaries of the Republic of Turkey (see The Armenian weekly (December 2016)).

[40]The adoption of a relevant law in Turkey in August 2011 is one of the main positive preconditions of the request. Nevertheless, there are also a number of practical legal and political obstacles which severely hinder the issue of property return. Among the legal obstacles are the issue of the legal status of the churches (as some religious communities are not recognized by the Turkish State), the limitations of retroactivity (as the law is applied to properties confiscated after 1936, while most of the church properties were confiscated between WWI and 1936) and the fact that some properties have been sold. On the issue see Hovyan (2015).

[41]Cited by Kebranian (2016), p. 45.

serious and massive intentional destruction of cultural properties by ISIS and other homologous fundamentalist groups[42]; States are also under the duty to actively protect, preserve and present cultural heritage in the interest of the whole international community—at least all the States Parties to the UNESCO 1972 World Heritage Convention share this duty, including Armenia, Turkey and Azerbaijan.[43] Hence, behaviour such as the progressive destruction of the Armenian kachkars of Djulfa in Azerbaijan or the corresponding destruction of historical islamic sites in Armenia, condemned by the European Parliament, cannot be justified, but also the abandonment of outstanding cultural sites to disrepair when domestic resources or international cooperation are available is against international law.

The fortunate opportunity we have today for a definite break from the mistakes of the past and for the opportunity of taking care of those elements of the Armenian cultural heritage that have been bequeathed to us is due to the inalienable resilience inherent to cultural heritage. Today the international recognition and protection of the Armenian cultural heritage through its multiple and diverse elements can also allow us, in some way, to revive what has been lost despite the serious damage suffered by the whole international Community because of these losses. This occurred in 2010, through the inclusion in the UNESCO Representative List of the Intangible Cultural Heritage of the "Armenian cross-stones art. Symbolism and Craftmanship of Kachkars", five years after the total destruction of the Djulfa cemetery.[44]

---

[42]The UNESCO 2003 Declaration concerning the Intentional Destruction of Cultural Heritage affirms both State responsibility and individual criminal responsibility and specifically refers to general international law: the General Conference is 'mindful of the development of the rules of customary international law as also affirmed by the relevant case-law, related to the protection of cultural heritage in peacetime as well as in the event of armed conflict'. Very recently, in September 2016, the International Criminal Court delivered the first decision of an international criminal tribunal in a case completely dedicated to acts directed against cultural heritage (ICC, Trial Chamber VIII, Judgment and Sentence in the case of The Prosecutor v. Ahmad Al Faqi Al Mahdi (Situation in the Republic of Mali), 27 September 2016, No. ICC-01/12-01/15). The places where ISIS has damaged cultural heritage include also some routes of the Armenian deportation in 1915; in 2014 ISIS also destroyed the Armenian Genocide Memorial Church in Syria (see The Armenian Weekly (September 2014)).

[43]In 2001, UNESCO, with the support of UNDP and in co-operation with the Armenian government, prepared a Donors' Conference as part of a larger program designed to strengthen national capacity for the preparation of well-designed projects aimed at attracting external funds (see UNESCO, UNDP and Republic of Armenia (2001)).

[44]On the inscription relating to the previous destruction of the kachkars in the Djulfa cemetry, see Bachoian (2011). Thanks to an ongoing research project of the Australian Catholic University - the Julfa Cemetery Digital Repatriation Project - the entire medieval cemetery is being digitally recreated in three interactive installations, two of them to be positioned respectively in Yerevan and in Sydney and one international touring installation (see Institute for Religion and Critical Inquiry). For a photographic journal of the first stages of the project see Crispin (2013).

The positive, active, role of territorial States in the protection of cultural heritage is indispensable towards making international cooperation work; but also the positive involvement of civil society in making choices and starting initiatives is fundamental towards ensuring that cultural heritage has a contemporary role in the life of local communities. The renewed attention of Turkey to the protection of certain specific Armenian sites, in particular through the inscription of the archaeological site of Ani in the World Heritage List in July 2016, is undoubtedly positive, and the recommendation by the World Heritage Committee to

> ensure the involvement of all relevant stakeholders in the management of the property, as well as international cooperation for conservation and restoration work

calls for a very far-sighted and mature approach to the management of the site.[45] It stresses the natural vocation of cultural heritage to express identity, at the same time highlighting connections with other cultures. This is the role of UNESCO.

Today's action can shed light on the facts of the past and open new paths of knowledge, development and dialogue for the future. This is true of cultural heritage in general, and is particularly true with reference to the Armenian cultural heritage. The way we deal with cultural heritage is extremely relevant in the perspective of the protection of human rights. As the first paragraph of the Preamble of the ICC Statute clearly states, States Parties are

> Conscious that all peoples are united by common bonds, their cultures pieced together in a shared heritage, and concerned that this delicate mosaic may be shattered at any time.

So, how to define genocide?

> Bloody corpses are signs of homicide. An abundance of them is evidence for genocide.

But

> What have cultural diversity and common heritage – this delicate mosaic – to do with international criminal law? Whatever the answer, something other than human life in the physical sense is undoubtedly at stake.[46]

[45]See World Heritage Committee, Decision 40 COM 8B.28. An interesting example of input from civil society concerns the site of Ani: it is the project to rebuild a 10th century bridge which crossed the Akhurian River and connected the Turkish border to the Armenian medieval capital. It was suggested in 2010 by Armenia's International Council of Monuments and Sites (ICOMOS), in conjunction with the Economic Policy Research Foundation of Turkey (TEPAV) (see Orenstein (2010)).

[46]Clavero (2008), Introduction.

References

Aleksanyan NG, Drake M, Renold M-A (2016) Canon Tables—Western Prelacy of the Armenian Apostolic Church of America and J. Paul Getty Museum. Platform Ar Themis. http://unige.ch/art-adr, Art-Law Centre, University of Geneva

Akande D (2011) Are extraterritorial armed conflicts with non-state groups international or non-international? EJIL: Talk. http://www.ejiltalk.org/are-extraterritorial-armed-conflicts-with-non-state-groups-international-or-non-international. Accessed 19 Jan 2017

Armenpress (20 July 2016) Inclusion of Ani in UNESCO World Heritage Sites creates guarantees of its conservation. https://armenpress.am/eng/news/854764/inclusion-of-ani-in-unesco-world-heritage-sites-creates-guarantees-of-its-conservation.html. Accessed 19 Jan 2017

Armenpress (7 December 2016) Live: Catholicosate of Cilicia briefs on ECHR lawsuit against Turkey. http://armenpress.am/eng/news/870865/live-catholicosate-of-cilicia-holds-press-conference-on-submitting-legal-case-against-turkey-to-echr.html. Accessed 19 Jan 2017

Bachoian M (2011) The destruction of Djulfa. Law J Soc Justice. https://ljsj.wordpress.com/2011/04/06/the-destruction-of-djulfa. Accessed 19 Jan 2017

Bassiouni MC (2011) Crimes against humanity: historical evolution and contemporary application. Cambridge University Press, New York

Casini L (2011) "Italian Hours": the globalisation of cultural property law. Int J Constit Law 9 (2):369–393

Clavero B (2008) Genocide or ethnocide, 1933–2007, how to make, unmake and remake law with words. Giuffrè, Milano

Cooper B, Taner A (2005) Turks, Armenians and the "G-Word". World Policy J 22(3):81–93

Crispin J (2013) Recovering a lost Armenian cemetery at Djulfa by way of 3D projections. Magnet Galleries, Melbourne

Dupuy P-M (1999) Reviewing the difficulties of codification: on Ago's classification of obligations of means and obligations of result in relation to state responsibility. Eur J Int Law 10(2):371–385

Ekmanian H (2010) Detailed report: the Mass in Akhtamar, and what's next. The Armenian Weekly. http://armenianweekly.com/2010/09/30/detailed-report-the-mass-in-akhtamar-and-what%E2%80%99s-next. Accessed 19 Jan 2017

Fiks D (1973) The Saga of Armenia's lost manuscripts. The UNESCO Courier: A Window Open on the World XXVI(7):26–31

Finkel I (2016) Getty displays Medieval illuminated pages after legal battle finally ends. The Art Newspaper. http://theartnewspaper.com/news/getty-displays-medieval-illuminated-pages-after-legal-battle-finally-ends. Accessed 19 Jan 2017

Francioni F, Lenzerini F (2003) The destruction of the Buddhas of Bamiyan and international law. Eur J Int Law 14(4):619–651

Halperin J (2015) Getty becomes first museum to restitute Armenian art removed during genocide. The Art Newspaper. http://theartnewspaper.com/news/museums/getty-becomes-first-museum-to-restitute-armenian-art-removed-during-genocide/

Hovyan V (2015) The issue of church property restitution as a constituent element of Armenian demands. Haigatian Armenol Rev 35:605–622

Institute for Religion and Critical Inquiry. https://irci.acu.edu.au/research/julfa-cemetery-digital-repatriation-project

Jakubowski A (2015) State succession in cultural heritage. Oxford University Press, Oxford

Kazanjian D (2011) Re-flexion: genocide in ruins. Discourse. J Theor Stud Media Cult 33(3), art. 4. http://digitalcommons.wayne.edu/discourse/vol33/iss3/4. Accessed 19 Jan 2017

Kebranian N (2016) Cultural heritage and the denial of genocide law. In: Demirdjian A (ed) The Armenian genocide legacy. Palgrave Macmillan, New York, pp 243–254

Lemkin R (1933) Les actes constituant un danger général (interétatique) considerés comme délits de droit des gens, Rapport spécial présenté à la V-me Conférence pour l'Unification du Droit Pénal à Madrid (14–20.X.1933) (explications additionnelles). Lemkin Collection, American

Jewish Historical Society. P-154, Box 1/11 and Box 5/3. Trans. Prevent Genocide International website. http://www.preventgenocide.org/lemkin/madrid1933-english.htm. Accessed 19 Jan 2017
Lemkin R (2008) Axis rule in occupied Europe: laws of occupation, analysis of government, proposals for redress. Second edition with introductory essays by Power S, Schabas WA. The Lawbook Exchange Limited, Clark, New Jersey
Moses AD (2008) Empire, colony, genocide: keywords and the philosophy of history. In: Dirk Moses A (ed) Empire, colony, genocide. Conquest, occupation and subaltern resistance in world history. Berghahn Books, New York/Oxford, pp 3–54
Moses AD (2010) Raphael Lemkin, culture and the concept of genocide. In Bloxham D, Dirk Moses A (eds) The Oxford handbook of genocide studies. Oxford University Press, New York, pp 19–41
Mucci F (2016) Intentional destruction of cultural heritage by ISIS: the reaction of the international community against this specific aspect of the aggression to peace and human rights. Peace Process Online Rev 2(1):1–15. http://www.peaceprocesses.it/images/pdf/federica_mucci_-_massive_intentional_destruction_of_cultural_heritage_by_isis.pdf
Novic E (2016) The concept of cultural genocide: an international law perspective. Oxford University Press, New York
Nowlan J (1993) Cultural property and the Nuremberg war crimes trial. Humanitäres Völkerrecht 4:221–223
O'Keefe R (2014) Protection of cultural property. In: Clapham A, Gaeta P (eds) The Oxford handbook of international law in armed conflict. Oxford University Press, New York, pp 492–520
Orenstein N (2010) Bridging nations no longer a figurative task. Newsdesk.org. http://newsdesk.org/2010/07/01/bridging-nations-no-longer-a-figurative-task. Accessed 19 Jan 2017
Peters R (2012) "Remedying Historical Injustice": ethical and historical considerations in returning cultural materials. In: Borrelli S, Lenzerini F (eds) Cultural heritage, cultural rights, cultural diversity: new developments in international law. Martinus Nijhoff Publishers, Leiden/Boston, pp 141–156
Riedlmayer A (2002) Destruction of cultural heritage in Bosnia-Herzegovina, 1992–1996: A Postwar survey of selected municipalities. http://archnet.org/system/publications/contents/3481/original/DPC1420.pdf?1384775281. Accessed 19 Jan 2017
The Armenian Weekly (21 September 2014) Isis destroys Armenian Genocide Memorial Church in Der Zor. http://armenianweekly.com/2014/09/21/der-zor/. Accessed 19 Jan 2017
The Armenian weekly (5 December 2016) Return of Sis Catholicosate case to be formally submitted to the European Court of Human Rights. Aram I: 'Recognition and reparation: This is our clear and firm position as a people and a Church'. http://armenianweekly.com/2016/12/05/sis-echr. Accessed 19 Jan 2017
UNESCO, UNDP and Republic of Armenia (2001) Regeneration through culture. Cultural projects for development. Print Info JV LLC, Armenia
Walasek H (ed) (2015) Bosnia and the destruction of cultural heritage. Routledge, Farnham/Burlington
Yeginsu C (2016) Turkey's Seizure of Churches and land alarms Armenians. The New York Times. http://www.nytimes.com/2016/04/24/world/europe/turkeys-seizure-of-churches-and-land-alarms-armenians.html?_r=1. Accessed 19 Jan 2017

What Reparations for the Descendants of the Victims of "the Armenian Genocide"?

David Donat Cattin

Contents

1 Introduction 182
2 Legal Bases 183
3 What Forms of Reparations? 185
4 Multi-generational Legacy of Victimization and Types of Reparations Aimed at Addressing It 188
References 191

Abstract The essay argues that the legal qualification of the widespread and systematic inhumane conduct that characterized the Armenian genocide as "war crimes" may constitute an appropriate legal basis for reparations in addition to the one provided by the law of State responsibility, at least to strengthen claims based on either domestic or international law that may not derogate from the general principle of law of non-retroactivity. Reparations—including restitution, compensation, rehabilitation, satisfaction and guarantees of non-repetition—may be characterized as essentially twofold, when referred to the status of the victims' descendants: those aimed at partially restoring the harm and losses of victims through material and immaterial means of reparation provided to their descendants and those aimed at preventing that atrocities are repeated in the future, also via the proper memorialization. They should be carefully tailored to address multi-generational harm. In this connection, ratification of the Rome Statute of the International Criminal Court by both Armenia and Turkey would be a meaningful and effective step to guarantee non-repetition, "never again".

D. Donat Cattin (✉)
Center for Global Affairs, New York University (NYU), New York, USA
e-mail: ddc4@nyu.edu

D. Donat Cattin
Parliamentarians for Global Action (PGA), New York, USA

F. Lattanzi and E. Pistoia (eds.), *The Armenian Massacres of 1915–1916 a Hundred Years Later*, Studies in the History of Law and Justice 15,
https://doi.org/10.1007/978-3-319-78169-3_8

1 Introduction

The principles and norms of International Law may not be applied retroactively to facts that occurred before the formation of such norms and principles. Legal consequences for violations of the law may only be determined on the basis of norms and principles that were legally binding when violations occurred. This hard reality is the starting point of this brief article, through which an investigation is made on the concrete legal bases for a legally enforceable case in support of reparations for the descendants of the Armenian genocide. However, it is not the intention of this author to exhaustively address the matter of State's responsibility for the enormous harm and losses that the Armenian populations suffered from the Ottoman Empire, bearing in mind that the principle of continuity of States' obligations is also attributing the responsibility of the Ottoman Empire's acts to its successor State, Turkey.[1] The goal of this article is to address inter-individual reparations and the multi-generational dimension of victimization as founding elements for State's reparations. The article will conclude that relevant remedial action by the States exercising their sovereign jurisdiction on the descendants of the victims and, most importantly, on the descendants of the alleged perpetrators is required.[2]

As evidenced by Professor Lattanzi's contribution in this volume, States' responsibility in the critical area of reparations can be found in a number of international legal sources, including the unapplied findings of the Report of the "Commission on the Responsibility of the Authors of the War and on Enforcement of Penalties" and, above all, the unenforced provisions of the Sèvres Peace Treaty signed by Turkey, the Allied Powers (UK, France, Italy, Japan) and the other so-called Allied Associated Powers, which included the Independent State of Armenia.

[1]Many profiles on the Turkish State's responsibility to repair Armenian victims, either directly or through the facilitation of the State of Armenia, are covered by the voluminous on-line report entitled "Resolution with Justice – Reparations for victims of the Armenian Genocide. The Report of the Armenian Genocide Reparations Study Group" (March 2016), available at www.armeniangenocidereparations.info. None of the observations contained in this brief article shall be interpreted as a limitation to the findings of this Report in the area of States' responsibility stemming from breaches of international law caused by acts of State.

[2]Regarding the victims' right to reparation in an historic perspective, reference is made to Roht Arriaza (2010). On the subject-matter of victims' rights in international criminal law, including the right to apply for reparations, reference may be made to: Donat Cattin (1998, 1999, 1999/2008/2015).

2 Legal Bases

Given that the Genocide Convention was adopted in 1948 and that the hard notion of crimes against humanity—from which genocide stems—was affirmed in the Moscow Declaration of the Allied Powers of 1943 and defined in the Charter of the International Military Tribunal (the IMT, better known as the Nuremberg Tribunal) of 1945, both these categories of core crimes under International Law may not be applied to the mass atrocities that occurred in Armenia and against Armenians during World War I, even if the underlying facts, should they had occurred after 1948 and during World War II respectively, could have squarely fallen under the definitions of genocide and crimes against humanity. The general principle of non-retroactivity under International Law, which backs the contemporary principle of legality in penal matters (*nullum crimen, nulla poena sine lege*), as defined in relevant International Criminal Law instruments that have arisen to the status of customary law, prohibits such an application while it recognizes the irrelevance of the lack of domestic criminalization (Nuremberg Principle No. 1).

In this respect, an essential distinction must be made between the two categories of individuals who are the primary subjects of crimes under International Law, namely those who commit the crimes, the perpetrators, and those who suffer the consequences of the crimes, the victims. In accordance with the definition of victims of crimes under International Law (genocide, crimes against humanity, war crimes and crimes against the peace or crime of aggression, in line with the Nuremberg Charter of the IMT or the Rome Statute of the ICC), individual victims have the right to be recognized as such regardless of the fact that a perpetrator of the crimes that victimized them has been found guilty or not.[3] Victims include dependents, descendants and other family members, as well as

> where appropriate […] persons who have suffered harm in intervening to assist victims in distress or to prevent victimization.[4]

[3]According the definition of victims unanimously adopted by the UN General Assembly in its pivotal Declaration of principles on victims' rights of 1985: "A person may be considered a victim, under this Declaration, regardless of whether the perpetrator is identified, apprehended, prosecuted or convicted and regardless of the familial relationship between the perpetrator and the victim." Cf. UN doc. A/RES/40/34 of 29 November 1985, Declaration of Basic Principles for Justice for Victims of Crimes and Abuse of Power, Annex, Section A.2.

[4]Ibidem. Reference is also made to the preparatory works of the Rome Statute of the ICC. When States participating in the Rome Diplomatic Conference Working Group in Procedural Matters adopted Article 75 on reparations to victims, they inserted a footnote (by general agreement) in the Working Group's report to orient the interpretation of the statutory language on reparations for victims and "*in respect of victims*" (Cf. Article 75, Rome Statute). Due its importance, the footnote is hereby reproduced: "Such a provision refers to the possibility for appropriate reparations to be granted *not only to victims* but also to others such as the victims' families and *successors*. For the purposes of interpretation of the terms 'victims' and 'reparations', definitions are contained in the text of article 44, paragraph 4 of the Statute [corresponding to article 43.6 of the Rome Statute], article 68, paragraph 1, and its accompanying footnote, the Declaration of Basic Principles of Justice for Victims of Crime and Abuse of Power (General Assembly resolution 40/34 of 29

However, until an individual perpetrator is found guilty, he or she shall be defined as alleged perpetrator. This is line with the general principle of law on the presumption of innocence. This distinction and separation of planes between individual criminal responsibility of perpetrators and the recognition of status of victims is the reflection of the separation between criminal and civil responsibility. Whereby the finding of individual criminal responsibility may automatically trigger the obligation to establish principles relating to reparations for the benefit of victims participating in trial proceedings, as per Article 75 of the Rome Statute of the ICC, the lack of such a finding in criminal proceedings does not erode the right of victims to apply for reparations on the basis of civil law and, if applicable, administrative law.[5] In all cases in which victimization is caused by acts carried out by State officials (security forces, law-enforcement authorities, the Judiciary, etc.), the application of administrative law is essential to provide effective reparations to victims whose fundamental rights may be only reinstated and reintegrated by State action (e.g. reintegration of a University Professor in a public institution from which he was expelled in furtherance of the crime against humanity of persecution and reinstatement of relevant pension rights).

Political recognitions of the Armenian "genocide", as such, may not provide for a legal basis as satisfactory as the one provided for by the Martens clause of The Hague Convention of 1907 on "the laws of humanity and the dictates of the public conscience" combined with prohibitions in the law of armed conflict, regarding which the obligation to repair was also connected with the responsibility for war crimes under International Law by the first wave of post-World War I peace-treaties, in particular Article 230 of the Sèvres Peace Treaty. Contemporary public statements, resolutions or political agreements affirming the "Armenian genocide" may, as such, be an acceptable and feasible form of collective reparation provided by the entity that is adopting them, but do not replace the application of the fundamental principle of responsibility for crimes under international law, even when such statements or resolutions would represent the formal and univocal position of States, including the States that had been most connected with the crimes themselves. The law of armed conflict, instead, already existed in 1915 and it may provide with the firmest additional legal basis for claims to obtain forms of reparations that may be inherited by descendants of victims, who are all deceased, vis-à-vis the law of State responsibility. Given that the Ottoman Empire characterized the Armenian communities as enemies in the framework of World War I,

November 1985, annex) and the examples in paragraphs 12 to 15 of the revised draft basic principles and guidelines on the right to reparation for victims of gross violations of human rights and humanitarian law (E/CN.4/Sub.2/1996/17)." (Emphasis added by the author.)

[5]As one of the most authoritative scholars in this field has written, "[a]dministrative reparations programs generally provide either a lump sum of money, services, and/or a pension for survivors or their family members. They may be the product of executive decrees or legislation. They generally do not try to put victims where they would have been absent the violation [of human rights or international humanitarian law], but rather to serve as modest acknowledgement of wrongdoing." Cf. Roht Arriaza (2010), p. 663.

even if the context of international armed conflict was utilized as nominal excuse to justify a criminal policy of mass-extermination, there are objective elements of evidence that may be produced to prove that the Ottoman Empire intended to attack the Armenians in the framework of its war efforts. As such, the targeting of civilians was specifically prohibited and criminalized by the Hague Conventions of 1907, which contained the well-known Martens clause and absolute prohibitions of conduct under Articles 23, 25, 26, 27 and 28. Such prohibitions were used to justify the existence of individual criminal responsibility for war crimes in post-World War I treaties, including with reference to the Armenians. The legal qualification of the widespread and systematic inhumane conduct that characterized the Armenian genocide as "war crimes" would have been sufficient to underpin inter-individual (civil law) and administrative reparations and, *a fortiori*, represents now a further legal basis for reparations to be provided by the relevant State. War crimes are applicable to the anti-Armenian mass-violence notwithstanding the facts that (i) the existence of the group as such is not the protected-interest safeguarded by war crimes (genocide protects the existence of a religious, national, ethnic or racial group, as a whole or in part, or as such) and (ii) the primary purpose of war crimes is not the protection of humanity as such (crimes against humanity reflect primarily this need in relation to widespread or systematic attacks directed against any civilian population). However, any violent attack against a civilian that is not justified by the principle of military necessity and that does not respect the principle of proportionality is prohibited under International Humanitarian Law. No State that participated in World War I negated or objected to this normative framework. Even if not comprehensive as the crimes of genocide and against humanity, the category of war crimes is sufficient to declare unlawful and criminal under International Law all the main atrocities that affected Armenian victims during, or in connection with, WWI.

3 What Forms of Reparations?

According to the Sèvres Peace Treaty, the general principle of law of *restitutio in integrum*[6] should have been applicable to the Armenian massacres perpetrated during World War I, regardless of the legal characterization of the facts by the

[6]*Case concerning the Factory at Chorzów (Claim for Indemnity) (Germany* v. *Poland)*, 13 September 1928, Permanent Court of International Justice, Merits, Collection of Judgments, Series A, No. 17, p. 29: "It is a principle of international law, and even a general conception of law, that any breach of an engagement involves an obligation to make reparation." The Chorzow Factory case has been cited consistently in the jurisprudence of international tribunals. For example, in its most famous and cited Judgement on the right to justice for victims gross human rights' abuses, the Inter-American Court of Human Rights affirmed that "[r]eparation of harm brought about by the violation of an international obligation consists in full restitution (*restitutio in integrum*), which includes the restoration of the prior situation, the reparation of the consequences of the violation, and indemnification for patrimonial and non-patrimonial damages, including

criminal law of the territorial state given that war crimes were grave breaches of International Law at the time in which they were committed. In accordance with jurisprudence of the Permanent Court of International Justice, reaffirmed by the International Court of Justice and other authorities,

> reparation must, as far as possible, wipe out all consequences of the illegal act and re-establish the situation which would, in all probability have existed if that act had not been committed.[7]

However, it is extremely difficult to conceive concrete modalities through which to "repair the irreparable" caused by criminal conduct such as mass murder and extermination. Hence, the *restitutio in integrum* must be understood *cum grano salis*, as it may only regard certain types, or forms, of reparation. Restitution of material loss, including restitution of stolen property, could have taken place in pursuance to the literal interpretation of this principle, while material and immaterial forms of compensation and rehabilitation could have been employed to provide partial reparation to the immense harm suffered by the survivors of the Armenian community and, in particular, the descendants of the community's members who lost their life in the course of the genocidal campaign against them.

Until today, the principle of *restitutio in integrum* and the consequent legal regime for reparations operate primarily on an inter-state level, not inter-individual.[8] In the aftermath of World War I, the filter of States was a necessary condition (although almost always *not* a sufficient condition) to permit that the victims of serious violations could find some form of reparation and recognition as "rights-bearers". Notwithstanding the fact that the death of all direct perpetrators

emotional harm": *Velásquez Rodríguez Case [Compensatory Damages]*, 21 July 1989, Inter-American Court of Human Rights, Series C, No. 7 [1990], Paragraphs 6, p. 25–26.

[7] *Case concerning the Factory at Chorzów (Claim for Indemnity) (Germany v. Poland)*, 13 September 1928, Permanent Court of International Justice, Merits, Collection of Judgments, Series A, No. 17, p. 47.

[8] While individual victims are rights' bearers vis-à-vis individual perpetrators in specific treaty-based systems (e.g. the Rome Statute of the International Criminal Court), this is not yet the case in general international law. Several universal standards on victims' rights are contained in non-legally-binding instruments, such as UN General Assembly resolutions. Conversely, under International Human Rights Law and International Humanitarian Law, there is no doubt that individual victims are rights' holders vis-à-vis the State that is most connected with the phenomenon of victimization, primarily, the territorial State and/or the State on behalf of which the authors of the violations were acting.

Also the duty to prosecute alleged perpetrators of international crimes, which constitutes an essential element of the right to justice for victims of crimes that may not be severed from the right to know the truth and to reparations, must be exercised by relevant States, in accordance with the jurisdictional criteria established by National Law or by applicable treaties. In the aftermath of World War I, this duty had been established only for war crimes under the relevant peace treaties combined with the Hague Convention of 1907, which reflected customary international law.

and their accomplices may render moot the quest for inter-individual reparations, the finding that State's responsibility derives from the commission of crimes of concern to the International Community as a whole (i.e. war crimes) may give a firm legal basis or, at a minimum, strengthen the claims of victims' successors. The consequent responsibility of relevant States regards two major forms of reparations: (I) those aimed at trying to partially restore the harm and losses of victims through material and immaterial means of reparation provided to their descendants; and (II) those aimed at preventing that atrocities are repeated in the future, also via the proper memorialization and recognition of the gross abuses of the past and the enactment of strict guarantees of non-repetition through legislative means and international cooperation against impunity for international crimes. While the first form of reparations must be inevitably undertaken by the State that succeeded in the rights and obligations of the State of nationality of the alleged perpetrators (State-actors of the Ottoman Empire, now Turkey), the second form of forward-looking reparations must also be undertaken by the territorial State, Armenia, which shall find any adequate ways and means to honour the victims.

According to the normative framework contained in various international instruments,[9] the types of reparation available to victims of crimes under International Law are restitution, compensation, rehabilitation, guarantees of non-repetition and satisfaction.[10] Some non-binding instruments refer to the notion of assistance to victims, which in substance corresponds to rehabilitation. In the view of this author, which is informed by a victims' rights perspective, guarantees of non-repetition and satisfaction[11] fall under the broad category of rehabilitation, which is aimed at addressing the traumatic consequences of atrocity-crimes and aggression on affected communities of victims, including in their multi-generational and institutional dimension.

[9]An overview of the existing International Instruments can be found in Brikci and Laucci (2016).

[10]For a detailed definition of these forms of reparation, reference is made to the last UN instrument on this subject-matter and the first decision of the International Criminal Court establishing principles relating to reparations, namely: M.C. Bassiouni, The right to restitution, compensation and rehabilitation for victims of gross violations of human rights and fundamental freedoms – Final report of the Special Rapporteur, UN Doc. E/CN.4/2000/62 (this report reflects also the content of report by previous rapporteur T. van Boven) and Prosecutor v. Thomas Lubanga Dyilo, No. ICC-01/04-01/06-2904, Trial Chamber I, Decision Establishing the Principles and Procedure to be applied in Reparations, 7 August 2012.

[11]Satisfaction as type of reparation for the benefit of victims of crimes under International Law does not correspond to the notion of satisfaction within the framework of the law on State responsibility as established in its codification by the International Law Commission in the Draft Articles on State Responsibility, UN Doc. A/56/10 (2001). The UN General Assembly, in its resolution 56/83 of 2001, commended the draft to the attention of governments "without prejudice to the question of their future adoption or other appropriate action".

4 Multi-generational Legacy of Victimization and Types of Reparations Aimed at Addressing It

Multi-generational harm and the need to put in place adequate measures of reparation have been studied by the psycho-social doctrine that investigated and researched into the profound impact that atrocity-crimes may have on the development of peaceful and open societies.[12] Studies have evidenced how the multi-generational dimension of trauma has impacted resilience and sustainability of societies in which the new generations inherited from their victimized parents and communities a sense of injustice and un-satisfaction that characterized their individual existences and the very identity of their "people" or "nation", especially with respect to unfriendly relations with other peoples and/or nations harbouring alleged perpetrators and/or their successors. Affected communities of victims and their descendants tried to fill the gap of impunity, injustice and grievances coming from a traumatic past in ways that at times have been peaceful and at times were characterized by violence—not necessarily retaliatory violence—and discrimination —not necessarily targeted to the communities of the alleged perpetrators of un-redressed atrocities. In this way, the unpredictable cycle of violence and conflict has brought about the victimization of new individuals, new groups and new peoples, dramatically enlarging the scope of the multi-generational legacy of impunity.

Against this background, both the Turkish State and the Armenian State may undertake a number of meaningful measures that can try to address the consequences of the harm suffered by Armenians during the I World War.

First of all, in the realm of restitution, an effort shall be made by relevant authorities to identify all stolen property, as difficult as it may be, with the view of creating an inventory for restitution to the successors of the victims in all cases in which there are not third parties that acquired such properties in good faith in the course of the last 100 or more years. The Turkish State should create a fund through which to provide monetary compensation for all property that may not be returned. In a purely legal perspective, as re-affirmed by Article 75 of the Rome Statute of the ICC on reparations to victims, it is not possible to confiscate and return illegally obtained property without safeguarding the rights of *bona fide* third parties. It appears self-evident that after 100 years of possession of land by third parties, a vast number of these proprietors may be considered third parties that acquired real estate and/or land property or other stolen goods in good faith. However, once it would be determined that the land and real estate properties or other goods of Armenian victims of atrocities were destroyed or unlawfully taken during World War I and that they are currently in the portfolio of *bona fide* third parties, the restitution of such properties or goods shall be transformed into compensation through an amount of money that would be deemed commensurate to the harm

[12]Reference is made to the pivotal work of Dr. Yael Danieli: See, in particular, Danieli (2007a, b, 2009).

currently suffered by the descendants of the victims. As no perpetrator may be accountable for the harm caused, the subsidiary responsibility to compensate shall be exercised by the States having jurisdiction over territories where properties are located and/or where the descendants of alleged perpetrators are present.

Secondly, a compensation scheme shall be created by the Turkish State for all alleged individuals who were killed or otherwise victimized by agents of the Ottoman Empire or by member of organized groups that were operating with the support or acquiescence of the Ottoman apparatus. While the amount of compensation to be received by any family member who inherited the traumatic impact of atrocities suffered by their ancestors may be symbolic, such an individual scheme for compensation might represent the most formidable means of healing of past wounds that still remain open, and may help communities affected by the WWI atrocities to move forward towards more peaceful relations, cooperation and integration, which are useful dynamics in an International Community characterized by the globalization of financial markets and other key aspects of the economic, cultural and social life, especially communications.

Thirdly, in the realm of rehabilitation, an emphasis has been made by authors and relevant bodies on the importance of public apologies, admissions of historic responsibility and other immaterial forms of collective reparations, which can entail the naming of streets and buildings to honour the memory of victims, the elaboration of history books and institutional celebration and remembrance of the victims. All these means of rehabilitation may have a special significance for the victims' successors if the descendants of the alleged perpetrators, especially via their State authorities, would undertake these extremely significant and powerful collective measures, which are retrospective. However, equally serious forward-looking and preventative efforts to provide strong guarantees of non-repetition to fulfil the moral imperative of "never again" ("nunca mas") must be undertaken by both the State of nationality of the alleged perpetrators (Turkey) and the territorial State in which serious atrocity-crimes occurred (Armenia). Both States should make a political determination about the historical record of the past atrocities and recognize the *jus cogens* obligation to prevent the re-occurrence of the most serious crimes of concern to the International Community as a whole, including genocide, crimes against humanity and war crimes. As such, both Turkey and Armenia, through separate and uniquely meaningful acts, should ratify the Rome Statute of the International Criminal Court and extend the protection that the Hague-based Court provides to their civilian populations in case there would be impunity for crimes that would be committed after the entry into force of the Statute in their territories or by their nationals, in accordance with Article 12 of the Statute. This legally-binding measure would have an enormous, immediate impact on the intergenerational trauma of Armenians who live in Armenia, as well as on Armenians who are part of the diaspora but follow closely the institutional developments of their country of origin, as it would entrench the "never again" principle in the State-policy. Therefore, ratification of the Rome Statute should be first and foremost undertaken by the Republic of Armenia. In this respect, it is rather surprising to note that such a measure is not even considered in the recommendations of the voluminous Report published on the occasion of the 100 anniversary of the *Metz Yeghern.*[13] It is also disheartening to notice that the Presidency of the Republic of Armenia decided to expunge the text of an "ICC-clause" from the package of constitutional reforms proposed by a Special Commission set up to revise the Constitution in 2015, 100 years after the "Armenian genocide".[14] Such an amendment to Articles 91 and/or 92 of the Constitution regarding "judicial sovereignty" has been deemed as necessary precondition for Armenia to ratify the Rome Statute of the ICC by an opinion of the Armenian Constitutional Court in 2004.[15] According to internal sources of the European Union, which is in a regular political dialogue with Third States on the ICC to implement the goals of the EU Decision on the ICC,[16] the Government of Armenia revealed to an EU delegation in Yerevan in January 2017 that Armenia was still supportive of the ICC and would have continued to consider to join the Rome Statute system against impunity in its capacity as signatory state. On the contrary, Turkey appeared very far from a positive decision to this effect notwithstanding a relevant constitutional reform. In fact, in 2003/2004 the Grand Assembly of Turkey revised the Constitution to align certain aspects of its basic law to fundamental human rights, as negotiated with the EU and within the Council of Europe. The Grand Assembly, on the basis of a report by Mr. Haluk Ipek, MP, adopted an amendment to Article 38 of the Constitution, which is similar to an amendment to the German Constitution, that stipulates as follows:

> No citizen shall be extradited to a foreign country because of an offence, except under obligations resulting from being a party to the International Criminal Court.[17]

However, such an important interim development was not followed-up by the commencement of an actual legislative process to authorize the ratification of the Rome Statute, and the Government of Turkey appeared to have motivated its

---

[13]The Report of the Armenian Genocide Reparations Study Group" (March 2016), available at www.armeniangenocidereparations.info.

[14]A copy of the draft ICC-clause proposed for inclusion in the amendments' package by a Commission of Experts convened by the Armenian Ministry of Justice is on file with the author.

[15]Relevant information may be found on the website of the European Commission for Democracy through Law – the Venice Commission – of the Council of Europe, including all the commentaries made by the Venice Commission to the 2015 drafted and adopted constitutional reforms: See www.venice.coe.int/WebForms/members/countries.aspx?id=42. Relevant information on the Armenian ICC process is available on the website of Parliamentarians for Global Action: See www.pgaction.org/campaigns/icc/cis/armenia.html.

[16]Council Decision 2011/168/CFSP of 21 March 2011 on the International Criminal Court and repealing Common Position 2003/444/CFSP, OJ L 76/56 of 22 March 2011.

[17]Article 38 ("Principles relating to offences and penalties"), Constitution of Turkey, as amended on May 7, 2004 by Act No. 5170 of the Grand Assembly of Turkey, available at https://global.tbmm.gov.tr/docs/constitution_en.pdf.

objection to joining the Rome Statute system on basis of an insurmountable and rather contradictory argument vis-à-vis the formulations of its new Article 38 of the Constitution, namely, the lack of ICC jurisdiction over the crime of terrorism.[18]

References

Brikci S, Laucci C (2016) Protecting/promoting the rights of victims in international law: some achievements and ways forward. In: Acconci P, Donat Cattin D, Marchesi A, Palmisano G, Santori V (eds) International law and the protection of humanity: essays in honour of judge Flavia Lattanzi. Brill/Nijhoff, Leiden/Boston, pp 306–322

Danieli Y (2007a) Multicultural, multigenerational perspectives in the understanding and assessment of trauma. In: Wilson JP, So-Kum Tang CC (eds) The cross-cultural assessment of psychological trauma and post-traumatic stress studies. Springer, New York, pp 65–89

Danieli Y (2007b) Multigenerational legacies of trauma. New Jersey Psychol 57:23–26

Danieli Y (2009) Massive trauma and the healing role of reparative justice. In: Ferstman C, Goetz M, Stephens A (eds) Reparations for victims of genocide, crimes against humanity and war crimes: systems in place and systems in the making. Martinus Nijhoff, The Hague, pp 41–78

Donat Cattin D (1998) The role of victims in the proceedings before the ICC. In: Lattanzi F (ed) The International Criminal Court: comments to the Draft Statute. Editoriale Scientifica, Napoli, pp 251–272

Donat Cattin D (1999) The role of victims in ICC proceedings. In: Lattanzi F, Schabas W (eds) Essays on the Rome Statute of the International Criminal Court, vol I. Il Sirente, Ripa di Fagnano Alto, 251–277

Donat Cattin D (1999/2008/2015) (I/II/III edition) Article 68—protection of victims and witnesses and their participation in the proceedings. In: Triffterer O (ed) (III ed Co-ed Ambos K) Commentary on the Rome Statute of the International Criminal Court, observers' notes, article by article. Nomos/Hart, Baden-Baden/Munich/Oxford

Donat Cattin D (1999/2008/2015) (I/II/III edition) Article 75—reparations to victims. In: Triffterer O (ed) (III ed Co-ed Ambos K) Commentary on the Rome Statute of the International Criminal Court, observers' notes, article by article. Nomos/Hart, Baden-Baden/Munich/Oxford

Roht Arriaza N (2010) Reparations in international law and practice. In: Cherif Bassiouni M (ed) The pursuit of international criminal justice: a world study on conflicts, victimization and post-conflict justice. Intersentia, Antwerp/Oxford/Portland, pp 655–698

[18]International terrorism is a transnational crime, not a crime under International Law. As such, all the general principles of international criminal law codified in Part III of the Rome Statute are not applicable to terrorism, which was not incorporated in the Rome Statute's subject-matter jurisdiction. Needless to say, should individuals belonging to a terrorist group commit genocide, crimes against humanity or war crimes, the ICC may exercise the relevant jurisdiction.

Part III
Denying the Armenian Massacres

The Armenian Massacres and the Price of Memory: Impossible to Forget, Forbidden to Remember

Agostina Latino

> *I think memory interacting with perception together with the things undergone in connection with them write as it were statements in our minds.*
> *When what is undergone writes the truth we acquire true judgements or statements;*
> *when this as it were internal scribe of ours writes falsehoods, the result is the opposite of the truth.*
>
> (*Philebus,* 39a; trans. By J. C. B. Gosling)

Contents

1 Introduction 196
2 Right to Truth and to Memory in International Law 199
3 International Practice Concerning the Massacres of the Armenians 204
4 The (Non)-Right to Memory of the Armenian Massacres in Turkish Law 221
5 Concluding Remarks 226
References 233

Abstract This contribution is aimed at assessing the right to truth and the right to memory of the Armenian people and of Armenians as individuals, drawing from a legal framework first developed in regional and local contexts and further elaborated at the level of the United Nations. It provides an in-depth picture of the widespread practice concerning the recognition of the massacre of the Armenians in the International Community, which includes various statements and actions by national and international institutions. It also examines the position of Turkey on the matter. As a conclusion, it puts forward some proposals *de jure condendo* with a view to contribute towards identifying the appropriate instruments to bring Turks and Armenians from conflict to dialogue. This would lead to the achievement of a shared memory based on a reconstruction of the events accepted by both sides, while being respectful of the historical truth.

A. Latino (✉)
University of Camerino, Camerino, Italy
e-mail: agostina.latino@unicam.it

F. Lattanzi and E. Pistoia (eds.), *The Armenian Massacres of 1915–1916 a Hundred Years Later*, Studies in the History of Law and Justice 15,
https://doi.org/10.1007/978-3-319-78169-3_9

1 Introduction

In the last decade of the past century, the list of human rights has been enriched with the right to memory,[1] together with the right to justice and to truth.[2]

The role of this right has four different aspects: curative for those affected and their relatives, judicial in the courts, pedagogical for the future generations and cultural for historians to whom it represents a source of reliable evidence to narrate the past. As correctly recognized by Farida Shaheed, Special Rapporteur in the field of cultural rights for the Human Rights Council,

> The goals assigned to memorialization processes are thus multi-faceted and, regardless of diversity in form and shape, memorials have both private/reflective and public/educative purposes. They are geared not only towards the past (recalling events, recognizing and honoring victims and enabling stories to be related), but equally to the present (healing processes and rebuilding of trust between communities) and the future (preventing further violence through education and awareness-raising).[3]

The right to memory encompasses a private and a public dimension and is therefore both an individual right and a collective one. From the first point of view, the right to memory belongs to the subjective dimension of each human being who can eventually choose a different path, such as that of oblivion.[4] But from the second point of view, its establishment ensures that a community (a people, a minority, an ethnical, religious group, etc.) satisfies the need to defend its roots, which are the basis of various kinds of identities, so that the removal of memory

---

[1]The right to memory, concerning mass-scale crimes, has emerged since the '80s: *ex plurimis* Gensburger and Lavabre (2004). This tendency to so-called memorialization has been institutionalized, in an increasingly similar manner between 1997 and 2005 with the involvement of multiple actors and States in different forums, as a propulsive mechanism to improve situations of conflict or repression, through the commitment to active commemorative policies. This has led some authors to speak of "malaise de la mémoire" (Rousso 1987) or "commemorative obsession" (Traverso 2006).

[2]The application was first received by the Inter-American Commission on Human Rights: "Every society has the inalienable right to know the truth about past events, as well as the motives and circumstances in which aberrant crimes came to be committed, in order to prevent repetition of such acts in the future", Annual Report of the Inter-American Commission on Human Rights 1985–1986, OEA/Ser.L/V/II.68, Doc. 8 rev. 1, 26 September 1986, p. 193, see at: https://www.cidh.oas.org/annualrep/85.86eng/toc.htm.

[3]Human Rights Council Twenty-fifth session, Agenda item 3, Promotion and protection of all human rights, civil, political, economic, social and cultural rights, including the right to development, A/HRC/25/49, 23 January 2014, §13.

[4]On the relationship between oblivion and memory, especially with regard to International Law, see Della Morte (2014).

threatens the knowledge and the judgments of future generations.[5] The right to memory is nonetheless strictly linked with the right to truth, whose private and public dimensions are indivisible. This implies that the grief borne by individuals and communities should be recognized in order to allow the full knowledge of the circumstances and the reasons for their grievances.

The close link between the right to truth and the right to memory clarifies one aspect which, at first glance, may seem paradoxical: in some cases, we should refer to the *right to memories* rather than the *right to memory*. This means that a single and shared memory is often triggered by a negotiating process between opposing parties, i.e. between those who claim to have suffered abuse and violence and those who deny having inflicted them.[6] The right to memory can therefore represent the aim rather than the starting point in ascertaining the historical event. "Memory" must not be used as a synonym of "history": the former is immanent, full of emotions that make the remembering eternal; the latter is the result of a study of sources (archival documents, oral testimonies, iconographies and audio-visual materials), i.e. an intellectual work of critical reflection, that secularizes the event.

A shared memory does not mean a more or less forced operation to reset the identities and hide the differences as if it were a "negotiated forgetfulness", a communion in the lack of memory. According to the well-known platonic distinction, it is necessary to distinguish between *anamnesis* and *mneme*, whereby the first word means the recovery (necessarily subjective) of what has previously been experienced and the second one refers to the stratification of something objective as it actually happened. A shared memory means reaffirming that the plurality of perspectives, readings, interpretations and historical narratives which arises does not necessarily imply the adoption of a relativism indifferent to the search of truth. The *mneme* is therefore the sensible memory, which strikes us without the involvement of willingness, while the *anamnesis* refers to a trained memory, an active and voluntary research, so that the main function of memory results in a "devoir de ne pas oublier".[7] In these terms, shared memory is to be regarded as an integral part of social claim mechanisms. Memory is in turn a key element not only to support and claim the experience of victims and survivors as the hub of the reconstruction of the social fabric and in the search for political solutions to the

[5]Giuva (2014), p. 16; Gallant (2009).

[6]According to Tomuschat (2006), the right of the victims to truth – if met – produces an effect of national cohesion, since a shared truth-memory is reconstructed.

[7]Ricoeur (2000).

conflict, but also as the central element in the building of a shared identity based on the respect of human rights.[8]

The dual right to memory and to truth emerges as an indispensable prerequisite for peace, in particular in cases of systematic and gross violations of human rights, so that the obligation to allow its full realization will be responsibility of the State which committed (or failed to prevent) such violations and, secondly, of each member of the International Community, given the *erga omnes* nature of this obligation.[9] In fact, if every State has a legal interest in the protection of this right,[10] it also has the *obligation to fulfil* by adopting positive measures in view of its full and concrete implementation.

In this paper we will try in the first place to reconstruct the notion and the legal-international function of the right to truth and to memory on the basis of the sources and the relevant international practice. Secondly, in the perspective of this right, we will address the issue of the Armenian massacres, which represent one of the darkest events in the history of the twentieth century. These events need to be addressed with a communication process between the opposing parties—Turks and Armenians—which should eventually result in a shared memory.

In fact both Turks and Armenians constitute social groups formed as "communities of memory" aimed at preserving their past (assumption of maintaining their identity) in the perspective of their own continuity and specificity.

Historians do not deny that hundreds of thousands of Armenians were massacred in the Ottoman Empire during the First World War; however, there is no agreement as to whether there was an intention "to destroy, in whole or in part, a national, ethnical, racial or religious group", as stated in Article 2 of the Convention on the prevention and punishment of the crime of genocide, recalled in Article 6 of the Statute of the International Criminal Court of 1998 and in the Statutes of the International Criminal Tribunal for former Yugoslavia and of the International Criminal Tribunal for Rwanda.[11] In this context we will avoid describing the events as "genocide": on the correctness (or not) of such a qualification of the Armenian

---

[8]Nevertheless, as pointed out by Damaška (2006), p. 17 when talking about the functions of International Criminal Justice, the pressing need to carry out historical research does not match the ability of judges to satisfy it. One reason is that they have to operate within time limitations and must produce stable decisions on which action is then taken: the *res* on which they focus must become *judicata* without undue delay. Historians, conversely, are not subject to the limitations of readiness and determination: they do not need to reach a decision quickly and can afford to follow the slow flow of history. Historians are free to change their findings. The *res judicata o*n historical issues is therefore nothing less than nonsense: history cannot be stopped by an ukase.

[9]In general, re the *ergaomnes* obligations that, on the one hand, erode and reduce the domestic jurisdiction of States and, on the other hand, imply obligations of *facere* for the subjects of the International Community, according to the principle of solidarity, see *ex plurimis* Picone (2013); Cannizzaro (2011); Tomuschat and Thouvenin (2006).

[10]International Court of Justice, Judgment of 5 February 1970, *Barcelona Traction, Light and Power Company Limited* (*Belgium* v. *Spain*), ICJ Reports 1970, 3 ss, § 33–34.

[11]It is, for instance, denied by Lewy (2005). For the opposite view see Flores (2006), as well as the Introduction of this Volume.

massacre we must refer to a very wide literature on the subject, as well as to some of the essays in this Volume. We will deliberately use neutral language functional to our goal, namely that of trying to subsume these events under the right to memory. In particular, on the one hand we will examine the widespread practice in the international community's recognition of the massacres of the Armenians (with positions and activities carried out at various levels both by national and international institutions) especially in the perspective of the right to truth and to memory; on the other hand, we will give an account of Turkey's position on the matter. Finally, we will try to draw some brief conclusions and formulate some proposals *de jure condendo* on the proper instruments to bring Turks and Armenians from the arena of conflict to the level of exchange of views, in order to reach a shared memory based on a reconstruction of the tragic events that can be accepted by both sides but does not deny the truth.

2 Right to Truth and to Memory in International Law

In the framework of the United Nations (UN), on the *soft law* level, many instruments have been adopted which include the right to memory among innovative forms of reparation, regarded as a form of satisfaction and of guarantees of non-repetition in the event of gross violations of human rights.

The Special Rapporteur of the Sub-Commission on Prevention of Discrimination and Protection of Minorities, Louis Joinet, drafted the Set of Principles for the protection and promotion of human rights through actions to combat impunity (hereafter Set of Principles)[12] in which, assuming that "before a new leaf can be turned the old leaf must be read",[13] the four rights-pillars of transitional justice are enucleated: the right to know the facts and the right to justice, the consequent right to compensation and guarantees of non-repetition. The *right to know* is defined not only as an individual right of each victim to know what really happened (*the right to truth*), but also as a collective right "drawing upon history to prevent violations from recurring in the future".[14]

[12]Louise Joinet, The Administration of Justice and the Human Rights of Detainees – Question of the impunity of perpetrators of human rights violations (civil and political), E/CN.4/Sub.2/1997/20/Rev.1.

[13]Ibidem, para. 50.

[14]Ibidem, para. 17.

The *Set of Principles* has been included and developed in the reports of the Special Rapporteur of the Sub-Commission, Theo van Boven,[15] and in the reports of Cherif Bassiouni, the Special Rapporteur of the Commission on Human Rights.[16]

The Set of Principles was updated by Diane Orentlicher[17] with the Updated Set of Principles for the Protection and Promotion of Human Rights through Action to Combat Impunity (hereafter Updated Set of Principles).[18] In the Updated Set of Principles, after affirming the inalienable right to the truth of

> "every people [...] about past events concerning the perpetration of heinous crimes and about the circumstances and reasons that led, through massive or systematic violations, to the perpetration of those crimes" it is stressed that "full and effective exercise of the right to the truth provides a vital safeguard against the recurrence of violation"[19] (Principle 2).

The right to truth is therefore conceived as a form of guarantee of non-repetition. It should also be noted that the right to know in this context is not limited to judicial truth, since Principle 4 states that it is

> irrespective of any legal proceedings.[20]

As for the right to the preservation of memory of the history of oppression suffered, as part of one's heritage, the obligation of the State

> to preserve archives and other evidence concerning violations of human rights and humanitarian law[21] (Principle 3).

is stressed. In the *Updated Set of Principles* we find both the two-way relationship of the right to memory with the right to truth since the one right depends on the other, and the restorative function of these rights. Thus, the overcoming of the centrality of victims *uti singulus* and the resulting peculiarity of the right to memory are also reflected on the function of (possible) punishment: its usual and "classical" aims and canons (general and specific deterrence, retribution-proportionality) are

---

[15]The Sub-Commission on Prevention of Discrimination and Protection of Minorities entrusted in 1989, by its resolution 1989/13 of 31 August 1989, a Special Rapporteur, Theo van Boven, with the task of undertaking a study concerning the right to restitution, compensation and rehabilitation for victims of gross violations of human rights and fundamental freedoms with a view to exploring the possibility of developing basic principles and guidelines on the issue.E/CN.4/1997/104. See the Final report submitted by Special Rapporteur Theo van Boven, Study Concerning the Right to Restitution, Compensation and Rehabilitation for Victims of Gross Violations of Human Rights and Fundamental Freedoms, E/CN.4/Sub.2/1993/8.

[16]Special Rapporteur Bassiouni, The Right to Restitution, Compensation and Rehabilitation for Victims of Gross Violations of Human Rights and Fundamental Freedoms, E/CN.4/2000/62.

[17]Diane Orentlicher was appointed by UN Secretary-General as Independent Expert to update the *Set of Principles*.

[18]The Updated Set Principles (UN Doc. E/CN.4/2005/102 and Addendum) were endorsed by the UN Commission on Human Rights at its 2005 session (CHR resolution 2005/81).

[19]Ibidem.

[20]Ibidem.

[21]Ibidem.

accompanied by *extraordinary purposes* (stigmatization, repair, compensation, reconciliation).

The inclusion of the right to truth and to memory among the forms of reparation is even more clearly reaffirmed in Resolution 60/147 by which the General Assembly of the UN adopted the Basic Principles and Guidelines on the Right to a Remedy and Reparation for Victims of Gross Violations of International Human Rights Law and Serious Violations of International Humanitarian Law (the so-called UN Basic Principles).[22] Here, in addition to "traditional" forms such as the verification of facts and the public dissemination of the truth the need for an official declaration or a judicial decision aimed at restoring the dignity of the victims and their relatives is recalled, together with a public apology, in which what must emerge clearly is the recognition of the facts and the assumption of responsibility, as well as commemorations and tributes to the victims and an accurate report of the violations of human rights and of international humanitarian law to be used as teaching material at all levels of education.[23] In this respect it should be noted that, according to the Chairperson-Rapporteur Alejandro Salinas, the UN Basic Principles

> did not introduce new principles of international law, but rather consolidated and clarified already existing obligations.[24]

The combination between the right to truth and the right to memory found its widest application on the one hand in Latin America, in the practice of the Inter-American Court of Human Rights (IACHR),[25] and on the other hand in

---

[22]The United Nations General Assembly adopted in 2005 by consensus the Basic Principles and Guidelines on the Right to a Remedy and Reparation for Victims of Gross Violations of International Human Rights Law and Serious Violations of International Humanitarian Law (General Assembly resolution 60/147 of 16 December 2005) (reparation principles) and in the same year the then United Nations Commission on Human Rights (succeeded by the Human Rights Council in 2006) endorsed the Updated Set of Principles for the Protection and Promotion of Human Rights through Action to Combat Impunity, E/CN.4/2005/102/Add.1.

[23]The resolution recommends States to take the UN Basic Principles into account, promote respect thereof and bring them to the attention of members of the governments.

[24]Report on the third consultative meeting, UN doc E/CN.4/2005/59, § 10–11.

[25]Ex plurimis, in the sentence *Miguel Castro-Castro Prison* v. *Peru*, judgment of 25 November 2006, para. 463, the Court ordered the building of a monument dedicated to the victims of the Peruvian Civil War, stating that Peru "must guarantee, within a one-year period, that all persons declared as deceased in the present Judgment are represented in the monument called The Eye that Cries"; in the case *Street children v. Guatemala* of 1999 concerning the violation of the right to life, and the prohibition of torture and slavery, the Court ordered the creation of an educational centre with a memorial plaque dedicated to the victims; in the case *Serrano Cruz sisters* v. *El Salvador* of 2005 a day of remembrance was established to commemorate the children who disappeared in an armed conflict; in the sentence *Huilca-Tecse v. Perù* of 2005 the Court ordered the establishment of a university course entitled to the victim; in the case *Masacres de Río Negro* v. *Guatemala*, Judgment of 4 September 2012, para. 279 e 28, related to the killing of 19 merchants in Colombia, the Court ordered Guatemala to build a memorial. As Farida Shaheed says: "Thus, Courts may also see their role as memorial facilitators and national authorities may see their approach contested by new actors actively engaged in shaping the memorial landscape",

post-dictatorial situations or in a context of *transitional justice*,[26] with particular regard to Commissions of truth and reconciliation.[27]

In the first context, the tendency towards *memorialization* led the IACHR to affirm the inadmissibility of amnesties and prescriptions, as well as causes precluding liability that prevent the investigation and the punishment of those responsible for gross violations of human rights: such measures, according to the IACHR, are devoid of legal effects because they deprive the victims of their rights such as, *inter alia*, the right to truth and to memory.[28]

Where the Commissions of truth and reconciliation are concerned (the practice of the right to memory, the ownership of which is at the same time subjective and diffuse) it is worth recalling, *ex plurimis,* the Commission for Historical Clarification in Guatemala which, in order to preserve "the historical memory, both individual and collective" as a "basis of national identity", recommended, *inter alia*, the building of monuments and the naming of parks and public buildings to the

Principles for the Protection and Promotion of Human Rights through Action to Combat Impunity, E/CN.4/2005/102/Add.1, §. 38.

[26]The *transitional justice*, as defined by the Secretary General of the United Nations, is "the full range of processes and mechanisms associated with a society attempts to come to terms with a legacy of large-scale past abuses, in order to ensure accountability, serve justice and achieve reconciliation. These may include both judicial and non-judicial mechanisms, with differing levels of international involvement (or none at all) and individual prosecutions, reparations, truth-seeking, institutional reform, vetting and dismissals, or a combination thereof". In this light, following the investigation of such gross and systematic violations, "reparations programs (that) seek to redress systemic violations of human rights by providing a range of material and symbolic benefits to victims can be arranged. Reparations can include monetary compensation, medical and psychological services, health care, educational support, return of property or compensation for loss thereof, but also official public apologies, *building museums and memorials, and establishing days of commemoration*". Italics added. Guidance Note of the Secretary-General on United Nations Approach to Transitional Justice, March 2010, § 3. https://www.un.org/ruleoflaw/files/TJ_Guidance_Note_March_2010FINAL.pdf.

[27]See, for example, the *Truth and Reconciliation Commission* (or, in afrikaans, *Waarheid-en-versoeningskommissie*), i.e. the extraordinary Commission established in South Africa after the end of the *apartheid* regime, known as the *starting point* of the so-called *Restorative Justice*, i.e. the justice which chooses the path of building a dialogue between victims and perpetrators, the antithesis of the justice of the victors over the losers, aimed at punishing the culprits.

[28]*Barrios Altos* v. *Perú* of 14 March 2001, § 41–44. Seem to welcome this motion, the so-called *juicios por la verdad*, i.e. the tools used in Argentina to judge the crimes committed during the military dictatorship (1976–1983) that are reopening the trials for the crimes of the military dictatorship, following the annulment of the Supreme Court of the Laws of *Obediencia debida* (Law 23.521 of 4 June 1987 which imposed an absolute presumption of "Absolute Obedience" in relation to the crimes committed by the subordinate members of the Armed and Security Forces) and *Punto Final* (Law 23.492 of 23 December 1986 under which a deadline of 60 days was established to prescribe punishment and to open proceedings against the alleged perpetrators of the crimes committed during the military dictatorship). Although such proceedings resolved under the auspices of the Federal Court of La Plata, the Capital of the Province of Buenos Aires, eminently served the purpose of ascertaining the truth, so that on completion of the process no "typical" penalty was imposed. See Andriotti Romanin (2013).

victims.[29] Furthermore, the Commission on the Truth for El Salvador recommended the building of a national monument which would contain the names of all the victims of the conflict, the recognition of their good name and the serious crimes they had suffered and, finally, the establishment of a national holiday to their memory as a symbol of reconciliation.[30] Other Commissions have also recommended that the places of detention of the victims be turned into places of memory: for example, one of the first inquiry commissions in Africa (1990–1992), in Chad, besides ordering the building of a memorial for the victims of the repression carried out by the government of Hissène Habré and requesting that the second Sunday of December be declared a day of prayer and memory, recommended that the former headquarters of the Direction de la Documentation et de la Sécurité (i.e. the headquarters of the secret services) be transformed from an illegal prison into a museum, "to remember the dark reign".[31] Similarly, in Morocco, the Equity and Reconciliation Commission recommended in its final report the transformation of the old illegal detention centers into projects to preserve memory.[32]

As a confirmation of the crystallization of the right to memory, let us mention, with particular reference to the European Union (EU), the Council Framework Decision 2008/913/JHA on combating certain forms and expressions of racism and xenophobia by means of criminal law. In fact, this decision requires member States to adopt the measures necessary to ensure that intentional conduct is made punishable: in particular, condoning, denying or grossly trivializing crimes of genocide, crimes against humanity or crimes of war, as defined in Articles 6, 7 and 8 of the Statute of the International Criminal Court; and secondly, condoning, denying or grossly trivializing the crimes defined in Article 6 of the Statute of the International Military Tribunal, annexed to the London Agreement of 8 August 1945.[33] Among the EU member States France in particular should be mentioned: since the '90s it has played a key role by implementing an advanced policy concerning the

[29]Report of the Commission for Historical Clarification, Conclusions and Recommendations, p. 49, available from https://hrdag.org/wp-content/uploads/2013/01/CEHreport-english.pdf. The Report pays particular attention to the need to give due consideration to the multilateral nature of the Guatemalan Nation and to promote and authorize the creation of monuments and municipal graveyards, developed according to the forms of the collective Maya memory.

[30]From Madness to Hope: the 12-year war in El Salvador: Report of the Commission on the Truth for El Salvador, S/25500, p. 186, see at: http://www.usip.org/sites/default/files/file/ElSalvador-Report.pdf.

[31]See Abakar (2006), pp. 110–111.

[32]Equity and Reconciliation Commission, final report, Truth, Equity and Reconciliation, vol. 1, in specie, pp. 92 and 99, available from http://www.ccdh.org.ma/IMG/pdf/rapport_ang_1.pdf. According to Farida Shaheed "Recommendations by truth and reconciliation commissions are important landmarks, helping civil society organizations to keep memorial issues on the agenda. Those recommendations often limit the choice of action by a Government, which might otherwise be tempted to destroy places of suffering and, in doing so, erase the memories attached to them", Principles for the Protection and Promotion of Human Rights through Action to Combat Impunity, E/CN.4/2005/102/Add.1, § 44.

[33]See http://eur-lex.europa.eu/LexUriServ/LexUriServ.do?uri=OJ:L:2008:328:0055:0058:it:PDF.

protection of the right to memory, with the adoption both of the so-called *lois mémorielles* or *lois compassionélles* (as defined to emphasize empathy with the victims), which recognize genocides and other similar tragic historical events and of which the *Loi Gayssot* of 1990[34] was the forerunner, and measures introducing the crime of Holocaust denial: the first category of laws are bound to require "the necessity to remember", while the laws belonging to the second category are designed to impose a penalty on those claiming to remember in a different way.

3 International Practice Concerning the Massacres of the Armenians

And so *quid iuris* in relation to the massacre of the Armenians?

It seems appropriate to refer briefly to the events.[35] As we know, the massacres of the Christian population (Armenians, Syrian Catholics, Syrian Orthodox, Assyrian, Chaldean and Greek) that occurred between 1915 and 1916 are remembered as the *Metz Yeghern*, "the great crime" or "the great evil".[36] The killings began on the night between 23 and 24 April 1915[37] when the first arrests were carried out among the Armenian elite of Constantinople upon order of the Ottoman empire's government, led by the "three pasha" (Talât,[38] Enver[39] and Cemal), the triumvirate who had taken power in a coup in January 1913. The operation continued in the following days. In a month more than two thousand

[34]About which see Kahn (2016); Nora (2011); Weil (2009).

[35]For an analytical reconstruction, see ex plurimis, Flores D'Arcais (2006); Introduction of this Volume.

[36]Bozarlsan et al. (2015).

[37]On 24 April 1915, the Interior Minister Mehmed Talât signed the order to arrest 2,345 prominent intellectuals, businessmen and people of culture from Constantinople and lead them to detention centres. They were followed by several hundreds more people. A few weeks later, Talât signed the law Tehcir, which decreed the expulsion of the Armenian population from the Empire. Armenians were forcibly removed and their property was confiscated. Ottoman soldiers devastated the Armenian villages, killing residents, taking them by force to concentration camps or burying them in mass graves. On this issue see Dadrian (2005).

[38]Mehmed Talât Pascià, (Edirne, 1874 – Berlin 1921), one of the leaders of the *Young Turks*, i.e. of the *Committee of Union and Progress* (CUP) party, which had gained through a coup d'état in 1913 control of the empire and established a military dictatorship. Mehmed Talât Pascià was the Interior Minister and Secretary-General of the CUP and, in 1917, the Grand Vizier, who ordered the closure of all Armenian political organizations in the empire and the relocation of Armenians. He was a major supporter of the Ottoman Empire's entry into the First World War alongside Germany, during which he contributed to the organization of the massacres of the Armenians.

[39]Ismail Enver, also known as Ismail Pascià or Enver Pashaor Enver Bey (Istanbul, 1881–1922), the Minister of War, de facto Commander of the Ottoman Army and Commander of the Third Army in Eastern Anatolia, leader of the Young Turks, had a leading role in the last period of the Ottoman Empire. It has been established that he planned and facilitated the elimination of non-Turkish population in the territory of the Ottoman Empire.

Armenian intellectuals, including journalists, writers, poets, public officials and parliamentarians were deported to the interior of Anatolia since they were regarded as a terrorist group. The aim of the Young Turks, i.e. the Committee of Union and Progress (CUP) (the nationalist organization founded in the early twentieth century) was to establish a Turkish National State, following the example of the new European countries, and to make it the leader of the Turkish-speaking world in central Asia, with the ultimate purpose of re-founding former Turkestan. In fact, until the late nineteenth century the Christian and Jewish communities in the Ottoman Empire had enjoyed certain rights under the *millet* system (non-Muslim religious and national communities), which had ensured the peaceful coexistence of Jews, Christians and Muslims. The Armenian and Indo-European community,[40] the largest among the non-Muslim communities, was the most evident obstacle to realizing the nationalist dream of an immense territory from the Mediterranean to Chinese Xinjiang. The best opportunity for resolving what was called the "Armenian question" and implement this plan arose as a result of the defeats suffered at the beginning of the First World War against the Russian Army, in which battalions of (Russian) Armenian volunteers operated and were potentially attractive for (Ottoman) Armenians settled on the Eastern border of the Ottoman Empire. This occasion arose especially as a result of the intention of the Ottoman government to expel the Armenian population from the Eastern part of the Empire bordering with Russia, its great enemy, because it feared that, in the chaos of the war, the country would instigate the Armenians to revolt, with risks of further fragmentation of the Ottoman Empire, while its armies clashed with Russia's allies, namely Great Britain and France. The defeats suffered led to the Ottoman Empire's decision to implement—in cooperation with its ally Friedrich Bronsart von Schellendorf, Major General of Wilhelm the Second's Reich, attached to the Military Mission to the Empire from 1913–1917—the extermination and the mass deportation of Western Armenia's Christian population. Since the beginning of 1915 the male Armenians of age for military service were concentrated in "labor battalions" of the Turkish Army and then killed, while the rest of the population was deported to the region of Deirez Zor in Syria with the death marches which involved more than one million people: hundreds of thousands died from starvation, illness, exhaustion or were massacred along the way.[41] On 24 May 1915 the Triple Entente Allies reacted to the violence carried out by the *Sublime Porte* against the

[40]The Armenian *millet* included about 3 million people, mostly allocated in the South-Eastern area of the Anatolian peninsula and present also in areas such as the *vilayet* (administrative divisions, or provinces) on the Caucasian border (in the hands of the Tsar), in Persia and, in small numbers, in the big cities.

[41]According to an eyewitness, the German missionary Johannes Lepsius (1858–1926), who reported in his writings that the massacres amounted to 2,493 villages looted and destroyed; the same fate fell to 568 churches and 77 convents; 646 villages converted to Islam; 191 clerics were brutally assassinated; 55 priests converted to Islam; 328 churches were transformed into mosques; 546 thousand people were reduced to misery and starvation, with a total of more than 200 thousand victims and 100 thousand refugees in Transcaucasia: Lepsius (1916).

Armenians with the Joint Declaration of France, Great Britain and Russia, where the massacres were described as

> new crimes of Turkey against humanity and civilization.[42]

In response, on 27 May 1915, the Ottoman government adopted the "temporary law of deportation"[43] and, on June 10 of the same year, the Parliament approved the "temporary law of expropriation and confiscation".[44] The former provided military authorities with the legal grounds for the forced transfer of the Armenian population from Anatolia and Cilicia for security, strategy and military reasons[45]; the latter allowed the sale of all the property of the deportees. The Joint Declaration may have had a boomerang effect on the Armenians who, on the contrary, were supposed to be protected by it: since the Allies condemned the Armenian massacres and the connivance of the Ottoman authorities,[46] the leaders of the CUP had nothing to lose and consequently decided to resolutely proceed in a massive and systematic way.[47]

The number of Armenians who died in this massacre is controversial. Turkish sources place the number of deaths at 300 thousand, while the Armenian sources speak of 2.5 million. Historians estimate that figures range between 500 thousand

---

[42]The text is available on http://www.armenian-genocide.org/Affirmation.160/current_category.7/affirmation_detail.html. The *Joint Declaration,* drafted during a month of negotiations by top-level diplomats of France, the United Kingdom and the Russian Empire, was conceived by the Chancellor's offices of the Entente (animated mainly by an initiative of the Czarist Empire) and made public on 24 May 1915 in the Capitals of the three States. Schabas (2009), stresses the importance of this statement since it represents the first instrument of international law in which the term "crimes against humanity" is used.

[43]Since it considered it a purely governmental act, it was possible for the Ottoman Parliament to repeal this law at the resumption of its work, on 4 November 1918, because of the unconstitutionality due to the lack of parliamentary ratification.

[44]It was expected that the measures of the law would have ensured the preservation of the assets of the deportees, thus facilitating their restitution at the end of the war. As the Constitution of 1876 provided, the law was promulgated and at the same time presented in Parliament to be discussed and eventually amended or repealed. Given the heated parliamentary debate that ensued, it was approved only at the end of the year by which time its effects had largely run their course.

[45]The planning of the removal and liquidation of the Armenians was implemented on the basis of detailed scheduling which took account of distances and geographic and logistical factors (shape of the land, seasons, major roads, etc.): evacuation of Cilicia (April-May), the eastern regions and the Syrian coast, the regions of central Anatolia and south-eastern borders (August and September).

[46]In fact the Joint Declaration stated that "the Allied governments announce publicly to the Sublime-Porte that they will hold personally responsible [for] these crimes all members of the Ottoman government and those of their agents who are implicated in such massacres".

[47]Bloxham (2005) believes that the *Joint Declaration* helped to precipitate the events against the Armenians instead of providing them protection which might have proved effective only at military level. See Flores, Introduction in this Volume.

and 2 million deaths, but the toll of 1.5 million is the most widespread and appears to be the closest to the truth.[48]

Immediately after its defeat, the Ottoman Empire recognized the massacres of Armenians and prosecuted some alleged perpetrators.[49] Other Turks—more than 100—accused of war crimes were deported by the British to be tried in a more impartial environment in Malta, but they were released and repatriated in the context of an exchange with 22 British prisoners held by the Turkish government of Mustafa Kemāl Atatürk (1881–1938, President of the Turkish Republic from 1923 until his death).[50]

---

[48]*Ex plurimis*, see Hovannisian (1981).

[49]In the first trial the so-called executioner of Yozgat, i.e. the local governor of the city, Mehmed Kemal (5 February–7 April 1919) was prosecuted and charged of plotting the deportation and/or the killing of the Armenian ethnicity in the district. After his decisions to that effect, only 88 Armenians out of 1,800 survived. The judgment, delivered on April 8th, sentenced Mehmed Kemal to death by strangulation, and he was executed in the first half of the same month. The second trial took place in Trebisonda from 26 March to 20th May 1919: two out of nine indicted were sentenced to death and the other seven to several years in prison. Other trials against local officials were those of Harpout, Baibourt and Erzindjan. The main trial, conducted against the other officials of the State, opened in Istanbul on 28 April 1919 and ended on 5 July of the same year with sentences which condemned to death in absentia the "three pashas" (Talât, Enver e Cemal), while it decreed sentences of 15 years imprisonment for three other officials of the *Ittihad* party and acquitted two (the former Minister of Finance Djavit Bey and the former Minister of Trade and Agriculture, Mustafa Şeref Bey). In particular, as regards Talât, the Atatürk revolution which overthrew the political order of Turkey allowed him to escape abroad but during a trip to Berlin he was assassinated by Soghomon Tehlirian, a survivor of the Armenian genocide and member of the *Nemesi* Project. Tehlirian was put on trial for murder but was acquitted by the jury. His three defense lawyers, including Theodor Niemeyer, a professor of law at Kiel University, called to testify in his favor survivors of the Armenian massacre such as Grigoris Balakian, and eyewitnesses of the massacres such as Johannes Lepsius and Liman von Sanders, the German General engaged on the Ottoman front during the First World War. Therefore the trial was not primarily based on the murder of Talât by Tehlirian but also and especially on the state of mind of the people caused by the Armenian massacres of whom Talât was one of the main perpetrators. When asked by the judge if he felt any sort of guilt, Tehlirian remarked: "I do not consider myself guilty because my conscience is clear […] I have killed a man. But I am not a murderer". It took the jury slightly over a hour to render a verdict of "not guilty": Vartabedian (2007).

[50]The British forces that were supposed to exercise jurisdiction as occupying forces, aware of the growing and insurmountable difficulties involved in proceeding against the alleged perpetrators, decided the exchange on November 1st, 1921. The failure of the Malta trial, which left open the issue of the Armenian massacres, was due to the competence *ratione materiae* of the British military tribunals which was limited to three cases – violation of the armistice terms, hindrance to its execution and ill-treatment of prisoners of war – with regard to the occupied territories. All other crimes, including crimes committed against the Armenian population, represented "a legal nightmare, a *terra incognita* that for a first time challenged legal minds to figure out solutions to phenomena unfamiliar before in the history of warfare and its aftermath": Bonello (2008). In fact, in the Histories of Malta the judge of the European Court of Human Rights, Giovanni Bonello, stated that the *legal vacuum* encountered in 1919 meant that the post-World War I Malta Trial failed to play a similar role to that of the Nuremberg Trials after the Second World War, i.e. to revolutionize the fundamental principle of *nullum crimen sine lege*. For a summary

The massacres of the Armenians were qualified as crimes against humanity[51] in the Peace Treaty of Sèvres of 10 August 1920, concluded between the Main Allied Powers of the First World War—United Kingdom, French Third Republic, Italy, Japan and Serbia[52]—and the Ottoman Empire which had fought on the side of the Central Powers. Article 230 of the Treaty followed the work of the Commission on the Responsibility of the Authors of the War and on Enforcement of Penalties established by the Paris Peace Conference.[53] It required the Turkish government to hand over to the Allies those charged with massacres committed during the war, as well as to recognize the judgments of the courts established by the Allies themselves or, eventually, by an international Tribunal created by the League of Nations for the punishment of crimes perpetrated not only against Allied civilians and military (for so-called war crimes), but also to the detriment of Ottoman citizens themselves (crimes against humanity).[54] In addition to ratifying this obligation and recognizing Armenia as an independent State (Article 88), the Treaty of Sèvres defined the new borders of the Ottoman Empire. Here the decisions were very unfavourable to the Ottoman Empire, since the territorial clauses of the Treaty took away from the former Ottoman Empire about four-fifths of its territory which was

see: http://www.independent.com.mt/articles/2012-04-19/news/turkeys-eu-minister-judge-giovanni-bonello-and-the-armenian-genocide-claim-about-malta-trials-is-nonsense-308828/.

[51]Already the Joint Declaration stated that "For about a month the Kurd and Turkish populations of Armenia have been massacring [killing] Armenians with the connivance [approval] and often assistance of Ottoman authorities".

[52]Other Allied Powers are: The First Republic of Armenia, Belgium, The First Czechoslovak Republic, Greece, Hejaz, The Second Polish Republic, The First Portuguese Republic, The Kingdom of Romania.

[53]Commission on the Responsibility of the Authors of the War and on Enforcement of Penalties, The American Journal of International Law 1920, Vol. 14, pp. 95–154.

[54]In the Treaty of Sèvres, five articles concerned the administration of justice against those charged of committing war crimes or related crimes: Article 226 "The Turkish Government recognizes the right of the Allied Powers to bring before military tribunals persons accused of having committed acts in violation of the laws and customs of war. [...]"; Article 227: "Persons guilty of criminal acts against the nationals of one of the Allied Powers shall be brought before the military tribunals of that Power [...]"; Article 228: "The Turkish Government undertakes to furnish all documents and information of every kind, the production of which may be considered necessary to ensure the full knowledge of the incriminating acts, the prosecution of offenders and the just appreciation of responsibility"; Article 229: "The provisions of Articles 226 to 228 apply similarly to the Governments of the States to which territory belonging to the former Turkish Empire has been or may be assigned, in so far as concerns persons accused of having committed acts contrary to the laws and customs of war who are in the territory or at the disposal of such States"; Article 230: "1. The Turkish Government undertakes to hand over to the Allied Powers the persons whose surrender may be required by the latter as being responsible for the massacres committed during the continuance of the state of war on territory which formed part of the Turkish Empire on August 1, 1914. 2. The Allied Powers reserve to themselves the right to designate the tribunal which shall try the persons so accused, and the Turkish Government undertakes to recognize such tribunal. 3. In the event of the League of Nations having created in sufficient time a tribunal competent to deal with the said massacres, the Allied Powers reserve to themselves the right to bring the accused persons mentioned above before such tribunal, and the Turkish Government undertakes equally to recognize such tribunal".

reduced to the Anatolian peninsula. The stipulations of Sèvres—which became outdated as a result of the independence War led by Atatürk—left the new Turkish leadership with the memory of an attempted break-up of the Empire planned by the European powers, which had received support from the Christian communities in the Ottoman territory. Therefore the term "Sèvres syndrome" has been commonly used to refer to a latent encirclement "psychosis" which characterized the Turkish conception of national security, considered to be endangered both from outside and from inside the country.[55] The Treaty, negotiated by Sultan Memed VI, never entered into force because it was strongly opposed by Atatürk, who won the Turkish Independence War and forced the former Allied Powers to return to the negotiating table. It is important, for our purposes, that the Armenian massacres were taken for granted: in the Treaty of Sèvres they were not called into question by any Contracting Party, since the Treaty only described and established the operational arrangements to bring the alleged perpetrators to justice.

Three years later the Treaty of Sèvres was replaced by the Treaty of Lausanne which, instead, did not make any mention of the Armenians. This Treaty, concluded between Turkey and the Entente Powers on July 24, 1923, put an end to the bloody Greek-Turkish conflict and set the borders between Greece, Bulgaria and Turkey, as well as determining the end of the Turkish claims on Cyprus, Iraq and Syria. The Treaty had a significant (negative) impact on the Armenian community since, in accordance to Articles 37–45 of the Section III, it generally recognized only the rights of "Turkey's non-Muslim subjects", thus depriving the Armenians of all the specific protections they earlier enjoyed in the Ottoman Empire and denying them those that were foreseen in the Treaty of Sèvres.[56] The Treaty of Lausanne did not contain provisions for the punishment of war crimes, but was indeed accompanied by a Declaration of Amnesty for all the crimes committed between 1 August 1914 and 20 November 1922. It seems appropriate to point out that the willingness to forget is clearly affirmed in the Preamble of the Declaration of Amnesty: it states that

[55]Schmid (2014).

[56]Winston Churchill said with regard to this: "In the Lausanne Treaty, which established a new peace between the Allies and Turkey, history will search in vain for the name Armenia": Churchill (1929), p. 408. On the peace treaties between the Ottoman Empire and the European powers, see generally Ziegler (2004). For a discussion of the general debate on the issue of the protection of Armenians during the Lausanne Conference and the subsequent request to create an "Armenian hearth" in the Caucasus presented by the Italian government in the course of the session of the League of Nations' Assembly on 25 September see: http://www.prassi.cnr.it/prassi/content.html?id=1857.

> The Powers signatory of the Treaty of Peace signed this day being equally desirous to cause the events which have troubled the peace in the East to be forgotten [...][57]

and—*ça va sans dire*—it is possible to forget what happened!

Later, the issue of the extermination of the Armenians was muted and more and more neglected.

In relation to the right to truth and to memory these precedents are relevant in several respects. First, the Joint Declaration is a document that establishes and defines the massacre of the Armenians as "crimes against humanity and civilization" which does not correspond to a position of the Ottoman Triumvirate aimed at denying that assessment. Secondly, even an instrument negotiated by the Ottoman Empire itself, the Treaty of Sèvres, recalled the events and described them as "massacres", providing for the prosecution of those responsible. Thirdly, in fact at the end of the war the Ottoman Empire prosecuted some of the people responsible, which clearly led to the establishment of the truth about the massacres and was thus formally recognized within the Empire itself.

Only political reasons—which unfortunately were also useful to the victorious Powers and were so formalized in the Treaty of Lausanne and in the annexed *Declaration of Amnesty*—made it possible to bring down the curtain on facts previously objectively established and accepted even by those who today deny them. This acknowledgment could currently well represent the premise for the Armenians to claim the recognition of the right to memory, memory which must be ensured in the first place to the victims and to their heirs; the same memory should also be taken in charge by the International Community as a whole.

In fact, since the 70s, the situation seems to register a move in this direction: the Armenian issue emerged again in 1971 when the UN Commission on Human Rights asked the Sub-Commission on Prevention of Discrimination and Protection of Minorities—made up of independent experts—decided to carry out a Study of the question of the prevention and punishment of the crime of genocide. In 1973

[57]The Declaration of Amnesty attached to the Treaty of Lausanne states that: "[...] III Full and complete amnesty shall be respectively granted by the Turkish Government and by the Greek Government for all crimes or offences committed during the same period which were evidently connected with the political events which have taken place between the 1st August, 1914, and the 20th November, 1922. IV Turkish nationals, and reciprocally nationals of the other Powers signatory of the Treaty of Peace signed this day who may have been arrested, prosecuted or sentenced by the authorities of the said Powers or by the Turkish authorities respectively, for reasons of a political or military nature previous to the 20th November, 1922, on territory which remains Turkish in accordance with the said Treaty of Peace, shall benefit from the amnesty, and, if they are detained, shall be handed over to the authorities of the States of which they are the nationals. [...] V All sentences pronounced for the above reasons shall be annulled, and any proceedings already instituted shall be stayed. [...] VII The British, French, and Italian Governments, [...] declare that they are prepared to adopt, subject to reciprocity on the part of the Turkish Government, the same measures for the benefit of such Turkish prisoners of war and interned civilians as may still be in their hands, with the exception of those who may have committed crimes and offences against ordinary law since the 20th November, 1922." http://www.mfa.gov.tr/viii_-declaration-of-amnesty.en.mfa.

and 1975 the two interim reports submitted to the Sub-Commission by Rwandan Nicodeme Ruhashyankiko evoked

> the existence of fairly abundant documentation relating to the massacre of the Armenians, considered as the first genocide of the twentieth century.[58]

Unfortunately, in the final report,[59] submitted to the Commission in 1979, the reference cited above was omitted due to the pressure of the Turkish delegation, which basically relied on three arguments: (1) the alleged facts were distorted compared to historical truth; (2) the qualification of genocide was not relevant, since it was about facts of war; (3) finally, recalling facts occurred at the beginning of the century would have only contributed to the awakening of appeased conflicts. Such arguments, however, do not imply the denial of anti-Armenian violence, but only its deformation and therefore basically a confirmation of the tragic events, so that they are relevant for the reconstruction of the (right to) memory.

Subsequently, in 1983, a new Special Rapporteur was appointed on the same theme. In the Revised and Updated Report on the Question of the Prevention and Punishment of the Crime of Genocide,[60] drawn up by the British expert Benjamin Whitaker and adopted by the Sub-Commission with a majority of 15 votes, in addition to the genocide committed by the Nazis, the Ottoman massacre of the Armenians is evoked as one of the cases of genocide in the twentieth century.[61] In the debates within the Sub-Commission for the adoption of the Report it was emphasized by some participants that the Special Rapporteur had correctly interpreted his mandate in referring to specific cases of allegations of genocide in the past, and, with reference to the Armenian massacre they expressed the view that such massacres indeed constituted genocide, as was well documented by the Ottoman military trials of 1919, eyewitness reports and official archives. In this regard it is very significantly stated that

> the lessons of history were indispensable to keep the conscience of the world alive, and prevent the recurrence of that odious crime.[62]

Some speakers, however, pointed out that the Special Rapporteur should have dealt exclusively with the problem of preventing future genocides, without referring to past events which were difficult or impossible to investigate and argued that the Armenian massacre was not adequately documented and that certain evidence had

---

[58]UN Doc. E/CN.4/Sub.2/L.583, para. 30.

[59]E/CN.4/Sub.2/416, 4 July 1979.

[60]U.N. ESCOR Commission On Human Rights, Sub-Commission on Prevention of Discrimination and Protection of Minorities, (Agenda Item 4), Revised and updated report on the question of the prevention and punishment of the crime of genocide prepared by Mr. B. Whitaker, 2 July 1985, 38th Session, Doc. E/CN.4/Sub.2/1985/6.

[61]Ibidem, para 24.

[62]Report of the Sub-Commission on Prevention of Discrimination and Protection of Minorities on its Thirty-Eight Session, 4 November 1985, UN Doc, E/CN.4/Sub.2/1985/SR.57, paragraphs 41, 42. See: Toriguian (1988), p. 170.

been forged.[63] This debate led the Sub-Commission to accept the "softer" position, where Whitaker is thanked for his commitment and the divergent opinions expressed during the debate are merely recorded.[64] Beyond the qualification of massacres, i.e. whether or not they can be defined as "genocide", a theme that is out of our field of inquiry, both the Whitaker Report itself and the debate within the Sub-Commission and the subsequent soft position taken by the Sub-Commission show that, at the time, there was not yet a historical certainty about the 1915 events.[65]

Furthermore, in more recent times, several national and international institutions, both intergovernmental and non-governmental, have recognized and condemned the Armenian massacres, sometimes qualifying them as "genocide". By way of example, it can be remembered the Permanent Peoples' Tribunal—an opinion tribunal, which is enriched by the work of a group of intellectuals—that, in the judgment adopted at the session of April 1984 devoted to this event, as a result of an in-depth analysis "in fact" and "in law" of the events *de qua*, argued among other things that

> the extermination of the Armenian population groups through deportation and massacre constitutes a crime of genocide

and stressed that this implies

> first and foremost the obligation to recognize officially the reality of this genocide and the consequent damages suffered by the Armenian people.[66]

The "judgment" of the opinion Tribunal also pointed out, very significantly, the duty of the UN as a whole and each of its members

> to demand this recognition and to assist the Armenian people to that end,[67]

according to a logic, we would say today, of Responsibility to Protect.

Also in this context, the European Parliament, at its meeting on 18 June 1987, recognized the Armenian genocide—taken for granted, because "historically proven". The Parliament did not limit itself to condemn the attitude of Turkey, but also called upon member States to dedicate a date to the victims of the Armenian (and

---

[63]Ibidem.

[64]UN Doc E/CN.4/Sub.2/1985/SR.36/Add.1, para. 57. As well highlighted by Schabas "An attempt to strengthen the resolution by expressing the Sub-Commission's thanks and congratulations for 'some' of the proposals in the report was resoundingly defeated": Schabas (2009), p. 467.

[65]Today this historical certainty seems to be real: Flores, Introduction of this Volume.

[66]Permanent Peoples' Tribunal, Verdict of the Tribunal, April 16, 1984, See more at: http://www.genocide-museum.am/eng/1984.php#sthash.ym52MYqz.dpuf. For an in-depth discussion about the contribution and the value of the decisions of the Permanent People's Tribunal see Simm (2016). According to the Author "the decision of international courts and tribunals affect how we read history (but) alternative tribunals, such as peoples' tribunals, attempt to write alternative histories to counter the official versions".

[67]Ibidem.

Jewish) genocide.[68] It should be stressed that in the Resolution of the European Parliament the condemnation of Turkey is restricted to the failure to recognize the anti-Armenian violence and does not extend (*rectius*: it excludes *expressis verbis*) to the possibility that these facts can legitimize requests or monetary claims towards the current State of Turkey.

On the contrary, the decision of Aram I, Armenian Apostolic Catholicos of the "Great House of Cilicia" headquartered in Antelias in Lebanon, should be reported. He announced, on 6 December 2016, his commitment to ask the Court of Strasbourg to impose the restitution of the former residences and properties belonging to the Catholicosate and located in Sis, in Turkish territory, after both the Turkish Ministry of Justice and the Turkish Constitutional Court rejected the application (filed 28 April 2015) aimed at discussing and solving, under the Turkish legal system, the dispute on the property of the Catholicosate's historical buildings.[69]

Moreover, in consideration of the Turkish attitude towards the massacre of the Armenians, the European Parliament has indicated, as a pre-condition for the admission of Turkey into the European Union, the recognition of this event—qualified as "genocide"—as an action perpetrated by the Turkish State. The European Parliament stated that the Turkish refusal of such recognition

> continues to deprive the Armenian people of the right to their own history[70]:

What else is the right to one's own history if not the fusion between the right to truth and the right to memory?

The European Parliament returned to the issue with the Resolution on the 1999 Regular Report from the Commission on Turkey's progress towards accession of 15 November 2000 calling on the Turkish Government and the Turkish Grand National Assembly to give fresh support to the Armenian minority as an important part of Turkish society, in particular by public recognition of the genocide which that minority suffered before the establishment of the modern state of Turkey and also suggesting that the Turkish Government launch a dialogue with Armenia aimed in particular at re-establishing normal diplomatic and trade relations between the two countries and lifting the current blockade.[71] These requests were repeated in the European Parliament resolution on the opening of the negotiations with Turkey

---

[68]European Parliament, Resolution on a Political Solution to the Armenian Question, 18 June 1987, Doc. A2-33/87, OJ C 190/119-190/121 of 20 July 1987.

[69]The text of the message of Aram I, which reaffirmed that "The Armenian cause is the case of justice. It is the cause of violations of human rights. It is the cause of our people. We never forget the Armenian Genocide. Recognition and reparation: this is our clear and firm position as a people and a church. […] Justice – we want *justice* from the international community. That is the clear and firm position of our people", available on http://armenianweekly.com/2016/12/05/sis-echr/

[70]Ibidem, point E.

[71]European Parliament resolution on the 1999 Regular Report from the Commission on Turkey's progress towards accession, 15 November 2000, A5-0297/2000, *in specie* points 10 and 21.

of 18 September 2005[72] and in the European Parliament resolution on Turkey's progress towards accession of 27 September 2006.[73] In the year of the centenary, after the Resolution on the Annual report on human rights and democracy in the World 2013 and the EU policy on the matter of 12 March 2015,[74] the European Parliament finally adopted on 15 April the Resolution on the centenary of the Armenian Genocide in which the Parliament confirmed the qualification of genocide for the massacres committed in 1915 against the Armenians and condemned any attempts to deny the commission of genocides and crimes against humanity.[75] In the first resolution it also condemned historical revisionism[76] and each Member State and the Union as a whole was invited to recognize the Armenian genocide. In the second Resolution, in addition to recognizing the Armenian genocide, the Parliament paid tribute to the victims and proposed the establishment of a European day of remembrance since there can be no reconciliation without truth and remembrance.[77] The Resolution also strongly deplored any attempts at their denial and commended the Declaration of 12 April 2015 in which Pope Francis

[72]European Parliament resolution on the opening of the negotiations with Turkey, 28 September 2005, Doc. P6_TA(2005)0350, point 5.

[73]European Parliament resolution on Turkey's progress towards accession, 27 September 2006, Doc. P6_TA(2006)0381, in particular point 56, which takes note of Turkey's proposal to establish a commission of experts for the investigation of the facts that occurred in 1915–1916. The European Parliament states that, although the recognition of the Armenian genocide as such is formally not one of the Copenhagen criteria, it is essential that a country committed on its accession to the EU comes to terms and recognizes its past. For this reason, it requires the Turkish authorities to facilitate the work of researchers, intellectuals and scholars who are investigating the issue.

[74]Resolution on the Annual Report on Human Rights and Democracy in the World 2013 and the European Union's policy on the matter, 12 March 2015, Doc. P8_TA(2015)0076.

[75]European Parliament, Resolution on the centenary of the Armenian Genocide, 15 April 2015, Doc. P8_TA(2015)0094.

[76]Resolution on the Annual Report on Human Rights and Democracy in the World 2013, point 10.

[77]European Parliament's Resolution of 15 April 2015 on the centenary of the Armenian genocide (2015/2590(RSP)). Even the European Parliamentary Assembly, with the Resolution on the centennial of the Armenian genocide, 17 March 2015, Doc. 2015/C 315/05, given that "the denial of genocide is widely recognized as the final stage of genocide", urges Turkey "to come to terms with its past".

commemorated the centenary of the genocide,[78] the first of the twentieth century, in a spirit of peace and reconciliation.[79]

The Council of Europe also, although with acts adopted not unanimously and not related to the Organization as a whole, has qualified the Armenian massacres as genocide. We should mention, inter alia, the Resolution on Commemoration of the Armenian genocide of 1915, Written Declaration n. 275 of 1998, in which the events of 1915 are recalled

> paying tribute to the memory of its victims.[80]

Later, on 14 May 2001, 85 members of the Assembly of the Council of Europe —commemorating with the Recognition of the Armenian genocide, Written Declaration n. 320, the anniversary of what once again is referred to as the first genocide in the twentieth century—appealed to all the members of the Assembly to work towards the recognition of the Armenian genocide. According to the Declaration, a widespread recognition in the International Community would induce Turkey to admit the facts, facilitating a détente in the relations between Turkey and Armenia, and fostering also a peace, security and stability process on the territory.[81] Again, on 29 April 2010, 95 years after the events, 26 members of the Assembly of the Council of Europe renewed the same appeal to the Assembly with the Written Declaration n. 440, *Recognition of the Armenian genocide.*[82] And again, in the year of the centenary, on 23 April 2015, with the Declaration *Commemoration of the Centennial of the Armenian genocide,* 171 members of the Assembly condemned the denial of the genocide and criticized the failure to

---

[78]The term genocide, used for the first time by Karol Wojtyla in 2001 to refer to the Armenian massacres (Common Declaration of His Holiness John Paul II and His Holiness Karekin II at Holy Etchmiadzin, Republic of Armenia), also appears in the joint statement of the current Pope with the Catholicos of all the Armenians, Karekin II, who spoke of "persistent denial" towards this page of history: Common Declaration of his Holiness Francis and his Holiness Karenin II at Holy Etchmiadzin, Republic of Armenia, Etchmiadzin, Apostolic Palace Sunday, 26 June 2016: http://www.armenian-genocide.org/uploads/Affirmation/551.pdf during the Holy Mass for the devotees of the Armenian rite, in the greeting at the beginning of the celebration, on 12 April 2015, Pope Bergoglio insisted on the need to remember the victims of the Armenian massacres: "It is necessary, and indeed a duty, to honour their memory, for whenever memory fades, it means that evil allows wounds to fester. Concealing or denying evil is like allowing a wound to keep bleeding without bandaging it!"

[79]European Parliament's Resolution of 15 April 2015 on the centenary of the Armenian genocide (2015/2590(RSP), § E.

[80]Council of Europe, Parliamentary Assembly, Resolution on Commemoration of the Armenian genocide of 1915, Written Declaration n. 275, Doc. 8091, 24 April 1998: "the date of 24 April 1915 marked the beginning of the implementation of the plan to exterminate Armenians living in the Ottoman Empire. Today we commemorate the anniversary of what has been called the first genocide of the 20th century, and we salute the memory of the Armenian victims of this crime against humanity".

[81]Written Declaration n. 320, Recognition of the Armenian genocide, 14 May 2001, Doc. 9056, 2nd ed.

[82]Written Declaration n. 440, Recognition of the Armenian genocide, 29 April 2010, Doc. 12232.

condemn the Armenian genocide in a timely manner, stating, among other things, that this omission has contributed *inter alia* to facilitating the commission of further crimes, such as the *Shoah*, given the substantial impunity for the anti-Armenian violence; both the material perpetrators and the State as a whole have benefited of such impunity.[83] In fact, according to a version supported by some historians, in order to reassure those advancing concerns about the campaign to exterminate the Jews in Poland, Adolf Hitler said in his speech to the commanders in chief of the German army in Obersalzberg on 22 August 1939:

> Who, after all, speaks today of the annihilation of the Armenians?[84]

A memory which restores transparency to the facts over which a leaden opacity weighs can then emerge in all its clarity as a bridge between a past to remember and a future in which the imperative is to avoid the recurrence of tragic events. This approach was reiterated in Resolution n. 591, adopted on 16 July 2016, in which the Council of Europe reaffirmed that:

> The absence of unequivocal and timely condemnation of the Armenian genocide largely contributed to the failure to prevent future crimes against humanity […]. The undersigned parliamentarians pay tribute to the memory of innocent victims and condemn all forms of crimes against humanity and genocide and deeply deplore attempts at their denial. (…). [The Council of Europe] should encourage its member States to come to terms with their own past and prepare grounds for future reconciliation between peoples.[85]

The *trait d'union* between the right to memory and the guarantees on non-repetition is thus clear.

However, there are several national Parliaments (including the Italian Parliament) and individual organizations or administrations[86] which officially

---

[83]Written Declaration n. 591. Commemoration of the Centennial of the Armenian genocide, 23-4-2015, Doc. 13770.

[84]This episode is reported in Bardakjian (1985); Dadrian (1996); Id. (7); Melson (2001). The text is the English version of the German document handed to Louis P. Lochner in Berlin. It first appeared in Lochner's What About Germany? (New York: Dodd, Mead & Co., 1942), pp. 1–4. The Nuremberg Tribunal later identified the document as L-3 or Exhibit USA-28. Two other versions of the same document appear in Appendices II and III. For the German original cf. Akten zur Deutschen Auswartigen Politik 1918–1945, Serie D, Band VII, (Baden-Baden, 1956), p. 171–172.

[85]Written Declaration n. 591, Recognition of the Armenian genocide, Doc. 13770, Second Edition 16 July 2015.

[86]For example, regional Parliaments, like those of Ontario and Quebec in Canada, New South Wales in Australia, and 38 U.S. States have condemned the extermination of the Armenians, qualified as genocide. In Italy, the Armenian genocide has been recognized by the city council of various cities: among others, Rome, Milan, Genoa, Florence, Venice, Padua, Parma, Ravenna, Belluno, Udine, Viterbo, as well as Italy's National Association of Municipalities (ANCI-Associazione Nazionale Comunid'Italia).

recognize the Armenian massacres, sometimes qualifying them as genocide.[87,88] It is worth remembering, *inter alia,* the Russian Duma (unanimously), the Bulgarian Parliament, the Cypriot Parliament; in 1996 the Greek Parliament; in 1997 the Lebanese Parliament; in 1998 the Belgian Senate and the Argentine one[89]; in 1998 (and again in 2001) the French National Assembly (unanimously); in 2000 the Swedish Parliament, the Parliament of Uruguay, the French Senate, the Vatican; in 2002 the Canadian Senate; in 2003 the Swiss Parliament; in 2004 the Canadian House of Commons (Parliament); in 2005 the Polish Parliament (*Sejm*), the Parliament of Venezuela, the Lithuanian Parliament; in 2007 the Senate of Chile; in 2010 the Swedish Legislative Assembly (Riksdag) and the Bolivian Cámara de Diputados; in 2015 the Austrian Parlaments klub der Österreichischen Volkspartei, the Grand Duchy of Luxembourg Chamber, the Senado Federal of Brazil and the Senado de la Republica of Paraguay.

Finally, on 2 June 2016, the German Bundestag passed a resolution whose title explicitly refers to the "Erinnerung und Gedenken an den Völkermord an den Armeniern und anderen christlichen Minderheiten in den Jahren 1915 und 1916"[90] (Remembrance and commemoration of the genocide of the Armenians and other

[87]For a list of the countries and organizations see Resolutions, Laws, and Declarations, Genocide 2015: http://www.armenian-genocide.org/current_category.7/affirmation_list.html.

[88]Italy Chamber of Deputies Resolution, Session n. 813 of 11/17/2000, see at: http://leg13.camera.it/_dati/leg13/lavori/stenografici/sed813/s420r.htm. Although the proposal for the recognition of the Armenian genocide had been submitted to the Chamber of Deputies in September 1998 by more than 170 parliamentarians from all the political groups in Parliament, the motion, voted by a large majority, produced a Resolution which was the result of distinction, symbol of concern about the future relations with Turkey. A long list of commemorative laws adopted in our country is provided by De Luna (2011), p. 82 who speaks about "overflowing bulimic memory, which is likely to favour oblivion, totally subordinated to the political aims of the moment" (for this reason, he uses the expression of "disposable past"). In this way, however, "from a memory that can reduce complexity, able to absorb the centrifugal forces of a reassuring national narrative, it turned into a memory that swells and is nourished by an uncontrolled proliferation of identity memories" (p. 39).

[89]It is important to remember that, precisely in relation to the *jucios por la verdad* cited above, footnote 28, and to the Armenian massacres, on 1 April 2011 the examining Magistrate N. Oyarbide pronounced, following the petition of *Gregorio* and *Luisa Hairabedian,* Argentinian citizens descendants of some of the victims survived at the massacre of the Armenians in 1915 and sheltered in Argentina, a declarative Resolution, with purely symbolic value, where such killings are qualified as "genocide", assigning the liability to the Turkish State, *Juzgado Criminal y Correccional Federal n. 5 de Buenos Aires,* judge N. Oyarbide, *Resolucióndeclarativa de lossucesoshistóricosconocidoscomo el genocidio del pueblo armenio – años 1915–1923*, obrados n° 2.610/2001 caratulados Imp. N.N. s/ suDenuncia. Querellante: Hairabedian, Gregorio. 01.04.201. http://www.iri.edu.ar/images/Documentos/documentos/boletin112/fallo_genocidio_armenio.pdf.

[90]See at http://dip21.bundestag.de/dip21/btd/18/086/1808613.pdf.

Christian minorities in the years 1915 and 1916).[91] The Resolution—strongly supported by three Parliamentary groups (Christian Democratic Union, Social Democratic, Greens)—in addition to recalling the systematic extermination of the Armenians perpetrated by the Ottoman regime, focuses on the serious responsibility of the Deutsches Reich, the empire of Wilhelm II allied with the Ottoman Empire in the First World War. In the text approved by the Bundestag the term Genozid recurs four times as well as the bluntly inglorious role of the German Empire, which, as a principal ally of the Ottoman Empire, did not try to stop these crimes against humanity despite explicit information regarding the organized expulsion and extermination of Armenians.[92] The text of the German Resolution continues:

> Germany's own historical experience shows how difficult it is for a society to face the dark chapters of its own past. However, an honest appraisal of history is the most important basis for reconciliation within a society as well as with others [...] The remembrance of the past also reminds us to stay alert and to prevent that hatred and destruction threaten people and nations over and over again.[93]

This Resolution, too, reiterates the central role that the right to truth and the right to memory has within the framework of the guarantees of non-repetition.

I would like to refer briefly to what happened, *in specie*, in France in an attempt to criminally condemn the denial of the Armenian genocide. On 22 December 2011, the French National Assembly overwhelmingly approved a bill which provided for an amendment to the 29 July 1881 Law on freedom of the press, art. 24*ter*, extending the punishment (with a penalty up to one year of imprisonment and a sanction up to EUR 45 thousand) to all those "contestant ou minimisant de

[91]In Germany the first to openly define the Armenian massacres as a genocide was the President of the Federal Republic. In fact, Joachim Gauck, in a speech held in Berlin Cathedral in April 2015, hence a hundred years after the events, stated that: "The fate of the Armenians stands as exemplary in the history of mass exterminations, ethnic cleansing, deportations and yes, genocide, which marked the 20th Century in such a terrible way (because the 1915 atrocity was a) planned and systematic mass murder": see at http://www.bbc.com/news/world-europe-32437633.

[92]The German complicity in the massacres of the Armenians was the matter of investigation by some authors, like Dadrian (1997).

[93]The Resolution, as the similar ones adopted by other countries, has immediately resulted in a negative reaction from Turkey: Turkish President Recep Tayyip Erdoğan has said Ankara will take retaliatory measures after the German parliament voted to recognize as 'genocide' the Armenian massacre of 1915. Turkey has already recalled its ambassador Huseyin Avni Karslioglu to Germany in protest. Turkey has also decided to summon Germany's chargé d'affaires to the Foreign Ministry in Ankara following the vote. President Erdoğan has said the German resolution will seriously impact relations between the two countries. Prime Minister Binali Yildirim condemned the German parliamentary vote and said in a speech in the Turkish capital that a "racist Armenian lobby" was responsible for the decision. the Anadolu Agency reported that he added that these were "ordinary events that could take place in any society or any country… in 1915, under conditions of World War I". The ruling AK Party in Turkey said the move had seriously damaged relations between the two countries, while Turkish Deputy Prime Minister Numan Kurtulmus was equally scathing, calling the resolution a "historic mistake". See at: http://www.bbc.com/news/world-europe-36433114.

façon outrancière un genocide reconnu comme tel par la loi française": i.e. the Armenian genocide, the only one recognized by French law, besides the *Shoah.*[94] This proposal was approved by the Senate on 23 January 2012, becoming law n. 647 "visant à réprimer la contestation de l'existence des genocides reconnus par la loi". Law n. 647 was repealed by the French *Conseil Constitutionnel* on 28 February 2012 because it was considered contrary to the Constitution, *in specie* Article 11 which affirms the freedom of expression and art. 6 according to which the law is expression of a general will.[95] In particular, the second argument against the law is based on the following reasoning: law 647 would not be the result of general will because it introduces incrimination *par ricochet which*, identifying as worthy of protection only genocides recognized by the legislator and implies that the lawmaker itself establishes the facts, taking this duty away from the judge who should be responsible according to law. This would violate the principle of separation of powers since the task of ascertaining the facts (judge's jurisdiction) would be assigned to the legislator (and to its discretion).[96] In fact in France the anti-revisionism jurisprudence concerning the qualification of the Armenian massacres started in the '90s with the controversial decision of the Paris Court of Appeal in the Bernard Lewis case.[97] The influential historian, invited by a journalist of *Le Monde* to express his views on why Turkey had not yet recognized the Armenian genocide, stated:

> Vous voulez dire reconnaître la version arménienne de l'affaire. […] Mais si l'on parle de génocide cela implique qu'il y ait eu une politique délibérée, une décision d'anéantir systématiquement la nation arménienne. Cela est fort douteux. Des documents turcs prouvent une volonté de déportation, pas une volonté d'extermination.[98]

Invested of a claim for civil liability brought under Article 1382 c.c. by an association representing the interests of the Armenian population—allegedly injured by the fact that the historian had doubted that the Turkish persecution was part of a plan aimed at the annihilation of the Armenian people (i.e. "technically" a

[94]Commission des lois, Répression de la contestation de l'existence du génocide arménien - Examen du rapport de M. Jean-Jacques Hyest sur la proposition de loi n° 607 (2009–2010), présentée par M. Serge Lagauche et plusieurs de ses collègues, 13 April 2011.

[95]See http://www.conseil-constitutionnel.fr/conseil-constitutionnel/francais/page-d-accueil.1.html.

[96]It is interesting to note how in Italian law, with reasoning equivalent to that set up by the French *Conseil Constitutionnel*, was a court to "refuse" this role: see Tribunale di Torino, sez. VII, 27 November 2008, n. 7881, in Giurisprudenza costituzionale 2009, 5, pp. 3949 ss., with a note by Lisena (2009). The Union of the Armenians in Italy and the Stefano Serapian Foundation denounced the violation of the right to personal identity that would have been caused by the failure to mention – as distinguished from explicit denial – the massacres of 1915–16 in a historical-literary work. The Court rejected the application because, among other things, the power to ascertain history is not one of the tasks assigned by the legislator to a court. See Fronza (2012), p. 104 ff.

[97]Forum des Associations Arméniens de France c. Lewis, TGI Paris, 21 June 1995, in Les petites affiches, 29 September 1995, n. 117, 17.

[98]Langellier and Peroncel-Hugoz (16 November 1993).

genocide), thus causing "grievous prejudice to truthful memory"—the Court condemned the defendant to pay a symbolic franc. The judges motivated the decision according to the principle that, in the case of a dispute concerning the interpretation of a past event, the historian does not have the freedom to silence the existence of different readings apart from the one considered most reliable and must give an account of the historiographical debate; otherwise the historian would be violating the duties of objectivity and prudence to which he is bound.

The survey carried out so far on the practice in the international community and in national legislation (which also has indirect impact at an international level) can lead to some considerations. In the first place, the massacres are beginning to be remembered both by International Organizations, entities and State authorities and —more generally—by members of so-called civil society. Often this memory has resulted in statements, resulting in *soft law*, almost always adopted by an overwhelming majority and at times unanimously, where the events are often taken for granted without the need for confirmation by historical and historiographical documents.[99] This can be read as the result of a superficial attitude or, on the contrary, as concrete evidence of the alleged facts which would not need to be supported by further evidence with respect to those already easily available and shared in several studies and earlier documents. Secondly, it is interesting to note that this exercise of memory is not limited to relations between Turkey (a State which claims to be the successor of the Ottoman Empire)[100] and Armenians, i.e. between (alleged successors of) perpetrators of criminal acts *de qua* and victims. On the contrary, it involves agencies, institutions and administrations completely extraneous to the facts under debate, which nonetheless have a core interest in the recognition of the right to truth and memory concerning such tragic events, even though distant from them in time and space. Thus, we may infer that the right to truth and memory are perceived as fundamental rights with *erga omnes* effects, particularly if they are linked with the commission of offences qualified as *crimes against humanity*.

[99]For example in the Written declaration No. 542, Doc. 13192, of 24 April 2013 of the Parliamentary Assembly of the Council of Europe it is stated (dogmatically) that: "The fact of the Armenian Genocide by the Ottoman Empire has been documented, recognized, and affirmed in the form of media and eyewitness reports, laws, resolutions, and statements by the United Nations, the European Parliament and Parliaments of the Council of Europe member States".

[100]That Turkey represents the Ottoman Empire's successor State is a shared opinion by the greater part of international law scholars: *ex plurimis* see Dumberry (2013), according to whom "Turkey has the same legal identity as the Ottoman Empire and [...] accordingly it should be held responsible for all internationally wrongful acts committed by the Empire against the Armenian population before, during and after the War", *in specie* p. 165. On this point, see the debate between Avedian (2012), on the one hand, and Tacar and Gauin (2012), on the other.

4 The (Non)-Right to Memory of the Armenian Massacres in Turkish Law

The Armenian massacres are neither acknowledged nor condemned by Turkey. On the contrary, the Country keeps on denying that they ever occurred "as such",[101] although, as we have mentioned, in the aftermath of the armistice and before the Treaty of Sèvres, the Ottoman Empire had brought to trial on its territory some of the alleged perpetrators, its organs issuing convictions in some cases.

The refusal of the Turkish government to qualify the events as genocide or even as "mere" massacres is based mainly on three arguments: the number of deaths that, according to Turkish historians, would amount to "only" 300 thousand Armenians; the responsibility of the "Armenian revolutionaries" and the consequent shift of guilt[102]; the lack of premeditation.[103] Basically it would not have been a systematic and deliberate extermination of a community, but rather a side effect of a population transfer operation which would have been perfectly legitimate in a context of war, where the Armenian minority might have acted as an internal enemy against the integrity of the then Ottoman Empire. In line with this reconstruction of events, in Istanbul and Ankara streets and squares were dedicated to the main persons responsible for the extermination of the Armenians: for instance, in Istanbul a mausoleum was built in honour of Talât Pascià; in 1996 the earthly remains of Enver Pascià, were transferred from Central Asia and buried in Turkey with top honours and the presence of the President of the Republic and the highest officials of the Turkish State, even though, as we mentioned, both Talât Pascià and Enver Pascià had been sentenced to death *in absentia* in the trial held in Istanbul in 1919. Essentially, a sort of "inverted" right to memory, where the (alleged) perpetrators are remembered and not the victims. It should be noted that the *damnatio memoriae* which Turkey is carrying out against the Armenians—including the situation of neglect of Armenian cultural monuments and religious buildings, and even their desecration[104] and destruction—sometimes goes beyond "bizarre" limits: the reference here is to the attempt of the *Turkish Environment and Forest Ministry* to

---

[101]According to some scholars there would even be evidence of financing by Turkey in order to commission studies consistent to such a position of denial: see Smith et al. (1995).

[102]As revealed by Göçek (2011), "(in) the transition from Ottoman to the Turkish nation-state, the official attribution of responsibility for the crimes gradually shifted from the perpetrators to the victims" and this reversal "both legitimated what happened to the Anatolian Armenians and took pains to demonstrate that the same, if not more, happened to Turks as well": *in specie* respectively pp. 46 and 52.

[103]*Ex plurimis*, the historian Yusuf Halacoglu, of the Turkish Historical Society, denies that there was a genocide of the Armenians and justifies the deportation with the theory of "treason", arguing that "the Armenians have attacked the Turks behind", fighting more or less directly for the Russian enemy under the scepter of the Tsar: Halacoglu (2008). For a more analytical framework on the Turkish denial motives: http://frontierenews.it/2015/04/genocidio-degli-armeni-su-cosa-si-fonda-il-negazionismo-turco/.

[104]Polatel et al. (2012); Banco (2015).

eradicate Armenian terms from the Latin classification of animal species, so that for example, according to Turkey, the native sheep *Ovis Armeniana* should have been called *Ovis Orientalis Anatolicus.*[105]

From the legal point of view, the drift of memory or, at least, the removal of the past becomes State truth so that those who question or doubt this truth can be indicted for conduct of "affirmationism".[106] In fact, after the proclamation of the Republic of Turkey a wide plan of reforms was launched, including a new penal code (hereafter referred to as Cpt) which came into force on 1 July 1926 and has been modified several times. The reformulated norms included the then Article 159 Cpt which punished certain forms of public defamation against the "Turkish nation" and several public institutions. Since then, Article 159 Cpt has been amended several times, gradually expanding the objects of protection.

In the Cpt of 2005, Article 301 provided the same offence[107] punishing it with imprisonment from six months to three years, which were increased by a third if the offence was committed abroad by a Turkish citizen (Article 301 Cpt, para 3). It punishes "public contempt" of "Turkishness, the Republic or the Grand National Assembly of Turkey" (Article 301 Cpt, para 1), as well as "the Government of the Republic of Turkey, the judicial bodies of the State or the military or security organizations of the State" (Article 301 Cpt, para 2). According to this norm a large number of journalists and writers such as the writer Elif Şafak[108] and the journalist Hrant Dink[109] were brought to trial and the case of the Nobel Prize for literature Orhan Pamuk is famous. He was indicted for violation of Article 301 Cpt, in December 2005—even though the trial was first suspended and then definitively

[105]The attempt, which coincided with the 95th anniversary of the massacres, was annulled by the United Nations Development Programme, the appropriate international Authority for this purpose: Separatist animals curbed, Hürriyet Daily News, 7 March 2005; www.hurriyetdailynews.com/default.aspx?pageid=438§n=separatist-animals-curbed-2005-03-07.

[106]See Fronza (2012), pp. 54–58.

[107]The former version, which came into force in 2005, established that: "1. A person who publicly vilifies Turkishness, the Republic or the Grand National Assembly of Turkey shall be punished by imprisonment for a term of six months to three years. 2. A person who publicly denigrates the Government of the Republic of Turkey, the judicial bodies of the State or the military or security organizations of the State shall be punished by imprisonment for a term of six months to two years. 3. In cases where denigration of Turkishness is committed by a Turkish citizen in a foreign country the punishment shall be increased by one third. 4. Expressions of thought for the purpose of criticism shall not constitute a crime". Code No. 5237, Turkish Official Gazette No. 25611, 12 October May 2004.

[108]Elif Shafak, one of the most important voices of Turkish narrative as well as the best-selling author in the country, was tried, with the request for a sentence of three years in prison for "insulting the good name of Turkey" with her novel The bastard of Istanbul. In her second novel, written in English and enthusiastically welcomed by the critics as the best-seller in Turkey in 2006, a character qualifies the massacre of the Armenians as a genocide. The novel sparked controversy in Turkey and the author was blamed by the ultranationalist lawyer Kemal Kerincsiz for an "attack against Turkish identity" under Article 301 Cpt. The investigation was closed on 21 September 2006.

[109]Cf. infra.

dismissed by the Court on 22 January 2006—because, in an interview with the Swiss weekly Das Magazin in February of that year, he had declared that

> Thirty thousand Kurds and one million Armenians were killed in these lands and nobody but I dares to talk about it.[110]

Article 301 Cpt in its 2005 version triggered findings of violation by the Court of Strasbourg, *inter alia,* of Article 10 of the Convention for the Protection of Human Rights and Fundamental Freedoms (ECHR) on freedom of opinion. In the *Dink* v. *Turkey* case,[111] for instance, the Court found a violation of that article and of Articles 2 (right to life and to an effective investigation into the causes of death); 13 (right to an effective remedy). The claimants were the relatives of the journalist Hrant Dink, who was murdered in 2007. Between 2003 and 2005 Dink published a series of articles in the Turkish-Armenian magazine *Agos* in which he spoke of the continuous engagement of the Armenian people for the recognition of their *status* as victims of a genocide, claiming that the denial of such events remains an open wound in spite of the indifference of the Turkish people. In particular, in one article Dink described Armenian blood as being "poisoned" by Turkish blood, referring in fact to the poison due to the Armenian "obsession" and not to the Turkish people themselves.[112] This expression provoked the reaction of the Turkish authorities who claimed that it denigrated Turkish identity (*Turkishness*): Dink was put on trial under art. 301 (pre-reform) and convicted, becoming a target of Turkish nationalists. On 19 January 2007 Dink was murdered with three shots in the head. The police had been informed of Dink's imminent murder, but no preventive measures were taken. After his death, the Strasbourg Court, on the strength of Dink's own appeal unified with the one raised by his family, condemned Turkey both for failing to protect Dink in the face of a real and imminent threat to the journalist's life—confirmed by accurate information—and for the lack of an effective investigation aimed at punishing the negligent management of information about the risks Dink

[110]Beachler (2011). However, Kemal Kerinçsiz, the lawyer who had originally pressed charges against Pamuk, appealed to the Supreme Court of Appeal which ordered the court in Şişli to re-open the case. On 27 March 2011, Pamuk was found guilty and ordered to pay 6,000 liras in total compensation to five people for, among other things, having insulted their honor: Hurriyet Daily News, Orhan Pamuk to pay compensation for his words, Court decides, Hurriyet Daily News, 27 March 2011, http://www.hurriyetdailynews.com/default.aspx?pageid=438&n=orhan-pamuk-will-pay-compensation-for-his-words-court-decided-2011-03-27.

[111]Application no. 2668/07, 6102/08, 30079/08, 7072/09, Judgment of 14 September 2010.

[112]Dink long objected to the idea of using outside pressure – through international governmental, parliamentary, and other institutional resolutions – to force the Turkish state and society to recognize the Armenian genocide. He believed history could not be legislated. Support for reconciliation and recognition would have to come from within Turkey. In his articles, Dink advocated for an open democratic dialogue about the events of 1915 to provide the Turkish public with a more informed understanding of the events. He encouraged closer societal contacts between Armenia and Turkey, which he considered crucial to a deeper comprehension of the complexities of the past by both sides: To Unlock and Transcend History, in Agos, 27 May 2005. Translation provided by Hrant Dink Foundation.

was facing.[113] More relevant for our purposes, concerning freedom of expression as restrained by Article 301 Cpt, the Court specified that the protection of the law involves a positive obligation of the State to take steps to ensure freedom of expression against all forms of attacks, including those on private individuals; this obligation was not fulfilled by Turkey, which was thus found in violation—also—of Article 10 of the EHCR.

Following those rulings, Article 301 Cpt was modified in 2008. The Parliament of Ankara has adopted a package of amendments that partially reform that article.[114] Under this reform, approved with 250 votes against 65, those who offend the Turkish State and the State bodies are punishable [thus no longer generically "Turkish identity" ("Turkishness"—*Türklük*), but rather the "Turkish Nation" (*TürkMilleti*)] (Article 301 Cpt, para 1), while the authorization for a possible opening of legal proceedings belongs to the Ministry of Justice (Article 301 Cpt, para 4). Finally, the maximum penalty was reduced, passing from three to two years in order to allow convicts to take advantage of the suspension of the sentence (Article 301 Cpt, paras 1–2). The conduct has been redefined in terms of "defamation" (*aşağılamak*), while in previous versions Turkish verbs corresponding to "mock" and "insult" (*tahkir* e *tezyif*) were used. Regardless of the persistent vagueness of the object protected, it has been argued that the use of the word "denigrate" does not respect the root "vilify", thus extending the punishment to conduct of scorn though lacking in "insult".[115] And so, Article 301 Cpt remains applicable to those who mention the Armenian massacres because these claims undermine the fundamental roots of Turkey: the 'removal' of such massacres allows to postulate Anatolian homogeneity from which Turkish nationalism takes breath and body, in line with the already mentioned syndrome of Sèvres. It is a known fact that the desire to forget rather than the duty to remember has dominated Turkish society: generally speaking, Turkey's position seems to embrace entirely the maxim

[113]Given this tragic precedent, it is surprising and regretful that the news that on 29th November 2016 two militants of a Turkish ultranationalist organization, responsible of threats and intimidation against the Agos newspaper, have been released. Agos reports this news, (http://www.agos.com.tr/en/article/17058/the-threat-against-agos-goes-unpunished), confirming that the Turkish judicial authorities have ordered the release of the two responsible of intimidation since the words and deeds attributed to these persons "do not represent a real threat". The ultra-nationalist militants, as confirmed by the Director of Agos, Yetvart Danzikyan, laid a funeral wreath of black flowers in front of the newspaper office, and said: "One night, we might come to visit you unexpectedly". The same words – noted Danzikyan – which had been uttered by unknown provocateurs against Hrant Dink, assassinated outside the headquarter of the newspaper.

[114]At Article 301, as amended in 2008 reads: "1. A person who publicly denigrates the Turkish Nation, the State of the Republic of Turkey, the Grand National Assembly of Turkey, the Government of the Republic of Turkey or the judicial bodies of the State, shall be punished by imprisonment for a term of six months to two years. 2. A person who publicly denigrates the military or security organizations of the State shall be sentenced to a penalty according to the first paragraph. 3. Expressions of thought for the purpose of criticism shall not constitute a crime. 4. The investigation of this offence shall be subject to the permission of the Minister of Justice." Code No. 5759, Turkish Official Gazette No. 26870, 8 May 2008.

[115]Algan (2008), pp. 2245 ss.

formulated by Hobbes: *auctoritas, non veritas facit legem*, despite the right to memory for which the determination of the truth is a necessary premise.

In fact, the 2008 reform of Article 301 Cpt appears to be more an operation of *maquillage* than of substance: the Court of Strasbourg seems to be of this opinion, given that, in a recent decision, it indicated that the existence of Article 301 Cpt *in re ipsa*, even in this watered down version, violates freedom of expression. The case *Altug Taner Akcam* v. *Turkey* is relevant in this respect.[116] The applicant was a sociologist—well-known for his views on the events concerning the Ottoman Armenians (which differ from the official position of Turkey)—who complained that Article 301 Cpt as such violated his freedom of speech. According to the applicant he feared prosecution for the crime under Article 301 Cpt, because of his views on the Armenian question which would have prevented him from continuing to write on that issue. In fact, following a complaint, an investigation against him was in course but the prosecutor decided not to pursue the matter, considering that his opinions were within the limits of his freedom of expression. Thus, although art. 301 Cpt was never applied against the applicant, the ECHR was of the opinion that the risk of being investigated on the basis of Article 301 Cpt represents a violation of Article 10 of the ECHR. The reasoning of the Court was based on three arguments: first, the concepts used in Article 301 Cpt violate the principle of *lex certa*[117]; second, the Turkish Courts interpret the facts *de qua* broadly[118]; third, the authorization provided by the Ministry of Justice does not constitute sufficient certainty since the attitudes and inclinations of the Minister may change depending on the political climate in Turkey.[119] The Court of Strasbourg, in accepting the complaint, stated that the Turkish criminal law does not respond to conventional requirements of accessibility and prevision, since national courts, punishing the expression of any opinion contrary to the government, give it an arbitrary interpretation (as already stated in the cited judgment *Dink* v. *Turkey*).[120]

---

[116] *Akcam* v. *Turkey,* Application no. 27520/07, Judgment of 25 October 2011.

[117] Ibidem, para. 87.

[118] Ibidem, para. 93.

[119] Ibidem, paras. 78, 94.

[120] It is useful to think for example that the Association of Turkish historians asked the Education Board (YÖK) to ensure that the individual universities and the individual teachers take the names of the students that write theses on the Armenian issue, communicating the title and all the information relevant about the elaborate. The official reason is to make the Association aware about the state of the research on the topic. In force of Article 301 Cpt, it can be observed how this "profiling" may be potentially harmful for scholars and teachers not fully in line with the official thesis.

5 Concluding Remarks

The following essential points seem to emerge from the examination conducted in the previous pages.

The regulatory framework of the "traditional" consequences triggered by gross violations of human rights has been enriched in recent decades with the right to truth and the inalienable right to memory of victims in the broad interpretation given in the first paragraph of this paper, i.e. a right belonging not only to those who have directly suffered such violations, but also to the family, the heirs, the community/the people/the ethnicity/the group they belong to. In the case of gross violations of human rights the legal interest rests with the International Community as a whole. The right to memory and the right to truth would then be seen in the context of "aggravated" responsibility arising from the infringement of interests and values felt as essential by the International Community as a whole. Therefore Article 41(1) and (2) of the Draft Articles on State Responsibility adopted by the International Law Commission in 2001 are relevant,[121] since in addition to the "ordinary" consequences of the offence, an infringement of this kind triggers even further consequences: the obligation for the States to cooperate in order to achieve the cessation of the infringement; the obligation for the States not to recognize a situation established through a serious violation of the essential interests of the International Community, as well as the obligation not to provide assistance or help in the maintenance of that situation. The conduct of the States must follow models of cooperation which can ensure a collective form of reaction. The *right* of each State to react to breaches of an obligation *erga omnes* thus turns into an *obligation* of reaction. However, the content of this obligation is weak, i.e., the duty of all States is to cooperate in order to bring an end to the offence, though unfortunately, as evinced by practice, only those States which have a real, specific "unmoved mover" interest in decentralized reactions, tend to take action to that effect. This also explains why, in the case of the events of 1915–1916, national institutions, internal organs, local authorities and representatives of civil society—and not the States *tout court*—were often the organisations that "fought" for the recognition of the right to truth and the right to memory concerning the massacres of the Armenians. This implies that the offence would be attributed to the lack of recognition of the events by Turkey, the Ottoman Empire's successor State. And this leads to another consideration: the right to truth and the right to memory have a "double soul", since they are both a primary obligation—which it is incumbent on the State to preserve—and the consequence of an "aggravated" responsibility.

[121]Text adopted by the Commission at its fifty-third session, in 2001, and submitted to the General Assembly as a part of the Commission's report covering the work of that session. The report, which also contains commentaries on the draft articles, appears in Yearbook of the International Law Commission, 2001, vol. II (Part Two). Text reproduced as it appears in the annex to General Assembly resolution 56/83 of 12 December 2001, and corrected by document A/56/49(Vol. I)/Corr.4.

Furthermore they are a recent development of well-established rights and obligations which are an integral part of the protection of the rights of human beings. This explains why, according to the logic of the Copenhagen criteria, only recently has the European Parliament urged Ankara to "come to terms with its past". According to this reconstruction, beyond the fact that the international obligations violated by the Ottoman Empire did or did not exist as such in 1915, today the emergence of the right to truth and the right to memory require that Turkey accept the legacy of the events and take action to that effect.

Thus it can be said that the right to memory is expressed in a collective dimension that goes beyond the mere Turkey-Armenia relationship so that the "legal" sanctions give way to a "social" sanction the goal of which is a reconstructed and shared memory which cannot be achieved with amputations, indulgences or even denials since the right to memory represents and embodies a peremptory invitation to justice. But, as has been pointed out, at the same time Turkey has rejected any wrongdoing and adopted a truth of State which, in the reconstruction of the events, has reversed the roles that the Armenian community and the CUP played in 1915 and compressed freedom of expression and attempts to search for the truth.

How can the deadlock caused by these parallel narratives which represent a real war of memories be overcome?

In the first place the relevance of the Updated Set of Principles,[122] especially Principle n. 2 which establishes the inalienable right to truth, Principle n. 3, concerning the right to the preservation of memory and Principle n. 4, linked to the hypothesis of a denied or adulterated memory, must be considered. In the first place this Principle emphasizes the imprescriptible nature of the right, which is not extinguished either by the mere passage of time or as a result of State efforts to temporarily compress it; secondly, it clearly mentions disappearances—a particularly massive phenomenon in the context of the Armenian massacres.[123] According to the Updated Set of Principles framework the right to know in order to preserve memory, may still call, in the case of the Armenian genocide, for judicial and administrative procedures, such as commissions of truth and justice and

[122]E/CN.4/2005/102/Add.1.

[123]According to Principle 4, registered: The victim's right to know, "Irrespective of any legal proceedings, victims and their families have the imprescriptible right to know the truth about the circumstances in which violations took place and, in the event of death or disappearance, the victims' fate." We should bear in mind, where this is concerned, the International Convention for the Protection of All Persons from Enforced Disappearance, which entered into force in December 2010. Armenia became a party on 2 July 2012, together with 32 other countries; however, Turkey has neither signed, nor ratified the Convention.

commissions of inquiry, which must be open to the victims, in accordance with the provisions of Principle n. 32.[124]

In the case of the Armenian massacres it would therefore be desirable that the United Nations Human Rights Council set up a Commission of Inquiry[125] which should however have access to all relevant archives,[126] as provided for by the High Commissioner of the United Nations[127] in accordance with Principle 5 of the Updates Principles to Combat Impunity.[128] The proposed solution shifts the dialectic plan and the *ratio* underlying the right to memory from a polemic to a

[124]"Reparation procedures: All victims shall have access to a readily available, prompt and effective remedy in the form of criminal, civil, administrative or disciplinary proceedings subject to the restrictions on prescription set forth in principle 23. In exercising this right, they shall be afforded protection against intimidation and reprisals. Reparations may also be provided through programmes, based upon legislative or administrative measures, funded by national or international sources, addressed to individuals and to communities. Victims and other sectors of civil society should play a meaningful role in the design and implementation of such programmes. Concerted efforts should be made to ensure that women and minority groups participate in public consultations aimed at developing, implementing, and assessing reparation programmes. Exercise of the right to reparation includes access to applicable international and regional procedures."

[125]Frappi (2015). In fact according the Author: "It seems naive or specious to believe that the matter can be settled by a joint commission of historians, as traditionally proposed by the Turkish authorities. For the same reasons it appears equally naive to believe that Ankara might recognize the genocidal nature of the facts subsequent to April 1915 in response to pressure exerted from outside and out of a clear and broader agreement on possible consequences of the recognition. Until the Turkish-Armenian 'push towards reconciliation' insists on this level it is therefore highly unlikely that they can be successful." In this sense Avedian (2013) stated: "there has already been such a commission, namely the *Turkish Armenian Reconciliation Commission* (TARC), which existed between 2002 and 2004 with the aim to bring Armenia and Turkey closer to each other. In order to resolve the question of the genocide, TARC asked an independent organization, *International Center for Transitional Justice* (ICTJ), to examine the events in accordance with the current United Nations' Convention on the Prevention and Punishment of Genocide. In its turn, ICTJ asked an independent legal council to conduct and compile an analysis, which resulted in a seventeen page report. The report was summarized by the following conclusion: 'the Events, viewed collectively, can thus be said to include all the elements of the crime of genocide as defined in the Convention, and all legal scholars as well as historians, politicians, journalists and other people would be justified in continuing to so describe them' (International Center for Transitional Justice, The Applicability of the United Nations' Convention on the Prevention and Punishment of Genocide to the Events which Occurred During the Early Twentieth Century Legal Analysis, 2002. ictj.org/sites/default/files/ICTJ-Turkey-Armenian-Reconciliation-2002-english.pdf). Thus, an 'impartial and scientific examination of the historical records' would be yet another wild goose chase fitting well into the denialist game in the search of the ultimate evidence and would at its best result in "agree to disagree", i.e. the status quo": p. 84.

[126]Naturally and in the first place, the Turkish archives, since the Armenian Republic, not existing at the time of the massacres, has very little documentation but also, according to the *erga omnes* declination of the right to memory we tried to reconstruct, even the archives of each State which may help to establish the facts, such as Russia and the Vatican.

[127]Right to the truth, Report of the Office of the High Commissioner for Human Rights, A/HRC/12/19 21 August 2009, §§ 6, 7, 10.

[128]The Principles require the State to "ensure the preservation of, and access to, archives concerning violations of human rights and humanitarian law" (E/CN.4/2005/102/Add.1 cit.).

hieratic plain: in other words, the fracture between winners and losers is not politically and symbolically (re)proposed, with the inevitable political and social effects which affect the way towards elaborating the past collective memory in terms of conflict; on the contrary, it adheres to a reconciling model which, by suspending the judicial logic, pursues the political and symbolical goal of promoting inclusion rather than exclusion.

This hypothesis was aired in the Protocol on Development of Relations between the Republic of Armenia and the Republic of Turkey and in the Protocol on the Establishment of Diplomatic Relations between the Republic of Armenia and the Republic of Turkey[129] signed in Zurich between Turkey and Armenia on 10 October 2009. In the Protocols, which never entered into force, provision was made for the establishment of a Commission to undertake

> a dialogue on the historical dimension with the aim to restore mutual confidence between the two nations, including an impartial scientific examination of the historical records and archives to define existing problems and formulate recommendations.

An appendix was attached to the first Protocol which set an accurate timetable for its implementation, providing for the establishment of the Commission within three months from the entry into force of the Protocol. Moreover, the creation of a "mixed" Commission was perceived—both in Armenia as well as in the diaspora—as a yielding to the official position of Turkey.[130] In fact the real goal of the Protocols was the search for a solution for the conflict over the region of Nagorno-Karabakh, populated by a large majority of Armenians and in Soviet times included in the territory of Azerbaijan with the *status* of autonomous region. Although this conflict, which exploded in 1988 and became open war after the dissolution of the USSR and the independence of Azerbaijan and Armenia in 1991, officially concerned only to the Armenians of Nagorno-Karabakh and Azerbaijan, in reality it significantly involved Armenia too. The hostilities came to an end in 1994 with a "cease-fire" which made the success of the Armenians clear; in fact, besides controlling the contended region, they had also occupied largely ethnically Azeri territories. The conflict resulted in the displacement of about one million people, both Armenians and Azerbaijanis. Following the conflict, Armenia has been subjected to block not only by Azerbaijan but also by Turkey, which has closed the common border since 1993.[131]

The Protocols of 2009 have never been ratified and they definitely failed in February 2015 as a result of Erdoğan's decision to fix the 24 April as commemorative day of the battle of Gallipoli (instead of the traditional 25), in order to—

[129]See http://www.europarl.europa.eu/meetdocs/2009_2014/documents/d-tr/dv/1006_10_/1006_10_en.pdf.

[130]See the petition "Votch" [i.e. "Not" in Armenian], which explains the reasons of such disagreement and collects signatures to oppose the protocols. (http://www.votch.org/index.php?option=com_petitions&view=petition&id=34&Itemid=53&lang=en.) In the literature see Avedian (2013), pp. 83–84.

[131]On this, see Ferrari (2009).

quite clearly—silence the celebration of the centenary of the Armenian massacres.[132] The Armenian President Serge Sarkissian, following Erdoğan's decision, noted in a letter addressed to the President of the Armenian Parliamentary Assembly

> l'absence de volonté politique du gouvernement turc, l'altération constant qu'il cause à l'esprit et aux termes du protocole.[133]

For this reason he decided not to submit the Zurich Protocols for ratification by the National Assembly.

Another way which has been suggested for the reconstruction and the qualification of the massacres seems to be less viable: it would consist in a petition to the International Court of Justice.[134] Indeed the 72 States which have deposited the unilateral declaration of acceptance of the competence of the Court under Article 36.2 of the Statute do not include either Turkey or Armenia, nor do there appear to exist international agreements with legal stipulations applicable *ratione personae* to Turkey or to Armenia and *ratione materiae* to the right to truth and/or to the right to memory of the Armenian case.

Rather, the ICJ could be asked to express an advisory opinion pursuant to Article 96 of the Statute in order to clarify from a legal point of view the qualification of the events of 1915–1916, if required to do so by the General Assembly or by the Security Council, and the will of the majority of the members could coagulate to that effect.[135] Devolving to the ICJ the legal question concerning the qualification of the Armenian massacres in the light of the right to truth and to memory could be a way forward in the face of the increasingly widespread practice of their recognition in the International Community. This would involve the most authoritative

---

[132] Tacconi (2015). It is sad to think how this constitutes a step backward with respect to, in our opinion, the right direction taken in April 2014 by Erdoğan. In an official message (for which translation is available on the Turkish government website http://www.basbakanlik.gov.tr) the President of Turkey, in recognizing the importance of April 24th for the Armenians, referred to historical events as "inhuman" and presented his condolences to the grandchildren of those who had lost their lives. Although Erdoğan's statement did not constitute an "official apology" nor even the recognition of the Armenian genocide as such, it represented a fundamental change in the way of understanding and treating the events of 1915 by Turkey.

[133] See http://www.hebdo.ch/news/politique/erevan-se-retire-des-protocoles-de-zurich-sur-une-normalisation.

[134] Pinton (2012), p. 70, which takes a similar position expressed by Pietrobon (2007).

[135] This hypothesis also suggested in the final document produced following the International Conference Armenian Genocide: From Recognition to Reparation, Catholicosate of Cilicia, Antelias, Lebanon, 23–25 February 2012, convened by His Holiness Aram I. Moreover, as has been pointed out "yet another side effect of the Turkish denial has been the acquaintance of the third parties, namely the world community and especially the major powers which have been playing a central role in this triangle drama. By focusing on the Turkish denial, the third-party states have acquitted themselves from any responsibility in that aspect, arguing that 'the problem between Turkey and Armenia must be resolved between the two countries' (U.S. Assistant Secretary of State: Turkey, Armenia must themselves solve their problems, Trend.az, 18 March, 2010; en.trend.az/regions/scaucasus/Armenia/1655960.html)". Avedian (2013), p. 80.

judicial body of the United Nations by taking away the dispute about the Armenians massacres from the bilateral approach, based on relations between Ankara and Yerevan, and promoting a solution for the spiral of polarization that has so far characterized the issue.[136] As a relevant international instrument, the International Covenant on Civil and Political Rights,[137] ratified by Armenia in 1993 and by Turkey in 2003, should be mentioned in particular with regard to the compatibility of Article 301 Cpt with the Covenant. In fact, according to General comment No. 34 of the Human Rights Committee:

> Laws that penalize the expression of opinion about historical facts are incompatible with the obligations that the Covenant imposes on States parties in relation to the respect for freedom of opinion and expression. The Covenant does not permit general prohibition of expressions of an erroneous opinion or an incorrect interpretation of past events. Restrictions on the right of freedom of opinion should never be imposed […].[138]

Still, on a regional level, when additional Protocol n. 16 to the ECHR enters into force, an opinion could be asked of the Strasbourg Court on the compatibility of Article 301 Cpt with the Convention.[139]

At present, unfortunately, such an option seems to be more distant considering the State of emergency decided on 20 July 2016 by President Erdoğan in response to an attempted coup d'etat[140] pursuant to Article 120 of the Turkish Constitution

[136] In general, for a review of the remedial measures in response to the Armenian massacres, we note the interesting survey of the studies on the subject by Theriault (2014).

[137] Adopted and opened for signature, ratification and accession by General Assembly resolution 2200A (XXI) of 16 December 1966, entry into force 23 March 1976.

[138] 102nd session, Geneva, 11–29 July 2011 on Article 19: Freedoms of opinion and expression, §49.

[139] The text of Protocol n. 16 is available on www.echr.coe.int/Documents/Protocol_16_ENG.pdf. It also stressed "It is one thing, in fact, to ascertain an infringement consequent to the exhaustion of domestic remedies, another the expression of an opinion 'for a trial under way' in which, ultimately, the European Court will not have to evaluate a final decision of the national judge but will have to express an opinion on the request of that judge on whom rests the last word, except if one of the parties requires a new intervention according to the EHCR provisions": Conti (2014).

[140] The repression of President Erdoğan in response to the attempted coup of 15 July 2016 scored, so far, 105 thousand public officials dismissed, 76 thousand holdings for questioning or garde a vue, 35 thousand arrests (including 2,745 judges) for suspected links with the movement of Fethullah Gulen, considered responsible for the attempted coup. On 9 November 2016, President Theodor Meron presented the fourth Annual Report of the Mechanism for International Criminal Tribunals (MICT) to the United Nations General Assembly and briefed the Assembly on the ongoing detention of a Judge of the Mechanism, 76 year old Judge Aydin Sefa Akay of Turkey, by Turkish authorities. Expressing his personal concern for the welfare of Judge Akay, the President also reported to the Assembly that the UN Office of Legal Affairs, on behalf of the Secretary-General, had formally asserted diplomatic immunity, in accordance with the MICT's Statute, and, as a consequence, had requested Judge Akay's immediate release from detention and the cessation of all legal proceedings against him. In that regard, President Meron expressed regret that the Government of Turkey has not as yet acted upon this formal request. http://www.unmict.org/en/news/president-meron-presents-fourth-annual-report-united-nations-general-assembly-and-calls-turkey.

("State of Emergency Declaration because of widespread acts of violence and serious deterioration of public order").[141] The deputy Prime Minister Kurtulmuş announced the temporary suspension by Turkey of the European Convention for the Protection of Human Rights and Fundamental Freedoms, invoking Article 15 of the Convention.[142] In October the state of emergency was extended, causing the concerned reactions of the Council of Europe[143] and the request of the European Parliament to suspend negotiations with Turkey on its accession to the European Union.[144]

So, both civil society[145] and the subjects of the International Community—considering the correct understanding of the right to memory as a right *erga omnes*—will have to intervene to (eventually) ascertain the Armenian massacre. It is worth to remembering that the attempts to resolve the *impasse*—involving only Turkey and Armenia—have always failed. However even prior to the aforementioned Protocols of Zurich, in April 2005 Prime Minister Erdoğan offered to make available (to a joint Armenian-Turkish Commission) undisclosed diplomatic documentation in order to allow the study of the controversial events after 1915.[146] Although the Armenian President Kocharian, accepted in principle the proposal to set up such a joint Commission, the Turkish counteroffer changed both the composition and the issues to be examined. An inter-governmental Commission rather than a historical one responsible for addressing the entire spectrum of issues

[141]B.B.C. News, *Turkey coup attempt: State of emergency announced*, http://www.bbc.com/news/world-europe-36852080; Shaheen (21 July 2016a). The state of emergency was approved by Parliament on 21 July, with 346 votes in favor and 115 against.

[142]Article 15.1: "Derogation in time of emergency: In time of war or other public emergency threatening the life of the nation any High Contracting Party may take measures derogating from its obligations under this Convention to the extent strictly required by the exigencies of the situation, provided that such measures are not inconsistent with its other obligations under international law".

[143]Memorandum on the human rights implications of the measures taken under the state of emergency in Turkey, by Nils Muižnieks, Council of Europe Commissioner for Human Rights, Comm DH(2016)35, Strasbourg, 7 October 2016.

[144]The resolution of 24 November 2016 on the relations UE-Turkey (2016/2993(RSP)) was approved with 470 votes in favor, 37 votes against and 107 abstentions and it is available on http://www.europarl.europa.eu/sides/getDoc.do?pubRef=-//EP//TEXT+TA+P8-TA-2016-0450+0+DOC+XML+V0//IT&language=IT.

[145]An example of a push "from the bottom" is the "I apologize" campaign (2008) - an online initiative led by a group of Turkish intellectuals to reject the official denial of the massacres and offer an apology. See: www.ozurdiliyoruz.com The full text reads: "My conscience cannot accept the ignorance and denial of the Great Catastrophe that the Ottoman Armenians were subjected to in 1915. I reject this injustice and – on my own behalf – I share the feelings and pain of my Armenian brothers and sisters – and I apologize to them". The petition initially provoked strong outcries from Erdoğan and Turkish nationalists but has been signed by over 32,000 Turks. See Aktar (2014).

[146]For the text of the letter of Prime Mister Erdoğan addressed to Kocharian, President of Armenia, proposing to form a joint historical commission with Armenia see: http://www.mfa.gov.tr/data/DISPOLITIKA/text-of-the-letter-of-h_e_-prime-minister-recep-tayyip-erdogan-addressed-to-h_e_-robert-kocharian.pdf.

between the two countries was proposed.[147] So the long-awaited meeting between the parties did not occur, thus formalizing the reopening of the vicious circle of reciprocal accusations, which was hoped had been overcome.

In fact, although Turkey seems to still be influenced by the so-called Syndrome of Sèvres, a permissive attitude of the International Community and civil society could hinder and slow down the process of leading Turkey into recognizing itself in the fundamental values fostered by the Council of Europe and the European Union and encouraging the full development of democracy and civil liberties in that country. Unfortunately, in the current situation, the "shared memory" that would allow processing the heavy legacy of the past seems to be moving further away. The invitation to dialogue between Turkey and the Armenians over the exact reconstruction and characterization of the facts of 1915–1916 could lay the groundwork for an alternative form of conflict resolution. This alternative form of management could allow for a deeper understanding of the facts rather than the traditional logic of punishment in a perspective which, far from judging and condemning, aims at explaining and understanding the complexity of the question,[148] while at the same time meeting the needs of narration and shared truth about serious facts that should not be forgotten.[149] Thus, what has been defined as the "dark side" of memory, i.e. the ability to nurture a sense of enmity and the persistence of old resentments that could hinder the reconciliation and the solidarity essential to the building of a functional society in the present time, could be enlightened in order to ensure that the memory of past injustice is not used instrumentally to maintain these old divisions and hatreds. This is probably the most important aspect of the right to truth and the right to memory: that of being useful for dealing with the past, a result which unfortunately still seems unreachable for Turks and Armenians.[150]

References

Abakar MH (2006) Chronique d'une enquête criminelle nationale. Le cas du régime de Hissène Habré, 1982–1990. L'Harmattan, Paris

Aktar C (2014) Turkish civil society: driving the politics of memory. Turk Policy Q 13(1):79–86

Algan B (2008) The brand new version of Article 301 of Turkish Penal Code and the future of freedom of expression cases in Turkey. Ger Law J 12:2237–2251

Andriotti Romanin E (2013) Decir la verdad, hacer justicia: Los Juicios por la Verdad en Argentin. Eur Rev Latin Am Caribb Stud 94:5–23

Aram I (2014) The Armenian genocide: from recognition to reparations. Int Crim Law Rev 14:233–241

[147]The text of Kocharian's answer is available on: https://wikileaks.org/plusd/cables/05YEREVAN769_a.html.

[148]That is an investigation of what some, with a happy expression, calls "tragic responsibility": Speziale Bagliacca (1998), p. 69.

[149]Osiel (2005), p. 106.

[150]Francioni (2008), p. 51.

Archiyan YE (2011) Turkey and European Union: an association in making. J Int Law Pract 20:117–148
Avedian V (2012) State identity, continuity and responsibility: the Ottoman Empire, The Republic of Turkey and the Armenian genocide. Eur J Int Law 23:797–820
Avedian V (2013) Recognition, responsibility and reconciliation: the trinity of the Armenian genocide. Eur Ethica 70(3/4):77–86
Bardakjian K (1985) Hitler and the Armenian genocide. Zoryan Institute, Cambridge, Massachusett
Beachler DW (2011) The genocide debate: politicians, academics and victims. Palgrave Macmillan, New York
Banco E (2015) Armenian genocide: 100 years later, Turkey replaces Armenian memories with "restored", whitewashed sites. International Business Times. http://www.ibtimes.com/armenian-genocide-100-years-later-turkey-replaces-armenian-memories-restored-1889898?utm_source=internal&utm_campaign=incontent&utm_medium=related1
Binder B (2001) Jahrestag. In: Pethes N, Rüchatz J (eds) Gedächtnis und Ennirerung. Ein Interdisziplinäres Lexikon. Rowohlt, Reinbek; Italian edition: Binder B (2005) Luogo della memoria. In: Dizionario della memoria e del ricordo. Mondadori, Milano, pp 291–293
Bloxham D (2005) The great game of genocide. Imperialism, nationalism and the destruction of the Ottoman Armenians. Oxford University Press, Oxford
Bonello G (2008) The "Malta Trials" and the Turkish-Armenian question. In: Bonello G (ed) Histories of Malta—confessions and transgressions, vol 9. Fondazzjoni Patrimonju Malti, pp 180–227
Bozarlsan H, Duclert V, Kévorkian RH (2015) Comprendre le génocide des arméniens. 1915 à nos jours. Tallandier, Paris
Bozbayındır AE (2012) Denigration of the Turkish Nation, the Turkish Republic, the Institutions and the Organs of the State: an unjustifiable offence? In: Riondato S, Alagna R (eds) Criminal law of the Republic of Turkey. Padova University Press, Padova, pp 235–248
Cannizzaro E (ed) (2011) The law of treaties beyond the Vienna Convention. Oxford University Press, Oxford
Cassese A (2009) Armenians (massacres of). In: Cassese A (ed) The Oxford Companion to International Criminal Justice. Oxford University Press, Oxford, p 249
Churchill WS (1929) The world crisis, vol 5: The Eastern Front. Thornton Butterworth Limited, London
Conti R (2014) La richiesta di "parere consultivo" alla Corte europea delle Alte Corti introdotto dal Protocollo n. 16 annesso alla Cedu e il rinvio pregiudiziale alla Corte di Giustizia Ue. Prove d'orchestra per una nomofilachia europea, Testo dell'intervento al Convegno su La richiesta di pareri consultivi alla Corte di Strasburgo da parte delle più alte giurisdizioni nazionali. Prime riflessioni in vista della ratifica del Protocollo 16 Cedu, Università di Milano Bicocca e dalla Scuola Superiore della Magistratura. http://www.giurcost.org/studi/conti2.pdf.
Dadrian VN (1996) The comparative aspects of the Armenian and Jewish cases of genocide: a socio-historical perspective. In: Rosenbaum AS (ed) Is the Holocaust unique?. Westview Press, Boulder Colorado, pp 101–135
Dadrian VN (1997) German responsibility in the Armenian genocide: a review of the historical evidence on Germany complicity. Blue Crane Books, Watertown, MA
Dadrian VN (2005) The history of Armenian genocide. Ethnic conflict from the Balkans to Anatolia and Caucasus, revised and expanded 7th edition. Berghahn Books, Providence/Oxford
Damaška M (2006) L'incerta identità delle corti penali internazionali. Criminalia 9–55
De Luna G (2011) La Repubblica del dolore: le memorie di un'Italia divisa. Feltrinelli, Milano
Della Morte G (2014) International law between the duty of memory and the right to oblivion. Int Crim Law Rev 14:427–440
Dumberry P (2013) Responsibility for crimes committed by the Ottoman Empire against the Armenian population: are the rules of state succession to international responsibility of any use? Hague Yearb Int Law 26:141–167

Dumberry P (2014) The consequences of Turkey being the "continuing" State of the Ottoman Empire in terms of international responsibility for internationally wrongful acts. Int Crim Law Rev 14:261–273

Ferrari A (2009) I protocolli armeno-turchi e il nodo dell'Alto Karabakh. ISPI - Policy Brief 164:1–6

Francioni F (2008) Riparazione per le violazioni dei diritti dei popoli indigeni: quale ruolo per il diritto internazionale? In: Palmisano AL, Pustorino P (eds) Identità dei Popoli Indigeni: aspetti giuridici, antropologici e linguistici. IILA, Roma, pp 33–51

Flores D'Arcais M (2006) Il genocidio degli armeni. il Mulino, Bologna

Frappi C (2015) Oltre il genocidio. La dimensione politica e regionale della questione turco-armena. ISPI Commentary. www.ispionline.it.

Fronza E (2012) Il negazionismo come reato. Giuffrè, Milano

Gallant KS (2009) The principle of legality in international and comparative criminal law. Cambridge University Press, Cambridge

Gensburger S, Lavabre M-C (2004) Entre "devoir de mémoire" et "abus de mémoire": la sociologie de la mémoire comme tierce position. In: Müller B (ed) Histoire, Mémoire et épistémologie. A propos de Paul Ricoeur. Éditions Payot, Lausanne

Göçek FM (2011) Reading genocide Turkish historiography on 1915. In: Suny RG, Göçek FM, Naimark NM (eds) A question of genocide: Armenians and Turks at the end of the Ottoman Empire. Oxford University Press, Oxford, pp 42–54

Giuva L (2014) Art. 12: il Diritto alla memoria e alle memorie. In: Melograni PS (ed) Manuale dei Diritti fondamentali e desiderabili. Oscar Mondadori, Milano, pp 15–19

Halaçoğlu Y (2008) The story of 1915: what happened to the Ottoman Armenians?. Turk Hist Soc, Ankara

Hovannisian RG (1981) The Armenian Holocaust. Armenian Heritage Press, Cambridge

Kahn RA (2016) Does it matter how one opposes memory bans? A commentary on Liberté Pour L'Histoire. Wash Univ Glob Stud Law Rev 15(1):55–92

Langellier J-P, Peroncel-Hugoz J-P (16 November 1993) Un entretien avec Bernard Lewis. Le Monde.

Leotta C (2013) Il genocidio nel diritto penale internazionale. Dagli scritti di Raphael Lemkin allo Statuto di Roma. Torino, Giappichelli

Leotta C (2016) Profili penali del negazionismo. Riflessioni alla luce della sentenza della Corte EDU sul genocidio armeni. CEDAM, Padova

Lepsius J (1916) Berichtüber die Lagedes Armenischen Volkes in derTürkei. Tempelverlag, Postdam

Lewy G (2005) The Armenian massacres in Ottoman Turkey: a disputed genocide. The University of Utah Press, Salt Lake City

Lisena F (2009) Spetta allo Stato accertare la "verità storica"? Giurisprudenzacostituzionale 54:3959–3968

Melson RF (2001) Revolution and genocide, on the origins of the Armenian genocide and the Holocaust. The University of Chicago Press, Chicago

Nora P (2011) History, memory and the law in France, 1990–2010, posted on the Liberté website www.lphasso.fr/index.php?option=com_content&view=article&id=159%3Apierre-nora-qlhistoire-la-memoireet-la-loi-en-france-1990-2008q&catid=53%3Aactualites&Itemid=170&lang=en

Osiel MJ (2005) Politica della punizione, memoria collettiva e diritto internazionale. In: Baldissarra L, Pezzino P (eds) Giudicare e punire. L'ancora del Mediterraneo, Napoli, pp 105–118

Picone P (2013) Comunità internazionale e obblighi "erga omnes", III edn. Jovene, Napoli

Pietrobon A (2007) Un giudice internazionale per il negazionismo? Forum di Quaderni costituzionali — Papers, 1–9. http://www.forumcostituzionale.it/

Pinton S (2012) The Armenian massacres in international law. In: Forlati MLP (ed) Rassicurazione e memoria. Per dare un futuro alla pace. CEDAM, Padova, pp 45–73

Polatel M, Mildanoğlu N, Leman Eren Ö, Atılgan M (2012) The 2012 declaration: the seized properties of Armenian Foundations in Istanbul. Hrant Dink Foundation Publications, Istanbul
Ricoeur P (2000) La mémoire, l'histoire, l'oubli. Editions du Seuil, Paris
Roscini M (2014) Establishing state responsibility for historical injustices: the Armenian case. Int Crim Law Rev 14:291–316
Rousso H (1987) La syndrome de Vichy (1944–1987). Éditions du Seuil, Paris
Schabas WA (2009) Genocide in international law: the crimes of crimes. Cambridge University Press, Cambridge
Schmid D (2014) Turquie: le syndrome de Sèvres ou la guerre qui n'en finit pas. Politique étrangère 1:199–213
Shaheen K (21 July 2016a) Turkey coup attempt: Erdoğan declares three-month state emergency. The Guardian.
Shaheen K (21 July 2016b) Turkey approves state of emergency bill allowing rule by decree. The Guardian.
Simm G (2016) The Paris peoples' tribunal and the Istanbul trials: archives of the Armenian genocide. Leiden J Int Law 29:245–268
Smith RW, Markusen E, Lifton RJ (1995) Professional ethics and the denial of Armenian genocide. Holocaust Genocide Stud 9:1–22
Speziale Bagliacca R (1998) Esiste una logica della colpa? Materiali per una storia della cultura giuridica 28:69–92
Tacar P, Gauin M (2012) State identity, continuity and responsibility: the Ottoman Empire, the Republic of Turkey and the Armenian genocide: a reply to Vaghagn Avedian. Eur J Int Law 23:821–835
Tacconi M (2015) Armeni, la memoria negata nel centenario del genocidio. Resetdoc on http://www.reset.it/reset-doc/centenario-genocidio-armeno
Taubira C (2006) Le droit à la mémoire. Cités 25:164–166
Theriault HC (2014) Legal avenues for Armenian genocide reparations. Int Crim Law Rev 14:219–231
Tomuschat C (2006) National. Prosecutions, truth. Commissions and International Criminal Justice. In: Werle G (ed) Justice in transition—prosecution and amnesty in Germany and South Africa. Berliner Wissenschafts-Verlag, Berlin, 157–168
Tomuschat C, Thouvenin J-M (2006) The fundamental rules of the international legal order. Martinus Nijhoff Publishers, Leiden, Boston
Toriguian S (1988) The Armenian question and international law, 2nd edn. University of La Verne Press, La Verne, CA
Traverso E (2006) Il Passato. Istruzioni per l'uso. Storia, memoria, politica. Ombre Corte, Verona
Vartabedian S (2007) Commemoration of an Assassin: representing the Armenian genocide. University of North Carolina, Chapel Hill
Weil P (2009) The politics of memory: bans and commemorations. In: Hare I, Weinstein J (eds) Extreme speech and democracy. Oxford University Press, Oxford, pp 562–579
Wilson RJ (2014) Restoration of historical memory and dignity for victims of the Armenian genocide. Int Crim Law Rev 14:332–342
Ziegler K-H (2004) The peace treaty of the Ottoman Empire with European Christian powers. In: Lesaffer R (ed) Peace treaties and international law in European history. Cambridge University Press, Cambridge, pp 338–364

Denying the Armenian Genocide in International and European Law

Monica Spatti

Contents

1 Introduction 237
2 International Acts that Criminalize Denial Conduct 239
3 Framework Decision 2008/913/JHA of the European Union 241
4 The Case-Law of the European Court of Human Rights 242
5 The Main Difficulties in the Criminalization of Denial Conduct in the Light of International Practice 245
6 Concluding Observations 247
References 248

Abstract Several international and European legal instruments, both binding and non-binding, call on or allow for the criminalization of speech that denies, condones or minimizes international crimes. The aim of this essay is to verify the extent of those instruments, particularly the definitions of punishable behaviours and the identification of the object/target of such behaviours, with a view to ascertain whether the instruments apply to the Armenian massacres of 1915–1916.

1 Introduction

Since the 1990s several European countries have introduced the criminalization of conduct such as the denial or condoning and minimization of the Holocaust or, more generally, of international crimes. Today this kind of offence is present in most countries on the continent, with significant differences concerning the conduct

M. Spatti (✉)
University "Cattolica del Sacro Cuore", Milan, Italy
e-mail: monica.spatti@unicatt.it

F. Lattanzi and E. Pistoia (eds.), *The Armenian Massacres of 1915–1916 a Hundred Years Later*, Studies in the History of Law and Justice 15,
https://doi.org/10.1007/978-3-319-78169-3_10

itself, requirements to make such conduct criminal and consequences of the conduct.[1] The spread of this criminalization was encouraged by the European Union which, through the Joint Action 96/443/JHA, invited Member States to cooperate in the pursuit of punishing behaviours such as public condoning and public denial of international crimes.[2] This Joint Action was followed by Framework Decision 2008/913/JHA, which imposes criminalization on denial statements.[3]

While many European countries, if not yet all, recognize the criminalisation of denial conduct, there is one country, Turkey, that introduced a sort of crime of recognition. In Turkey those who speak of genocide towards the Armenian massacres could be punished by imprisonment due to the application of Article 301 of the Turkish penal code, which makes the denigration of Turkishness a criminal offence.[4]

In international law there are several relevant instruments relating to this issue. First of all, we have to consider the Additional Protocol to the Convention on Cybercrime, concerning the criminalisation of acts of a racist and xenophobic nature committed through computer systems. This Protocol came into force on 28 January 2003 and imposes the criminalization of the denial of certain international crimes.[5] Furthermore, the pronouncements of various international bodies must be considered, such as the General Assembly, the UN Committee on the Elimination of Racial Discrimination and the UN Human Rights Committee, all of which have made their positions clear on this matter. Of particular importance is the case-law of the European Court of Human Rights, which has issued many judgements regarding the legitimacy of sanctions imposed on persons who have justified or minimized the Holocaust.

The aim of this analysis is to verify the extent of the obligations established in international and European norms regarding the criminalisation of denial conduct, with a view to ascertain whether they apply to the Armenian massacres. After reviewing international and European acts and case-law on the subject, the analysis will focus on the main problem areas, in particular the definition of punishable conduct and the identification of the target of the conduct itself.

---

[1]See the report from the Commission to the European Parliament and the Council of 27 January 2014 on the implementation of the Council Framework Decision 2008/913/JHA on combating certain forms and expressions of racism and xenophobia by means of criminal law, COM(2014) 27 final, paras 3.1.3–3.1.5. For scholarly writings, see, *inter alia*: Bazyler (2009); Hennebel and Hochmann (2011); Kahn (2004); Fronza (2006), p. 617 et seq.

[2]Joint action of 15 July 1996 adopted by the Council on the basis of Article K.3 of the Treaty on European Union, concerning action to combat racism and xenophobia, OJ L 185, 24 July 1996, p. 5 et seq.

[3]Council Framework Decision of 28 November 2008 on combating certain forms of racism and xenophobia by means of criminal law, OJ L 328 of 6 December 2008, p. 55 et seq.

[4]On this topic see Tate (2008), p. 181 et seq.

[5]Adopted in Strasbourg and entered into force 1 March 2006.

2 International Acts that Criminalize Denial Conduct

Within the body of international law, the only provision that criminalizes denial conduct is included in the Additional Protocol to the Convention on Cybercrime. According to Article 6.1, States parties must consider as criminal offences the distribution to the public, through a computer system, of "material which denies, grossly minimises, approves or justifies action constituting genocide or crimes against humanity," as recognized by decisions of the International Military Tribunal of Nuremberg or any other international court whose jurisdiction is recognized by the State party. The inclusion of denial conduct in an instrument concerning the criminalisation of acts of racist and xenophobic nature is driven by the consideration that such conduct is able to inspire racist and xenophobic behaviours.[6] It should be noted, however, that States Parties, according to Article 6.2.a, are allowed *not* to apply this provision. Among the twenty-four countries that have ratified the Protocol—all members of the Council of Europe, even if it is also open to non-European countries—only three of them have expressed reservation to this provision.[7]

In international law, there are instruments that do not specifically concern denial conduct but which emphasize that denial conduct could incite hate or violence. According to Article 20.2 of the International Covenant on Civil and Political Rights (ICCPR), States parties have the duty to prohibit "[a]ny advocacy of national, racial or religious hatred that constitutes incitement to discrimination, hostility or violence."

The Human Rights Committee dealt with the relationship between this provision and that of Article 19, which recognizes freedom of expression. In General Comment No. 34 it established that "Laws that penalize the expression of opinions about historical facts are incompatible with […] the respect for freedom of opinion and expression," even if these opinions are erroneous or incorrect interpretations of past events.[8]

The same pronouncement comes from two other UN organs. First of all, the UN Special Rapporteur on the promotion and protection of the right to freedom of opinion and expression[9] which, in a report submitted to the General Assembly on 7 September 2012, recalls the position of the Human Rights Committee and confirms that "laws that penalize the expression of opinions about historical facts are

[6]See the explanatory report to the Additional Protocol, available at http://www.coe.int/en/web/conventions/full-list/-/conventions/treaty/189.

[7]Ibidem.

[8]General comment No. 34, Article 19, Freedoms of opinion and expression, 12 September 2011, CCPR/C/GC/34, para. 49.

[9]Established by the UN Commission on Human Rights with resolution 1993/45 of 5 March 1993, E/CN.4/RES/1993/45.

incompatible" with Article 19 ICCPR.[10] In the same way, the UN Independent Expert on the promotion of a democratic and equitable international order,[11] in a report of 1 July 2013 submitted to the Human Rights Council, affirmed that "memory laws and any laws that hinder open discussion of political and historical events" are incompatible with Articles 18 and 19 of the International Covenant on Civil and Political Rights concerning, respectively, the right to freedom of thought, conscience and religion, and the right of freedom of expression.[12]

However, the Human Rights Committee in the General Comment No. 34 has also affirmed that "Articles 19 and 20 are compatible with and complement each other" and that "[i]t is only with regard to the specific forms of expression indicated in article 20 that States parties are obliged to have legal prohibition."[13] From these sentences, it can be deduced that national laws that criminalize the denial of international crimes are compatible with the obligations imposed by the Covenant only if they penalize the conduct that represents hate speech.

Another international provision that condemns incitement to hate or violence, in this case for racial reasons, is contained in Article 4.a of the International Convention on the Elimination of All Forms of Racial Discrimination (CERD).[14] This norm differs from Article 20 ICCPR in that while the latter contains a generic prohibition of hate speech, according to Article 4.a, States parties have the duty to consider this kind of conduct as an offence punishable by law. It therefore imposes the use of criminal prosecution in the case of hate speech.

The UN Committee on the Elimination of Racial Discrimination had the opportunity to speak about the compatibility of national laws criminalizing Holocaust denial with Article 4.a. Similarly to what was affirmed by the Human Rights Committee, it asserted in its General Recommendation No. 35 that:

> Public denials or attempts to justify crimes of genocide and crimes against humanity, as defined by international law, should be declared as offences punishable by law, provided that they clearly constitute incitement racial violence or hatred.[15]

The UN General Assembly has also ruled on the matter, but only with respect to one specific international crime: the Holocaust. According to resolution No. 60/7 of 1 November 2005,[16] the UN General Assembly claims to reject "any denial of the

[10] Report on the encouragement and protection of the right to freedom of opinion and expression, A/67/357, para. 55.

[11] Established by the Human Rights Council with Resolution 18/6 of 13 October 2011, A/HRC/RES/18/6.

[12] A/HRC/24/38, par. 56.e.

[13] Ibidem, paras. 50–52.

[14] Opened for signature in New York on 7 March 1966 and entered into force on 4 January 1969.

[15] General recommendation No. 35, Combating racist hate speech, 26 September 2013, CERD/C/GC/35, para. 14.

[16] UN Doc. A/RES/60/7.

Holocaust as an historical event."[17] In Resolution No. 61/255 of 26 January 2007,[18] it invites member States to do the same.

3 Framework Decision 2008/913/JHA of the European Union

The first instrument within the European integration organizations to deal with the phenomenon of negationism was the Joint Action of the Council 96/443/JHA, which aimed to improve judicial cooperation between Member States in the prosecution of offences based on racism and xenophobia. Among these, in Article A, (b) and (c), the Joint Action included the public condoning of crimes against humanity committed for a racist or xenophobic purpose, and the public denial of the crimes defined in Article 6 of the Charter of the International Tribunal of Nuremberg, provided that it comprised contemptuous or degrading behaviour against a group.

The implementation of the Joint Action revealed the existence of some problems, especially obstacles to judicial cooperation mainly based on the divergence of legal approaches between Member States.[19] For this reason, the European Commission proposed replacing the Joint Action with a new instrument which should more closely unify criminal laws, in particular to make punishment of certain conduct mandatory for all Member States. This harmonization should facilitate judicial cooperation among States and prevent criminals (and in particular, regarding the subject of this work, the deniers) from searching for a country where their conduct is not punishable.

In November 2001, the European Commission proposed to the Council the adoption of a "Framework Decision on combating racism and xenophobia" in order to render some behaviours punishable as criminal offences, including denial conduct.[20] It took seven years before the Council was able to adopt the act, because of the resistance of many Member States.[21] The main obstacle was the fear, expressed by some States, of unreasonably impairing the right to freedom of expression. The resistance was overcome only through a compromise (to be discussed, *infra*) and a reassurance about the compliance with the principle of freedom of expression. According to Article 7.2, "This Framework Decision shall not have the effect of

[17]See para. 3 of resolution No. 60/7, and para. 1 of resolution No. 61/255.

[18]Un Doc. A/RES/61/255.

[19]See the explanatory memorandum of the proposal, OJ 75 E of 26 March 2002, p. 269 et seq.

[20]The Framework Decision is based on the assumption that the denial statements nurture the dissemination of xenophobic and anti-Semitic ideologies. On the relationship between these elements, see Lipstadt (1993).

[21]On the Framework Decision see: Garman (2007); Lobba (2014); Renauld (2010).

requiring Member States to take measures in contradiction to fundamental principles relating to [...] freedom of expression."

The Framework Decision imposes the criminalization of the conduct of those who publicly condone, deny or trivialise the occurrence of international crimes as defined in the Charter of the International Military Tribunal of Nuremberg and in the Statute of the International Criminal Court; but only when the conduct is directed against a group of persons or a member of such a group and "when the conduct is carried out in a manner likely to incite violence or hatred against such a group or a member of such a group" (Article 1, (c) and (d)).

This broad definition is, however, accompanied by the possibility for Member States to restrict the field of action of the offence. We find in particular two clauses, referred to as the German and the French clauses because they typically occur in the formulation of the offence in Germany and in France, respectively. According to the so-called German clause, Member States are allowed to "choose to punish only conduct which is either carried out in a manner likely to disturb public order or which is threatening, abusive or insulting" (Article 1.2). This clause enables States to prosecute only the negationist conduct liable to create an atmosphere of hate and violence. The French clause (to be discussed, infra) allows Member States to condition the criminalization of denial conduct on the requirement that the international crimes to which they refer "have been established by a final decision of a national court of this Member State and/or an international court, or by a final decision of an international court only" (Article 1.4).

4 The Case-Law of the European Court of Human Rights

The criminalization of denial statements is clearly a restriction of the right to freedom of expression, which is a fundamental right enshrined in all the most important instruments concerning human rights, including the following: Article 19 of the Universal Declaration of Human Rights; Article 19 of the International Covenant on Civil and Political Rights; Article 10 of the European Convention on Human Rights (ECHR) and Article 11 of the Charter of Fundamental Rights of the European Union. As can be seen from reading these norms, freedom of expression is a fundamental right, but not an absolute one; it can be limited when the restriction is prescribed by law and is necessary to pursue a legitimate aim.

The European Court of Human Rights has often been called upon to decide the compatibility of the convictions of negationists with the European Convention on Human Rights. First of all, it was the old European Commission that was faced with applications from persons, condemned for having pronounced denying or revisionist statements of the Holocaust, who complained of the infringement of Article 10. The European Commission established compatibility of the convictions with the provision concerning the freedom of expression.[22] In a practice then confirmed and further developed by the European Court, the European Commission introduced a reference to Article 17 ECHR concerning the abuse of rights, using this rule as a useful tool for the interpretation and application of Article 10.[23] According to this rule, it is not possible to use the provisions of the European Convention in order to "engage in any activity or perform any act aimed at the destruction of any of the rights and freedoms set forth herein." The European Commission stated that "freedom of expression as expressed in Article 10 of the Convention may not be invoked in a sense contrary to Article 17."

The European Court's case-law relating to the denial of the Holocaust has confirmed reference to Article 17 ECHR and has recently arrived at the point of applying the provision in a way that produces the so-called "Guillotine" effect, thereby dismissing the applications, and thus excluding consideration on the merits.[24] According to the European Court it is, therefore, perfectly legitimate to sanction those who make denial or revisionist statements of the Holocaust. And it is equally legitimate to do this without considering factors such as the capacity of these statements to incite to hate or violence, or the ability of the statements to reach a large or small audience or, again, the notoriety or the role of those who pronounce the disputed statements and, even, the nature of the sanction imposed. These elements must instead be taken into consideration if the Court applies Article 10 ECHR and, therefore, verifies whether the restrictive measure is necessary to achieve the objective.[25]

As already emphasized, the European Court case-law on negationism has always been about the Holocaust. In the only case in which the Court was faced with a case of denial regarding a different event, it followed a different path. This refers to the case *Perinçek v. Switzerland,* which concerns the conviction of a person who relativized the Armenian massacres, when both the second section of the Chamber and the Grand Chamber decided not to apply Article 17, but Article 10.[26] The Court (for reasons of conciseness the reference is made solely to the Grand Chamber's judgement) therefore verified the compliance of the three conditions for the lawfulness of the restriction, according to paragraph 2 of Article 10 ECHR. In particular, in assessing the necessity of the restrictive measure, the Court ascertained

[22]See decisions of 6 September 1995, *Remer v. Germany*, application No. 25096/94, and of 18 October 1995, *Honsik v. Austria*, application No. 25062/94.

[23]See decisions of 11 January 1995, *Walendy v. Germany*, application No. 21128/93; of 16 January 1996, *Rebhandl v. Austria*, application No. 24398/94; of 24 June 1996, *Marais v. France*, application No. 31159/96; of 26 June 1996, *D.I. v. Germany*, application No. 26551/95; and of 9 September 1998, *Nachtmann v. Austria*, application No. 36773/97. See Frowein (2000), p. 33 et seq.; Van Drooghenbroeck (2001).

[24]See decisions of 24 June 2003, *Garaudy v. France*, application No. 65831/01, and of 13 December 2005, *Witzsch v. Germany*, application No. 7485/03. Among the literature see: Cannie and Voorhoof (2011), p. 62 et seq.; Keane (2007), p. 641 et seq.; Lobba (2015), p. 246 et seq.

[25]See Tulkens (2012), p. 288 s.; and Weber (2009), p. 33.

[26]Judgements of 17 December 2013 and of 15 October 2015, application No. 27510/08.

whether the statements at issue had incited to hate or violence. To this end, it took into account the political and social context in which they were made, their ability to harm, and the intention of the person who had pronounced the contested statements.[27]

This means that the memory of the Armenian massacres does not deserve the same protection accorded to the massacre of Jews. The Grand Chamber justifies this different treatment on the basis of two reasons that lend themselves to criticism. One reason, of an historical and geographical nature, relies on the fact that these events did not take place on European soil, and in relation to which there is no question of any form of involvement of responsibility on the part of the defendant State (paras. 242–248). The other reason, of a temporary nature, is based on the consideration that the facts are so dated that the survivors are no longer alive (paras. 249–254). As noted by some judges in their dissenting opinion, this approach contrasts with the universal and *erga omnes* scope of human rights and with the non-applicability of statutory limitations to war crimes and crimes against humanity (paras. 6–8 of the dissenting opinion annexed to the judgement).[28]

Even the UN Committee for Human Rights has found itself deciding on the compatibility with the provision on freedom of expression of a criminal sentence imposed against a person who had denied the existence of gas chambers as part of the plan to exterminate the Jews. In the case *Faurisson v. France*, the Committee considered the national sentence compatible with Article 19 of the International Covenant on Civil and Political Rights.[29] Although also available in the Covenant (Article 5.1), the norm concerning the abuse of rights did not find any applicability here, and the Committee thus verified the fulfilment of the conditions required for the restriction of the right of freedom of expression. In particular, it examined the question of whether the restriction was provided by law, pursued a legitimate aim and was necessary to the pursued aim, as laid down in par. 3 of Article 19. Even when applying Article 20.2, which requires States to prohibit speech inciting to hate and violence, the UN Committee has determined that any restriction on freedom of expression must be examined in light of the three conditions for lawfulness laid down in par. 3 of Article 19,[30] though not explicitly foreseen in the provision.

[27]See paras. 204–208 and 231–233 of the Grand Chamber's judgement.

[28]See Borgna (2015); Daniele (2016); Della Morte (2016); Garibian (2016); Gonzalez (2016), Leotta, in this book.

[29]Decision of 8 November 1996, communication No. 550/1993.

[30]See decision of 18 October 2000, *Ross v. Canada*, communication No. 736/1997, paras. 10.6, 11.1–11.6, and the General Comment No. 34, paras. 50–52.

5 The Main Difficulties in the Criminalization of Denial Conduct in the Light of International Practice

The criminalization of denial conduct as configured in the international acts and case-law that we have considered in the previous paragraphs touches on several problematic issues; among them the following aspects need to be considered in particular: the definition of punishable behaviours and the identification of the object of the punishable conduct.

The first issue concerns the kind of conduct that may be criminalized, since international practice differs on this point. According to Article 1.1, (c) and (d), of the Framework Decision 2008/913/JHA, the punishable conduct consists of those behaviours that are public and consist of condoning, denying and grossly trivialising crimes of genocide, crimes against humanity and war crimes as defined in the Statute of the International Criminal Court or in the Charter of the International Military Tribunal of Nuremberg. Primarily, it is important to clarify the meaning of the words used in the norm. While "to condone" means the justification or the exaltation of certain events, "to deny" indicates the disclaiming of the existence of those events. "To trivialize" means, instead, the activity of reducing the importance or the seriousness of the events. The latter is certainly hazy in its definition.[31] The European Union legislature intended to better define the case by adding the adjective "grossly." This addition should eliminate the risk that an historical analysis calling into question certain aspects of events which have been qualified as international crimes could be criminalized.

Article 6.1 of the Additional Protocol to the Convention on Cybercrime has a similar formulation, but it does not mention war crimes. The most significant difference between the two acts in question concerns, however, the different emphasis given to the ability of the denial conduct to instigate hate and violence. For the Framework Decision, denial behaviours can only be criminalized if they are made in public and are "carried out in a manner likely to incite to violence or hatred" against a group of persons or a member of that group "defined by reference to race, colour, religion, descent or national or ethnic origin."

Therefore, the mere act of denying, minimizing or justifying an international crime is not enough. Because it can become punishable, it is necessary that the behaviour "is likely to incite to violence or hatred"; that means that it should be capable of causing violence or hatred, regardless of the actual realization of that outcome.

In contrast, under the Additional Protocol this element is not necessarily an integral part of the offence. It falls within the powers of the States parties to include the incitement factor in the offence.[32]

---

[31] Pech (2009), p. 44 s.

[32] See Article 6.2, (a).

Moving on to the UN bodies, it has already been said that for the UN Human Rights Committee and the UN Committee on the Elimination of Racial Discrimination, the denial behaviours should be criminalized precisely when they are an incitement to hate and violence.

With regard to the European Court case-law, when it was called upon to assess the legitimacy of convictions related to the denial, minimization or justification of the Holocaust, the Court has never conducted a specific investigation to verify the intention of the author of the statement to incite to violence or hatred or the ability of the statement to achieve that goal. Only in the recent ruling *Perinçek v. Switzerland*, unlike what was done in the cases concerning the Holocaust, the Court specifically investigated the above elements by concluding that neither the intent of the applicant nor the content of his statements were somehow acts to incite hatred and violence.[33]

The other main problem concerning the criminalization of denial behaviours is the identification of their object. According to Article 1.1, (c) and (d), of the Framework Decision 2008/913/JHA, the punishable conduct is the public "condoning, denying or grossly trivialising" of crimes of genocide, crimes against humanity and war crimes as defined in the Statute of the International Criminal Court and in the Charter of the International Military Tribunal of Nuremberg. The European legislature has thus decided not to typify the object of punishable conduct, as, in contrast, many national legislations do, when they criminalize only the denial of some well-identified historical events, usually the Holocaust, but not exclusively. The provision under examination exceeds the paradigm of the uniqueness of the Holocaust, according to which the genocide of the Jews would have had some unique characteristics that make the Holocaust different and, if possible, more serious than other crimes and, therefore, its remembrance would need a stronger criminal protection.

The position of the European Court of Human Rights is different. In the case *Perinçek c. Switzerland*—the only one having to do with behaviour not concerning the Holocaust—the Court concluded, as already said, by denying to the memory of the Armenian massacres the same protection accorded to the memory of the Holocaust.

Article 6.1 of the Additional Protocol to the Convention on Cybercrime shares with the Framework Decision the same openness to all crimes, but submits it to the condition that the crime is recognized as such by "final and binding decisions of the International Military Tribunal" of Nuremberg or "of any international court established by relevant international instruments and whose jurisdiction is recognized by that Party." In order to criminalize the denial conduct, therefore, not only is the existence of a final and binding judgement of an international tribunal that has ascertained the international crime necessary, but the international tribunal must also be recognized by the State.

[33]Paras. 204–208 and 231–233.

Subordinating the possibility to employ the criminal prosecution against denial conduct only in presence of a previous judgement means depriving of criminal protection the memory of those international crimes that, even if historically documented, have not been recognized by an international judge. We have to consider that the possibility that an international court would rule on and ascertain the existence of an international crime depends on various factors, not necessarily related to the irrefutability of the events. Such is the case of the Armenian massacres that have not been crystallized by an international court, although they are clearly established historical facts. With regard to the Armenian Massacres there are instead judgements adopted at the national level. Between 1919 and 1920 in Turkey several trials took place and led to the convictions of some perpetrators of the Armenian massacres.[34]

The Framework Decision contemplates the element of the existence of a previous international decision of an international court as merely optional. As already noted, according to the so-called French clause (Article 1.4), Member States are allowed to submit the criminalization of the denial conduct to the condition of the existence of a final decision of an international, or national, tribunal. The Framework Decision thus allows considering judgements adopted at the national level but only when the decision that ascertains the international crime is "of a national court of this Member State." This means that those States that adopted the French clause could not invoke the Ottoman rulings.

6 Concluding Observations

The review of the international provisions and case-law concerning negationism shows the existence of a general stigmatization of the phenomenon. States are urged, in some cases obliged, to criminalize denial conduct.

Although it is clear that the main reason that prompted the adoption of these provisions is the fight against the negationism of the Holocaust, they can be suited to combat the denial of the Armenian genocide. The only significant obstacle is the clause—mandatory for the Additional Protocol, and optional for the Framework Decision—which allows States to condition the criminalization of denial conduct only to those cases in which there are international, or national, decisions that have established the existence of the international crime. There is no international judgement regarding the Armenian massacres, nor can the Ottoman military court rulings be of any use as long as denial is criminalized in States other than Turkey.

Even if there are significant differences with regard to the definition of punishable behaviours and the identification of the object of the punishable conducts, the relevant provisions and case-law share relevant elements.

---

[34]See Dadrian (1989), and Marchesi and Flores in this book.

A first matter on which the tools analysed tend to converge regards the relationship between the criminalization of denial conduct and the protection of the right to freedom of expression. From the study of the UN practice, as well as under the Framework Decision and the European Court judgement in the case *Perinçek c. Switzerland*—with the exception, therefore, of the Holocaust denial for which the Court configures a different regime—it can safely be affirmed that if national laws should include penalties for denial statements or, conversely, for "recognition" statements, (as in the case of the Turkish law related to denigration of Turkishness), without verifying the capability of these to incite to hate or violence, they would not comply with the international standards of protection of the right to freedom of expression.

Another element on which the international practice converges regards the temporal factor. With the exception of the *Perinçek c. Switzerland* case, none of the analysed instruments gives prominence to the time elapsed since the event. The criminalization of the denial behaviours thus turns out to be a useful tool for safeguarding the memory of the Armenian victims even "one hundred years later."

References

Bazyler MJ (2009) Holocaust denial laws and other legislations criminalizing the promotion of Nazism. A lecture at Yad Vashem. http://www1.yadvashem.org/yv/en/holocaust/insights/pdf/bazyler.pdf

Borgna G (2015) Il genocidio armeno (non) passa in giudicato: in margine al caso "Perinçek". Diritti umani e diritto internazionale 9:697–704

Cannie H, Voorhoof D (2011) The abuse clause and freedom of expression in the European Human Rights Convention: an added value for democracy and human rights protection? Neth Q Hum Rights 29:54–83

Dadrian VN (1989) Genocide as a problem of National and International Law: The World War I Armenian case and its contemporary legal ramifications. Yale J Int Law 14:221–334

Daniele L (2016) Disputing the indisputable: genocide denial and freedom of expression in Perinçek v Switzerland. Nottm Law J 25:141–151

Della Morte G (2016) Bilanciamento tra libertà di espressione e tutela della dignità del popolo armeno nella sentenza *Perinçek c. Svizzera* della Corte europea dei diritti dell'uomo. Rivista di diritto internazionale 99:183–190

Fronza E (2006) The punishment of negationism: the difficult dialogue between law and memory. Vt Law Rev 30:609–626

Frowein JA (2000) Incitement against democracy as a limitation of freedom of speech. In: Kretzmer D, Hazan FK, Stiftung FE (eds) Freedom of speech and incitement against democracy. Martinus Nijhoff Publishers, The Hague, pp 33–40

Garibian S (2016) On the breaking of consensus: the Perinçek case, the Armenian genocide and International Criminal Law. In: Willems J, Nelen H, Moerland R (eds) Denialism and Human Rights. Intersentia, Cambridge, pp 212–221

Garman JJ (2007) The European Union combats racism and xenophobia by forbidding expression: an analysis of the framework decision. Univ Toledo Law Rev 39:843–860

Gonzalez G (2016) Quel gènocide arménien? Revue trimestrielle des droits de l'homme 108:1019–1036

Hennebel L, Hochmann T (eds) (2011) Genocide denials and the law. Oxford University Press, Oxford

Kahn RA (2004) Holocaust denial and the law. A comparative study. Palgrave Macmillan, New York

Keane D (2007) Attacking hate speech under Article 17 of the European Convention on Human Rights. Neth Q Hum Rights 25:641–663

Lipstadt DE (1993) Denying the holocaust: the growing assault on truth and memory. Penguin Books, New York

Lobba P (2014) Punishing denialism beyond holocaust denial: EU framework decision 2008/913/ JHA and others expansive trends. New J Eur Crim Law 5:58–78

Lobba P (2015) Holocaust denial before the European Court of Human Rights: evolution of an exceptional regime. Eur J Int Law 26:237–253

Pech L (2009) The law of holocaust denial in Europe: towards a (qualified) EU-wide criminal prohibition. Jean Monnet working paper. https://doi.org/10.2139/ssrn.1536078

Renauld B (2010) La decision-cadre 2008/913/JAI du Conseil de l'Union européenne. Revue trimestrielle des droits de l'homme 81:117–140

Tate J (2008) Turkey's Article 301: a legitimate tool for maintaining order or a threat to freedom of expression? Georgia J Int Comp Law 37:181–217

Tulkens F (2012) When to say is to do: freedom of expression and hate speech in the case-law of the European Court of Human Rights. In: Casadevall J, Myjer E, O'Boyle M, Austin A (eds) Freedom of expression. Essays in honour of Nicolas Bratza. Wolf Legal Publishers, Oisterwijk, pp 279–295

Van Drooghenbroeck S (2001) L'article 17 de la Convention européenne des droits de l'homme est-il indispensable? Revue trimestrielle des droits de l'homme 46:541–546

Weber A (2009) Manuel sur le discours de haine. Martinus Nijhoff Publishers, Leiden-Boston

Criminalizing the Denial of 1915–1916 Armenian Massacres and the European Court of Human Rights: *Perinçek* v *Switzerland*

Carmelo Domenico Leotta

Contents

1 The Exercise of the Freedom of Expression Under Article 10 of the European Convention on Human Rights: The Rights to Hold Opinions, to Impart and Receive Information and Ideas 252
2 The Legitimate Interference with the Right to Freedom of Expression Under Article 10(2) of the Convention 254
3 The Application of the "Abuse Clause" Provided by Article 17 of the Convention in Case of Denial of the Holocaust 257
4 The Justification of a Genocide as an Aim Pursued by the Author of a Negationist Statement—A Comparison Between the Spanish Constitutional Court and the ECtHR's Approach: The *Varela Geis* and *Perinçek* Cases 260
5 The *Perinçek* Case Solution: Freedom of Expression *v* Right to Respect for Private Life 263
6 Conclusions 268
References 270

Abstract In *Perinçek v Switzerland*, the Grand Chamber of the European Court of Human Rights strikes a delicate balance between the right to respect for private and family life (Article 8 ECHR) and the freedom of expression (Article 10 ECHR), and refers to the requirements of lawful limitations (interferences) in relation to the denial of the *Metz Yeghern*—perpetrated against the Armenians in 1915–1916—as a genocide. The case originated from an application against Switzerland lodged with the Court by Doğu Perinçek, a chairman of the Turkish Workers' Party, who during three public events in 2005 in Switzerland stated that the mass deportation and massacres suffered by the Armenians in the Ottoman Empire did not amount to genocide and were "an international lie." Perinçek was found guilty by the Swiss

C. D. Leotta (✉)
European University of Rome, Rome, Italy
e-mail: carmelo.leotta@unier.it

F. Lattanzi and E. Pistoia (eds.), *The Armenian Massacres of 1915–1916 a Hundred Years Later*, Studies in the History of Law and Justice 15,
https://doi.org/10.1007/978-3-319-78169-3_11

judges of the offence under Article 261bis(4), of the Criminal Swiss Code, which punishes "any person who [...] denies, grossly trivializes or seeks to justify a genocide or other crimes against humanity." He thus decided to apply to the ECtHR in 2008 alleging that his criminal conviction was in breach of his freedom of expression and his right not be punished without law. On 12 November 2013 the Second Section of the Court held that there had been a breach of Article 10 ECHR, and on 17 March 2014 the Swiss government requested to refer the case to the Grand Chamber. Finally, on 15 October 2015, the latter confirmed that the conviction of the applicant represented a limitation to his freedom of expression not necessary in a democratic society, in accordance with Article 10(2) ECHR.

1 The Exercise of the Freedom of Expression Under Article 10 of the European Convention on Human Rights: The Rights to Hold Opinions, to Impart and Receive Information and Ideas

The measures adopted by States to penalize those who deny a genocide or another crime against humanity, even if an obligation to prosecute such an expression is established in several international instruments,[1] constitute a limitation to the right to freedom of expression. In the regional human rights system based on the European Convention on Human Rights (ECHR), freedom of expression is protected by Article 10 and plays a central role, not only as a fundamental right in itself, but also as a component of other rights. These would include freedom of thought, conscience and religion (Article 9) and freedom of assembly and association (Article 11). Freedom of expression is, more generally, a requirement of a public organization respecting human dignity.[2] The Strasbourg Court itself in its seminal judgment—the *Handyside* case (1976)—affirmed that freedom of expression constitutes one of the essential foundations of a democratic society, "one of the basic conditions for its progress and for the development of every man."[3]

Article 10 reads as follows:

> 1. Everyone has the right to freedom of expression. This right shall include freedom to hold opinions and to receive and impart information and ideas without interference by public authority and regardless of frontiers. This Article shall not prevent States from requiring the licensing of broadcasting, television or cinema enterprises.

---

[1]Spatti, in this book.

[2]Macovei (2004), p. 1–15; Schabas (2015), p. 444–481.

[3]*Handyside v United Kingdom*, App. no. 5493/72 (ECtHR [GC], 7 December 1976), para. 49. More recently see *Lindon, Otchakovsky-Laurens and July v France*, Apps. nos. 21279/02 and 36448/02 (ECtHR [GC], 22 October 2007), para. 45; *Guja v Moldova*, App. no. 14277/04 (ECtHR [GC], 12 February 2008), para. 69.

2. The exercise of these freedoms, since it carries with it duties and responsibilities, may be subject to such formalities, conditions, restrictions or penalties as are prescribed by law and are necessary in a democratic society, in the interests of national security, territorial integrity or public safety, for the prevention of disorder or crime, for the protection of health or morals, for the protection of the reputation or rights of others, for preventing the disclosure of information received in confidence, or for maintaining the authority and impartiality of the judiciary.

Freedom of expression includes some specific rights guaranteed by Article 10 (1), namely:

(a) the right to hold opinions,
(b) the right to impart information and ideas, and
(c) the right to receive information and ideas.

The first one (the right to hold opinions) is the prior condition to the other freedoms protected by Article 10 and it cannot be restricted in any case. It implies that States cannot indoctrinate citizens and aliens and that they are not allowed to discriminate against individuals because of their opinions and ideas. The prohibition of discrimination on any grounds (*inter alia* for opinions expressed) is specifically provided by Article 14, which contains an autonomous provision against direct and indirect discrimination in enjoying the rights guaranteed by the Convention. Furthermore, a corollary to the right to hold opinions, under Article 10 (1), is that no one should be forced to express someone else own opinions.

The second right provided by Article 10(1) regards the faculty to impart information and ideas and it is directly connected to political life and to a State's democratic structure. Free political decisions, indeed, are not allowed without the possibility to criticize and disapprove of the government. For these reasons, in the *Lingens* case (1986) the Court stated, for example, that it is incumbent on the press "to impart information and ideas on political issues just as on those in other areas of public interest."[4] The right to impart information and ideas under Article 10(1) concerns not only political aspects of public life, but also economic matters and artistic creation and performance.

Regarding the right to impart information and ideas, the Court appropriately distinguishes information, whose objects are facts, and ideas, whose objects are value judgments: in the above-mentioned *Lingens* case, it clarified that the existence of facts can be demonstrated, but the truth of value judgments could not be proved.[5] For this reason, the manifestation of ideas deserves stronger protection than information. Nevertheless, also a value judgment requires a factual basis:

[4] *Lingens v Austria*, App. no. 9815/82 (ECtHR, Court Plenary, 8 July 1986), para. 41; *Sener v Turkey*, App. no. 26680/95 (ECtHR, Section III, 18 July 2000), para. 41; *Thoma v Luxembourg*, App. no. 38432/97 (ECtHR, Section II, 29 March 2001), paras. 58, 62; *Dichand and Others v Austria*, App. no. 29271/95 (ECtHR, Former Section III, 26 February 2002), para. 39.

[5] *Lingens v Austria*, App. no. 9815/82 (ECtHR, Court Plenary, 8 July 1986), para. 46; *Dichand and Others v Austria*, App. no. 29271/95 (ECtHR, Former Section III, 26 February 2002), para. 42.

> [E]ven where a statement amounts to a value judgment, the proportionality of an interference may depend on whether there exists a sufficient factual basis for the impugned statement, since even a value judgment without any factual basis to support it may be excessive.[6]

The distinction between information about facts, ideas and value judgments regards a relevant aspect in the analysis of the lawful limits to the denial of a historical event, because rejecting the legal qualification of a historical event does not *de plano* imply the denial of the event itself.

The third right provided by Article 10(1) is the freedom to receive information and ideas, which includes the right to gather and seek information in every lawful way. Although not explicitly mentioned, Article 10(1) is applicable to freedom of press[7]—which is a "political watchdog"[8]—and the freedom of radio and television broadcasting.[9]

As stated in the *Handyside* case, the right to freedom of expression,

> subject to paragraph 2 of Article 10 (art. 10-2), is applicable not only to 'information' or 'ideas' that are favourably received or regarded as inoffensive or as a matter of indifference, but also to those that offend, shock or disturb the State or any sector of the population. Such are the demands of that pluralism, tolerance and broad mindedness without which there is no "democratic society."[10]

2 The Legitimate Interference with the Right to Freedom of Expression Under Article 10(2) of the Convention

The right to freedom of expression, as required by Article 10(2), "carries with it duties and responsibilities" and it can be thus subjected to some "formalities, conditions and penalties" (generally called "interferences"). For this reason, domestic authorities in any Contracting State may impose measures that limit the exercise of the freedom of expression if three cumulative conditions exist: (a) the interference is prescribed by law; (b) it protects a legitimate aim; and (c) it is necessary in a democratic society.

In particular, the legal basis of the interference requires not only that the measure imposed by a State is provided by domestic law, but also that the rule contained in

[6] *Jerusalem v Austria*, App. no. 26958/95 (ECtHR, Section III, 27 February 2001), para. 43.

[7] *Thoma v Luxembourg*, App. no. 38432/97 (ECtHR, Section II, 29 March 2001), paras. 43–46.

[8] *Thorgeir Thorgeirson v Iceland*, App. no. 13778/88 (ECtHR, Chamber, 25 June 1992), para. 63.

[9] *Informationsverein Lentia v Austria*, Apps. nos. 13914/88; 15041/89; 15717/89; 15779/89 and 17207/90 (ECtHR, Chamber, 24 November 1993), paras. 30–44.

[10] *Handyside v United Kingdom*, App. no. 5493/72 (ECtHR [GC], 7 December 1976), para. 49.

the law in question is accessible and that its effects are foreseeable.[11] Regarding the requirement of a legitimate aim, it is notable that Article 10 on freedom of expression establishes a longer list than Article 8 (right to respect for private and family life), Article 9 (freedom of thought, conscience and religion) and Article 11 (freedom of assembly and association). Finally, the condition according to which the interference must be "necessary in a democratic society" implies that the limitations to the freedom of expression should respond to "a pressing social need"[12] and should not be greater than necessary.[13] In order to guarantee an effective exercise of the right to freedom of expression, and in particular to verify the existence of the above-mentioned requirement ("necessary in a democratic society"), the Strasbourg Court's task "is not to take the place of the competent national authorities but to review the decisions they made under Article 10."[14]

For these reasons, the Court should examine the limitation imposed by the State "in the light of the case as a whole and determine whether it was proportionate to the legitimate aim pursued and whether the reasons adduced by the national authorities to justify it were relevant and sufficient."[15]

As the Grand Chamber affirms in the *Perinçek* case, "there is a little scope under Article 10(2) of the Convention for restrictions on political expression or on debate on questions of public interest."[16]

In this sense—as already stated in the *Wingrove* (1996),[17] *Ceylan* (1999)[18] and *Animal Defenders International* (2013)[19] cases—interferences with the right to freedom of expression are tolerable as a truly exceptional remedy, if the discourse deals with questions of public interest. In particular, the interferences are legitimate if the statements could be considered as "hate speech"—for example, if "made

---

[11]*VgT Verein gegen Tierfabriken v Switzerland*, App. no. 24699/94 (ECtHR, Section II, 28 June 2001), para. 52; *Rotaru v Romania*, App. no. 28341/95 (ECtHR [GC], 4 May 2000), para. 52; *Amann v Switzerland*, App. no. 27798/95 (ECtHR [GC], 16 February 2000), para. 65.

[12]*Perinçek v Switzerland*, App. no. 27510/08 (ECtHR [GC], 15 October 2015), para. 196, ii); *Lehideux and Isorni v France*, App. no. 24662/94 (ECtHR [GC], 23 September 1998), para. 51.

[13]In *Perinçek v Switzerland*, App. no. 27510/08 (ECtHR [GC], 15 October 2015), para. 196, i), the Grand Chamber affirms besides that 'the need for any restrictions must be established convincingly'. About the requirement that an interference be 'necessary in a democratic society' see also *Animal Defenders International v The United Kingdom*, App. no. 48876/08 (ECtHR [GC], 22 April 2013), para. 100 and *Mouvement raëlien suisse v Switzerland*, App. no. 16354/06 (ECtHR [GC], 13 July 2012), para. 48.

[14]*Perinçek v Switzerland*, App. no. 27510/08 (ECtHR [GC], 15 October 2015), para. 196, iii).

[15]Ibidem.

[16]Ibidem, para. 197. See also *Lykin v Ukraine*, App. no. 19382/08 (ECtHR, Section II, 12 January 2017), para. 26.

[17]*Wingrove v The United Kingdom*, App. no. 17419/90 (ECtHR, 25 November 1996), para. 58.

[18]*Ceylan v Turkey*, App. no. 23556/94 (ECtHR [GC], 8 July 1999), para. 34.

[19]*Animal Defenders International v The United Kingdom*, App. no. 48876/08 (ECtHR [GC], 22 April 2013), para. 102.

against a tense political or social background"[20] or if they directly or indirectly instigate acts of violence or justify violence, intolerance or hatred,[21] such as in cases of "statements attacking or casting in a negative light entire ethnic, religious or other groups."[22]

In conclusion, in evaluating whether the interference is necessary in a democratic society, the Court adopts a "highly context-specific"[23] approach, which considers "the interplay between the various factors rather than any one of them taken in isolation that determined the outcome of the case."[24]

With regard to the exercise of the right to freedom of expression in relation to historical events, the Court generally recuses itself from the concerned debate[25] (without derogating from what will be said in the following paragraphs about the denial of the Holocaust). Nevertheless, interferences can be imposed on authors and

[20] *Perinçek v Switzerland*, App. no. 27510/08 (ECtHR [GC], 15 October 2015), para. 205. See also *Balsytė-Lideikienė v Lithuania*, App. no. 72596/01 (ECtHR, Section III, 4 November 2008), para. 78; *Soulas and Others v France*, App. no. 15948/03 (ECtHR, Section V, 10 July 2008), paras. 38–39; *Le Pen v France*, App. no. 18788/09 (ECtHR, Section V, 20 April 2010), para. 1 (*En droit*).

[21] *Perinçek v Switzerland*, App. no. 27510/08 (ECtHR [GC], 15 October 2015), para. 206. See also *Gündüz v Turkey*, App. no. 35071/97 (ECtHR, Section I, 4 December 2003), paras. 48, 51; *Féret v Belgium*, App. no. 15615/07 (ECtHR, Section II, 17 July 2009), paras. 69–73, 78; *Fáber v Hungary*, App. no. 40721/08 (ECtHR, Section II, 24 July 2012), paras. 52, 56–58; *Vona v Hungary*, App. no. 35943/10 (ECtHR, Section II, 9 July 2013), paras. 64–67; *Özgür Gündem v Turkey*, App. no. 23144/93 (ECtHR, Section IV, 16 March 2000), para. 64; *Hizbut-Tahrir and Others v Germany*, App. no. 31098/08 (ECtHR, Section V, 12 June 2012), para. 73.

[22] *Perinçek v Switzerland*, App. no. 27510/08 (ECtHR [GC], 15 October 2015), para. 206. See also *Kasymakhunov and Saybatalov v Russia*, App. nos. 26261/05 and 26377/06 (ECtHR, Section I, 14 March 2013), para. 106; *Norwood v The United Kingdom*, App. no. 23131/03 (ECtHR, Section II, 16 November 2004), para. 2; *Féret v Belgium*, App. no. 15615/07 (ECtHR, Section II, 17 July 2009), para. 71; *Soulas and Others v France*, App. no. 15948/03 (ECtHR, Section V, 10 July 2008), paras. 40, 43; *Le Pen v France*, App. no. 18788/09 (ECtHR, Section V, 20 April 2010), para. 1 (*En droit*); *Hizbut-Tahrir and Others v Germany*, App. no. 31098/08 (ECtHR, Section V, 12 June 2012), para. 73.

[23] *Perinçek v Switzerland*, App. no. 27510/08 (ECtHR [GC], 15 October 2015), para. 208.

[24] Ibidem. See also *Karataş v Turkey*, App. no. 23168/94 (ECtHR [GC], 8 July 1999), paras. 51–52; *Gündüz v Turkey*, App. no. 35071/97 (ECtHR, Section I, 4 December 2003), paras. 43–44; *Féret v Belgium*, App. no. 15615/07 (ECtHR, Section II, 17 July 2009), para. 76; *Fáber v Hungary*, App. no. 40721/08 (ECtHR, Section II, 24 July 2012), paras. 44–45; *Vona v Hungary*, App. no. 35943/10 (ECtHR, Section II, 9 July 2013), paras. 64–69.

[25] *Perinçek v Switzerland*, App. no. 27510/08 (ECtHR [GC], 15 October 2015), para. 214. See also *Lehideux and Isorni v France*, App. no. 24662/94 (ECtHR [GC], 23 September 1998), para. 47. In *Chauvy and Others v France*, App. no. 64915/01 (ECtHR, Section II, 29 June 2004), para. 69, the Chamber affirms: 'The Court considers that it is an integral part of freedom of expression to seek historical truth and it is not the Court's role to arbitrate the underlying historical issues, which are part of a continuing debate between historians that shapes opinion as to the events which took place and their interpretation.' See also *Monnat v Switzerland*, App. no. 73604/01 (ECtHR, Section III, 21 September 2006), para. 57; *Fatullayev v Azerbaijan*, App. no. 40984/07 (ECtHR, Section I, 22 April 2010), para. 87; *Giniewski v France*, App. no. 64016/00 (ECtHR, Section I, 31 January 2006), para. 51.

editors on the basis of the "interplay between the nature and potential effects of such statements and the context in which they are made."[26]

In such cases, it is necessary to mainly consider: (a) the manner in which the discourse is phrased and the way in which it is construed[27]; (b) the nature of interests or rights affected[28]; (c) the social impact of the statements and, in particular, if they can instigate hatred and intolerance[29]; (d) the lapse of time since the historical events to which the statement has been pronounced.[30]

In spite of the Court's intention not to investigate the content of the debate among historians about historical events and their interpretation, it is an ascertained principle of the Strasbourg's case law that the denial or revision of events which belong to the category of clearly established historical facts—such as the Holocaust —is removed from the protection of Article 10 by Article 17.[31] In light of this premise, it is worth analyzing which limits can be imposed on statements denying the Holocaust.

3 The Application of the "Abuse Clause" Provided by Article 17 of the Convention in Case of Denial of the Holocaust

As stated above, applying the criteria of "clearly established historical facts," the European Court of Human Rights—consistent with the European Commission of Human Rights[32]—constantly dismisses applications complaining about limitations

[26]*Perinçek v Switzerland*, App. no. 27510/08 (ECtHR [GC], 15 October 2015), para. 220.

[27]Ibidem, para. 216. See also *Lehideux and Isorni v France*, App. no. 24662/94 (ECtHR [GC], 23 September 1998), para. 53; *Orban and Others v France*, App. no. 20985/05 (ECtHR, 15 January 2009), paras. 46, 49, 51; *Stankov and the United Macedonian Organization Ilinden v Bulgaria*, Apps. nos. 29221/95 and 29225/95 (ECtHR, Section I, 2 October 2001), paras. 102, 106.

[28]*Perinçek v Switzerland*, App. no. 27510/08 (ECtHR [GC], 15 October 2015), para. 217. See also *Stankov and the United Macedonian Organization Ilinden v Bulgaria, cit.*, para. 106; *Orban and Others v France*, App. no. 20985/05 (ECtHR, 15 January 2009), para. 52.

[29]*Perinçek v Switzerland*, App. no. 27510/08 (ECtHR [GC], 15 October 2015), para. 218. See also *Stankov and the United Macedonian Organization Ilinden v Bulgaria, cit.*, paras. 102–103, 110.

[30]*Perinçek v Switzerland*, App. no. 27510/08 (ECtHR [GC], 15 October 2015), para. 219. See also *Lehideux and Isorni v France* [GC], App. no. 24662/94 (ECtHR [GC], 23 September 1998), para. 55; *Orban and Others v France*, App. no. 20985/05 (ECtHR, 15 January 2009), para. 52.

[31]*Lehideux and Isorni v France* [GC], App. no. 24662/94 (ECtHR [GC], 23 September 1998), para. 47.

[32]*B.H., M.W. and G.K v Austria*, App. no. 12774/87 (12 October 1989); *Wallendy v Germany*, App. no. 211182/92 (11 January 1995); *Remer v Germany*, App. no. 25096/94 (6 September 1995); *Honsik v Austria*, App. no. 25062/94 (18 October 1995); *Nationaldemokratische Partei Deutschlands, Bezirsverband München–Oberbayern v Germany*, App. no. 25992/94 (29 November 1995); *Rebhandl v Austria*, App. no. 24398/94 (16 January 1996); *Marais v France*,

imposed by a national State against the denial of the Holocaust.[33] For instance, the "abuse clause" has recently been applied in the *M'Bala M'Bala* case (2015), even though it referred to an episode of injury perpetrated on racial, ethnic or religious grounds. (This episode, however, had a strict connection with the phenomenon of the denial of the Holocaust, because of the participation of the French negationist author Robert Faurisson).[34]

In the Strasbourg case law related to the denial of the Holocaust, the inadmissibility of the complaint is grounded on the so-called "abuse clause" provided by Article 17 of the Convention, according to which:

> Nothing in this Convention may be interpreted as implying for any State, group or person any right to engage in any activity or perform any act aimed at the destruction of any of the rights and freedoms set forth herein or at their limitation to a greater extent than is provided for in the Convention.

In the *Perinçek* case, the Grand Chamber recalled its previous decisions and some of those of the European Commission of Human Rights, according to which:

> the reason why Article 17 had been included in it [the Convention] had been that it could not be ruled out that a person or a group of persons would attempt to rely on the rights enshrined in the Convention to derive the right to conduct activities intended to destroy these rights.[35]

In any case the Grand Chamber reaffirms that:

> Article 17 is [...] only applicable on an exceptional basis and in extreme cases,[36]

because:

> its effect is to negate the exercise of the Convention right that the applicant seeks to vindicate in the proceedings before the Court.[37]

In particular, considering the importance of freedom of expression as an essential component of a democratic society, the Court continues:

App. no. 31159/96 (24 June 1996); *D.I. v Germany*, App. no. 26551/95 (26 June 1996); *Nachtmann v Austria*, App. no. 36773/97 (9 September 1998).

[33] *Schimanek v Austria*, App. no. 32307/06 (ECtHR, Section I, 1 February 2000); *Garaudy v France*, App. no. 65831/01 (ECtHR, Section IV, 24 June 2003); *Witzsch v Germany (no. 2)*, App. no. 7485/03 (ECtHR, Section IV, 13 December 2005); *Gollnisch v France*, App. no. 48135/08 (ECtHR, Section V, 7 June 2011).

[34] *M'Bala M'Bala v France*, App. no. 25239/13 (ECtHR, Section V, 20 October 2015), paras. 32–39.

[35] *Ždanoka v Latvia*, App. no. 58278/00 (ECtHR [GC], 16 March 2006), para. 99.

[36] *Perinçek v Switzerland*, App. no. 27510/08 (ECtHR [GC], 15 October 2015), para. 114; *Paksas v Lithuania*, App. no. 34932/04 (ECtHR [GC], 6 January 2011), para. 87.

[37] *Perinçek v Switzerland*, App. no. 27510/08 (ECtHR [GC], 15 October 2015), para. 114. See also *Norwood v The United Kingdom*, *cit.*, para. 2. For a comment on Article 17 see Buyse (2014), 491–503; Cannie and Voorhoof (2011), 54–83; Keane (2007), 641–663.

> in cases concerning Article 10 of the Convention, it should only be resorted to if it is immediately clear that the impugned statements sought to deflect this Article from its real purpose by employing the right to freedom of expression for ends clearly contrary to the values of the Convention.[38]

Furthermore, in the European Court case law this decisional framework is constantly adopted in cases of claims against restrictive measures of Holocaustic negationism. It is based on the strict connection between the negationist statement —which is subjected to "interferences"—and the Nazi ideology expressed, and thus incompatible with the principles of the Convention.

In this regard, the *Garaudy* case (2003) is worth mentioning, in which the Court provides a well-structured opinion based on three main steps: (i) firstly, whoever denies the Holocaust does not intend to research the historical truth, but aims at rehabilitating the Nazi ideology, accusing the victims of having distorted historical facts[39]; (ii) secondly, acts of violence and discrimination could be instigated by Holocaust negationists[40]; and, (iii) thirdly, as stated in the *Garaudy* judgment:

> [L]a négation ou la révision de faits historiques de ce type remettent en cause les valeurs qui fondent la lutte contre le racisme et l'antisémitisme et sont de nature à troubler gravement l'ordre public. Portant atteinte aux droits d'autrui, de tels actes sont incompatibles avec la démocratie et les droits de l'homme et leurs auteurs visent incontestablement des objectifs du type de ceux prohibés par l'article 17 de la Convention.[41]

Despite these premises, the new approach introduced by the *Perinçek* case is related to the application of a different decisional paradigm, instead of the so-called "abuse clause," grounded on the balancing of the provisions of Articles 8 and 10 of the Convention. In fact, in judging the complaint of the Turkish politician, coherently with the declared exceptional nature of the "abuse clause" in the European Convention of Human Rights, the Grand Chamber states that:

> since the decisive point under Article 17 – whether the applicant's statements sought to stir up hatred or violence, and whether by making them he attempted to rely on the Convention to engage in an activity or perform acts aimed at the destruction of the rights and freedoms laid down in it – is not immediately clear and overlaps with the question whether the interference with the applicant's right to freedom of expression was 'necessary in a democratic society' […], the question whether Article 17 is to be applied must be joined to the merits of the applicant's complaint under Article 10 of the Convention.[42]

[38]*Perinçek v Switzerland*, App. no. 27510/08 (ECtHR [GC], 15 October 2015), para. 114. See also *Hizbut-Tahrir and Others v Germany*, App. no. 31098/08 (ECtHR, Section V, 12 June 2012), paras. 73–74, 78; *Kasymakhunov and Saybatalov v Russia*, App. nos. 26261/05 and 26377/06 (ECtHR, Section I, 14 March 2013), paras. 106–113.

[39]*Garaudy v France*, App. no. 65831/01 (ECtHR, Section IV, 24 June 2003), para. 1 (*En droit*).

[40]Ibidem.

[41]Ibidem.

[42]*Perinçek v Switzerland*, App. no. 27510/08 (ECtHR [GC], 15 October 2015), para. 115. See also *United Communist Party of Turkey and Others v Turkey*, App. no. 19392/92 (ECtHR [GC], 30 January 1998), para. 32; *Refah Partisi (the Welfare Party) and Others v Turkey*, Apps. nos. 41340/98, 41342/98, 41343/98 and 41344/98 (ECtHR [GC], 13 February 2003), para. 96; *Féret v*

Balancing the applicant's right to freedom of expression against the Armenians' right to respect for their private life (protected respectively by Article 10 and by Article 8 of the Convention), the Court of Strasbourg judges whether, in the present case, the interference imposed by the State is allowed because it is "necessary in a democratic society." To this aim, it applies seven criteria that will be analyzed hereinafter.

4 The Justification of a Genocide as an Aim Pursued by the Author of a Negationist Statement—A Comparison Between the Spanish Constitutional Court and the ECtHR's Approach: The *Varela Geis* and *Perinçek* Cases

Before analysing the balancing method between Articles 8 and 10 of the Convention applied in the *Perinçek* case, it can be appropriate to recall the specific jurisprudential approach that focuses on the aim pursued by the statement's author to evaluate the legitimacy of a limit imposed on freedom of expression. Such an approach, also retraceable in the ECtHR case law concerning the application of Article 10 in historical debates,[43] was recently adopted in the *Varela Geis* case, decided in 2007 by the Spanish Constitutional Court (*Tribunal Constitucional de España*), as well as in the *Perinçek* case of the ECtHR Grand Chamber.

In the *Varela Geis* case, the Spanish Constitutional Court declares the illegitimacy of Article 607(2) of the Spanish Criminal Code (in the formulation in force at that time), when it pursued those who merely denied a genocide. This provision, according to the Court of Madrid, was illegitimate because it violated Article 20(1) of the Spanish Constitution, which protects the right to freedom of expression.[44]

Belgium, App. no. 15615/07 (ECtHR, Section II, 17 July 2009), para. 52; *Vona v Hungary*, App. no. 35943/10 (ECtHR, Section II, 9 July 2013), para. 38; *Varela Geis v Spain*, App. no. 61005/09 (ECtHR, Section III, 5 March 2013), para. 31; *Soulas and Others v France*, App. no. 15948/03 (ECtHR, Section V, 10 July 2008), para. 23.

[43] *Lehideux and Isorni v France*, App. no. 24662/94 (ECtHR [GC], 23 September 1998), para. 53; *Orban and Others v France*, App. no. 20985/05 (ECtHR, 15 January 2009), paras. 46, 49, 51.

[44] Tribunal Constitucional de España, Sentencia 235/2007, de 7 de noviembre de 2007, Boletín Oficial del Estado, 10 December 2007, n. 295, Suplemento del Tribunal Constitucional, p. 42–59, available on http://www.boe.es. For a comment see Ramós Vazquez (2009), p. 120–137; Bilbao Ubillos (2009), p. 299–352.

However, Article 607 was successively modified by the *Ley Orgánica* no. 1 of 30 March 2015 and in its current formulation it punishes the crime of genocide, whereas Article 510(1)(c) of the Criminal Code—which entered into force on 1 July 2015—condemns the denial of international crimes (genocide, crimes against humanity and war crimes), if the denial incites discrimination or violence.[45]

The Spanish Court affirmed that the national criminal law may not prosecute those who merely deny a genocide or another international crime if the "incriminated statement" does not contextually express a value judgment about the fact denied. Differently, if the negationist statement amounts to hate speech—because it instigates violent acts against individuals or groups—it is not protected under Article 20 of the Spanish Constitution and may be banned by domestic law.

The freedom of historical research—as the *Tribunal Constitucional* explains—enjoys a wider protection than the freedom of expression and information; in fact:

> [S]ólo de esta manera se hace posible la investigación histórica, que es siempre, por definición, polémica y discutible, por erigirse alrededor de aseveraciones y juicios de valor sobre cuya verdad objetiva es imposible alcanzar plena certidumbre, siendo así que esa incertidumbre consustancial al debate histórico representa lo que éste tiene de más valioso, respetable y digno de protección por el papel esencial que desempeña en la formación de una conciencia histórica adecuada a la dignidad de los ciudadanos de una sociedad libre y democrática.[46]

For the same reasons, the Spanish Court states that Article 607(2) of the Spanish Criminal Code (in force at that time) did not violate Article 20 of the Constitution, when it pursues those who publicize ideas and doctrines justifying a genocide:

> siempre que tal justificación opere como incitación indirecta a su comisión; esto es incriminándose (y ello es lo que ha de entenderse que realiza el art. 607.2 CP) conductas que aunque sea de forma indirecta supongan una provocación al genocidio.[47]

The criterion that allows the distinction between the mere denial and the justification of a genocide—well-settled in the *Varela Geis* case—has also been applied in the *Perinçek* case by the ECtHR Grand Chamber, which cites *apertis verbis* the

[45]Article 510(1)(c) of the Spanish Criminal Code reads as follows: '*Quienes [...] públicamente nieguen, trivialicen gravemente o enaltezcan los delitos de genocidio, de lesa humanidad o contra las personas y bienes protegidos en caso de conflicto armado, o enaltezcan a sus autores, cuando se hubieran cometido contra un grupo o una parte del mismo, o contra una persona determinada por razón de su pertenencia al mismo, por motivos racistas, antisemitas u otros referentes a la ideología, religión o creencias, la situación familiar o la pertenencia de sus miembros a una etnia, raza o nación, su origen nacional, su sexo, orientación o identidad sexual, por razones de género, enfermedad o discapacidad, cuando de este modo se promueva o favorezca un clima de violencia, hostilidad, odio o discriminación contra los mismos.*'

[46]Tribunal Constitucional de España, Sentencia n. 235/2007, II, 8.

[47]Ibidem, II, 9. And it continued as follows: '*Por ello, el legislador puede, dentro de su libertad de configuración, perseguir tales conductas, incluso haciéndolas merecedoras de reproche penal siempre que no se entienda incluida en ellas la mera adhesión ideológica a posiciones políticas de cualquier tipo, que resultaría plenamente amparada por el art. 16 CE y, en conexión, por el art. 20 CE.*'

2007 Spanish Court's decision. The Strasbourg judges, by evaluating the applicant's statements regarding the massacres of the Armenians, holds that—because of the context in which they had been pronounced—these statements could not instigate hatred, violence and discrimination against the victims, and that they were not aimed at justifying the attempts to destroy the Armenian community perpetrated in 1915–1916. In fact, they state:

> genocide justification does not consist in assertions that a particular event did not constitute a genocide, but in statements which express a value judgement about it, relativising its gravity or presenting it as right.[48]

The decisional scheme described above—focused on the purpose of the statements pronounced—marks a deviation from a previous jurisprudential pathway of the Court, adopted for instance in the *Lehideux and Isorni* case (1998)[49] and in the *Garaudy* case (2003).[50]

In the former, the Court upheld the application because the interference imposed by the national authority was not necessary in a democratic society. The campaign promoted by the applicant for rehabilitating Philippe Pétain (1856–1951) was not intended to deny or revise any historical event (such as the Holocaust) belonging to the category of "clearly established historical facts;"[51] if so, the protection provided by Article 10 of the Convention would have been excluded by the abuse clause (Article 17). The same principle is present in the more recent *Garaudy* case, where the Court, applying Article 17 of the Convention, declared:

> la requête irrecevable[52]

because:

> [...] il ne fait aucun doute que contester la réalité de faits historiques clairement établis, tels que l'Holocauste, comme le fait le requérant dans son ouvrage [Les Mythes fondateurs de la politique israélienne, Paris, 1995] ne relève en aucune manière d'un travail de recherche historique s'apparentant à une quête de la vérité.[53]

Beyond the divergent conclusions of the above-mentioned cases—the former accepted, whilst the latter was rejected by the European Court of Human Rights—they are both strongly grounded on the same legal principle, already affirmed in the *Leugnung der Judenverfolgung* case, decided by the Bundesverfassungsgericht (the German Constitutional Court) in 1994. According to this principle, the denial of an

---

[48] *Perinçek v Switzerland*, App. no. 27510/08 (ECtHR [GC], 15 October 2015), para. 240.

[49] *Lehideux and Isorni v France*, App. no. 24662/94 (ECtHR [GC], 23 September 1998).

[50] *Garaudy v France*, App. no. 65831/01 (ECtHR, Section IV, 24 June 2003).

[51] *Lehideux and Isorni v France*, App. no. 24662/94 (ECtHR [GC], 23 September 1998), para. 47.

[52] *Garaudy v France*, App. no. 65831/01 (ECtHR, Section IV, 24 June 2003), para. 4 (*En droit*).

[53] Ibidem, para. 1 (*En droit*). And it continues as follows: '*L'objectif et l'aboutissement d'une telle démarche sont totalement différents, car il s'agit en fait de réhabiliter le régime national-socialiste, et, par voie de conséquence, d'accuser de falsification de l'histoire les victimes elles-mêmes*'.

ascertained historical event is incompatible with the correct enjoyment of the freedom of expression and cannot thus be protected under the European Convention.

In *Perinçek*, the European Court changes its decisional paradigm, at least in part: even if it underlines the continuity with its previous leading cases on the denial of the Holocaust, it states that:

> the justification for making its [the Holocaust's] denial a criminal offence lies not so much in that it is a clearly established historical fact but in that, in view of the historical context in the States concerned – the cases examined by the former Commission and the Court have thus far concerned Austria, Belgium, Germany and France […] –, its denial, even if dressed up as impartial historical research, must invariably be seen as connoting an antidemocratic ideology and anti-Semitism.[54]

According to this affirmation—which clearly outlines a deviation from the previous judgments—the punishment of the Holocaustic negationism could not be merely justified by the denial of ascertained historical facts, differently from the positions expressed in *Lehideux and Isorni v France* and in *Garaudy v France* cases. In fact, although the denial could be the result of research conducted in an empirical and scientific way, it contains anti-democratic and anti-Semitic features. The latter is the essential reason why this form of negationism could not be tolerated.

Considering the effective protection of freedom of expression, such a solution presents various complicated aspects. Indeed, whereas the criterion adopted in the previous leading cases is strictly connected to an objective element (namely, whoever denies ascertained historical facts cannot enjoy protection under Article 10 of the European Convention), in the *Perinçek* decision the Grand Chamber no longer focuses on the statement's mere content, but on the value judgment that it represents. This is the real criterion to be applied for considering the lawfulness of the interferences with the freedom of expression, even if the denial is dressed up as:

> impartial historical research.[55]

5 The *Perinçek* Case Solution: Freedom of Expression *v* Right to Respect for Private Life

In the *Perinçek* case, the Grand Chamber held that the applicant's conviction, delivered by Swiss judges, respects the requirements of "lawfulness of interference" and "legitimate aim" established by Article 10(2) of the Convention. Regarding the

[54]*Perinçek v Switzerland*, App. no. 27510/08 (ECtHR [GC], 15 October 2015), para. 243: 'Holocaust denial is thus doubly dangerous, especially in States which have experienced the Nazi horrors, and which may be regarded as having a special moral responsibility to distance themselves from the mass atrocities that they have perpetrated or abetted by, among other things, outlawing their denial'.

[55]Ibidem.

former, the Court holds that the limitation imposed on the applicant's right to freedom of expression has its legal basis directly in Article 261 *bis*(4) of the Criminal Code of Switzerland: the interference appears sufficiently foreseeable and it could be thus considered "prescribed by law," as required by Article 10(2). Even the requirement of the "legitimate aim" is satisfied, because the criminal penalty was intended to protect "the rights of others," namely the honour and the memory of the Armenians, victim of the massacres.[56] Interpreting the concept of "rights of others" within the meaning of Article 10(2) of the Convention, the Court explains:

> these [the rights of others] were the rights of Armenians to respect for their and their ancestors' dignity, including their right to respect for their identity constructed around the understanding that their community has suffered genocide.[57]

The evaluation of the third requirement—that the applicant's conviction is necessary in a democratic society—is more complex and, in carrying it out, the Grand Chamber strikes a balance between two rights deserving equal respect under the Convention. On the one hand lies the applicant's freedom of expression, protected by Article 10; on the other there is the right to respect for the Armenian group's private life, provided by Article 8, which safeguards their dignity, prohibiting offences to the group's sense of identity and to its members' feelings of self-worth and self-confidence.[58]

The judgment is based on balancing the following seven criteria:

(a) *The nature of the applicant's statements.*[59] This criterion makes it possible to distinguish between statements on matters of public interest and others lacking such a qualification, and to affirm that the former are

> in principle entitled to strong protection.

Even if in these circumstances the national authority's margin of appreciation is limited, statements on public matters can still be subjected to interference if they promote or justify violence, hatred or intolerance. If that occurs, indeed, the protection entitled by Article 10 is excluded. In the present case, the Court finds that the applicant's statements, on the one hand "had been of a historical, legal and political nature,"[60] and, on the other hand,

---

[56]Ibidem, paras. 137–140; 145–157.

[57]Ibidem, paras. 227, 252.

[58]An attack on the reputation of an ancestor can affect a person's right protected by Article 8. See *Perinçek v Switzerland*, App. no. 27510/08 (ECtHR [GC], 15 October 2015), para. 200–203 and *Aksu v Turkey*, Apps. nos. 4149/04 and 41029/04 (ECtHR [GC], 15 March 2012), paras. 58–61, 81; *Putistin v Ukraine*, App. no. 16882/03 (ECtHR, Section V, 21 November 2013), paras. 36–41; *Jelševar and Others v Slovenia*, App. no. 47318/07 (ECtHR, Section V, 11 March 2014), paras. 29–40.

[59]*Perinçek v Switzerland*, App. no. 27510/08 (ECtHR [GC], 15 October 2015), paras. 229–240.

[60]Ibidem, para. 231.

> read as a whole and taken in their immediate and wider context, cannot be seen as a call for hatred, violence or intolerance toward Armenians.[61]

In particular, the words pronounced by Perinçek cannot be considered as justifying genocide or other crimes against humanity. The Court concludes on this question:

> It follows that the applicant's statements, which concern a matter of public interest, were entitled to heightened protection under Article 10 of the Convention, and that the Swiss authorities only had a limited margin of appreciation to interfere with them.[62]

(b) *The context of interference*: "the geographical and historical factors" and "the time factor."[63] In judging if a pressing social need for interference really exists (and, thus, if the interference was necessary in a democratic society), the Court usually considers the context in which the statement has been pronounced and the interference has been imposed. In the *Perinçek* case, according to the Grand Chamber, there is not an evident and direct link between the place where the applicant pronounced his discourse (Switzerland) and the Armenian massacre, which occurred on the Ottoman Empire's territory. The Court is aware that "no message may be regarded as purely local;"[64] for this reason, it investigates whether the measure adopted by the Swiss authorities could be useful and proportionate to protect the Armenians' rights abroad, and in particular in Turkey. The judges of Strasbourg hold that:

> the broader concept of proportionality inherent in the phrase 'necessary in a democratic society' requires a rational connection between the measures taken by the authorities and the aim that they sought to realise through these measures, in the sense that the measures were reasonably capable of producing the desired result.[65]

Applying the described criterion, it appears that the applicant's conviction pronounced by the Swiss courts is not an incisive and proportionate measure for the Armenian community living in Turkey to feel safer. In the same way, it cannot be said that the hostilities existing in Turkey towards the descendents of the *Metz Yeghern*'s victims could be considered as being the consequences of the criminalised discourses. Finally, also "the lapse of time" between them and the massacres was very long:

> at the time when he [Perinçek] made the statements there were surely very few, if any, survivors of these events.[66]

---

[61]Ibidem, para. 239.

[62]Ibidem, para. 241.

[63]Ibidem, paras. 242–250.

[64]Ibidem, para. 246.

[65]Ibidem, para. 246.

[66]Ibidem, para. 250.

(c) *The extent to which the applicant's statements affected the rights of the members of the Armenian community.*[67] The statement that could be limited should represent a concrete offense for the community who suffered the events denied. The Court—being aware of the relevance given by the Armenian community to the recognition of the genocide—follows the interpretation according to which:

> statements that contest, even in virulent terms, the significance of historical events that carry a special sensitivity for a country and touch on its national identity cannot in themselves be regarded as seriously affecting their addresses. It has come to the same conclusion with respect to statements contesting the very identity of a national group.[68]

In this specific case, the Grand Chamber holds that there are two main reasons why Perinçek's statements could not be intended as having a significant upsetting meaning that could lead to a criminal offense. Firstly, the Turkish politician's words were not directed towards the Armenians, but towards the "imperialist powers" responsible for having used the Armenian community as a tool of propaganda against the Ottoman Empire and for having provoked the violence between Turks and Armenians. Secondly, the applicant's remarks did not lead to the conclusion that the Armenians deserved the atrocities that occurred in 1915–1916.

(d) *The existence of consensus among the High Contracting Parties.*[69] In a comparative perspective, the concept of "consensus" refers to the existence of common legal instruments criminalising negationism in European legal systems. The Court does not think the legal comparison could play a "weighty part" in the present case; nevertheless, it notes that Switzerland—criminalising the denial of any genocide without requiring that the denial itself incites hatred or violence—"stands at one end of the comparative spectrum."[70]
(e) *International law obligations.*[71] The fifth criterion, already retraceable in the Court's jurisprudence,[72] is aimed at verifying whether the interference that limits an individual's right protected by the Convention could be justified by the existence of an international law obligation for the State to pursue some facts or behaviours. It cannot be said that such an obligation derives either from customary international law or from conventional international law, even when specifically considering the International Convention on the Elimination of All Forms of Racial Discrimination (1965) and the International Covenant on Civil and Political Rights (1966). Therefore, the Grand Chamber arrives at the conclusion that:

[67]Ibidem, paras. 251–255.
[68]Ibidem, para. 253.
[69]Ibidem, paras. 255–257.
[70]Ibidem, para. 257.
[71]Ibidem, paras. 258–268.
[72]*Nada v Switzerland*, App. no. 10593/08 (ECtHR [GC], 12 September 2012).

> it cannot be said that the interference with the applicant's right to freedom of expression was required under, and could hence be justified by, Switzerland's international laws obligations.[73]

(f) *The method employed by the Swiss courts to justify the applicant's conviction.*[74] The sixth criterion does not require the European judges to evaluate the method applied by Swiss courts to reach the conclusion that the Armenians' massacres could be intended as a genocide as provided by the Swiss Criminal law (because it is a matter of interpretation of domestic law), but the effects that the decisions had on the applicant's right to freedom of expression. On this point the Grand Chamber observes that:

> it remained unclear whether the applicant was penalised for disagreeing with the legal qualification ascribed to the events of 1915 and following years or with the prevailing views in Swiss society on this point.[75]

In the latter hypothesis, a decision that condemns the applicant would conflict with the possibility, in a democratic society, to express diverging opinions from those stated by domestic authorities or any other sector of the population.

(g) *Severity of the interference.*[76] Applying the last balancing criterion, the Court analyses the concrete consequences of the interference and, as far as the present case is concerned, observes that a criminal conviction, such as that of the applicant,

> is one of the most serious forms of interference with the right to freedom of expression.[77]

Applying the seven criteria mentioned above, the Grand Chamber finally holds that Perinçek's conviction is in breach of Article 10 of the Convention, concluding that the Swiss authority has not explained why the limitation to the freedom of expression was necessary for a democratic society "in the specific circumstances."[78]

> Indeed an interference with the right to freedom of expression that takes the form of a criminal conviction inevitably requires detailed judicial assessment of the specific conduct sought to be punished.[79]

[73] *Perinçek v Switzerland*, App. no. 27510/08 (ECtHR [GC], 15 October 2015), para. 268.
[74] Ibidem, paras. 269–271.
[75] Ibidem, para. 271.
[76] Ibidem, paras. 272–273.
[77] Ibidem, para. 273.
[78] Ibidem, para. 275.
[79] Ibidem.

For these reasons, the Court concludes affirming that:

> it was not necessary, in a democratic society, to subject the applicant to a criminal penalty in order to protect the rights of the Armenian community at stake in the present case.[80]

6 Conclusions

In *Perinçek v Switzerland*, the Grand Chamber of the European Court of Human Rights—balancing the rights of the Armenians' community to respect for private life, protected by Article 8 of the Convention, and the freedom of expression of the applicant, protected by Article 10—confirms the judgment of the Second Section and arrives at the conclusion that Doğu Perinçek's conviction—pronounced by the Swiss courts—violated Article 10(2) because the criminal penalty represents an interference that is not necessary in a democratic society.

The judgment, in certain respects, deserves appreciation since it truly gives value to the freedom of expression provided by Article 10, not only as an individual right, but also—and perhaps especially—as a requirement of a public organization respecting human dignity and democratic order. In fact, the respect for freedom of expression, according to the European judges, is more urgent when, as in the present case, the statement concerns a political or historical matter or, more in general, a matter of public interest.

Nevertheless, the *Perinçek* case opens the possibility to some radical critiques, in particular regarding the balancing method it adopted. In fact, although Article 8 seeks to guarantee, as affirmed in the judgment, respect for a group's identity, historical memory and self-confidence, the Court's judgment does not lead to consequences that are coherent with this premise. In conclusion, it holds that the breach of Article 10(2) has occurred, not because the applicant's statements did not offend the Armenians' dignity, but because they were not aimed at promoting violence, hatred and discrimination.

By reaching such a conclusion, the Court has struck a balance not so much between the above-mentioned rights provided by Articles 8 and 10, but rather, more between freedom of expression and security of society and peaceful coexistence in the social context where the applicant pronounced his discourses. Certainly, the prevention of diffusing discrimination, hatred and violence is worth serious protection, but this interest is different from that of the group's dignity, which includes its members' feelings of self-worth and the feelings of others regarding the group's value. Upon closer inspection, indeed, anyone who denies that a genocide really took place offends the victim group's dignity and identity: even if the statement does not incite hate and violence, the denial itself, refuting a historical event, is generally an attempt to destroy—after the physical destruction of the group, in

[80] Ibidem, para. 280.

which the genocide consists—the identifying characters of the community grounded on the memory of the unforgettable crime suffered by the community.

From this point of view, and in light of the analysis conducted above, the judges' decision deserves a severe critique, because the Grand Chamber does not seriously investigate the issue of whether Perinçek's discourse had offended the dignity of the *Metz Yeghern* victims' descendants. In addition, the Court appears to be superficial when it excludes that Perinçek's discourse could attempt to justify the Armenian genocide[81] and that it was not directed towards the Armenians themselves, but towards the imperialist States,[82] even if the applicant had stated:

> the allegations of the Armenian genocide are an international lie. Can an international lie exist? Yes, once Hitler was the master of such lies; now it's the imperialists of the USA and the EU! […]. The Great Powers, which wanted to divide the Ottoman Empire, provoked a section of the Armenians, with whom we had lived in peace for centuries, and incited them to violence. The Turks and Kurds defended their homeland from these attacks. […]. The lie of the Armenian genocide was first invented in 1915 by the imperialists of England, France and Tsarist Russia, who wanted to divide the Ottoman Empire during the First World War. As Chamberlain later admitted, this was war propaganda. […]. The lies about the Armenian genocide and the pressure linked to the Aegean and Cyprus are interdependent and designed to divide us and take us hostage. […]. Don't believe the Hitler-style lies such as that of the Armenian genocide.[83]

And further:

> even Lenin, Stalin and other leaders of the Soviet revolution wrote about the Armenian question. They said in their reports that no genocide of the Armenian people had been carried out by the Turkish authorities. This statement was not intended as propaganda at the time. In secret reports the Soviet leaders said – this is very important – and the Soviet archives confirm that at that time there were occurrences of ethnic conflict, slaughter and massacres between Armenians and Muslims. But Turkey was on the side of those defending their homeland and the Armenians were on the side of the imperialist powers and their instruments … and we call on Bern, the Swiss National Council and all parties of Switzerland: Please take an interest in the truth and leave these prejudices behind. That is my observation, and I have read every article about the Armenian question and these are merely prejudices. Please leave these prejudices behind and join (??), what he said about these prejudices, and this is the truth, there was no genocide of the Armenians in 1915. It was a battle between peoples and we suffered many casualties … the Russian officers at the time were very disappointed because the Armenian troops carried out massacres of the Turks and Muslims. These truths were told by a Russian commander […].[84]

A critical remark also arises from the consideration of the "time factor". In fact, if, on the one hand it could be affirmed that the lapse of time between the applicant's statements and the Armenian genocide was considerably long and that nowadays there are only a few survivors of the massacres, on the other hand it is

[81]Ibidem, para. 240.

[82]Ibidem, para. 252.

[83]Ibidem, para. 13.

[84]Ibidem, para. 16

true that negationism does not essentially offend the victims of a genocide, but the living people belonging to the group of those targeted by its perpetrators.

In conclusion, if the Grand Chamber had really balanced the freedom of expression with the Armenian group's right of identity and dignity and not merely with the risk of diffusion of violence and hatred, the affirmation contained in the judgment—according to which the Holocaust denial "must invariably be seen as connoting an antidemocratic ideology and anti-Semitism"[85]—it would appear to be gravely discriminatory because it would imply that, in a democratic society, some groups are more valuable than others.

References

Belavusau U (2013) Freedom of speech. Importing European and US Constitutional models in transitional democracies. Routledge, London

Belavusau U, Gliszczyńska-Grabias A (2017), Law and Memory: Towards Legal Governance of History, Cambridge University Press, Cambridge

Bilbao Ubillos JM (2009) La negación de un genocidio no es una conducta punible (comentario de la STC). Revista Española de Derecho Constitucional 85:299–352

Borgna G (2015) Il genocidio armeno (non) passa in giudicato: in margine al caso *Perinçek*. Diritti umani e diritto internazionale 9(3):697–704

Buyse A (2014) Dangerous expressions: the ECHR, violence and free speech. Int Comp Law Q 63:491–503

Cannie H, Voorhoof D (2011) The abuse clause and freedom of expression in the European Convention of Human Rights. Neth Q Hum Rights 29(1):54–83

Cascione CM (2016) Genocide denial and freedom of expression in the *Perinçek* Case: A European overruling or a new approach to negationism. Questions of International Law, Zoom in 28:5–18

Della Morte G (2016) Bilanciamento tra libertà di espressione e tutela della dignità umana nella sentenza *Perinçek*. Rivista di diritto internazionale 1:183–190

Directorate General of Human Rights (ed) (2001) Case law concerning Article 10 of the European Convention on Human Rights. Council of Europe Publishing, Strasbourg

Flauss J-F (2009) The European Court of Human Rights and the freedom of expression. Indiana Law J 84(3):809–849

Fronza E (2012) Il negazionismo come reato. Giuffrè, Milano

Fronza E (2018) Memory and Punishment. Historical Denialism, Free Speech and the Limits of Criminal Law, T.M.C. Asser Press, The Hague

Greer S (2006) The European Convention of Human Rights. Achievements, problems and prospects. Cambridge University Press, Cambridge-New York

Harris D, O'Boyle M, Carla W (2014) Law of the European Convention on Human Rights, 3rd edn. Oxford University Press, Oxford-New York

Hennebel L, Hochmann T (2011) Genocide denials and the law. Oxford University Press, Oxford-New York

Herz M, Molnar P (eds) (2012) The content and the context of hate speech. Cambridge University Press, Cambridge-New York

Hochmann T (2013) Le négationnisme face aux limites de la liberté d'expression. Pedone, Paris

[85]Ibidem, para. 253.

Kahn RA (2004) Holocaust denial and the law. A comparative study. Palgrave MacMillan, New York

Keane D (2007) Attacking Hate Speech under Article 17 of the European Convention on Human Rights. Neth Q Hum Rights 25:641–663

Kiska R (2012) Hate speech: a comparison between the European Court of Human Rights and the United States Supreme Court Jurisprudence. Regent Univ Law Rev 27:107–151

Leotta CD (2016) Profili penali del negazionismo. Riflessioni alla luce della sentenza della Corte EDU sul genocidio armeno. Wolter Kluwer-CEDAM, Padova

Leotta CD (2016b) Brief remarks on the balancing method 'truly' adopted by the ECtHR Grand Chamber in *Perinçek v Switzerland*. Questions Int Law Zoom 28:29–32

Lobba P (2017) Testing the "Uniqueness": Denial of the Holocaust vs Denial of Other Crimes before the European Court of Human Rights. In Belavusau U, Gliszczyńska-Grabias A (eds.), Law and Memory: Towards Legal Governance of History: 109–128, Cambridge University Press, Cambridge

Macaya A (2016) Focus sur Perinçek c Suisse. La question de la limitation à la liberté d'expression nécessaire dans une société démocratique. Questions Int Law Zoom 28:19–28

Macovei M (2004) Freedom of expression. A guide to the implementation of Article 10 of the European Convention of Human Rights, 2nd edn. Council of Europe Publishing, Strasbourg

Merrils JG, Robertson AH (2001) Human Rights in Europe. A study of the European Convention on Human Rights. Manchester University Press, Manchester and New York

Mowbray A (2012) Cases and materials on the European Convention on Human Rights, 3rd edn. Oxford University Press, Oxford-New York

Rainey B, Wicks E, Ovey C (2014) Jacobs, White & Ovey: The European Convention on Human Rights, 6th edn. Oxford University Press, Oxford-New York

Ramos Vázquez JA (2009) La declaración de inconstitucionalidad del delito de 'negacionismo' (art. 607.2 del Código Penal). Revista penal 23:120–137

Schabas WA (2015) The European Convention on Human Rights. Oxford University Press, A Commentary. Oxford-New York

Weber A (2009) Manual on hate speech. Council of Europe Publishing, Strasbourg

Part IV
The Armenian Massacres and the European Union: Active Player or *Festin de Pierre*?

Is the Denial of the "Armenian Genocide" an Obstacle to Turkey's Accession to the EU?

Pierluigi Simone

Contents

1 Introduction 276
2 Turkey–EU: An Unusual Accession Process 278
3 The "Armenian Genocide" and the Copenhagen Criteria 283
4 Guaranteeing the Freedom of Expression and Good Neighbourly Relations 289
5 Conclusions 293
References 296

Abstract The persistent refusal of the Turkish government to qualify the Armenian massacres performed in 1915–1916, during the Ottoman Empire, as a genocide is here taken into consideration from the point of view of the ongoing accession process of Turkey to the European Union (EU). Even if the recognition of the "Armenian Genocide" as such does not pertain to Article 49 TEU, is not included in Article 2 TEU and does not constitute one of the so-called "Copenhagen criteria", the criminalization in the Turkish legal order of any dissenting opinion on the matter could however indirectly affect the Copenhagen legal criteria (because of the compulsory nature of Framework Decision 2008/913/JHA) as well as Articles 2 and 49 TEU and the Copenhagen political criteria (because of the attenuation of the right of freedom of expression).

P. Simone (✉)
University of Rome "Tor Vergata", Rome, Italy
e-mail: pierluigi.simone@uniroma2.it

F. Lattanzi and E. Pistoia (eds.), *The Armenian Massacres of 1915–1916 a Hundred Years Later*, Studies in the History of Law and Justice 15,
https://doi.org/10.1007/978-3-319-78169-3_12

1 Introduction

On the night of 24 April 1915, known as "Red Sunday",[1] the Young Turk government of the Ottoman Empire engaged in World War I rounded up, arrested and deported a first wave of 235–270 Armenian intellectuals, clergy and community leaders from Constantinople and other cities to two holding centers near Ankara.[2] The majority of them were gradually murdered. After the approval by the Ottoman Parliament on 27 May 1915 of the Temporary Law of Deportation (*Tehcir* Law),[3] defined in the Republic of Turkey as "Relocation and Resettlement Law" (*Sevk ve İskân Kanunu*), authorising the punishment of anyone sensed as a threat to national security, the persecution of the Ottoman Empire's Armenian population was systematized and implemented until February 1916 (but probably pursued up to 1917) through the wholesale elimination of the able-bodied males, the disarmament of the Armenian soldiers in the Ottoman Armed Forces who worked to death in labour battalions or were outright executed in small batches, and the deportation of hundreds of thousands of women, children, infirms and the elderly on long forced marches leading out to the Syrian town of Deir ez-Zor and the surrounding inhospitable Mesopotamian desert. There is no evidence that the Ottoman government provided the extensive facilities and supplies that would have been necessary to sustain the life of the deportees. Driven by military escorts, they were deprived of food, water and shelter, and subjected to periodic robbery, rape and massacre. This "resettlement" campaign resulted in the death of an estimated number between 800.000 and over 1.800.000 civilians in what is commonly referred to as the "Armenian Genocide".[4] On 26 September 1915, the Ottoman Parliament also passed the "Temporary Law of Expropriation and Confiscation", otherwise said "Liquidation Law" (*Tasfiye Kanunu*), stating that all property, including land, livestock and homes belonging to Armenians, was to be confiscated by the Ottoman authorities.[5]

---

[1]This date (now observed as the "Armenian Genocide Remembrance Day") coincided with the British (Australian and New Zealander) Allied troops landings at Gallipoli after some unsuccessful naval attempts to break through the Dardanelles to Constantinople from 19 February to 18 March 1915.

[2]The total number of arrests, intended to deprive the Armenian population of leadership and a chance of resistance, amounted to 2.345.

[3]The Law was officially enacted on 1 June 1915 and was repealed on 21 February 1916. Cf. Lekka (2007), p. 138 et seq.; Engert (2016), p. 221.

[4]The literature on the "Armenian Genocide" is by now very extensive and extremely detailed. See, among the others, Hovannisian (1992); Melson (1996); Bryce et al. (2000); Bloxham (2005). Where the past few years are concerned, the studies of Kevorkian (2011); Akçam (2012); de Waal (2015); Flores (2015); Göçek (2015); Suny (2015); Gingeras (2016) are extremely significant.

[5]See Baghdjian (1987), p. 255 et seqq.; Dadrian (2003), p. 224; Lekka (2007), p. 138 et seq.; Engert (2016), p. 221.

To date, a few States and many State Parliaments have officially defined the above mentioned events as a genocide.[6] Most historians and scholars agree with this view. The Republic of Turkey, successor State of the Ottoman Empire, argues on the contrary that the word "genocide" is an unfounded classification.[7] In recent years Turkey has been faced with repeated calls to recognize the mass killings of Armenians as a genocide, but it has always refused, preferring instead to actively promote the use of more open expressions such as the "so-called Armenian Genocide" (*sözde Ermeni Soykırımı*), the "Armenian Question", the "Armenian Problem" or the "Armenian Tragedy" (suggesting, respectively, an indeterminate issue, an unfounded accusation and an accidental event).[8] In Turkey there is no official thesis on the Armenian issue. The formal stance is that the deaths of Armenians during the "relocation" or "deportation" cannot aptly be deemed "genocide" because of several diverging justifications: that the killings were neither deliberate nor systematically orchestrated or planned but rather "local" or "spontaneous"; that the killings were justified because Armenians were disloyal and were used by the Russian Empire for separatist purposes which obliged the Ottoman government to take legitimate action of military self-defence against the division of the homeland; that Armenians merely starved to death; and that Armenians were the target of "marauding gangs".[9] Turkish governmental sources have asserted that the historically demonstrated "tolerance of the Turkish people" itself renders the "Armenian Genocide" an impossibility. In 2005, the then Prime Minister Recep Tayyip Erdoğan and the Grand National Assembly of Turkey launched an "*Initiative to resolve Armenian Allegations regarding 1915*" by using archives in Turkey, Armenia and other Countries,[10] but the President of Armenia did not accept this offer. Since 2007, a circular made by the Prime Minister's Office calls on the government institutions to use the neutral-sounding phrase "*1915 olaylari*" ("Events of 1915").[11] Efforts by the Turkish government and its agents to quash

[6]According to the web sites of the National Assembly of the Republic of Armenia (www.parliament.am) and the Armenian National Institute (www.armenian-genocide.org), declarations, laws or resolutions recognizing the "Armenian Genocide" have been adopted in: Argentina, Austria, Belgium, Bolivia, Brazil, Bulgaria, Canada, Chile, Cyprus, Czech Republic, Denmark, France, Germany, Greece, Italy, Lebanon, Lithuania, Luxembourg, Netherlands, Paraguay, Poland, Russia, Slovakia, Sweden, Switzerland, Syria, United States of America, Uruguay and Venezuela. Resolutions in favor of recognition have also been approved by the Holy See, the Parliamentary Assembly of the Council of Europe, the European Parliament (European Union) and the Parliament of Mercosur. Cf. below, Sect. 3.

[7]Bayraktar and Seibel (2004), p. 393.

[8]Engert (2016), p. 226.

[9]Engert (2016), p. 225.

[10]See the text of the Letter of 10 April 2005 of H.E. Prime Minister Recep Tayyip Erdoğan addressed to H.E. President of Armenia Robert Kocharian, proposing to form a joint historical commission with Armenia, and the text of the Declaration by the Turkish Grand National Assembly supporting the Turkish proposal of 13 April 2005 to form a joint historical commission with Armenia, both available on the Internet at www.mfa.gov.tr.

[11]Engert (2016), p. 226.

mention of the "genocide" have resulted in numerous scholarly, diplomatic, political and legal controversies.[12] Prosecutors, acting on their own initiative, have used Article 301 of the Turkish Penal Code prohibiting "denigrating Turkishness" or the "Turkish nation" to silence prominent academics, human rights activists, journalists and novelists who have spoken of atrocities suffered by the Armenians.[13]

In the following pages, this persistent refusal to qualify the facts of 1915–1916 as a genocide is investigated from the particular point of view of Turkey's accession to the European Union (EU), in order to consider whether and to what extent this political attitude could contribute in (negatively) affecting negotiations. After giving an essential frame of the Turkey–EU accession process and its advancement (Sect. 2), the topic will be considered with reference to the Copenhagen criteria (Sect. 3). During negotiations (an open-ended process the outcome of which cannot be guaranteed beforehand) every candidate State should in fact demonstrate that it meets the political, economic and legal criteria set by the European Council of Copenhagen in 1993. The obligation to adequately ensure the right to freedom of expression and the necessity of good neighbourly relations as an essential element of the accession process, due to the important regional role played by Turkey, will also be focused (Sect. 4). Some concluding remarks will be drawn in Sect. 5.

2 Turkey–EU: An Unusual Accession Process

Among the Third Countries currently applying to join the EU, it is certainly a well-known fact that Turkey's negotiations are experiencing the major difficulties. This membership bid has become a major controversy within the ongoing enlargement of the EU, despite the fact that the process of rapprochement to Europe undertaken by this State is not at all recent.

In response to a specific request made on 31 July 1959 (shortly after the creation of the European Economic Community (EEC) in 1957) by the Turkish Prime

[12]Among the most recent diplomatic disputes, a famous one occurred in 2015, when Pope Francis said that the Armenian massacres of 1915–1916 were to be considered as "the first genocide of the 20th century". The word was not used again, due to a strong Turkish backlash, until 24 June 2016, when he reaffirmed and solidified his stance that this constituted a genocide and strongly condemned the enduring denial. Turkey responded by accusing the Pope of having a "crusader mentality" against the Country. The Holy See strongly denied this, claiming that the Pope had actually called for reconciliation between Armenians and Turks.

[13]For instance, Article 301 has been used to bring charges against five journalists who, in 2006, had criticized a Court order to shut down a conference in Istanbul about the Ottoman Armenian casualties in the Ottoman Empire during World War I; against Arat Dink, editor-in-chief of the Armenian bilingual weekly newspaper Agos, published in Istanbul, and its managing editor Serkis Seropyan, in 2007, for printing Dink's words that the killings of Armenians in 1915 were a genocide; and against the writer Orhan Pamuk for stating, in an interview of 2009 with the Swiss magazine Das Magazin, that "Thirty thousand Kurds have been killed here, and a million Armenians. [...]". Cf. Engert (2016), p. 228 et seq.

Minister Adnan Menderes, the first formalization of mutual contacts took place with the Agreement establishing an Association between the European Economic Community and Turkey. This was signed at Ankara on 12 September 1963 and entered into force on 1 December 1964.[14] This Agreement was then completed with an Additional and a Financial Protocol, both signed in Brussels on 23 November 1970; a Supplementary Protocol, signed in Ankara on 30 June 1973; a Financial Protocol, signed in Brussels on 12 May 1977; and an Additional Protocol, signed in Brussels on 29 July 2005.[15] A further, significant consolidation occurred later with the adoption, by the EC–Turkey Association Council (a body that operates within the Ankara Agreement itself), of Decision No. 1/95 of 22 December 1995 on implementing the final phase of the Customs Union, entered into force on 31 December 1995.[16]

The Agreement of 1963 thus initiated a process towards creating a Customs Union to help secure Turkey's full membership in the EEC. Significantly, its Preamble recognizes that

> […] the support given by the European Economic Community to the efforts of the Turkish people to improve their standard of living will facilitate the accession of Turkey to the Community at a later date;

while, pursuant to the subsequent Article 28,

> As soon as the operation of this Agreement has advanced far enough to justify envisaging full acceptance by Turkey of the obligations arising out of the Treaty establishing the Community, the Contracting Parties shall examine the possibility of the accession of Turkey to the Community.

The Preamble of Decision No. 1/95 cited above, also considers that

> […] the objectives set out by the Ankara Agreement, and in particular by its Article 28, which established the Association between Turkey and the Community maintain their significance at this time of great political and economic transformation on the European scene.

[14]See Council Decision 64/732/EEC of 23 December 1963. The English version of the Ankara Agreement is published in OJ C 113, 24 December 1973, p. 2 et seqq. Cf. also the web site of the Ministry of European Union Affairs of the Republic of Turkey (www.ab.gov.tr).

[15]See respectively: OJ C 113, 24 December 1973, pp. 18 et seqq. and 76 et seqq. (Council Regulation (EEC) No. 2760/72 of 19 December 1972); OJ L 361, 31 December 1977, p. 2 et seqq. (Council Regulation (EEC) No. 3026/77 of 28 November 1977); OJ L 67, 17 March 1979, p. 15 et seqq. (Council Decision 79/281/EEC of 5 March 1979); OJ L 254, 30 June 2005, p. 57 et seqq. (Council Decision 2005/672/EC of 13 June 2005). Cf. also on the Internet the web site www.ab.gov.tr.

[16]In OJ L 35, 13 February 1996, p. 1 et seqq. See also Türkiye-Avrupa Topluluğu Ortaklık Konseyi Kararları/Turkey-European Union Association Council Decisions, 1964–2000, Vol. 2, Ankara, 2001, p. 199 et seqq. (www.ab.gov.tr).

Full membership in the European Communities (now the EU) is therefore a clear and fundamental goal that both Turkey and its Community counterpart have faced since the beginning.[17]

The history of Turkey's candidacy can be easily summarized in its essential steps, as follows:

- on 14 April 1987, the application for formal membership in the European Communities was presented by the Turkish Prime Minister Turgut Özal[18];
- on 18 December 1989, the European Commission refused to immediately begin accession negotiations, citing Turkey's economic and political situation, poor relations with Greece and their conflict with Cyprus, but overall reaffirming the eventual membership as a goal[19];
- on 11 December 1999, the European Council of Helsinki recognized Turkey as a candidate on equal footing with other potential candidates[20];
- on 26 February 2001 Council Regulation (EC) No. 390/2001 on assistance to Turkey in the framework of the pre-accession strategy established an Accession Partnership that provides a single framework covering the priorities, as defined in the analysis of the situation in Turkey, on which preparations for accession must concentrate in view of the political and economic criteria and the obligations incumbent upon a EU Member State as defined by the European Council, and the financial resources for assisting Turkey to implement the priorities identified during the pre-accession period[21];

[17]Turkey's accession to the EU presents a fascinating case study for all those with an interest in europeanization. See Arikan (2006); Arvanitopoulos (2009); Nas and Özer (2012); Müftüler Baç (2016).

[18]See Council of the European Economic Community, Demande d'adhésion de la Turquie à la Communauté économique européenne (14 avril 1987), lettre adressée à Leo Tindemans, Ministre belge des Affaires étrangères et Président en exercice du Conseil des Communautés européennes, doc. 6012/87, reproduced at www.cvce.eu.

[19]Commission of the European Communities, Commission Opinion on Turkey's Request for Accession to the Community, doc. SEC(89)2290 final of 20 December 1989, available at www.cvce.eu. In accordance with the procedure set out at that time in Article 237 TEEC, the Council called on the European Commission (on 27 April 1987) to deliver an opinion on the application. The European Commission reaffirmed that Turkey was a natural candidate for full EU Member State status and took the view that closer relations should be encouraged. It pointed out, however, that no negotiations for Turkish accession to the EU should be contemplated until 1993 at the earliest; the major political priority in the meantime should be to further European integration with the completion of the internal market and progress towards Economic and Monetary Union. The European Commission considered that, until these aims could be judged to have been successfully achieved, it would be extremely unwise to begin enlargement negotiations.

[20]Helsinki European Council, 10 and 11 December 1999, Presidency Conclusions, point 12 (cf. www.consilium.europa.eu).

[21]The text of Council Regulation (EC) No. 390/2001 is available in OJ L 58, 28 February 2001, p. 1 et seqq. On its basis, an Accession Partnership with Turkey has been adopted in 2001 (Council Decision 2001/235/EC of 8 March 2001); in 2003 (Council Decision 2003/398/EC of 19 May 2003); in 2006 (Council Decision 2006/35/EC of 23 January 2006); and in 2008 (Council Decision 2008/157/EC of 18 February 2008). About Decision 2008/157/EC see furthermore below, Sect. 4.

- on 12 December 2002, the European Council of Copenhagen stated that
  If the European Council in December 2004, on the basis of a report and a recommendation from the Commission, decides that Turkey fulfils the Copenhagen political criteria, the European Union will open accession negotiations with Turkey without delay.[22];
- on 17 December 2004, the European Council of Brussels agreed to start negotiations.[23]

Negotiations officially began on 3 October 2005.[24] The European Commission pointed out that long transitional periods, derogations, specific arrangements or permanent safeguard clauses could have been considered in areas such as the free movement of persons, structural policies or agriculture. Furthermore, the decision-taking process regarding the eventual establishment of the free movement of persons should have allowed for a maximum role of individual Member States. As Turkey's accession could have had substantial financial consequences, the European Commission clarified also that negotiations could be concluded only after the establishment of the Financial Framework for the period from 2014 together with possible financial reforms. Any arrangements should have ensured that the financial burdens were fairly shared between all Member States.[25]

Since then, negotiations have been hampered by a series of problems, both internal and external to Turkey. To accede to the EU, Turkey must successfully complete negotiations with the European Commission on thirty-three thematic chapters of the *acquis* of the Union (the common rights and obligations that are binding on all EU Member States).[26] The opening of eight chapters has been frozen since 11 December 2006, over Turkey's rejection to grant its ports and airports to traffic from Cyprus.[27] Six other chapters do not proceed to the next stage in the

[22]Copenhagen European Council, 12 and 13 December 2002, Presidency Conclusions, doc. 15917/02, points 18 and 19 (cf. www.consilium.europa.eu).

[23]Brussels European Council, 16 and 17 December 2004, Presidency Conclusions, doc. 16238/1/04, point 22 (cf. www.consilium.europa.eu).

[24]Cf. European Commission, Negotiating Framework (Luxembourg, 3 October 2005), available at ec.europa.eu.

[25]Cf. European Commission, Negotiating Framework (Luxembourg, 3 October 2005), points 12 and 13.

[26]On the *acquis* of the Union see below, Sect. 3. For the general arrangement of chapters with the candidate States cf. below, footnote 60.

[27]These are: Chapters 1 (Free Movement of Goods), 3 (Right of Establishment for Companies and Freedom to provide Services), 9 (Financial Services), 11 (Agriculture and Rural Development), 13 (Fisheries), 14 (Transport Policy), 29 (Customs Union) and 30 (External Relations).

process because they are blocked by Cyprus.[28] Until now, sixteen chapters have been opened and so far only one of them has been closed.[29]

In 2007, Turkey stated that it was aiming to comply with EU law by 2013, but many people have reported a slowdown of the reforms that Turkey itself is called upon to introduce. In 2006, the President of the European Commission José Manuel Durão Barroso said that the accession process would take at least until 2021. In 2012, Prime Minister Erdoğan made clear that Turkey was expecting membership in the EU to be effective by 2023 (the 100th anniversary of the proclamation of the Republic of Turkey), implying that Turkey could end negotiations if the talks had not yielded a positive result by then. In 2013, Turkish President Abdullah Gül said that upon completing the accession process, Turkey would hold a referendum for its membership in the EU.

The conclusion of the Agreement between the European Union and the Republic of Turkey on the readmission of persons residing without authorization, signed at Ankara on 16 December 2013,[30] seemed to have given a new impetus to the accession negotiations. After signing the Readmission Agreement, the European Commissioner for Home Affairs Cecilia Malmström in fact launched a visa liberalization dialogue with Turkey including a "Roadmap towards the Visa-free Regime" aimed at ensuring Turkish citizens visa-free travels to the Schengen Area.[31] In line with the Conclusions of the European Council of Brussels of 15 October 2015,[32] both the EU–Turkey Statement approved by the Meeting of Heads of State or Government with Turkey, held in Brussels on 29 November 2015, and the EU–Turkey Statement of 18 March 2016 reconfirmed the commitment to re-energize the whole process.[33]

However, the repressive measures under the state of emergency declared by the Turkish government in the aftermath of the failed military coup of 15 July 2016,

[28]Since 8 December 2009, these are: Chapters 2 (Freedom of Movement for Workers), 15 (Energy), 23 (Judiciary and Fundamental Rights), 24 (Justice, Freedom and Security), 26 (Education and Culture) and 31 (Foreign, Security and Defence Policy).

[29]Currently, the open Chapters are the following: 4 (Free Movement of Capital), 6 (Company Law), 7 (Intellectual Property Law), 10 (Information Society and Media), 12 (Food Safety, Veterinary and Phytosanitary Policy), 16 (Taxation), 17 (Economic and Monetary Policy), 18 (Statistics), 20 (Enterprise and Industrial Policy), 21 (Trans-European Networks), 22 (Regional Policy and Coordination of Structural Instruments), 27 (Environment and Climate Change), 28 (Consumer and Health Protection), 32 (Financial Control) and 33 (Financial and Budgetary Provisions). Chapter 25 (Science and Research) was opened on 12 June 2006 and closed on the same day.

[30]Council Decision 2014/252/EU of 14 April 2014. See OJ L 134, 7 May 2014, p. 3 et seqq.

[31]Cf. European Commission, Roadmap towards the Visa-free Regime with Turkey (16 December 2013), available at ec.europa.eu.

[32]Brussels European Council, 15 October 2015, Presidency Conclusions, doc. EUCO 26/15, point 2 (www.consilium.europa.eu).

[33]See European Council, Meeting of Heads of State or Government with Turkey, EU-Turkey Statement, 29 November 2015, point 2; and European Council, EU-Turkey Statement, 18 March 2016, point 8. Both of them are available on the Internet at www.consilium.europa.eu.

carried out by a faction within the Turkish Armed Forces are calling everything into question. Serious concerns have been raised over the conditions of those detained and arrested following the attempted coup and over the severe restrictions on the freedom of expression and on the press and media in Turkey. In considering such measures disproportionate and in breach of basic rights and freedoms protected by the Turkish Constitution, of democratic values upon which the EU is founded and of the European Convention on Human Rights (ECHR) and the International Covenant on Civil and Political Rights (of which Turkey is a State Party), the European Parliament, with its resolution on EU–Turkey relations of 24 November 2016, albeit committed to keeping Turkey anchored to the EU, called on the European Commission and the Member States to initiate a temporary freeze of the ongoing accession negotiations with Turkey, and reiterated that a reintroduction of capital punishment by the Turkish government would have to lead to a formal suspension of the accession process.[34] On 13 December 2016, a Statement of the General Affairs Council said that no new chapters in Turkey's membership are considered for opening "under the current prevailing circumstances".[35] Turkey's path toward autocratic rule is making progress on accession to the EU extremely complicated.

3 The "Armenian Genocide" and the Copenhagen Criteria

Although from a formal point of view the negotiations with Turkey seem to respect the path already previously followed by other applicant Countries, from a substantive point of view they show some quite original characteristics, which combine skepticism and fears on the part of the public opinion of several EU Member States. In addition to the doubts linked to religion, culture and demographics, three unsolved and very delicate matters weigh on the negotiating table: the continuing Turkish occupation of the North-Eastern part of the island of Cyprus (where the self-declared Turkish Republic of Northern Cyprus, not recognized by the international community, extends since 1983) and the refusal of Turkey to acknowledge the Republic of Cyprus (Southern part of the island, where the Greek Cypriot ethnic group lives), which is a EU Member since 1 May 2004, as the sole existing territorial authority[36]; the condition of the Kurdish minority, given that, due to the

[34]European Parliament, Resolution of 24 November 2016 on EU-Turkey relations, doc. P8_TA (2016)0450, points 1 and 3 (see www.europarl.europa.eu). Cf. also the Foreign Affairs Council Conclusions on Turkey of 18 July 2016.

[35]Council of the European Union, Outcome of the Council Meeting, 3511st Council Meeting, General Affairs, Brussels, 13 December 2016, doc. 15536/16, point 23 (cf. www.consilium.europa.eu).

[36]From 1 July 2012 to 31 December 2012, Turkey froze its relations with the EU for the duration of the Republic of Cyprus's rotating Presidency.

large number of Turkish Kurds, the expression of a Kurdish identity is viewed as a potential threat to Turkish unity[37]; and the unwillingness to acknowledge the Armenian massacres as a genocide, in respect of which the above mentioned official position of Turkey has never changed over the years.[38]

Political stands on the issue of this lack of recognition, connected with Turkey's accession process to the Community and the EU, have been taken so far by some Member States parliamentary assemblies, which normally use the expression "Armenian Genocide". Here it is worth mentioning the decisions, motions and resolutions approved by the Parliaments of Germany, Italy, the Netherlands and Sweden.

Germany and Italy have spoken in general terms. A resolution of the Italian Chamber of Deputies of 16 November 2000 urged the Italian government

> […] to pursue energetically the easing of all tensions between peoples and minorities [in the Caucasus], in order to create […] pacific coexistence and respect for human rights, thereby expediting a more rapid integration of Turkey within the European Community.[39]

while in its motion of 15 June 2005, the German *Bundestag* stressed that the

> […] Turkish attitude is in opposition to the idea of reconciliation which guides the common values of the European Union.[40]

The Dutch and Swedish approaches have been more direct. The Second Chamber (House of Representatives) of the States General of the Netherlands, noting the start of the accession negotiations with Turkey, and being of the opinion that an honest acceptance of its own history is inextricably connected with the position of candidate Member State, with a motion of 21 December 2004 asked the Dutch government, within the framework of its dialogue with Turkey, to continuously and expressly raise the recognition of the "Armenian Genocide".[41] The Swedish *Riksdag* decision of 11 March 2010 affirms that

> As long as countries such as Sweden do not confront Turkey with the truth and the facts which are at hand, Turkey cannot go further on its path to a more open society, a better democracy and fully open its possibilities for a membership in EU.[42]

---

[37]The Kurdish issue has always been one of a particular importance in Turkish complex political life. The European Court of Human Rights (ECtHR) has condemned Turkey for thousands of abuses in respect of Kurdish people. The judgments are related to executions of civilians, torturing, forced displacements, destroyed villages, arbitrary arrests and trials, murdered and disappeared journalists. Among the latest judgments, cf.: ECtHR, 24 March 2014, No. 23502/06, *Benzer and Others* v. *Turkey*; ECtHR, 6 December 2016, No. 50171/09, *Belge* v. *Turkey*.

[38]See Sect. 1.

[39]See the web site of the Armenian National Institute (www.armenian-genocide.org).

[40]See the web site of the Armenian National Institute (www.armenian-genocide.org).

[41]See the web site of the Armenian National Institute (www.armenian-genocide.org).

[42]See the web site of the Armenian National Institute (www.armenian-genocide.org).

Moreover, France is the only EU Member State to have publicly acknowledged the "Armenian Genocide" by law.[43] In 2004 the French Minister of Foreign Affairs Michel Barnier stated that Turkey should have recognized the systematic massacres of Armenians as a genocide; he insisted that, even without setting a precondition for EU entry regarding the matter, France would however raise the issue during negotiations.

Setting aside what has just been examined, can the denial that the events of 1915–1916 represent a genocide create, in strictly legal terms, difficulties for Turkey's accession negotiations to the EU? As will be shortly explained, this policy, though not directly, can hinder negotiations also at the legal-normative level.

The entry of new States into the EU is currently governed by Article 49 TEU. This provision requires a "geographical condition" (which Turkey certainly meets), combining geographical, historical and cultural elements which all contribute to the European identity[44]; and a "political condition", namely the respect for, and the promotion of, the values referred to in Article 2 TEU, for the most part later enshrined in Article 6(1) TEU and in the Charter of Fundamental Rights of the European Union: human dignity, freedom, democracy, equality, the rule of law, human rights (including the rights of persons belonging to minorities), pluralism, non-discrimination, tolerance, justice, solidarity and equality between women and men.[45]

The State concerned addresses its application to the Council, which shall act unanimously after consulting the European Commission and after receiving the consent of the European Parliament. The conditions of eligibility agreed upon by the European Council must also be taken into account.[46] This last reference in Article 49 is due to the Lisbon Treaty and is based on the so-called "Copenhagen criteria" rules that were adopted by the European Council of Copenhagen of 21–22 June 1993 (from which they take their name) to define whether a Country is fit to

---

[43]See the law No. 2001-70 relating to the recognition of the Armenian Genocide of 1915 (loi relative à la reconnaissance du genocide arménien du 1915), of 29 January 2001, published in Journal Officiel de la République Française No. 25, 30 January 2001, p. 1590. A law of 2012 making a criminal offence "the denial or extreme minimization" of one or several genocide crimes (among those, the "Armenian Genocide"), has been censored by the French Constitutional Council (decision No. 2012-647 of 28 February 2012) and therefore has not been promulgated.

[44]Commission of the European Communities, Europe and the Challenge of Enlargement, Bulletin of the European Communities, Supplement No. 3, 1992, p. 11.

[45]On the origin and meaning of Article 2 TEU, and on and the characters of the outlined model of European society, see Priollaud and Siritzky (2008), p. 31 et seq.; Fischer (2010), p. 632; von Bogdandy et al. (2012), p. 490 et seqq.

[46]Article 49 (1) TEU. Para. 2 of the same provision also states that "The conditions of admission and the adjustments to the Treaties on which the Union is founded, which such admission entails, shall be the subject of an agreement between the Member States and the applicant State. This agreement shall be submitted for ratification by all the contracting States in accordance with their respective constitutional requirements." Cf. Priollaud and Siritzky (2008), p. 143 et seqq.; Pingel (2010), p. 236 et seqq.

join the EU. The main priority areas identified for each candidate State relate to the ability to take on some obligations. EU membership thus requires:

- that the candidate State has achieved stability of institutions guaranteeing democracy, the rule of law, human rights and respect for, and protection of, minorities;
- the existence of a functioning market economy, as well as the capacity to cope with competitive pressure and market forces within the EU;
- that all prospective Members make the law built up over the history of the European Communities and the EU part of their own national legislation, and accept what has been formerly known as the *acquis communautaire* and now as the *acquis* of the Union, in order to adhere to the aims of Political, Economic and Monetary Union.[47]

At its meeting in Madrid in 1995, the European Council also stressed the need for the candidate States to adjust their administrative structures to ensure harmonious operation of Community policies after accession,[48] and at Luxembourg, in 1997, it pointed out that the incorporation of the *acquis* into legislation is not in itself sufficient, being necessary to ensure that it is actually implemented.[49] The European Councils of Santa Maria da Feira and Göteborg, in 2000 and 2001 respectively, confirmed the vital importance of the applicant Countries' capacity to enforce the *acquis*, and added that this required important efforts by the applicants in strengthening and reforming their administrative and judicial structures.[50]

Useful items having specific reference to the Armenian massacres, their recognition and the Copenhagen criteria can definitely be found in the answers of the Council and the European Commission to written questions submitted by members of the European Parliament. Some resolutions adopted by the European Parliament itself since 1987 are also significant, notwithstanding, as the Court of First Instance (now, the General Court) and the Court of Justice have explained in the *Krikorian* case in 2003 and 2004, these are declarations of a purely political nature and cannot have binding legal consequences for their author nor for the other EU institutions.[51]

---

[47]Copenhagen European Council, 21–22 June 1993, Conclusions of the Presidency, doc. SN/180/1/93, point 7.A (cf. www.consilium.europa.eu).

[48]Madrid European Council, 15 and 16 December 1995, Presidency Conclusions, doc. SN/004/0/95, point III.A (cf. www.consilium.europa.eu).

[49]Luxembourg European Council, 12 and 13 December 1997, Presidency Conclusions, doc. SN/400/97, point 23 (cf. www.consilium.europa.eu).

[50]Santa Maria da Feira European Council, 19 and 20 June 2000, Presidency Conclusions, doc. SN/200/1/00, point 16; Göteborg European Council, 15 and 16 June 2001, Presidency Conclusions, doc. SN 200/1/01, points 7 and 8 (cf. www.consilium.europa.eu).

[51]See: Court of First Instance, order of 17 December 2003, Case T-346/03, *Krikorian and Euro-Arménie ASBL* v. *European Parliament, Council of the European Union and Commission of the European Communities*, para. 19 (Reports of Cases 2003, II-6037 et seqq.); Court of Justice, order of 29 October 2004, Case C-18/04P, *Krikorian and Euro-Arménie ASBL* v. *European Parliament, Council of the European Union and Commission of the European Communities*, para. 32 (not published).

The Council and the European Commission either have been evasive and have avoided addressing the issue on the merits; or have entrenched themselves behind the literal formalism represented by the Copenhagen criteria, which do not cover the "Armenian Genocide", essentially defining the topic as irrelevant.[52] The European Parliament, in particular with the resolution on the opening of negotiations with Turkey of 28 September 2005, appears to have interpreted the Copenhagen criteria: on this occasion, in calling on Turkey to recognize the "Armenian Genocide", it has expressly considered the recognition to be a prerequisite for accession to the EU.[53]

Despite what the European Parliament has pointed out in 2005 (and that seems to have been no (more) longer followed so explicitly in the subsequent years), it is quite clear that the recognition of the "Armenian Genocide" as such does not pertain to Article 49 TEU, because neither is it included in Article 2 TEU, nor does it constitute one of the Copenhagen political criteria. These should be read, in fact, in accordance with a democratic principle assessed on a both formal and substantial meaning: existence of a parliamentary body to which the executive is responsible; separation of powers and regular forms of popular consultation; stability of institutions, their long-standing tradition in political life and effectiveness of their functioning. Obviously, the Turkish refusal to classify the Armenian massacres as a genocide, as will be mentioned later, influences the current relations between Turkey and Armenia, and also the stability in the Caucasus.[54] However, it is hard to believe that what already occurred in the case of Croatia could be replicated for Turkey since, when evaluating Croatia's application to become a EU Member State, "Regional Issues and International Obligations" were considered among the Copenhagen political criteria.[55] At the time, a less than full cooperation of this latter State with the International Criminal Tribunal for the former Yugoslavia (ICTY) was viewed as eligible to affect the overall progress of accession negotiations (whose opening was postponed for this reason) and could have been grounds for their suspension.[56] At all events Croatia's case shows very relevant differences with Turkey's, since the collaboration with ICTY, the developments in war crimes trials, a special care in ensuring human rights and more generally the regional cooperation

[52]See Rosanò, in this book.

[53]European Parliament, Resolution of 28 September 2005 on the opening of negotiations with Turkey, doc. P6_TA(2005)0350, point 5 (www.europarl.europa.eu). Nevertheless, in the resolution on Turkey's progress towards accession of 27 September 2006 (point 56), the European Parliament stressed that, although the recognition of the "Armenian Genocide" as such is formally not one of the Copenhagen criteria, it is indispensable for a Country on the road to membership to come to terms with and recognize its past.

[54]Cf. below, Sect. 4. See also Pistoia, in this book.

[55]See Commission of the European Communities, Commission Staff Working Paper, Croatia, Stabilisation and Association Report, doc. SEC(2002)341 final of 4 April 2002, points 2.1.1. and 2.3.1.; European Commission, Croatia 2005 Progress Report, doc. SEC(2005)1424 final of 9 November 2005, points B.1. and B.1.3.

[56]Brussels European Council, 17 and 18 June 2004, Presidency Conclusions, doc. 10679/2/04, points 35 and 39; Brussels European Council, 16 and 17 December 2004, Presidency Conclusions, point 16; European Commission, Croatia 2005 Progress Report, point A.1.

are fundamental commitments of the EU policy, defined by the Stabilization and Association Process involving the whole Western Balkan area.[57] The "Armenian Genocide" could instead have a different, and indirect, impact on Article 2 TEU, quoted by Article 49(1) TEU, and the Copenhagen political criteria to the extent that the "human rights" protected by the rules mentioned above include a right to memory, perceived as a right, both individual and collective, with a pedagogical, therapeutic, legal and cultural function.[58] The best way to prevent the recurrence of genocide and other forms of mass violence promoted by a State is to cultivate a lasting collective memory of the horrors that have occurred. The regime of human rights provides a structure by which memory can be restored, and it is the role of human rights law never to forget.[59]

The Copenhagen legal criteria concerning the ability of alignment with the *acquis* of the Union, take a further indirect importance. As previously said, the *acquis* is constantly evolving and comprises the contents, principles and political objectives of the Treaties on which the EU is founded; the legislation adopted pursuant to the Treaties and the case-law of the Court of Justice, the General Court and the specialized Courts; the standards adopted and referred to in Community and EU legislation and international agreements; the declarations and resolutions adopted by the EU; the acts related to the Area of Freedom, Security and Justice; the instruments under the Common Foreign and Security Policy; the international agreements concluded by the Communities and the EU, the Communities and the EU jointly with their Member States and those concluded by the Member States among themselves within the sphere of the Communities and EU activities.[60]

All this concerns the acceptance of the real or potential rights and obligations inherent to the EU system and to its institutional framework. Therefore, one cannot help considering within this acceptance also Council Framework Decision 2008/913/JHA of 28 November 2008 on combating certain forms and expressions of racism and xenophobia by means of criminal law,[61] which provides that each Member State has to take the measures necessary to ensure the punishment of the intentional conduct of publicly condoning, denying or grossly trivialising crimes of genocide as defined in Article 6 of the Statute of the International Criminal Court

[57]Cf. Brussels European Council, 17 and 18 June 2004, Presidency Conclusions, points 35 and 39; Brussels European Council, 16 and 17 December 2004, Presidency Conclusions, point 15. See furthermore Pistoia, in this book.

[58]On the right of memory cf. Osiel (2005), p. 105 et seqq.; Taubira (2006), p. 164 et seqq.; Giuva (2013), p. 113 et seqq.; Wilson (2014), p. 332 et seqq.

[59]Osiel (2005), p. 109; Wilson (2014), p. 342.

[60]For the negotiations with Croatia (which joined the EU in 2013), Iceland (actually suspended), Turkey, Montenegro, Serbia and, in the future, with the former Yugoslav Republic of Macedonia and Albania (candidate Countries), the *acquis* is split up into thirty-five chapters (thirty-three thematic, one dedicated to "Institutions" and one to "Other Issues": see above, Sect. 2 and footnotes 27, 28 and 29), with the purpose of better balancing between the chapters: dividing the most difficult ones into separate chapters for easier negotiation, uniting some easier chapters, moving some policies between chapters, as well as renaming a few of them in the process.

[61]In OJ L 328, 6 December 2008, p. 55 et seqq.

(the "Armenian Genocide" is generally included among them), directed against a group of persons or a member of such a group defined by reference to race, colour, religion, descent or national or ethnic origin when the conduct is carried out in a manner likely to incite to violence or hatred against such a group or a member of such a group.[62] This Framework Decision should also be valued in the light of the "communitarization" of the former Third Pillar policies that leaks out in Articles 9 and 10 of Protocol No. 36 on transitional provisions annexed by the Lisbon Treaty to the TEU and the TFEU.[63] On the one hand, pursuant to Article 9,

> The legal effects of the acts of the institutions, bodies, offices and agencies of the Union adopted on the basis of the Treaty on European Union prior to the entry into force of the Treaty of Lisbon shall be preserved until those acts are repealed, annulled or amended in implementation of the Treaties. […].

On the other hand, according to the provisions of paras. 1 and 3 of Article 10, since 1 December 2014, with respect to the acts of the EU in the field of Police Cooperation and Judicial Cooperation in Criminal Matters which have been adopted before the entry into force of the Lisbon Treaty, the powers of the European Commission under Article 258 TFEU are applicable and the powers of the Court of Justice under Title VI of the TEU, in its previous version, have ceased.[64] This means that also Council Framework Decision 2008/913/JHA is currently under the supervision of the European Commission through the infringement procedure and to the full jurisdiction and competence of the Court of Justice.

4 Guaranteeing the Freedom of Expression and Good Neighbourly Relations

Some further elements useful for understanding what might be the effect of the Turkish refusal to regard the Armenian massacres as a genocide on Turkey's accession negotiations to the EU are offered by Council Decision 2008/157/EC of 18 February 2008 on the principles, priorities and conditions contained in the Accession Partnership with the Republic of Turkey.[65] Among the short-term priorities which are mentioned in the Annex to that Decision, in the section dedicated to "Human Rights and the Protection of Minorities", subsection on "Civil and Political Rights", there is the need that full respect for the freedom of expression be ensured; and in this optic, that freedom of the press, in line with the European

[62]See Article 1(1)(c) of Council Framework Decision 2008/913/JHA. For some comments on this act, cf. Garman (2008), p. 843 et seqq.; Mitsilegas (2009a), p. 98 et seqq. and (2009b), p. 530 et seqq.; Renauld (2010), p. 119 et seqq.

[63]In OJ C 202, 7 June 2016, p. 321 et seqq.

[64]See Article 35 TEU as in force before the Lisbon Treaty.

[65]In OJ L 51, 26 February 2008, p. 4 et seqq. See also above, footnote 21.

Convention on Human Rights and the case-law of the European Court of Human Rights, be reviewed and implemented; and that the situation of those persons prosecuted or sentenced for non-violent expression of opinion be remedied.[66]

In the European Convention on Human Rights, the right to freedom of expression and information, subject to restrictions that are "in accordance with law" and "necessary in a democratic society", is provided for by Article 10. This right includes the freedom to hold opinions, and to receive and impart information and ideas. The interpretation of Article 10 ECHR by the European Court of Human Rights, has shown for about twenty years a particular severity in respect of negationism, attributing to it a statute of exception that escapes the common guarantees recognized in the field of freedom of expression and solemnly proclaimed on other occasions.The Court has made it clear that the negation or revision of clearly established historical facts is removed from the protection of Article 10 by Article 17 ECHR, which is intended to prevent any State, group or person from inferring from the European Convention on Human Rights any right to engage in activities or perform acts aimed at the destruction of any of the rights and freedoms set forth therein or at their limitation to a greater extent than is provided for in the Convention.[67] The recent judgment delivered on 15 October 2015 in the *Perinçek* case, by which the applicant's conviction for denying the legal qualification of the Armenian massacres as a genocide, has been alleged to amount to a violation of the freedom of expression guaranteed by Article 10 ECHR and does not seem to be in contradiction with what has just been observed.[68] This judgment raises in fact several critical issues and leaves a number of unresolved questions (that cannot be detailed here) with particular reference, among the others, to those related to the distance, both spatial and temporal, between the applicant's statement and the events to which he referred.[69]

The freedom of expression guaranteed under Article 10 ECHR may thus not be invoked in conflict with Article 17. Consequently, a denialist position such as that relating to the "genocide" of the Armenians cannot be protected by the right to freedom of expression provided for by Article 10 ECHR and rather constitutes an abuse of rights under Article 17 ECHR. At the same time, Turkish legislation (mainly consisting in Article 301 of the Penal Code) which prosecutes anyone who

---

[66]See the Annex to Council Decision 2008/157/EC, point 3.1. Cf. also the Annexes to Council Decision 2001/235/EC (point 4.1), to Council Decision 2003/398/EC (point 4) and to Council Decision 2006/35/EC (point 3.1). All these acts have been already mentioned above, footnote 21.

[67]Cf. for instance: ECtHR, 23 September 1998, No. 24662/94, *Lehideux and Isorni* v. *France*, para. 47; ECtHR, decision of 24 June 2003, No. 65831/01, *Garaudy* v. *France*, para. 1; ECtHR, decision of 13 December 2005, No. 7485/03, *Witzsch* v. *Germany (No. 2)*, para. 3. The related texts are all available on the Internet at hudoc.echr.coe.int.

[68]ECtHR, 15 October 2015, No. 27510/08, *Perinçek* v. *Switzerland* (see hudoc.echr.coe.int).

[69]Ibidem, paras. 242–250. Cf. also the dissenting opinions of judges Isabelle Berro, Josep Casadevall, Vincent A. De Gaetano, Egidijus Kūris, Linos-Alexandre Sicilianos, Johannes Silvis and Dean Spielmann (hudoc.echr.coe.int). On the *Perinçek* case see Voorhoof (2014, 2015); Borgna (2015), p. 697 et seqq.; Tuncel (2015); Della Morte (2016), p. 183 et seqq.

does not agree with the governmental vision on the Armenian question (since a public reference to the "Armenian Genocide" is considered "an attempt to insult Turkish national identity" (*Türklük*) and is punishable by imprisonment), must be considered not suitable to the requirements of the European Convention on Human Rights, nor does it comply with the formalities, conditions, restrictions or penalties to which para. 2 of Article 10 ECHR allows to submit the freedom of expression itself.[70] This strong attenuation of the freedom of expression, linked to the legal classification attributable to the facts of 1915–1916, contrasts with the obligations imposed on Countries wishing to join the EU. Thus this establishes an indirect connection between the denial of the "Armenian Genocide" and the respect for "freedom", "democracy", "human rights" and "pluralism" cited among the values of Article 2 TEU, evoked by Article 49(1) TEU, and the Copenhagen political criteria.[71] This limitation of the freedom of expression also impairs the right to memory as a "human right", being obvious that if there is not a promotion of the event, those who are destined to gain knowledge of the event itself do not have, and will not have, any possibility to remember, celebrate, learn, study and elaborate it.[72]

Being a Contracting Party to the European Convention on Human Rights, Turkey is of course bound to respect the Convention and the case-law of the European Court of Human Rights even at this stage, independently and regardless of its (future) EU membership.[73] Moreover, Turkey's accession to the EU would result in the full acceptance of the Charter of Fundamental Rights of the European Union, solemnly proclaimed on 7 December 2000 and adapted on 12 December 2007, which has the same legal value as the Treaties in accordance with Article 6(1) TEU.[74] Article 11 of the Charter on the freedom of expression and information corresponds to Article 10 ECHR.[75] Pursuant to Article 52(3) of the Charter (equivalence clause), the meaning and scope of this right are the same as those

[70]See ECtHR, 10 February 2009, No. 27690/03, *Güçlü* v. *Turkey*, paras. 33–42; ECtHR, 20 May 2010, No. 2933/03, *Cox* v. *Turkey*, paras. 41–45; ECtHR, 14 September 2010, Nos. 2668/07, 6102/08, 30079/08, 7072/09 and 7124/09, *Dink* v. *Turkey*, paras. 128 and 135; ECtHR, 25 October 2011, No. 27520/07, *Altuğ Taner Akçam* v. *Turkey*, paras. 62–82 and 89–96 (hudoc.echr.coe.int).

[71]Cf. above, Sect. 3.

[72]Cf. above, Sect. 3.

[73]Turkey ratified the European Convention on Human Rights on 18 May 1954, and Protocol No. 11 of 11 May 1994 (by which the European Court of Human Rights has been given compulsory jurisdiction, since previously Member States could ratify the Convention without accepting the jurisdiction of the Court) on 11 July 1997.

[74]The text of the Charter of Fundamental Rights of the European Union is reproduced in OJ C 202, 7 June 2016, p. 391 et seqq.

[75]See the Explanations relating to the Charter of Fundamental Rights ("Explanation on Article 11–Freedom of Expression and Information"), published in OJ C 303, 14 December 2007, p. 17 et seqq. Although the Explanations do not as such have the status of law, they are a valuable tool of interpretation intended to clarify the provisions of the Charter itself.

guaranteed by the European Convention on Human Rights (and by the case-law of the European Court of Human Rights).[76] Furthermore, according to the compatibility clause laid down by Article 53 of the Charter, Article 11 cannot be

> [...] interpreted as restricting or adversely affecting human rights and fundamental freedoms as recognized, in their respective fields of application, by Union law and international law and by international agreements to which the Union or all the Member States are party, including the European Convention for the Protection of Human Rights and Fundamental Freedoms, and by the Member States' constitutions.

Therefore, it would be even more impossible for Turkey, as a EU Member State, to support its denial policy.

Finally, the recognition of the Armenian massacres as a genocide interacts with international and regional obligations which must be taken into account in the evaluation of the path towards accession to the EU of any applicant Country.

Concerning this, the Annex to Council Decision 2008/157/EC mentioned above (section on "Regional Issues and International Obligations", subsection on "Peaceful Settlement of Border Disputes"),[77] points out the need to unequivocally commit to good neighbourly relations; to address any sources of friction with neighbours; and to refrain from any threat or action which could adversely affect the process of peaceful settlement of border disputes.[78] Besides, regional cooperation, good neighbourly relations, promotion of reconciliation, peace-building and confidence-building measures are among the specific objectives the achievement of which is pursued through the Instrument for Pre-accession Assistance (IPA II) for the period from 2014 to 2020, established by Regulation (EU) No. 231/2014 of the European Parliament and of the Council of 11 March 2014,[79] with the aim of supporting Turkey and other States in adopting and implementing the political, institutional, legal, administrative, social and economic reforms required by them in order to comply with the EU values and to progressively align to the rules, standards, policies and practices that are necessary with a view to EU membership.[80] It is quite clear how the lack of recognition of the massacres against Armenians as a genocide affects still today the Southern Caucasian geopolitical context and the (almost inexistent) political relations between Turkey and Armenia.[81]

The Communication from the European Commission to the European Parliament, the Council, the European Economic and Social Committee and the Committee of the Regions on "EU Enlargement Policy" of 9 November 2016 is also still very relevant. With regard to Turkey, this document has upheld that good

---

[76]The limitations which may be imposed on it may therefore not exceed those provided for in Article 10(2) ECHR.

[77]Cf. footnotes 21 and 65.

[78]See the Annex to Council Decision 2008/157/EC, point 3.1. Cf. also the Annex to Council Decision 2006/35/EC, point 3.1.

[79]In OJ L 77, 15 March 2014, p. 11 et seqq.

[80]Articles 1 and 2(1)(a)(iii) and (iv), of Regulation (EU) No. 231/2014.

[81]See also above, Sect. 3.

neighbourly relations and regional cooperation are essential parts of the enlargement, stabilization and association processes, all preliminary elements to a full EU membership.[82] Turkey needs therefore to commit itself to a peaceful settlement of disputes in accordance with the Charter of the United Nations, having recourse, if necessary, to the International Court of Justice. The EU has expressed once again serious concern, and the European Commission, in particular, has urged the Turkish government to avoid any kind of threat, source of friction or actions that would jeopardize the achievement of the aforesaid objective.[83]

5 Conclusions

The mass killings of Armenians perpetrated in 1915–1916 remain a key political topic, which causes tensions and separation. The issue has also entered the European domain, becoming even more controversial as Turkey is in the process of (contested) accession negotiations to the EU. The common point of view in Turkey, despite the ongoing international condemnation, is that this historical event was simply the attempt to relocate the Armenian population because of domestic security reasons, the most important of which being a suspected collaboration with the Russian Empire (one of the members of the Triple Entente Alliance and consequently an enemy of the Ottoman Empire during World War I) when the two Countries were fighting each other in the Caucasus Campaign.[84] The pressure to recognize the "Armenian Genocide" is therefore perceived negatively and is considered an artificial obstruction to Turkey's EU accession plans created by hostile States. Turkey, however, has also witnessed the changing perceptions of intellectuals who advocate the recognition of the Armenian massacres as a genocide and speculate on whether EU membership or the attempt at accession may lead to a

---

[82] European Commission, Communication from the Commission to the European Parliament, the Council, the European Economic and Social Committee and the Committee of the Regions on "EU Enlargement Policy", COM(2016)715 final of 9 November 2016, pp. 10 and 19.

[83] See also in this sense: European Commission, Communication from the Commission to the European Parliament, the Council, the European Economic and Social Committee and the Committee of the Regions on "Enlargement Strategy and Main Challenges 2014–15", COM(2014) 700 final of 8 October 2014, pp. 22 and 50; European Commission, Communication from the Commission to the European Parliament, the Council, the European Economic and Social Committee and the Committee of the Regions on "EU Enlargement Strategy", COM(2015)611 final of 10 November 2015, pp. 12 and 33.

[84] The Caucasus Campaign comprised in fact armed conflicts between the Ottoman Empire and the Russian Empire (later including Azerbaijan, Armenia, the Central Caspian Dictatorship and the British Empire) as part of the Middle Eastern theatre during World War I. The "Armenian Genocide" is intertwined with the events of this Campaign, since Turkish Armenia was depopulated of its entire Christian Armenian population as part of an Ottoman plan to weaken the Russian-Armenian alliance, as only Muslims, who were loyal to Turkey, would remain. See also above, Sect. 1.

more open discussion and perhaps to an official acknowledgment by the Turkish government.[85]

Following on the question asked in Sect. 3 above and the considerations it led to, one might also ask: is a formal recognition of the "Armenian Genocide" an essential condition for Turkey's accession to the EU?

On the one hand, the declarations delivered by several EU Member States Parliaments indicate that such a recognition is not an official precondition for accession, but it is anyhow deemed essential in order to establish Turkey's viability as an open and more transparent democracy.[86] The resolutions of the European Parliament have steadily highlighted the importance of qualifying the Armenian massacres as a genocide: recognition is thus a "favored" (not required nor exigible) precondition for Turkey's accession to the EU and an unavoidable political factor to be taken into account for the enlargement.[87] States wanting to get EU membership should in fact accept and overcome the legacies of their past; the undertaking to promote reconciliation and to resolve bilateral disputes, which is among the main features of the accession process, would be otherwise disregarded.[88]

On the other hand, the recognition of the "Armenian Genocide" as such is formally set outside Article 2 (and Article 49) TEU, and is not one of the Copenhagen criteria. The "Armenian Genocide" cannot even be counted among the Copenhagen political criteria as an element of "Regional Issues and International Obligations" to be assessed in the same way as was done for Croatia's accession to the EU, due to significantly different historical, political and legal conditions.[89] The absolute denial of the Turkish government and especially the outlawing by the Turkish legal order of any accusation or mention of the Armenian massacres as a genocide, seem however not to be alien to Article 2 (and Article 49) TEU and to the Copenhagen criteria themselves. Turkish behaviour seems to fall indirectly within the Copenhagen legal criteria concerning the *acquis* of the Union, through the compulsory nature that should be attributed to Council Framework Decision 2008/913/JHA[90]; and within Article 2 (and Article 49) TEU as well as the Copenhagen political criteria. It should be emphasized that the scope of the terms under Article 301 of the Turkish Penal Code are too wide and vague to the point that this provision constitutes a continuing threat to the exercise of the right to freedom of expression.[91] In this regard, the right to freedom of expression under Article 10 ECHR and Article 11 of the Charter of Fundamental Rights of the European Union must undoubtedly be seen in relation to the "freedom", "democracy", "human

---

[85]See in this sense Souleimanov and Ehrmann (2014), p. 33.

[86]Souleimanov and Ehrmann (2014), p. 27. Cf. above, Sect. 3.

[87]Souleimanov and Ehrmann (2014), p. 27. Cf. above, Sect. 3. See furthermore Rosanò, in this book.

[88]See above, Sect. 4.

[89]Cf. above, Sect. 3.

[90]See above, Sect. 3.

[91]Cf. ECtHR, 25 October 2011, No. 27520/07, *Altuğ Taner Akçam* v. *Turkey*, para. 93.

rights" (including the right to memory) and "pluralism" encompassed both in Article 2 TEU (as recalled by Article 49(1) TEU) and in the Copenhagen political criteria, and also laid down in the Negotiating Framework with Turkey adopted by the European Commission in 2005.[92] Moreover this right, because it is mentioned in Article 10 ECHR and in Article 11 of the Charter, is a part of the heritage of binding values that current and future EU Member States cannot avoid selecting and implementing pursuant to Article 6 TEU.[93] Therefore, it is not the lack of recognition of the Armenian massacres as a genocide by the Turkish government as such that could probably risk compromising (or contribute towards compromising) Turkey's accession to the EU, but rather the imposition at national level of the official governmental belief on the matter through the criminalisation of any dissenting thought. All other internal practices contrary to the exercise of the freedom of expression should be likewise assessed, whatever the argument (not covered by Article 10(2) ECHR and by Article 11 of the Charter of Fundamental Rights of the European Union) put forward to justify them. Moreover similar cases could compel the European Parliament to deny its consent under the special legislative procedure provided for by Article 49(1) TEU.[94]

It is difficult to say whether or not the EU accession negotiations can lead Turkey to a more open discussion and to the development of a greater amount of self-criticism concerning the Armenian massacres. The answer depends upon Turkey's advancement in obtaining EU membership.[95] Turkey has traditionally been a Western-oriented Country and has performed for decades its tasks in political, military and economic European regional organizations.[96] Nevertheless, Turkey–EU relations are now marked with mutual distrust and a deep crisis of confidence. The continuous and growing obstacles to an integration into the EU have contributed to an increase of Euro-skepticism in the Turkish population, and have disappointed the Turkish government, driving it to try out alternatives to the Western world. There is therefore the risk of a double defeat: if EU loses Turkey, it will lose an important partner in the fight against terrorism and in the management of the immigration crisis; if Turkey loses its attachment to the EU, it could go towards an accentuated authoritarianism and reduce its force of attraction in the Middle East.

---

[92]European Commission, Negotiating Framework (Luxembourg, 3 October 2005), point 4.

[93]See above, Sect. 4.

[94]Cf. above, Sect. 3.

[95]See Souleimanov and Ehrmann (2014), p. 33 et seq.

[96]Turkey is a Member State of the Council of Europe since 9 August 1949; of the Conference on Security and Cooperation in Europe (CSCE), later of the Organization for Security and Cooperation in Europe (OSCE), since 25 June 1973; of the European Organization for the Safety of Air Navigation (Eurocontrol) since 1 March 1989. The Country is also part of the North Atlantic Treaty Organization (NATO) and of the Western Europe branch of the Western European and Others Group (WEOG) of the United Nations. It has been an Associate Member of the Western European Union (WEU) from 1992 to its abolition in 2011.

An open and honest dialogue between the Parties should be therefore established in order to start a new form of strategic partnership. As it has been rightly observed, in this renewed political dialogue EU should put more emphasis, among other things, on freedom of expression and bilateral cooperation in the field of education, with the aim of replacing the Turkish nationalistic historiography with a more critical one.[97] The intergovernmental channel which has already contributed to Turkey's overall democratization can offer its support also to overcoming the "Armenian Genocide" issue. Turkey and Armenia could thus live their bilateral relations without resentment and an "ideological stumbling block" for accession to the EU would have been eliminated.[98]

References

Akçam T (2012) The Young Turk's crime against humanity: the Armenian genocide and the ethnic cleansing in the Ottoman Empire. Princeton University Press, Princeton

Arikan A (2006) Turkey and the EU: an awkward candidate for EU membership? 2nd ed. Ashgate Publishing, Farnham, Burlington

Arvanitopoulos C (ed) (2009) Turkey's accession to the European Union: an unusual candidacy. Springer, Berlin, Heidelberg

Baghdjian KK (1987) La confiscation par le gouvernement turc des biens arméniens … dits "abandonnés". Bibliothèque Nationale du Canada, Montreal

Bayraktar S, Seibel W (2004) Das türkische Tätertrauma. Der Massenmord an den Armeniern von 1915 bis 1917 und seine Leugnung. In: Giesen B, Schneider C (eds) Tätertrauma. UVK, Konstanz, pp 381–398

Bloxham D (2005) The great game of genocide: imperialism, nationalism and the destruction of the Ottoman Armenians. Oxford University Press, Oxford

Borgna G (2015) Il genocidio armeno (non) passa in giudicato: in margine al caso *Perinçek*. Diritti umani e diritto internazionale 9:697–704

Bryce J, Toynbee A, Sarafian A (eds) (2000) The treatment of Armenians in the Ottoman Empire, 1915–1916: documents presented to Viscount Grey of Falloden. Princeton, Gomidas

Dadrian VN (2003) The history of the Armenian genocide: ethnic conflict from the Balkans to Anatolia to the Caucasus, 6th edn. Berghahn Books, New York, Oxford

Della Morte G (2016) Bilanciamento tra libertà di espressione e tutela della dignità del popolo armeno nella sentenza *Perinçek* c. *Svizzera* della Corte europea dei diritti umani. Rivista di diritto internazionale 99:183–189

de Waal T (2015) Great Catastrophe: Armenians and Turks in the shadow of genocide. Oxford University Press, Oxford

Engert S (2016) Turkey–Armenia: from denial to excuse? In: Daase C, Engert S, Horelt M-A, Renner J, Strassner R (eds) Apology and reconciliation in international relations. The importance of being sorry. Routledge, Abingdon, New York, pp 218–236

Fischer KH (2010) Der Vertrag von Lissabon. Text und Kommentar zum Europäischen Reformvertrag. Nomos Verlagsgesellschaft, Baden–Baden

Flores M (2015) Il genocidio degli Armeni, 2ª edizione. Il Mulino, Bologna

---

[97]Engert (2016), p. 230.

[98]See Souleimanov and Ehrmann (2014), p. 34; Engert (2016), p. 232.

Garman JJ (2008) The European Union combats racism and xenophobia by forbidding expression: an analysis of the framework decision. University of Toledo Law Review 39:843–860
Gingeras R (2016) Fall of the Sultanate: the great war and the end of the Ottoman Empire, 1908–1922. Oxford University Press, Oxford
Giuva L (2013) Il diritto alla memoria e alle memorie. In: Melograni PS (ed) Manuale dei diritti fondamentali e desiderabili. Mondadori, Milano, pp 113–115
Göçek FM (2015) Denial of violence: Ottoman past, Turkish present and collective violence against the Armenians, 1789–2009. Oxford University Press, Oxford
Hovannisian R (ed) (1992) The Armenian genocide: history, politics, ethics. St. Martin's Press, New York
Kevorkian R (2011) The Armenian genocide: a complete history. I.B. Tauris, London
Lekka A (2007) Legislative provisions of the Ottoman/Turkish Governments regarding minorities and their properties. Mediterr Q 18:135–154
Melson R (1996) Revolution and genocide: on the origins of the Armenian genocide and the holocaust. University of Chicago Press, Chicago
Mitsilegas V (2009a) EU Criminal Law. Hart Publishing, Oxford
Mitsilegas V (2009b) The third wave of third pillar law: which direction for EU Criminal Justice? Eur Law Rev 34:523–560
Müftüler Baç M (2016) Divergent pathways: Turkey and the European Union. Re-thinking the dynamics of Turkish–European Union relations. Barbara Buldrich Publishers, Leverkusen
Nas Ç, Özer Y (eds) (2012) Turkey and the European Union: processes of Europeanisation. Ashgate Publishing, Farnham, Burlington
Osiel MJ (2005) Politiche della punizione, memoria collettiva e diritto internazionale. In: Baldissarra L, Pezzino P (eds) Giudicare e punire. I processi per crimini di guerra tra diritto e politica. L'ancora del Mediterraneo, Napoli, pp 105–118
Pingel I (2010) De Rome à Lisbonne: Commentaire article par article des traités UE et CE, 2ème éd. Dalloz, Bruxelles: Bruylant, Bâle: Helbing Lichtenhahn Verlag, Paris
Priollaud F-X, Siritzky D (2008) Le traité de Lisbonne: Commentaire, article par article, des nouveaux traités européens (TUE et TFUE). La Documentation française, Paris
Renauld B (2010) La décision–cadre 2008/913/JAI du Conseil de l'Union Européenne: du nouveau en matière de lutte contre le racisme? Revue trimestrielle des droits de l'homme 81:119–140
Souleimanov E, Ehrmann M (2014) The issue of the recognition of the Armenian genocide as a political phenomenon. Middle East Rev Int Affairs 18:25–37
Suny RG (2015) "They can live in the desert but nowhere else": a history of the Armenian genocide. Princeton University Press, Princeton
Taubira C (2006) Le droit à la memoire. Cités 25:164–166
Tuncel TK (2015) The judgment of the European Court of Human Rights Grand Chamber on Perinçek v. Switzerland Case in perspective: 1. preliminary remarks; 2. three disqualified arguments and "the prevention of disorder". Center of Eurasian Studies/Avrasya İncelemeleri Merkezi (avim.org.tr)
von Bogdandy A, Kottmann M, Antpöhler C, Dickschen J, Hentrei S, Smrkolj M (2012) Reverse Solange-protecting the essence of fundamental rights against EU Member States. Common Market Law Rev 49:489–519
Voorhoof D (2014) Criminal conviction for denying the existence of the Armenian "genocide" violates freedom of expression. Strasbourg Observers (strasbourgobservers.com)
Voorhoof D (2015) Criminal conviction for denying the Armenian genocide in breach with freedom of expression, Grand Chamber confirms. Strasbourg Observers (strasbourgobservers.com)
Wilson RJ (2014) Restoration of historical memory and dignity for victims of the Armenian genocide: a human rights law approach to effective reparations. Int Crim Law Rev 14:332–342

The European Parliament as the Human Rights Gatekeeper of the Union?

Alessandro Rosanò

Contents

1 Introduction ... 300
2 Turkey's Accession and the Armenian Genocide: The Position of the European Parliament ... 302
3 Turkey's Accession and the Armenian Genocide: The Position of the European Council and the European Commission ... 304
4 Krikorian ... 305
5 Conclusion ... 306
References ... 309

Abstract The question that is addressed in this paper relates to the relevance that the choice made by the Turkish Government not to recognise the Armenian Genocide may have with regard to Turkey's accession to the European Union. On the one hand, the European Parliament considers this to be a key issue, as is confirmed by many resolutions passed over time. On the other hand, in the light of a strictly literal interpretation of the Copenhagen criteria, the European Council and the European Commission have ruled out that the refusal expressed by Turkey to recognise those facts could negatively affect the accession process. The purpose of this paper is to prove that the European Parliament has introduced a new *ad hoc* criterion to be imposed on Turkey because of the gravity of the Armenian genocide, and to provide a further element that may confirm the theory of the development *par autoconstitution* of the European Union legal system.

A. Rosanò (✉)
University of Turin, Turin, Italy
e-mail: alrosano@unito.it

F. Lattanzi and E. Pistoia (eds.), *The Armenian Massacres of 1915–1916 a Hundred Years Later*, Studies in the History of Law and Justice 15,
https://doi.org/10.1007/978-3-319-78169-3_13

1 Introduction

The accession of new States to the European Union (hereinafter EU) may be regarded as the litmus test of the success of the European project, the tangible evidence of the results achieved by a united Europe over the years and the milestone of key events in its history. As this phenomenon has become paramount in EU policies over time,[1] it is easy to understand the reasons behind the choice made by the EU which—like any club worthy of the name—has set some requirements for the accession of other members.

As we know, the eligibility criteria were established in Copenhagen in 1993[2] and later specified in Madrid in 1995 and it is to those criteria that—albeit indirectly—Article 49 TEU refers to.[3] Namely, they are: (a) the stability of institutions guaranteeing democracy, the rule of law, human rights and respect for and protection of minorities (political criteria); (b) the existence of a functioning market economy and the capacity to cope with competitive pressure and market forces within the Union (economic criteria); (c) the ability to take on the obligations deriving from the *acquis communautaire*, including adherence to the aims of political, economic and monetary union; and (d) the fact that the States have created the conditions for their integration through adjustment of their administrative structures.

[1]The European Council has quite often stressed the importance it attaches to the enlargement of the European Union. Over time, there were statements such as: "Enlargement is both a political necessity and a historic opportunity for Europe [because] it will ensure the stability and security of the continent and will thus offer […] new prospects for economic growth and general well-being" (Madrid European Council, 15 and 16 December 1995 – Presidency Conclusions, http://www.europarl.europa.eu/summits/mad1_it.htm#enlarge (accessed 10 August 2017); "Extending the European integration model to encompass the whole of the continent is a pledge of future stability and prosperity" (Luxembourg European Council, 12 and 13 December 1997 – Presidency Conclusions, http://www.europa.eu/rapid/press-release_DOC-97-24_en.pdf (accessed 10 August 2017); "The European Council reaffirms the historic significance of the European Union enlargement process and the political priority which it attaches to the success of that process" (Nice European Council, 7–10 December 2000 – Presidency Conclusions, http://www.europarl.europa.eu/summits/nice1_en.htm#II (accessed 10 August 2017).

[2]Copenhagen European Council, 21 and 22 June 1993 – Presidency Conclusions, http://www.consilium.europa.eu/en/european-council/conclusions/pdf-1993-2003/presidency-conclusions_-copenhagen-european-council_-21-and-22-june-1993/ (accessed 10 August 2017).

[3]Pursuant to Article 49 TEU, "(1) any European State which respects the values referred to in Article 2 and is committed to promoting them may apply to become a member of the Union. The European Parliament and national Parliaments shall be notified of this application. The applicant State shall address its application to the Council, which shall act unanimously after consulting the Commission and after receiving the consent of the European Parliament, which shall act by a majority of its component members. (2) The conditions of eligibility agreed upon by the European Council shall be taken into account. The conditions of admission and the adjustments to the Treaties on which the Union is founded, which such admission entails, shall be the subject of an agreement between the Member States and the applicant State. This agreement shall be submitted for ratification by all the contracting States in accordance with their respective constitutional requirements".

These criteria identify the areas in which the candidate countries must carry out reform and the objectives they have to pursue, laying the foundations of mutual trust with the Member States, and providing an effective guarantee of their institutional, economic, and legal-administrative stability.[4] At the same time, they can be considered as means to protect the European process of integration and diffuse a political, economic and legal model.[5] All the States wishing to join the EU have to comply with those criteria, without any distinction. Therefore, as they have been applied to the countries that came to join the EU in 2004, in 2007 and 2013, so all the pending and future applications will be assessed in the light of the same criteria.

The case of Turkey, whose relations with the European Communities date back to the late fifties,[6] makes no exception. In 2005, the negotiations for accession were opened but, at present, they are at a stalemate.[7] From a geopolitical point of view, there is no doubt that the EU and the Member States have strong interests in expanding the Union to Turkey especially in the light of the problems posed by international terrorism and the crisis of migrants,[8] but the understandable security reasons that lie behind this choice clash with the political, economic, and legal requirements underlying the Copenhagen criteria.[9]

Thus, the question that will be addressed in this paper relates to the relevance of the choice not to recognise the Armenian Genocide and, over time, may take with regard to Turkey's accession to the EU. As a matter of fact, as is explained below, the European Parliament (hereinafter EP) considers this to be a key issue, as is confirmed by a number of resolutions passed over time. This leads many to believe that, should the Turkish government not change its mind, it would not be possible

---

[4]Nascimbene (1992).

[5]Smith (2003). On the enlargement, see Sadurski (2012); Lang (2010); Kochenov (2008); Rizzo (2006); Bifulco (2005); Sanna (2005); Nelli and Feroci (2005); Micheletta (2005); Rizzo (2004); Sinagra (2004); Bonini (2003); Kellerman et al. (2001); Jovanovic (1998).

[6]On the relationship between the European Union and Turkey, see Baracani (2008); Yildiz and Müller (2008); Cerruti (2007); Zijal (2006).

[7]That is because the Turkish government has not agreed on the implementation of the Additional Protocol to the Ankara Agreement (Council Decision No 64/732/EEC of 23 December 1963 on the conclusion of the Agreement establishing an Association between the European Economic Community and Turkey, in OJ 217 of 29 December 1964, p. 3685) with regard to Cyprus. The Ankara Agreement was followed by an Additional Protocol signed in Brussels on 23 November 1970 and concluded, approved, and confirmed on behalf of the Community by Council Regulation (EEC) No 2760/1972 of the Council of 19 December 1972 concluding the additional protocol and the financial protocol signed on 23 November 1970 and annexed to the Agreement establishing an Association between the European Economic Community and Turkey and relating to the measures to be taken for their implementation. On the long negotiations between Turkey and the European Union, see European Commission, Turkey 2015 Report, http://ec.europa.eu/enlargement/pdf/key_documents/2015/20151110_report_turkey.pdf (accessed 10 August 2017); http://ec.europa.eu/enlargement/countries/detailed-country-information/turkey/index_en.htm (accessed 10 August 2017); Panebianco (2005); Kuneralp (2001).

[8]Byman (2016); Nigro (2016); Salomoni (2016); Picone (2015); Santoro (2015).

[9]On the cultural issues related to Turkey's accession, see Susuzlu (2009); Calchi Novati (2001). On the concept of Europe, see Ferraris (2001); Chabod (1959, 2011).

to obtain the consent by the EP as provided under Article 49 TEU (para 1). On the other hand, the European Council and the European Commission seem to have adhered to a strictly literal interpretation of the Copenhagen criteria, therefore ruling out that the refusal expressed by Turkey to recognise the Armenian genocide could negatively affect the accession process (para 3). After addressing the issue of the legal values of the acts adopted by the institutions with regard to this topic, especially as far as the EP resolutions are concerned (para 4), the paper aims to support the idea that the EP has introduced a new *ad hoc* criterion which is imposed on Turkey because of the gravity of the Armenian genocide. In turn, this may be regarded as a feature which confirms the theory of the development *par autoconstitution* of the EU legal system (para 5).

2 Turkey's Accession and the Armenian Genocide: The Position of the European Parliament

In 1987, the members of the EP strongly expressed their beliefs with regard to Turkey's accession to the European Communities and the importance they attached to the recognition of the 1915 Armenian genocide in evaluating whether Turkey should be accepted into the European Community. Indeed, it was stated that the events in 1915–1917 involving the Armenians living in the territory of the Ottoman Empire constitute genocide within the meaning of the UN Convention; that the refusal expressed by the Turkish government had deprived and continued to deprive the Armenian people of the right to their own history; that the recognition of the Armenian genocide by Turkey should have been viewed as a profoundly human act of moral rehabilitation towards the Armenians; that the Armenian question and the question of minorities in Turkey should have been resituated within the framework of relations between Turkey and the European Community; and that the refusal by the Turkish government to acknowledge the genocide was an insurmountable obstacle to consideration of the Turkish application.[10] In addition to that, Turkey was urged to fairly treat the Armenian minority with regard to their identity, language, religion, culture, and school system and preserve the Armenian historical and artistic heritage.[11]

[10]Recitals E and G and paras. 1, 2 and 4 of the European Parliament resolution of 18 June 1987 on a political solution to the Armenian question, in OJ C 190 of 20 July 1987, p. 119. Under para. 4, the reluctance of Turkish government to apply the principles of international law in its disputes with Greece, the maintenance of Turkish occupation forces in Cyprus, the denial of the existence of the Kurdish question, the lack of true parliamentary democracy, and the failure to respect individual and collective freedoms, especially freedom of religion, are identified as insurmountable obstacles to Turkey's accession.

[11]Para. 6 of the above-mentioned resolution. Under paras. 10 and 11, the EP expressed its concern with regard to the difficulties experienced by the Armenian minority in Iran and the Soviet Union.

In addition to that, two resolutions that were subsequently passed must be taken into account. In the former, the EP highlighted a number of political problems Turkey had to deal with before joining the EU. In fact, the EP called on Turkey to solve the Cyprus dispute, stressing that

> a rapid normalisation of relations between Turkey and all EU Member States, including Turkey's recognition of the Republic of Cyprus, is a necessary component of the accession process; and that Turkey's recognition of the Republic of Cyprus can in no way be the subject of the negotiations;

and

> failure to do so will have serious implications for the negotiation process and could even lead to a halting of the negotiation process.[12]

Furthermore, the EP expressed concern about the protection of fundamental rights in Turkey, especially with regard to freedom of opinion and religious freedom.[13] Finally, the EP took a significantly uncompromising position, defining the recognition of the Armenian genocide,

> a prerequisite for accession to the European Union.[14]

In the latter, Turkey was criticized for the slowing down of the reform process,

> as reflected in persistent shortcomings or insufficient progress in particular in the areas of freedom of expression, religious and minority rights, civil-military relations, law enforcement on the ground, women's rights, trade union rights, cultural rights and the swift and correct enforcement of court rulings by State services.[15]

As far as the Armenian genocide is concerned, it was stated that both the Turkish Government and the Armenian Government had to continue their process of reconciliation; the work of researchers, intellectuals and academics working on the issue had to be facilitated, ensuring them access to the historical archives and providing them with all relevant documents; and most of all, although the recognition of the Armenian genocide was not one of the Copenhagen criteria, it was recognized as indispensable for Turkey as a country on the road to membership to come to terms with it and recognise its past.[16]

In 2015, two more resolutions concerning this matter were approved. First, ahead of the 100th anniversary of the Armenian genocide, the EP called on all the

[12]Para. 8 of the European Parliament resolution of 28 September 2005 on the opening of negotiations with Turkey, http://www.europarl.europa.eu (accessed 10 August 2017).

[13]Ibidem, para. 10.

[14]Ibidem, para. 5.

[15]Para. 2 of the European Parliament resolution of 27 September 2006 on Turkey's progress towards accession, http://www.europarl.europa.eu/ (accessed 10 August 2017).

[16]Ibidem, para. 56.

Member States to acknowledge it and encouraged them and the EU institutions to contribute further to its recognition.[17] Then, the EP encouraged Turkey

> to use the commemoration of the centenary of the Armenian Genocide as an important opportunity to continue its efforts, including the opening of the archives, to come to terms with its past, to recognise the Armenian Genocide, and thus to pave the way for a genuine reconciliation between the Turkish and Armenian peoples.[18]

3 Turkey's Accession and the Armenian Genocide: The Position of the European Council and the European Commission

The clash between the position taken by the EP and that expressed by the European Council and the European Commission could not be more evident. Most of all, the silence of the European Council on the Armenian genocide with regard to Turkey's accession could not be more deafening.

In the Presidency Conclusions of the Helsinki European Council (1999), at paragraph 12, Turkey was recognized as a candidate country. Moreover, it was made clear—as mentioned above—that Turkey would have joined the EU on the basis of the same criteria as applied to other candidate States and that it would have benefited from a pre-accession strategy to stimulate and support the reforms deemed necessary, especially with regard to the protection of human rights and the solution of the Cyprus issue.[19]

In 2002, the Copenhagen European Council praised the reform process undertaken by Turkey and pointed out that if Turkey had complied with the political criteria functional to accession, the EU would have opened negotiations without delay.[20]

Two years later, the meeting of Heads of State and Government once again expressed appreciation for the progress made by Turkey in the reform process and invited the Commission to present to the Council a proposal for a framework for negotiations, requesting the Council to agree on that framework so that negotiations

[17]Para. 77 of the European Parliament resolution of 12 March 2015 on the Annual Report on Human Rights and Democracy in the World in 2013 and European Union's policy on the matter, http://www.europarl.europa.eu (accessed 10 August 2017).

[18]Para. 5 of the European Parliament resolution of 15 April 2015 on the centenary of the Armenian Genocide, http://www.europarl.europa.eu (accessed 10 August 2017).

[19]Helsinki European Council, 10 and 11 December 1999 - Presidency Conclusions, http://www.europarl.europa.eu/summits/hel1_it.htm (accessed 10 August 2017).

[20]Copenhagen European Council, 12 and 13 December 2002 – Presidency Conclusions, http://www.consilium.europa.eu/en/european-council/conclusions/pdf-1993-2003/presidency-conclusions_copenhagen-european-council_-12-and-13-december-2002/ (accessed 10 August 2017).

could be opened on October 3, 2005.[21] However, in none of these documents can one find a specific reference to the Armenian genocide and its recognition.

For what concerns the European Commission, it is enough to recall the answers given by Günther Verheugen—European Commissioner for Enlargement in the executive led by Romano Prodi—and Stefan Füle—Commissioner for Enlargement in the second Barroso Commission—to the written questions submitted by some members of the EP with regard to Turkey's accession negotiations and the recognition of the Armenian Genocide: according to the Commission, the topic is not relevant since it is not part of the Copenhagen criteria.[22]

4 Krikorian

A case brought before the Court of First Instance of the European Communities—as it was called at that time—can help understand the legal value of the acts that have been mentioned so far—particularly with regard to the EP resolutions.

In 2003, an association and two natural persons brought an action for damages in which they sought compensation for the non-material harm suffered by them on account of the recognition of Turkey's status as a candidate for accession to the EU. Because of that and because of the accession partnership that was set up by the EU,[23] the EP, the European Council and the European Commission had allegedly infringed the 1987 EP resolution which had clearly set a special condition for Turkey's accession, that is to say, the prior recognition of the Armenian Genocide. According to the applicants, EP resolutions should have been regarded as legal acts which could produce legally binding effects: therefore, the mere fact that the EP resolution had been disregarded sufficiently proved that there had been a serious breach of Community law. That conduct would have been an affront to the

[21]Brussels European Council, 16 and 17 December 2004 – Presidency Conclusions, http://www.consilium.europa.eu/ueDocs/cms_Data/docs/pressData/en/ec/83201.pdf (accessed 10 August 2017).

[22]Written Question E-012658/11 Mario Borghezio (EFD) to the Commission. Failure to recognise the Armenian genocide, OJ C 66 E of March 7 March 2013, p. 119, Written Question E-2038/03 by Miquel Mayoli Raynal (Verts/ALE) to the Commission. Turkey and the denial of the Armenian genocide, OJ C 51 E of 26 February 2004, p. 184, Written Question P-3186/00 by Marie-Arlette Carlotti (PSE) to the Commission, OJ C 151 E, 22 May 2001, p. 87. On the topic, see also Written Question E-0229/01 by Roberto Bigliardo (TDI) to the Commission. Turkey's application for EU membership, OJ C 187 of 3 July 2001, p. 203.

[23]See Council Regulation (EC) No 2500/2001 of 17 December 2001 concerning pre-accession financial assistance for Turkey and amending Regulations (EEC) No 3906/89, (EC) No 1267/1999, (EC) No 1268/1999 and (EC) No 555/2000, OJ L 342 of 27 December 2001, p. 1, Council Regulation (EC) No 390/2001 of 26 February 2001 on assistance to Turkey in the framework of the pre-accession strategy, and in particular on the establishment of an Accession Partnership, OJ L 58 of 28 February 2001, p. 1, Council Decision 2001/235/EC of 8 March 2001 on the principles, priorities, intermediate objectives and conditions contained in the Accession Partnership with the Republic of Turkey, OJ L 85 of 24 March 2001, p. 13.

applicants' dignity as Armenians which would have brought about marginalisation and a feeling of inferiority within the Armenian community.

First of all, the Court of First Instance recalled the settled case-law according to which, for the Community to incur non-contractual liability, three conditions must be satisfied: the illegality of the conduct alleged against the institutions, the fact of damage, and the existence of a causal link between the alleged conduct and the damage complained of.[24] If any of those conditions is not satisfied, the action must be dismissed.

With regard to the recognition of Turkey's status as a candidate for accession to the EU, that was an act of the European Council which, at that time, was not an institution of the Community.[25] As a result, its conduct could not give rise to the non-contractual liability of the Community.

For what concerns the accession partnership, the applicants' claim was based on the fact that the conduct of the institutions would have been unlawful in that it was contrary to the 1987 EP resolution. According to the Court, an EP resolution is a document containing declarations of a purely political nature, which may be amended by the EP at any time. Therefore, it cannot have binding legal consequences for its author and, *a fortiori*, for other institutions.[26]

In the light of the above and in the light of the fact that the applicants were not able to prove the existence of a causal connection between the conduct and the damage, the action was dismissed.[27] This outcome was later confirmed by the Court of Justice.[28]

5 Conclusion

First of all one must underline that the decision passed by the Court seems to be legally unchallengeable as it confirms well-settled case-law and is based on a correct assessment of the legal value of the EP's resolutions. However, this does not mean that there are no other analyses to be carried out.

---

[24]See, among others, Case 4/69 *Lütticke* [1971] ECR 326, paras. 10–11. On the topic, see Craig (2012); Heukels and McDonnell (1997); Venturini (1980).

[25]In light of the reform introduced by the Treaty of Lisbon, and pursuant to Article 13(1) TEU, the European Council is an EU institution but, at the time when the case was brought before the Court of First Instance, it was not considered as part of the institutional framework (see Article 7 of the Treaty establishing the European Community).

[26]EP resolutions are not legally binding, thus the other EU institutions are not obligated to comply with them. However, they are a means to direct the political action of the EU since they can have a political impact on the position of other institutions and, above all, support the action of the European Commission (see, Strozzi and Mastroianni 2013). On the effects of EP resolutions, see Case 230/81 *Luxembourg v European Parliament* [1983] ECR 258.

[27]Case T-346/03 *Krikorian* [2003] ECR II-6040.

[28]Case C-18/04 P *Krikorian* [2004] not published in the ECR.

With specific regard to *Krikorian*, it is true that EP resolutions contain declarations of a merely political nature as it is undeniable that these documents may be amended by the EP at any time. However, one should wonder whether the Court of Justice might come to the same decision should the EP deny its consent to Turkey's accession under Article 49, paragraph 1, TEU. In fact, when it comes to a State's application to become a member of the Union, the Council of the European Union needs to receive EP consent, which is expressed—or denied—in a resolution.[29] In this specific case, the EP resolution would be a binding instrument that would have binding legal consequences for the Council, which could not act, and for the accession process, which would be blocked. This might lead to a very different outcome, as far as the Court of Justice's case-law on non-contractual liability is concerned, but most of all, as far as the enlargement of the EU is concerned. In fact, thanks to the Lisbon Treaty, the EP has been granted a sort of veto power,[30] which would make it possible for its members to make the accession conditional upon the compliance with some new criteria the EP might decide to introduce, should the actual situation require it. This line of reasoning seems to be validated by an analysis of the former Treaty provisions concerning enlargement: In fact, Article 237, first paragraph, of the former Treaty establishing the European Economic Community as amended by the Single European Act and Article 49 of the former Treaty on the European Union provided for a sort of all-or-nothing co-decision procedure, granting the EP the power to assent or dissent with the position adopted by the Council.

In light of what has been underlined earlier in this paper, one can say that the European institutions seem to have reached a consensus on the relevance of the Copenhagen criteria as the main reference for the purpose of new States' accession to the EU. Yet, focusing on the issue of recognition of the Armenian genocide, it is highlighted what the position taken by the EP has constantly been. One can also add that, in the framework of a different institutional reality, it was argued that the denial of genocide is the final stage of genocide itself, because it enshrines impunity for its perpetrators and paves the way for future genocide, whereas the absence of unequivocal and timely condemnation of the Armenian genocide has contributed, to a large extent, to the failure to prevent future crimes against humanity.[31]

---

[29]See European Parliament legislative resolution of 1 December 2011 on the accession to the European Union of the Republic of Croatia, http://www.europarl.europa.eu/ (accessed 10 August 2017).

[30]See Puglia (2014).

[31]Recital C of the European Parliamentary Assembly resolution on the centennial of the Armenian genocide, OJ C 315 of 23 September 2015, p. 23. The Euronest Parliamentary Assembly was established in Brussels in 2011 as a meeting place between the EU and Armenia, Azerbaijan, Belarus, Georgia, Moldova, and Ukraine within the Eastern partnership. Both members of the EP and representatives of the parliaments of the six countries involved take part in its activities. On this topic, see the Constituent Act of the Parliamentary Assembly Euronest, OJ C 198 of 6 July 2011, p. 4.

It also seems appropriate to recall that the European Council urged the candidate countries to cooperate in order to promote good neighbourly relations.[32] With specific reference to Turkey, it was highlighted that the progress of the negotiations was conditional upon not only the compliance with the Copenhagen criteria but also the unequivocal commitment to good neighbourly relations and resolution of any border issues in conformity with the principle of peaceful settlement of disputes in accordance with the United Nations Charter.[33] Therefore, it seems quite difficult to speak of a normalization of relations between Armenia and Turkey when the latter has not recognized the Armenian genocide.[34]

Thus, it is doubtful that Turkey will join the EU without first having complied with the EP resolutions. In fact, the EP has risen to the status of moral authority of the Union thanks to its activism and the choices it has made with reference to the most important international issues, especially those related to the protection of human rights. For what concerns enlargement, it is worth remembering that, in 1969, it was the EP that prevented the European Communities from maintaining friendly relations with Greece, stressing that fundamental freedoms should have first be restored in that country.[35] That happened at a time when the EP powers were particularly limited,[36] yet this did not prevent the assembly from taking such a strong position. Thus, *a fortiori*, one can hardly believe that today, in a completely reformed institutional framework, the EP would give its approval to Turkey's accession as provided under Article 49 TEU while the Turkish government has not acknowledged the Armenian genocide and, in general, where a State has not complied with the ideas expressed by the EP with regard to the protection of human rights. It is apparent that the recognition of that event and those values has become a non-negotiable condition for entry.

Finally, this topic should be placed in the context of a broader discussion which concerns the process of development *par autoconstitution* of the European

---

[32]Essen European Council, 9 and 10 December 2004 – Presidency Conclusions, http://www.europarl.europa.eu/summits/ess1_en.htm#ext (accessed 10 August 2017).

[33]European Commission, Turkey – Negotiating Framework, 3 October 2005, http://ec.europa.eu/enlargement/pdf/turkey/st20002_05_tr_framedoc_en.pdf (accessed 10 August 2017).

[34]On this point it should be considered that the EP too has called for a normalization of relations between Turkey and Armenia: see paragraph 8 of the European Parliament resolution of 14 April 2016 on the 2015 Report on Turkey, http://www.europarl.europa.eu/sides/getDoc.do?pubRef=-//EP//TEXT+TA+P8-TA-2016-0133+0+DOC+XML+V0//EN (accessed 10 August 2017) and para. 49 of the European Parliament resolution of 10 June 2015 on the 2014 Commission Progress Report on Turkey, http://www.europarl.europa.eu/sides/getDoc.do?pubRef=-//EP//TEXT+TA+P8-TA-2015-0228+0+DOC+XML+V0//EN (accessed 10 August 2017).

[35]Raspadori (2007).

[36]One should remember that, without prejudice to the functions of political control that it already carried out, the EP was given the power to reject the Community budget with the Treaty of Brussels of 22 July 1975. With regard to the EP powers at the time, see Pocar (1981). On the role of the EP, see Delledonne (2014); Fasonea and Lupo (2012); Fabbrini (2011); Piroddi (2011); Raspadori (2009); Mangiameli (2008); Pinelli (2005); Ninatti (2004); Dìez Parra (2002); Garabello (1998).

supranational legal system.[37] The Court of Justice of the European Union has played a key role in this process thanks to a number of judgments it has passed over time, starting with *van Gend en Loos* and *Costa v. ENEL*,[38] but one should also take into proper account how the EP has been able to gradually achieve a significant position in that process. For instance, one may think of the approval of the Draft Treaty on European Union (so-called Spinelli Treaty) of 1984,[39] the practice of the trialogue and the way the European political parties identified the candidates to the post of President of the European Commission before the European elections of 2014. Initiatives of this kind—which are neither expressly permitted nor expressly prohibited by the Treaties, and should be qualified as *praeter legem*—have helped shape the European Union legal system almost independently from the constituent power conferred on the Member States by the Treaties, thus further enhancing its *sui generis* feature.

Therefore, the position expressed by the European Parliament with regard to Turkey's accession to the EU and the recognition of the Armenian genocide should be regarded not only as a brave choice in favour of a higher ideal of justice, but also as a further step in the process of development *par autoconstitution* that has constantly marked the history of European integration.

References

Baracani E (2008) Unione europea e democrazia in Turchia. Rubbettino, Soveria Mannelli

Bifulco D (2005) Com'è difficile dirsi 'europei' … Spunti di riflessione circa l'art. 49 del Trattato UE e l'allargamento dell'Unione europea agli Stati dell'Europa centro-orientale. Rassegna di diritto pubblico europeo 4:11–53

Bonini M (2003) La costruzione della 'nuova' Europa: l'impatto dell'allargamento a est sulla cornice giuridica dell'Unione e della Comunità europea. Rivista italiana di diritto pubblico comunitario 13:271–275

Byman D (2016) ISIS goes global. Foreign Affairs 95:76–85

Calchi Novati G (2001) Un candidato controverso e la forza della Storia. In: Novati GC, Di Casola MA (eds) L'Europa e i ruoli della Turchia. Giuffrè, Milano

Cerruti T (2007) L'apertura dei negoziati di adesione all'Unione europea della Turchia e della Croazia. Quaderni costituzionali 27:93–112

Chabod F (1959) Storia dell'idea di Europa. Laterza, Bari-Roma

Chabod F (2011) Idea d'Europa e civiltà moderna. Sette saggi inediti. Carocci editore, Roma

Cortese B (2014) À la recherche d'un parcours d'autoconstitution de l'ordre juridique interindividuel européen: essay d'une lecture pluraliste 50 ans après van Gend en Loos et Costa c. ENEL. In: Cortese B (ed) Studi in onore di Laura Picchio Forlati. G. Giappichelli editore, Torino, pp 301–339

Craig P (2012) EU administrative law. Oxford University Press, Oxford

Dìez Parra I (2002) Il Parlamento europeo nel trattato di Nizza. Il diritto dell'Unione europea 7:368–382

[37]See Picchio Forlati (1999).

[38]See Cortese (2014).

[39]Draft Treaty establishing the European Union, OJ C 77 of 19 March 1984, p. 33.

Delledonne G (2014) Elezione del Parlamento europeo e politicizzazione dell'Unione di nuovo al vaglio del Bundesverfassungsgericht. Quaderni costituzionali 3:690–693
Ferraris LV (2001) La geografia e i valori dell'Europa di fronte all'allargamento. In: Novati GC, Di Casola MA (eds) L'Europa e i ruoli della Turchia. Giuffrè, Milano, pp 103–117
Fasone C, Lupo N (2012) Il Parlamento europeo alla luce delle novità introdotte nel Trattato di Lisbona e nel suo regolamento interno. Studi sull'integrazione europea 7:329–357
Fabbrini F (2011) La composizione del Parlamento europeo dopo il Trattato di Lisbona. Rivista trimestrale di diritto pubblico 3:787–802
Garabello R (1998) I nuovi poteri del Parlamento europeo nel quadro delle riforme istituzionali apportate dal Trattato di Amsterdam. La comunità internazionale 53:271–294
Heukels T, McDonnell A (eds) (1997) The action for damages in community law. Wolters Kluwer, The Hague
Jovanovic MN (1998) 'Festina lente': prospettive e limiti dell'allargamento ad Est dell'Unione europea. La comunità internazionale 53:529–544
Kellerman AE, de Zwaan JW, Czuczai J (2001) EU enlargement: The constitutional impact at EU and national level. Springer, The Hague
Kochenov D (2008) EU enlargement and the failure of conditionality: pre-accession conditionality in the fields of democracy and the rule of law. Wolters Kluwer, Aalphenaan den Rijn
Kuneralp S (2001) Joining the European Union: a process underway. In: Novati GC, Di Casola MA (eds) L'Europa e i ruoli della Turchia. Giuffrè, Milano, pp 65–72
Lang A (2010) La politica di allargamento dell'Unione europea. Studi sull'integrazione europea 5:477–491
Mangiameli S (2008) Il ruolo del Parlamento europeo e il principio della democrazia rappresentativa. Teoria del diritto e dello Stato 1(3):491–509
Micheletta L (2005) Ex pluribus… 25 e più: l'allargamento dell'Unione europea in una prospettiva storica. La comunità internazionale 60:245–267
Nascimbene B (1992) La procedura di adesione all'Unione europea. In: Ganino M, Venturini G (eds) L'Europa di domani: verso l'allargamento dell'Unione. Giuffrè, Milano, pp 9–10
Nelli Feroci F (2005) L'Unione europea: tra la crisi del Trattato costituzionale e i dilemmi dell'allargamento. La comunità internazionale 60:597–606
Nigro R (2016) La risoluzione del Consiglio di sicurezza delle Nazioni Unite n. 2249 (2015) e la legittimità dell'uso della forza contro l'ISIS in base al diritto internazionale. Diritti umani e diritto internazionale 10:137–156
Ninatti S (2004) Le attribuzioni del Parlamento europeo nel trattato costituzionale. Quaderni costituzionali 24:870–874
Panebianco S (2005) L'allargamento dell'Unione al Mediterraneo. In: Scartezzini R, Milanese JO (eds) L'allargamento dell'UE nello scenario geopolitico europeo. Franco Angeli, Milano, pp 128–135
Picchio Forlati L (1999) Il diritto dell'Unione europea fra dimensione internazionale e transnazionalità. Jus 1999:461–473
Picone P (2015) Unilateralismo e guerra contro l'ISIS. Rivista di diritto internazionale 98:5–27
Pinelli C (2005) Ruolo e poteri del Parlamento europeo secondo il Trattato costituzionale europeo. Il diritto dell'Unione europea 10:171–185
Piroddi P (2011) Il Parlamento europeo nel Trattato di Lisbona tra democrazia rappresentativa e democrazia partecipativa. Rivista italiana di diritto pubblico comunitario 21:801–837
Pocar F (1981) *Parlamento europeo*. In: Enciclopedia del diritto, vol. XXXI. Giuffrè, Milano, pp 864–866
Puglia M (2014) Commento all'art. 49 TUE. In: Tizzano A (ed) Trattati dell'Unione europea. Giuffrè, Milano, p 337
Raspadori F (2007) La politica estera dell'Unione europea: istituzioni e strumenti di pace. Morlacchi, Perugia, p 122
Raspadori F (2009) Il deficit di rappresentatività del Parlamento europeo: limiti e soluzioni. Studi sull'integrazione europea 4:121–132

Rizzo A (2004) L'allargamento ad Est dell'Unione europea: Problematiche del Trattato di adesione. Editoriale Scientifica, Napoli
Rizzo A (2006) Elementi di approfondimento e sviluppo del diritto comunitario e dell'Unione europea nel processo di allargamento. Studi sull'integrazione europea 1:281–307
Sadurski W (2012) Constitutionalism and the enlargement of Europe. Oxford University Press, Oxford
Salomoni F (2016) Turchia, migrazioni e crisi siriana. Il Mulino 483:173–181
Sanna C (2005) L'allargamento dell'Unione europea, la libera circolazione delle persone e la cooperazione nel settore della giustizia e affari interni. Rivista di diritto internazionale privato e processuale 41:282–287
Santoro D (2015) La Turchia, cuscinetto tra profughi siriani e 'Fortezza Europa'. Limes 6:173–184
Sinagra A (2004) Allargamento dell'Unione europea e cooperazione giuridica internazionale. Rivista di studi politici internazionali 71:403–414
Smith KE (2003) The evolution and application of EU membership conditionality. In: Cremona M (ed) The enlargement of the European Union. Oxford University Press, Oxford, pp 106–107
Strozzi G, Mastroianni R (2013) Diritto dell'Unione europea. Parte istituzionale. G. Giappichelli editore, Torino
Susuzlu S (2009) The identity clash of the European Union and Turkey. A cultural approach. VDM Verlag, Saarbrücken
Venturini G (1980) La responsabilità extracontrattuale delle Comunità europee. Giuffrè, Milano
Yildiz K, Müller M (2008) The European Union and Turkish accession. Pluto Press, Human Rights and the Kurds. London-Ann Arbour
Zijal U (2006) L'ingresso della Turchia nell'Unione europea. Rivista della cooperazione giuridica internazionale 8:167–171

The EU and the Turkish Recognition of the Armenian "Genocide" in the Broader Framework of the EU External Action: A Tale of Possibilities Yet to Be Explored

Emanuela Pistoia

Contents

1 Introduction ... 314
2 The Affaire of the Recognition of the "Genocide" in EU/Turkey Bilateral Relations: A Few Weak Traces in the Community's Association with Turkey Before the Treaty of Maastricht ... 315
3 Availability of Tools Versus Lack of Action Post Treaty of Maastricht ... 319
4 The Union and Turkey/Armenia Relations: Watching from a Distance ... 323
5 Conclusions ... 328
References ... 330

Abstract Throughout decades of partnership, the European Union (EU) has never opened a dialogue with Turkey regarding its refusal to recognise the 1915–1916 "genocide." This paper evaluates this lack of action against a multilevel legal background: in bilateral relations with Turkey, the European Economic Community lacked powers in the field of foreign policy until the Treaty of Maastricht, although an association agreement was operational; since 1993, a full-fledged external-action machinery became available; in multilateral relations, the EU developed a policy vis-à-vis its Eastern neighbourhood, which evolved over the years. As remarkable as it may be as the only act produced outside the framework of Turkey's accession process, the European Parliament's resolution on the "genocide" centenary also constitutes a missed opportunity. Despite the current difficult stage of relations between Turkey and the EU, some tools towards a possible solution are still available.

E. Pistoia (✉)
University of Teramo, Teramo, Italy
e-mail: epistoia@unite.it

F. Lattanzi and E. Pistoia (eds.), *The Armenian Massacres of 1915–1916 a Hundred Years Later*, Studies in the History of Law and Justice 15,
https://doi.org/10.1007/978-3-319-78169-3_14

1 Introduction

Two things are crystal clear to anyone who is even minimally familiar with the discourse on the Armenian massacres of 1915–1916: that Turkey has constantly refused to admit that a "genocide" of the Armenian people took place while the former Ottoman government bears precise responsibilities for its planning and execution, and that the Armenian community all around the world, including but not at all limited to the Republic of Armenia, steadily struggles for such an admission.

Turkey's position is in itself a breach of the obligation to provide satisfaction for the international wrongdoings committed by the Ottoman Empire in connection to the 1915–1916 massacres,[1] as well as a breach of a self-standing right to memory which is emerging in general international law over the last decades.[2] Yet it also brings about breaches of other secondary obligations of reparation[3] and, even more importantly, several breaches of primary international obligations imputable to Turkey. In 1926, the newly-born Republic passed legislation through which it got directly involved in the follow-up activities of the 1915–1916 massacres.[4] In later decades and still in current times, the refusal to "recognise the Armenian genocide" is behind Turkey's breach of civil, political and cultural rights, a number of which are related to the memory of Armenians, as described in a recent report on memorialization processes developed in the framework of the United Nations Human Rights Council.[5]

Far from being forgotten history, the disagreement between Turkey and the Armenians still has severe consequences on the current relationship between the two States: they have no diplomatic relations and their border is closed. Admittedly, the "genocide *affaire*" is not alone in keeping the two countries far apart: the other hot dossier is the conflict in Nagorno-Karabakh, as better explained below. Yet it certainly plays a huge role in keeping their relationship icy. This state of affairs in turn deeply affects the overall international relations of small and landlocked Armenia, as the isolation from neighbouring dynamic Turkey makes it vital for the Caucasian State to eagerly pursue alternative commercial partnerships to develop a languishing economy.

Turkey has been a partner of the European Union (EU) for decades, beyond the accession process, which started officially only in 2005. Soon after Armenia gained independence from the former Soviet Union, in 1991, it developed relations with

[1]See, in this book, Lattanzi and Gianelli in relation to the international law applicable to the massacres; Lattanzi and Latino for the recognition of the relevant international wrongdoings as a form of satisfaction due by Turkey as the successor State of the Ottoman Empire.

[2]Reading (2011); Latino, in this book.

[3]Lattanzi and, extensively, Donat-Cattin in this book.

[4]Lattanzi, in this book.

[5]Report of the Special Rapporteur in the field of cultural rights, Farida Shaheed – Memorialization processes, A/HRC/25/49, 23 January 2014, especially paras. 45–46.

the EU, which led to the signature of a bilateral Partnership and Cooperation Agreement in 1999.

Against this background, it is interesting to consider the Union's stance on the issue. Given that the European Council and the Commission chose to keep Turkey's refusal to "recognise the genocide" out of the accession process,[6] has it ever been given room in another context? On top of that, has the Union ever taken steps to pursue the right of memory that is apparently due to Armenians? Concerning the tensions between Turkey and the Armenians and Armenia, has the Union been ignoring the dispute? Or has it ever sought to make a reconciliatory effort?

The present essay is devoted to assessing the Union's course of action vis-à-vis the foregoing options. It will consider the legal toolkit available to the Union and its use in the bilateral relations with Turkey as well as in policies towards the Eastern neighbourhood. Due attention will be paid to the major changes that this legal toolkit has undergone over the years.

2 The Affaire of the Recognition of the "Genocide" in EU/Turkey Bilateral Relations: A Few Weak Traces in the Community's Association with Turkey Before the Treaty of Maastricht

Unlike States and typically like international organizations, the EU takes action on the grounds of competences and powers and with a view towards pursuing objectives respectively set out in its establishing Treaties. Hence, while for States the decision on addressing the Armenian "genocide" affaire is entirely a matter of discretion and policy, for the EU it is, besides that, also a matter of consistency with the Treaties' objectives and values and extent of competences and powers. At the present stage of the European integration, the latter is soon settled, as the topic fits within the external action of the Union, i.e., either into its common foreign policy (CFSP) or within one of the areas covered by Part Five of the Treaty of the Functioning of the European Union (TFEU), depending on the specific action under consideration. For instance, urging the Turkish government to fully acknowledge the extent and the real features of the Armenian massacres is a political move that falls within the scope of the CFSP; conditionality aimed at that purpose, or alternatively at having Turkey improve the treatment of the Armenian minority and cultural heritage or respect freedom of expression in the matter, etc., would be covered by the applicable external policy (commercial policy, development, association agreements). I will further discuss this point in the next Section, since the Union was conferred the powers to take certain actions and pursue certain purposes only in the Nineties.

[6]In this book, Simone and Rosanò.

It follows that the earlier lack of action in connection with the Armenian "genocide" affaire could be justified based on the said lack of powers, particularly if assuming that, being an international organization, the then European Economic Community (EEC) had no full legal personality in international law. Such a concept of international capacity of international organizations was first put forward by the International Court of Justice in 1949[7] and is apparently the most widely accepted in legal literature. Yet the EEC carried out a number of activities in its external relations with no basis whatsoever in its establishing treaty, thus providing good evidence to the contrary concept of international capacity of international organizations, sharing the same preconditions and requirements as States'.[8] However, even in this perspective the EEC's lack of action with regard to the Turkish recognition of the Armenian "genocide" may have a legal justification: in fact, human rights awareness in the EEC's external relations arose only in the early Nineties.[9] Moreover, in the absence of explicit powers, a dispute arising from events that had occurred decades earlier and attributable to States that no longer existed, even including the EEC's follow-up actions regarding human-rights breaches by modern Turkey, obviously did not make the top of the Community's international agenda.

Interestingly, in the late Eighties/early Nineties the EEC's Member States took several diplomatic steps in connection with human rights abuses perpetrated by third States in the framework of the European Political Cooperation (EPC): public statements, public and confidential démarches.[10] They constitute implementation of the EPC's Declaration on Human Rights, adopted in 1986. This practice is perfectly coherent with the *Community*'s lack of action vis-à-vis Turkey regarding the Armenian massacres, as long as it could have consisted of diplomatic steps. Instead, the parallel lack of action in the framework of the EPC cannot be deemed fully consistent with the practice in this area, which focused on current breaches of human rights: as recalled in the Introduction, Turkey's refusal to "recognise the Armenian genocide" did bring about several contemporary breaches of civil, political and cultural rights.

Turning now to look more closely at EEC/Turkey relations pre-Nineties, the Ankara Agreement was concluded as early as 1963 on the basis of former Article 238 of the Treaty of Rome, which enabled the Community to conclude association

[7]ICJ, Advisory Opinion of 11 April 1949, *Reparation for Injuries Suffered in the Service of the United Nations*, ICJ Reports 1949, para. 179.

[8]Gianelli (2004a, b), pp. 102–107.

[9]European Council, Declaration on Human Rights, Annex V to the Presidency Conclusions, 28–29 June 1991. See Bartels (2005); Rossi (2010), pp. 519–522.

[10]King (1999), pp. 316–318. The Author clarifies that public statements and *démarches* were used as joint protests at human rights abuses, the latter when the situation in a particular country had grown serious. Public statements were rarely used to praise improvements in the human rights situation in a particular country.

agreements with third States.[11] For decades, Turkey's negative attitude vis-à-vis the Armenian "genocide" affaire did not play a role in slowing down the implementation of the Ankara Agreement, i.e., Turkey's approach process to the Community in view of a future accession. In other words, Turkey's reluctance to take responsibility for the Armenian massacres and to otherwise value the Armenian identity was never regarded as non-compliance with democratic principles and human rights, which was under scrutiny for other potential candidates associated with the Community already at that time. This inaction marked a difference with the 1961 Association Agreement with Greece, whose implementation was slowed down, if not completely suspended, under the Junta rule on such grounds. However, the overall political situation in Greece in the early Seventies was not comparable to the Turkish refusal to "recognise the Armenian genocide." At that time such a refusal, including its repercussions in terms of breach of freedom of expression and treatment of the Armenian minority, did not offer a straightforward link to democratic principles: the Armenian component of Turkish society was very small and Armenia was part of the Soviet Union, with little possibility for its population to interact with the outer world, while the Armenian diaspora did not appear to be very organized.

In addition to the lack of consequences on the Association Agreement, for decades not a move was taken within or outside the Association Council towards calling upon Turkey to admit the responsibilities of the Ottoman Empire for the Armenian massacres, as well as its own for the follow-ups of the massacres and for the subsequent breaches of human rights related thereto. Nor was the implementation of the Ankara Agreement affected whatsoever by the Turkish denial of the Armenian "genocide" on grounds of general international law. Possibly, the EEC might have contemplated countermeasures or even suspension of the treaty as consequences of human rights breaches carried out by Turkey.[12] This line of action would have been consistent with the Community's early practice; as an international legal subject, the EEC was surely an addressee of general international law norms, whatever concept of international legal personality one may prefer.

In the light of the foregoing remarks, it makes perfect sense that Turkey's refusal to recognise the Armenian "genocide" made its debut in Turkey/EEC relations as soon as Turkey applied for full membership of the Community. As explained in previous chapters,[13] the European Parliament (EP) passed a resolution on the matter shortly after Turkey put forward an official application to join the EEC, on 18 June 1987. The resolution firmly placed it in the context of Turkey's accession process:

---

[11]Council Decision, of 23 December 1963, on conclusion of the agreement creating an association between the European Economic Community and Turkey, OJ L 217, 29.12.1964, p. 3685. Article 238 later became Article 310 of the Treaty on the European Community and it currently corresponds to Article 217 TFEU.

[12]Gianelli (1997), pp. 791–800.

[13]Simone, Rosanò.

> The Parliament [...] [b]elieves that the refusal by the present Turkish Government to acknowledge the genocide against the Armenian people committed by the Young Turk government [and three other factors] [...] are insurmountable obstacles to consideration of the possibility of Turkey's accession to the Community (para 4).

Indeed, that resolution also put forward suggestions to deal with the issue in the context of the Association Agreement, by calling on the Community to extend it

> to the cultural field so that the remains of Christian or other civilizations such as the ancient classical, Hittite, Ottoman, etc., in that country are preserved and made generally accessible (para 9).

Interestingly, with the then-imminent entry into force of the Single European Act within weeks, on 1 July 1987, the Parliament was to acquire a crucial new role in the conclusion (and obviously the modification) of association agreements: from the former one of merely providing its opinion (which was normally sought only *after* the Council's decision!),[14] to that of *approving* such agreements in advance, as per the amendment of Article 238 of the Treaty of Rome. The amended provision did not confer a formal value to the Parliament's proposal, yet it surely increased its political weight. Needless to say, no amendment to the Ankara Agreement was ever proposed as a follow-up to the Parliament's above-indicated suggestion.

The 1987 resolution also identified a number of actions that Turkey should have taken in favour of the Armenian people. It included an invitation upon the Community to consider how it could contribute to a Turkish effort, which the Parliament urged, to ensure a "fair treatment" of the Armenian minority in the country (para 6).

All of those measures were clearly tools envisaged to soften Turkey's position vis-à-vis the past and to try and change the discourse on the Armenian massacres in the country. Among the institutions to which the resolution should be forwarded, the Parliament notably mentioned the EEC/Turkey Association Council (para 15). However, given the traditional inherent link of the association of third countries to their future accession to the Community/Union especially in the past decades, those provisions cannot be deemed as the Parliament's (unsuccessful) effort to trigger a dialogue on the recognition of the Armenian "genocide" outside of the framework of the Turkish accession process.

In any event, the Association Council did not bother to take the resolution into account.

The next time the issue surfaced within the Union, namely by means of another Parliamentary resolution, in 2005, it was again in connection with Turkey's membership ambitions.[15]

---

[14]Pocar (1991), pp. 70–71.

[15]Resolution adopted on 8 September 2005.

3 Availability of Tools Versus Lack of Action Post Treaty of Maastricht

Since the inclusion of the CFSP in the European integration process, the Union acquired all necessary tools to engage in a dialogue with Turkey aimed at changing its position on the Armenian "genocide" issue.

In terms of competences, in the framework of the CFSP the Union became capable of making statements and using political pressure to influence the Turkish government. Although the Treaty of Lisbon made the CFSP more advanced and sophisticated, those moves were certainly feasible already under the Treaty of Maastricht.

In terms of inspiring principles and purposes, since the outset the CFSP was aimed at developing and consolidating democracy and respect of human rights and fundamental freedoms.[16] The recognition of the Armenian "genocide" by the successor State of the Ottoman Empire clearly has strong connections with both. Knowing and acknowledging the truth about massive human rights violations perpetrated in the past is essential to democracy, especially when the victims belonged to a minority group, and the political and constitutional identity of the State where the atrocities were perpetrated (*rectius*, whose authorities are responsible for perpetrating the atrocities) mainly relies on the majority group. Such acknowledgement is the long-term tool to quell nationalism and hence to favour the consolidation of a balanced society and stable institutions. Likewise, taking responsibility for the Armenian "genocide" is heavily related to human rights: both indirectly, as a reparation to tremendous human rights' abuses, and directly, as an expression of the right to memory of that minority. Moreover, other well-established rights are affected by Turkish denial. For instance, over the decades the denial has regularly led to serious breaches of the right of expression, even in the form of criminal sanctions for the dissenting press/authors, as well as of cultural and minority rights.

To give a full picture, I should also mention that the Treaty of Lisbon added "international law principles" to the values at which the Union's external actions should be aimed.[17] Moreover, the TEU currently details the principles upon which such actions should be based, in Article 21. They include the indivisibility of

---

[16]Article J.1 (later Article 11), para. 1, last indent, of the Treaty of Maastricht. Since the Treaty of Lisbon, developing and consolidating democracy and respect of human rights and fundamental freedoms are purposes of the Union's external action (Article 21(2)(b) TEU), the CFSP being a part thereof (Articles 23–46 TEU). The CFSP should pursue the purposes of the Union's external action (Article 23 TEU). On the EU's actions aimed at the protection of human rights in the early years of the CFSP, Flauss (1999), pp. 145–156; (1999), pp. 324–335. On the central role of human rights already in the European Political Cooperation (EPC), King (1999), pp. 316–324.

[17]Article 21(2)(b) TEU.

human rights, respect for human dignity as well as for the principles of the United Nations and international law.[18]

To date, the Union has never taken advantage of its CFSP tools in its relations with Turkey, which have been monopolized by the accession process, especially after the accession negotiations officially started, in 2005. That year, the European Parliament passed another resolution on the matter: unsurprisingly, it was entirely related to Turkey's membership ambitions.[19]

From the point of view of the present essay, the Parliamentary resolution passed on the occasion of the "Genocide" centenary, on 15 April 2015, is more interesting. It is a straightforward and emotional text. After commending the statements of President Erdoğan and Prime Minister Davutoğlu "offering condolences and recognising atrocities," it encourages Turkey to take further steps in that direction[20] and to comply with its obligations on the protection of cultural heritage.[21] Yet, the resolution has nothing but a moral value. In legal terms, it does not convey the Union's point of view and will on the matter; through it, the Parliament speaks for itself, not on behalf of the Union. The reason is that the Council takes decisions that "define the approach of the Union to a particular matter of a geographic or a thematic nature" (Article 29 TEU). Moreover, the High Representative represents the Union for matters related to the foreign common and security policy and expresses the Union positions in international fora (Article 27 TEU).

However, the Parliament does not entirely lack tools. For instance, under Article 36 TEU the European Parliament may address questions or make recommendations to the Council: rather than putting forward recommendations to Turkey, through an act that has no legal value based on the Treaty for Turkey, the "Centenary" resolution should have urged the Council to recommend certain actions to Turkey. This would not have been binding on the Council, but at least it would have had a legal value. Instead, the hidden face of the "Centenary resolution" is that of a missed opportunity.

Also, in the aftermath of the Maastricht Treaty the EEC expanded the scope and the purposes of association agreements in such a way as to try and build up a common framework of values and a political partnership with associated countries.[22] A staple of the new trend is the "essential element" clause, i.e., a provision stating that respect for the democratic principles and human rights as proclaimed in the 1948 Universal Declaration and defined in the Helsinki Final Act and in the Charter of Paris for a new Europe, as well as respect for international law, the rule of law and the principles of market economy, constitute an "essential element" of the agreement. Such phrasing echoes Article 60 of the Vienna Convention on the Law of the Treaties, which allows the suspension or the termination of a treaty as a

[18]Cremona (2011), p. 280.

[19]Resolution adopted on 8 September 2005.

[20]Para. 5.

[21]Para. 7.

[22]Cremona (2011), p. 292; Cannizzaro (2015), p. 380.

result of a material breach thereof.[23] The purpose of the clause is precisely to lay down a ground for suspending an association agreement should the counterparty of the Union and its Member States seriously disregard democratic principles or breach human rights, international law principles and/or the rule of law. Interestingly, the "essential element" clause was included even in association agreements with candidate countries whose respect for the said principles was already monitored (or was to be monitored) in the framework of the accession negotiations. For instance, in the Stabilisation and Association Agreement (SAA) with Croatia, signed on 29 October 2001 and entered into force on 1 February 2005, a classic "essential element" clause was included in Article 2.[24] Upon signature, Croatia was only months away from becoming a candidate country, as foreshadowed by the conclusion of the SAA itself.[25] Accordingly, Croatia's advancement in the areas covered by the clause was assessed in the framework of the accession process.[26] The European Council's decision on Croatia's status as a candidate State, on 17–18 June 2004, made the cooperation with the International Tribunal for the Former Yugoslavia (ICTY) a condition for officially starting negotiations as an essential part of the said advancement.[27] Specifically, such a cooperation was part of the political criteria for membership.

[23]The Court of Justice noted that the human rights clause could prove "an important factor for the exercise of the right to have a development cooperation agreement suspended or terminated where the non-member country has violated human rights": Case C-268/94 *Portugal* v. *Council* [1996] ECR I-6177, para. 27. In legal literature, Brandtner and Rosas (1998), p. 474; Flauss (1999), pp. 161–162; Gianelli (2004a, b), p. 102.

[24]OJ L 26, 28.1.2005, p. 3. The Council of the European Union decided to systematically apply conditionality in its relations with all countries in South-Eastern Europe in 1997: Council Conclusions on the Application of Conditionality with a View to Developing a Coherent EU Strategy for the Relations with the Countries in the Region, 2003rd Council Meeting – General Affairs, Luxembourg 29–30 April 1997, Annex III. The purpose was to promote "democracy, the rule of law, higher standards of human and minority rights", as well as transformation towards market economy and greater cooperation between the concerned countries. At that time the concerned countries (Albania, Bosnia-Herzegovina, Croatia, FYROM and FRY) were without association agreements and conditions applied to trade preferences, financial assistance, economic cooperation and contractual relations. The Stabilization and Association Process was created in 1999 with the purpose of providing a solid framework to the Western Balkans countries' motivation to carry out the reforms that the Union expected from them. Hence, conditionality was made a cornerstone of the process and extended to SAAs.

[25]Schenker (2008), p. 1. The Author underlines that Croatia was the only country included in the Stabilization and Association process at combining full implementation of a SAA with application as a candidate State (p. 6).

[26]Cf. especially European Commission, Croatia – 2005 Progress Report, COM(2005) 561 final, 9 November 2005, pp. 10–34 and, in parallel, 2nd Meeting of the EU-Croatia Stabilisation and Association Council, Luxembourg, 10 April 2006, Joint Press Release. The accession negotiations with Croatia and with Turkey were the first to include a specific chapter on fundamental rights (along with judiciary): Editorial Comments (2012), p. 481 et seq.

[27]Presidency Conclusions of the Brussels European Council (17–18 June 2004), para. 35, and, explicitly, Presidency Conclusions of the Brussels European Council (16–17 December 2004), para. 16.

The Union institutions went so far as to postpone the opening of the accession negotiations until a Tribunal Chief Prosecutor's report declared that Croatia's cooperation with ICTY had become satisfactory, on 3 October 2005.[28] By no means was the SAA "essential element" clause felt as a duplication of this pattern; indeed, it was fully part of it.

Against this background, the EU-Turkey Association Agreement could have been amended appropriately, so that it could prove to be a tremendous tool for tackling the many facets of Turkish negative legacy vis-à-vis the Armenian massacres. As shown by the precedent of Croatia, a parallel accession process could not have been an obstacle.[29]

However, upon closer consideration of Croatia's case, the Union's lack of action in relation with the Ankara Agreement could be consistent with the very choice of keeping the Armenian "genocide" issue out of the accession negotiations (even though an "essential element" clause would obviously cover a number of topics beyond the said issue). Hence, such choice proved twice as fatal: any different path to obtain the much longed-for Turkish recognition was precluded.

Another tool left unused is financial conditionality, i.e., conditioning the Union's financial assistance upon the respect by the recipient country of certain pre-requisites. The Union did activate its well-tried conditionality vis-à-vis Turkey on a number of topics, which do not include putting pressure on the government to recognise the Armenian "genocide." However, like any other move taken vis-à-vis this country in the past, conditionality is placed in the framework of the accession process, i.e., it is used to support the full implementation of the Copenhagen criteria,[30] which in the interpretation of the Commission and the European Council do not cover Turkish recognition of the Armenian "genocide." Yet, the EU-Turkey conditionality covers priorities such as freedom of expression in line with the ECHR and the legal protection of minorities, particularly as regards the peaceful enjoyment of possessions in accordance with Protocol 1 to the ECHR.[31]

---

[28]European Commission, Croatia – 2005 Progress Report, 9 November 2005, COM (2005) 561 final, p. 23.

[29]The inclusion of human rights clauses in agreements concluded by the EEC caused a lively debate on the Community's competence to conclude agreements aimed at human rights protection and, more broadly, to develop external human rights policy: Brandtner and Rosas (1998), pp. 473–477; Flauss (1999), pp. 163–164; Cannizzaro (2002), pp. 308–317.

[30]Council Decision of 18 February 2008, 2008/157/EC, on the principles, priorities and conditions contained in the Accession Partnership with the Republic of Turkey and repealing Decision 2006/35/EC, OJ L 51, 26.2.2008, p. 4. Conditionality is laid down in the annexed Turkey 2007 Accession Partnership, Section 6.

[31]See Turkey 2007 Accession Partnership, Section 6, read in combination with Chapter 3.1.

4 The Union and Turkey/Armenia Relations: Watching from a Distance

Armenia became independent from the former Soviet Union in 1991. This certainly fueled the international relevance of the Turks/Armenians disagreement on the "genocide *affaire*" because for the first time the Armenians' claim could be voiced by an international subject with an Armenian identity. Also, an independent Armenia interacting with Turkey expanded the diplomatic toolkit for having the latter make progress towards the recognition of the "genocide." Obviously, the closer their relations would be, the lower the tensions between their respective civil societies would become, and the easier the Turkish attitude vis-à-vis a bit of the country's history, which would prove to be truly nation-building. In any event, the Republic of Armenia started making a point about Turkey to recognize "the genocide" only in 1998, when the new President Robert Kocharian decided to put the issue at the top of the country's foreign policy agenda.[32]

The beginnings of the relationship between Turkey and the newly-born Republic of Armenia were promising: Turkey was among the first countries to recognise the newly-independent State;[33] reportedly, it soon reopened the historic railway connecting the two countries and informal contacts were started, which brought the two governments very close to establishing diplomatic relations and agreeing on their international border.[34] The outbreak of the conflict in Nagorno-Karabakh abruptly brought this progress to an end, in 1993.[35] Since then, the main feature of the relationship between the two countries is the unilateral closure of their border by the Turkish authorities, which Armenian sources refer to as an economic blockade imposed by Turkey on the Caucasian Republic.[36] Turkey reopened its airspace to air traffic to/from Yerevan in 1995. The Turkish blockade forms a common strategy with the Azerbaijani blockade on Armenia in the context of the conflict in

[32]Shahnazaryan (2014), pp. 46–47.

[33]Moffatt et al. (2015), p. 6; Sahakyan (2014); Shahnazaryan (2014), p. 46.

[34]Moffatt et al. (2015), p. 6.

[35]Nagorno-Karabakh was an autonomous province of the former Soviet Republic of Azerbaijan, which declared its independence from Azerbaijan on 2 September 1992, following the proclamation by the Azerbaijani Republic of the "restoration of the 1918–1920 state independence" from the former Soviet Union, earlier in August: Potier (2001), p. 41. As Azerbaijan opposed this development, armed hostilities broke out between the national army and local organized forces, which were supported by Armenia. An assessment of the conflict in Nagorno-Karabakh in international law is in Ronzitti (2014). To date, the conflict remains unsettled and no States or other international entities recognize Nagorno Karabakh as a State: Ronzitti (2014), p. 18–22. In 2015, the European Court of Human Rights found that Armenia exercises effective control over Nagorno-Karabakh and the surrounding regions, thanks to the "significant and decisive influence" on them since the early days of the conflict and the high degree of integration in "virtually all important matters" between Armenia and the secessionist region: ECtHR [GC], 16 June 2015, *Chiragov and Others v Armenia*, App. no. 13216/05 (quotes are from para. 186).

[36]Moffatt et al. (2015), p. 8; Sahakyan (2014), who engage in a comprehensive analysis of the Turk-Azerbaijani blockade on Armenia in international law.

Nagorno-Karabakh. Although the border is sealed, the trade between Turkey and Armenia is not banned, as it takes place through the territory of Georgia. However, the Georgian journey obviously makes trade slow, costly, difficult and therefore limited. Moreover, following the 2008 Russian-Georgian war, the Georgian route became unviable.[37] The reopening of the border has long been a priority for the Armenian government, and it still is.

For many years, the only real sign of openness on the Turkish side has been the liberalization of visas for Armenian nationals, which made it possible for some thousands of Armenians to join the labour market in Turkey, albeit illegally. At a certain point—and this might be regarded as another sign of openness, even if indirectly—undocumented workers were allowed to regularize their positions.

In what looked like a real turning point, Armenia and Turkey signed two Protocols on 10 October 2009. The signing was the highlight of what at the time was referred to as the "normalization process" of the relations between the two countries, or even their "reconciliation." On the Turkish side, the Protocols were part of the new "zero problems with neighbours" policy; on the Armenian side, they were regarded as vital for breaking the country's isolation. In the first Protocol the two governments agreed to establish diplomatic relations. The second Protocol was more far-reaching, as it aimed at developing relations between the two countries. It covered a variety of topics: the opening of the common border within two months after its entry into force; the conduct of regular consultations between the Ministries of Foreign Affairs; the making of the "best possible use" of existing transport, communication and energy infrastructures and networks; the development of a "bilateral legal framework" in order to foster cooperation; cooperation in the fields of science and education; the establishment of consular relations; trade, tourism and economic cooperation, which the parties committed themselves to develop; environmental protection. The "genocide" issue was not mentioned. Yet it clearly stood behind the decision to "implement a dialogue on the historical dimension": the related aim "to restore mutual confidence between the two nations" spoke volumes, as did the proposed "impartial scientific examination of the historical records and archives to define existing problems and formulate recommendations" (Section 2, second indent). Those provisions gave rise to opposing interpretations. Some understood them as a success for Turkey, which had posed among the three preconditions for agreeing to the Protocols and opening the Armenian border that the Armenian claims on Turkey to recognise the 1915–1916 "genocide" in the international arena be given up. The Armenian hardliners also held that bringing up the involvement of historians was a concession to the Turkish position that historical facts are controversial.[38] Conversely, others estimated the said provisions were an

[37]Moffatt et al. (2015), p. 6.

[38]Cheterian (2009); Ferrari (2009), p. 2. The "historical" component of the Protocols is seen as a main reason for the failure of the political rapprochement between Turkey and the Republic of Armenia (namely, a ground of conflicting interests between the Armenian State and the Armenian diaspora) in Shahnazaryan (2014), pp. 48–49.

opportunity to establish an unprecedented dialogue between the two nations on the 1915–1916 massacres.

The two Protocols were relentlessly linked, since they were due to enter into force on the same day. Neither of them ever did, as neither party ratified them. Indeed, Armenia took some steps in this direction: the Constitutional Court released a favourable preventive opinion. However, in May 2015, President Sargsyan decided to withdraw the Protocols from the Parliamentary agenda as there was no sign towards ever starting the ratification procedure on the Turkish side. Reportedly, Turkey turned out to be politically committed to leave the Protocols a dead letter vis-à-vis Azerbaijan, whose position against Armenia in the Nagorno Karabakh situation Turkey steadily supports.[39] Indeed, that Turkey posed the settlement of the situation in the secessionist region as one of three preconditions in the Protocols negotiation process leaked ahead of the signature.

The two Protocols are currently believed to be history.

The EU has long been a spectator to the poor relationships between Turkey and Armenia. Likewise, in the Protocols' negotiation process and in its follow-ups, the Union stayed very much in the background. Other international actors played roles as stakeholders. Switzerland brokered the agreement between the parties—a role that is said to have started in 2007—[40] but also Russia acted as a mediator in the negotiation process, and the United States openly put pressure on both States to sign the Protocols. In any case, the then EU High Representative for CFSP, Mr. Javier Solana, was present at the signature ceremony in Zurich, along with the US Secretary of State. In the weeks ahead, the External Relations Commissioner, Benita Ferrero-Waldner, and the Enlargement Commissioner, Mr. Olli Rehn, had publicly commended the two Protocols as a decisive step to bring peace and stability in Southern Caucasus.[41] The EU High Representative for CFSP did the same, also acknowledging the mediation efforts of Switzerland.[42]

Admittedly, such a minor role is consistent with Armenia's geopolitical position. Although Armenia has taken the path to enter the Western European orbit since 1996,[43] Russia is still the reference power in the Caucasus and particularly Armenia

[39]Moffatt et al. (2015). On the Azerbaijani reaction to the Armenia-Turkey reapproachment and the signature of the Protocols, Ferrari (2009), p. 5. The Armenian parliamentary opposition and some commentators highlighted the strong link between the settlement (in favour of Azerbaijan) of the situation in Nagorno Karabakh and the Turkish signature, ratification and implementation of the Protocols even ahead of their final failure. The link made an argument against Armenian participation and/or hopes for the successful outcome of the normalization process. On the opposition to the Protocols in Turkey, insomuch as the related process left the situation in Nagorno-Karabakh aside, Ferrari (2009), p. 2.

[40]On the Swiss mediation, see Phillips et al. (2012), pp. 27–31.

[41]Turkey hopes to open Armenian border by the year-end, 1 September 2009, http://www.reuters.com.

[42]Javier Solana welcomes statement on normalization of Armenian-Turkish relations, 1 September 2009, https://armenpress.am.

[43]In 1996, Armenia applied for membership of the Council of Europe and signed a Partnership and Cooperation Agreement with the EU.

keeps on holding it as such even in very recent times.[44] Meaningfully, while negotiations for the conclusion of an association agreement with the EU started in 2010, following Russian pressure, Armenia ended up joining the Eurasian Economic Union in 2013, which in turn brought the EU association agreement negotiations to an end.[45] Russia's influence is sought also for security reasons: Armenia agreed on the enhancement of Russian military presence in its territory in August 2010.[46] Indeed, Russia was the mediator of the cease-fire agreement in Nagorno-Karabakh and neighbouring territories, known as the Protocol of Bishkek, in 1994.[47] Russia is also one of the three Co-Chairs of the Minsk Group of the OSCE (Organization for Security and Co-operation in Europe), entrusted with supporting the peaceful solution of the conflict in Nagorno-Karabakh.[48]

However, the fact remains that the Union entirely disregarded the relations between Turkey and Armenia, as well as those between Turkey and the other Southern Caucasian states, while developing its course of action concerning the area. Starting from the 1995 Commission Communication on EU relations with the Transcaucasian Republics,[49] through the development of bilateral relations with Armenia, Azerbaijan and Georgia by means of the Partnership and Cooperation Agreements (PCAs), in 1996,[50] the incorporation of the three Republics into the European Neighbourhood Policy (ENP), in 2004, and the launch of the Eastern Partnership in 2008,[51] the Union has never made a point about improving the relations between Turkey and those States, specifically Armenia. In the Union's perspective, they belong to two different paths, which run in parallel: Turkey is a candidate country, whereas neither the Eastern Neighbourhood at large nor

[44]The re-approachment between Turkey and Armenia is said not to meet Russian geopolitical interests in the region: Shahnazaryan (2014), pp. 49–50. Instead, the Turkish-Armenian re-approachment is seen as one of the few issues where Russian and US interests coincide in Mikhelidze (2010), p. 7. On the close ties between Russia and Armenia, see Phillips et al. (2012), pp. 10–13 and, for most recent developments, Kostanyan and Giragosian (2016), p. 3. More generally, on Russia's role in Southern Caucasus: Ghazaryan (2012), p. 228.

[45]Kostanyan (2015).

[46]The focus on the relations with Russia, to the detriment of those with Turkey, is said to be due to President Kocharian: Moffatt et al. (2015), p. 6.

[47]ECtHR [GC], 16 June 2015, *Chiragov and Others v Armenia*, App. no. 13216/05, para. 24.

[48]ECtHR [GC], 16 June 2015, *Chiragov and Others v Armenia*, App. no. 13216/05, paras. 29–31.

[49]European Commission, Towards A European Union Strategy for Relations with Transcaucasian Republics, 31 May 1995, COM(95) 205 final.

[50]The history of the relationship between the EU and the Southern Caucasus is divided into two stages in Ghazaryan (2012), p. 224. In the first stage, the three PCAs followed the same pattern as the Europe Agreements, except that they did not share the latter's objective of membership; their poor personality was probably the reason for their failure (pp. 228–229). The second stage started in 2004 with the inclusion of the Southern Caucasus into the ENP (pp. 235–239).

[51]European Commission, Communication to the European Parliament and the Council – Eastern Partnership, 3 December 2008, COM(2008) 823 final.

specifically the Southern Caucasus are an enlargement zone for the Union.[52] While the ENP, in the wake of the 2003 European Security Strategy, marked the Union's decision to focus on its own security and to contribute to stability in the neighbourhood on this ground,[53] little or no care has been attached to the relations between States belonging to different blocks in the geo-political area or between those blocks altogether. One reason is surely that the blocks are identified in the perspective of the Union's own security.[54] Last, with the launch of the ENP, in 2004, the Union started to insist that it would play a more active role in the management of conflicts in the ENP area[55]; this is also a leitmotiv of the Eastern partnership.[56] Letting aside the fact that Turkey is not covered by the ENP, since the long-time frozen relations between Armenia and Turkey fall short of a conflict, the rapprochement between the two countries is not a priority for the EU.

However, years ago the improvement of Turkey's relations with neighbouring countries had become a priority for the Union. In the words of the European Council:

> The European Council, while underlining the need for unequivocal commitment to good neighbourly relations welcomed the improvement in Turkey's relations with its neighbours and its readiness to continue to work with the Member States concerned towards resolution of outstanding border disputes in conformity with the principle of peaceful settlement of disputes in accordance with the United Nations Charter. In accordance with its previous conclusions, notably those of Helsinki on this matter, the European Council reviewed the situation relating to outstanding disputes and welcomed the exploratory contacts to this end. In this connection it reaffirmed its view that unresolved disputes having repercussions on the accession process should if necessary be brought to the International Court of Justice for settlement. The European Council will be kept informed of progress achieved which it will review as appropriate.[57]

It clearly emerges that good neighbourly relations were encouraged insofar as deteriorated relations could jeopardise the accession process: once again, the choice to keep the "Armenian genocide recognition" *affaire* out of this process proved fatal.

---

[52]This is true for all of the States covered by the ENP. While the latter shows strong similarities with the enlargement and pre-accession model, its main characteristic is that it is not aimed at the accession to the Union. This ambiguity, or lack of a precise identity, is regarded as a major weakness, which the Union has been working to improve in the last decade: Gebhard (2012), pp. 103–105.

[53]Ghazaryan (2012), p. 226.

[54]The ENP is regarded as "the operationalisation" of the objective of building security in the EU's neighbourhood, stated in the 2003 European Security Strategy: Biscop (2012), p. 73. In terms of security threats and related Union's strategy and/or action, this Author identifies the following areas: the Mediterranean neighbourhood, the eastern neighbourhood and "the broader region," which includes the Euro-Mediterranean countries and Southern Caucasus: ibidem, pp. 80–86.

[55]Biscop (2012), p. 83; Wolff and Peen Rodt (2012), pp. 128–131.

[56]Joint Declaration of the Eastern Partnership Summit (Riga, 21–22 May 2015), point 5.

[57]Presidency Conclusions of the Brussels European Council (16–17 December 2004), para. 20.

5 Conclusions

The foregoing analysis has shown how little the Union has done in the past decades and even recently in order to put pressure on Turkey to recognize the 1915–1916 Armenian "genocide," in whatever meaning this expression may have: from proper "genocide" recognition in a historical sense, to admitting size, modality and illegality of the massacres, involvement of Ottoman officials at the highest Government level, etc., with a view to obtaining the cessation of the international wrongdoings currently committed by modern Turkey upon the basis of the denial of any responsibility of the predecessor State for those events. This finding gives rise to two interrelated conclusive questions.

First, one should wonder whether the Union's lack of action is compliant with the Treaty on the EU, at least as it stands at present, i.e., *post* Lisbon. Invoking the cessation of internationally wrongful acts and assurances of non-repetition in pursuance with Article 48(2)(a) of the Draft Articles on State Responsibility is certainly not an obligation for States and other international entities. A decision to disregard such a course of action is perfectly compatible with international law. While this is true also for the EU based on customary international law, the same conclusion might not apply in relation to the Treaty on the EU, which sets out that the Union's contribution to the respect of international law and the principles of the United Nations Charter is a goal of the Union's external action. Indeed, the Union's objectives are relevant not only to establish the extent of the latter's powers, but also for the legality of their exercise.

It is here maintained that working towards Turkey's acknowledgement of the atrocities perpetrated in 1915–1916 is consistent with the EU Treaties. Moreover, based on the objectives and on the principles of the Union's external action laid down in Article 21 TEU, the decision to leave the topic behind is not an option for the Union. Being obliged to take action in a manner consistent with the Union's principles and objectives does not amount to being bound to exercise a competence established in the Treaties. The latter can obviously never be obligatory: a competence or power is just a legal tool made available to the Union and to all of its stakeholders (Member States, natural and legal persons, third States when relevant). However, insofar as it is exercised, an action should never depart from the principles and the objectives set out in the Treaties. It is here maintained that the Union has exercised its external powers and, therefore, that it has to do so in compliance with the purposes set out in the Treaties.

The problem with the Armenian "genocide" affaire is that whether the Union truly disregarded the said principles and objectives is unclear and virtually impossible to establish. Indeed, the Union has never officially approved Turkey's refusal to apologise or to take responsibilities for the 1915–1916 massacres, nor has it ever sympathized with the Turkish "negationist" attitude. Those actions would undoubtedly be in contrast with the TEU. As explained above, the Union's lack of direct action in the last two decades can be understood in the light of a number of factors: Turkey's reluctance vis-à-vis the issue, which makes a straightforward approach unwise, and Armenia's geopolitics. Moreover, reactions to the signature of the 2009 Protocols teach that the Turkish and Armenian societies are still torn regarding the Armenian massacres and far from reconciliation. In addition to those mentioned in the previous Section, I wish to recall the "Votch" ("No" in Armenian) campaign, aimed at collecting signatures to oppose ratification of the Protocols on the Armenian side.[58] In Turkey, the "societal component" of the recognition affaire is clearly behind the application of the Turkish criminal provision on the protection of "Turkishness" against those who write and speak on the 1915–1916 massacres[59] and the landmark killing of Hrat Dink in Turkey in 2007.[60] Dink was an ethnic Armenian journalist with Turkish citizenship, founder and leader of a bilingual magazine whose mission was societal reconciliation between Armenians and Turks. Also, a classic "reconciliation tool," i.e., the establishment of a bilateral commission entrusted with fact-finding and dialogue, has proved unsuccessful twice: the Turkish Armenian Reconciliation Commission (TARC), operational between 2002 and 2004 and composed by civil society representatives, and the governmental sub-commission envisaged in the second 2009 Protocol, which was never set up and raised countless criticisms, especially in Armenian society and in the diaspora.[61]

This leads me to the second question worth asking at the conclusion of the present analysis: in times when Turkey is losing interest in joining the Union, it shows a growing attention towards different partners, its respect of human rights is more and more doubtful and the international agenda in the Middle East is filled with other priorities, which tools are left for the Union to support the Armenian case? Societal reconciliation is clearly key. To this end, the winning card in the EU's sleeve could be supporting regional cooperation in the area, including by means of conditionality, in the context of its Eastern partnership but in such a way as to get Turkey involved.

A stable and lively regional cooperation is believed to be able to play a major role in de-escalating tension: over the years it should help finding a solution to the Nagorno-Karabakh conflict and, both in parallel and as a result thereof, achieving normalization of Armenia-Turkey relations. Indeed, particularly in a lessons-learnt perspective, the latter is the only credible tool for societal reconciliation: the closer mutual relations in trade and other areas of cooperation are, the easier it will be to overcome mistrust and biases. Admittedly, this was precisely the idea behind the determination of the Armenian Republic's leadership to the success of the 2009 Protocols.

The building of a multilateral framework is one of the highlights of the Eastern Partnership. "Multilateralism" is mainly understood as an alternative to "bilateralism," i.e., as being limited to the relations between the Union and the six States

[58]See http://www.votch.org, no longer live.

[59]Latino, in this book.

[60]On Dink's assassination see Phillips et al. (2012), pp. 35–38.

[61]For such criticism, see the previous Section. On both commissions, see Latino, in this book.

involved (the three Caucasian Republics, plus Belarus, Moldova and Ukraine).[62] However, the envisaged tools can be very promising, especially the creation of a "Neighbourhood Economic Community" involving the EU and all of its (Eastern) neighbours. This should be an advanced step of a process whose kick-off is to be the establishment of a deep and comprehensive free trade area (DCFTA) between the EU and each of the partner countries, in bilateral Association Agreements.[63] The long-term goal leading to the "Neighbourhood Economic Community" is the creation of a network of DCFTAs among the six "Eastern neighbours" or regional free-trade agreements based on the bilateral commitments undertaken in the DCFTAs with the EU.[64] The underpinning idea has been integrated into the ENP[65]: trade would bring along prosperity and stable relations. It should be implemented in a local, multilateral framework.[66]

The EU is familiar with such a pragmatic approach, which closely resembles that at the basis of the European integration itself.[67] Its implementation in those regions requires taking Russia's politics into due account, but no credible alternative seems feasible, neither yesterday in continental Europe, nor today or tomorrow in Anatolia and Southern Caucasus.

References

Adam R (1982) Le relazioni esterne. In: Pennacchini E, Monaco R, Bravo LF, Puglisi S (eds) Manuale di diritto comunitario. UTET, Torino

Archiyan YE (2011) Turkey and European Union: an association in making. J Int Law Pract 20:117–148

Bartels L (2005) Human rights conditionality in the EU's international agreements. Oxford University Press, Oxford

Biscop S (2012) The ENP, security and democracy in the context of the European security strategy. In: Whitman RG, Wolff S (eds) The European neighbourhood policy in perspective. Context, implementation and impact. Palgrave Macmillan, Houndmills, Basington, Hampshire and New York, pp 73–109

Blockmans S, Van Vooren B (2012) Revitalizing the European 'neighbourhood economic community': the case for legally binding sectoral multilateralism. Working Paper No. 91. Leuven Centre for Global Governance Studies

Brandtner B, Rosas A (1998) Human rights and the external relations of the European Community: an analysis of doctrine and practice. Eur J Int Law 9:468–490

---

[62]European Commission, Communication to the European Parliament and the Council – Eastern Partnership, 3 December 2008, COM(2008) 823 final, pp. 8–11.

[63]Ibidem, p. 4.

[64]Ibidem, p. 10.

[65]Blockmans and Van Vooren (2012), p. 4.

[66]Blockmans and Van Vooren (2012), argue that a method of real multilateralism should be adopted for developing a credible "Neighbourhood Economic Community" (see specifically p. 5) and propose a very interesting and realistic "legally binding sectoral multilateralism."

[67]Blockmans and Van Vooren (2012), p. 6.

Cannizzaro E (2002) The Scope of the EU Foreign Power: Is the EC Competent to Conclude Agreements with Third States Including Human Rights Clauses? In: Cannizzaro E (ed) The European Union as an actor in international relations. Kluwer Law International, The Hague, London, New York, Boston, pp 297–319

Cannizzaro E (2015) Il diritto dell'integrazione europea. L'ordinamento dell'Unione. Torino, Giappichelli

Cheterian V (2009) Armenia-Turkey: genocide, blockade, diplomacy. http://www.opendemocracy.net. Accessed 15 Jan 2017

Cremona M (2011) Values in EU Foreign Policy. In: Evans M, Koutrakos P (eds) Beyond the established legal orders. Hart Publishing, Oxford, Portland, pp 275–315

Comments E (2012) Fundamental rights and EU membership: do as I say, not as I do! Common Market Law Rev 49:481–488

Ferrari A (2009) I protocolli armeno-turchi e il nodo dell'Alto Karabakh. ISPI - Policy Brief 164:1–6

Flauss J-F (1999) Droits de l'homme et relations extérieures de l'Union européenne. In: Stéphane Leclerc, Jean François Akandji-Kombé and Marie-Joëlle Redor (eds) L'Union européenne et les droits fondamentaux. Bruylant, Bruxelles, pp 137–172

Gebhard C (2012) The ENP's strategic conception and design overstretching the enlargement template? In: Whitman RG, Wolff S (eds) The European neighbourhood policy in perspective. Context, implementation and impact. Palgrave Macmillan, Houndmills, Basington, Hampshire and New York, 89–109

Ghazaryan N (2012) The ENP and the Southern Caucasus: meeting the expectations? In: Whitman RG, Wolff S (eds) The European neighbourhood policy in perspective. Context, implementation and impact. Palgrave Macmillan, Houndmills, Basington, Hampshire and New York, pp 223–246

Ghazaryan N, Hakobyan A (2014) Legislative approximation and application of EU Law in Armenia. In: Petrov R, Van Elsuwege P (eds) Legislative approximation and application of EU Law in the eastern neighbourhood of the European Union. Towards a common regulatory space? Routledge, London and New York, pp 191–214

Gianelli A (1997) Adempimenti preventivi all'adozione di contromisure internazionali. Giuffré, Milano

Gianelli A (2004a) Aspects of the relationship between the law of the treaties and state responsibility. In: Giardina A, Lattanzi F (eds) Studi di diritto internazionale in onore di Gaetano Arangio-Ruiz. Editoriale scientifica, Napoli, pp 757–805

Gianelli A (2004b) Unione europea e diritto internazionale consuetudinario. Giappichelli, Torino

Gstöhl S (2014) Differentiated integration and the prospects of a neighbourhood economic community between the EU and its eastern partners. In: Petrov R, Van Elsuwege P (eds) Legislative approximation and application of EU Law in the eastern neighbourhood of the European Union. Towards a common regulatory space? Routledge, London and New York, pp 89–107

King T (1999) Human rights in European Foreign Policy: success or failure for post-modern diplomacy? Eur J Int Law 10:313–337

Kostanyan H (2015) The Rocky-Road to an EU-Armenia agreement: from U-turn to detour. CEPS commentary. www.ceps.eu. Accessed 15 Jan 2017

Kostanyan H, Giragosian R (2016) EU-Armenian relations: seizing the second chance CEPS commentary. www.ceps.eu. Accessed 15 Jan 2017

Lang A (2014) Gli atti della PESC. In: Lang A, Mariani P (eds) La politica estera dell'Unione europea, Inquadramento giuridico e prassi applicativa. Giappichelli, Torino, pp 31–50

Lawry-White M (2015) The reparative effect of truth seeking in transitional justice. Int Comp Law Q 64:141–177

Mariani P (2014) Profili istituzionali della PESC. In: Lang A, Mariani P (eds) La politica estera dell'Unione europea, Inquadramento giuridico e prassi applicativa. Giappichelli, Torino, pp 3–30

Mikhelidze N (2010) The Turkish-Armenian rapprochement at the deadlock. Documenti IAI 10/05

Moffatt A, Hill F, Kirişhi K (2015) Armenia and Turkey: from normalization to reconciliation. Turkish Policy Quarterly. https://brookings.edu. Accessed 15 Jan 2017

Phillips D, Lemmon M, de Waal T (2012) Diplomatic history: the Turkey-Armenia protocols. Carnegie Endowment for International Peace. http://carnegieendowment.org. Accessed 15 Jan 2017

Pippan C (2004) The Rocky Road to Europe: the EU's stabilisation and association process for the Western Balkans and the principle of conditionality. Eur Foreign Affairs Rev 9:219–245

Pocar F (1991) Diritto delle Comunità europee, 4th edn. Giuffrè, Milano

Potier T (2001) Conflict in Nagorno-Karabakh, Abkhazia and South Ossetia. A legal appraisal. Kluwer Law International, The Hague-London-Boston

Reading A (2011) Identity, memory and cosmopolitanism: the otherness of the past and a right to memory? Eur J Cult Stud 14:379–394

Ronzitti N (2014) Il conflitto del Nagorno-Karabakh e il diritto internazionale. Giappichelli, Torino

Rossi LS (2010) Democrazia e diritti fondamentali: coerenza dell'azione esterna dell'Unione europea e politica verso il Mediterraneo. In: Triggiani E (ed) Europa e Mediterraneo. Le regole per la costruzione di una società integrata. Editoriale scientifica, Napoli, pp 517–542

Sahakyan A (2014) Economic blockades and international law: the case of Armenia. The Armenian Weekly. http://armenianweekly.com. Accessed 15 Jan 2017

Schenken H (2008) The stabilization and association process: an engine of European integration in need of tuning. J Ethnopolit Minor Iss Eur 7:1–19

Schimmelfennig F (2008) EU political accession conditionality after the 2004 enlargement: consistency and effectiveness. J Eur Public Policy 15:918–937

Shahnazaryan N (2009) Breaking the nation's taboo. The *Meds Yeghern* and Turkish intellectuals, PONARS Eurasian Policy Memo No. 86. www.ponarseurasia.org. Accessed 15 Jan 2017

Shahnazaryan D (2014) Nervous neighbours: five years after the Turkey-Armenia protocols, Turkish Policy Quarterly. www.turkishpolicy.com. Accessed 15 Jan 2017

Wolff S, Peen Rodt A (2012) Lessons from the Balkans: the ENP as a possible conflict management Tool? In: Whitman RG, Wolff S (eds) The European neighbourhood policy in perspective. Context, implementation and impact. Palgrave Macmillan, Houndmills, Basington, Hampshire and New York, pp 113–134

Kolibri 360 GmbH
Ferdinand-Jühlke-Straße 7
99095 Erfurt, Deutschland
produktsicherheit@kolibri360.de